CAMBRIDGE SURVEYS OF ECONOMIC LITERATURE

ECONOMIC BEHAVIOR AND INSTITUTIONS

CAMBRIDGE SURVEYS OF ECONOMIC LITERATURE

Editors:
Professor Mark Perlman, University of Pittsburgh
Professor E. Roy Weintraub, Duke University
Editorial Advisory Board:
Professor A. B. Atkinson, London School of Economics and Political Science
Professor M. Bronfenbrenner, Duke University
Professor K. D. George, University College, Cardiff
Professor C. P. Kindleberger, Massachusetts Institute of Technology
Professor T. Mayer, University of California, Davis
Professor A. R. Prest, London School of Economics and Political Science

The literature of economics is expanding rapidly, and many subjects have changed out of recognition within the space of a few years. Perceiving the state of knowledge in fast-developing subjects is difficult for students and time-consuming for professional economists. This series is intended to help with this problem. Each book will be quite brief, giving a clear structure to and balanced overview of the topic, and written at a level intelligible to the senior undergraduate. The books will therefore be useful for teaching but will also provide a mature yet compact presentation of the subject for economists wishing to update their knowledge outside their own specialization.

Other books in the series
E. Roy Weintraub: Microfoundations: The compatibility of microeconomics and macroeconomics
Dennis C. Mueller: Public choice
Robert Clark and Joseph Spengler: The economics of individual and population aging
Edwin Burmeister: Capital theory and dynamics
Mark Blaug: The methodology of economics or how economists explain
Robert Ferber and Werner Z. Hirsch: Social experimentation and economic policy
Anthony C. Fisher: Resource and environmental economics
Morton I. Kamien and Nancy L. Schwartz: Market structure and innovation
Richard E. Caves: Multinational enterprise and economic analysis
Anne O. Krueger: Exchange-rate determination
James W. Friedman: Oligopoly theory
Mark R. Killingsworth: Labor supply
Helmut Frisch: Theories of inflation
Steven M. Sheffrin: Rational expectations
Sanford V. Berg and John Tschirhart: Natural monopoly regulation

Economic behavior and institutions

THRÁINN EGGERTSSON
University of Iceland

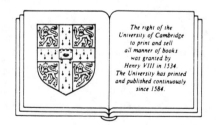

The right of the
University of Cambridge
to print and sell
all manner of books
was granted by
Henry VIII in 1534.
The University has printed
and published continuously
since 1584.

CAMBRIDGE UNIVERSITY PRESS

CAMBRIDGE

NEW YORK PORT CHESTER MELBOURNE SYDNEY

Published by the Press Syndicate of the University of Cambridge
The Pitt Building, Trumpington Street, Cambridge CB2 1RP
40 West 20th Street, New York, NY 10011, USA
10 Stamford Road, Oakleigh, Melbourne 3166, Australia

© Cambridge University Press 1990

First published 1990

Printed in the United States of America

Library of Congress Cataloging-in-Publication Data
Thráinn Eggertsson, 1941–
Economic behavior and institutions / Thráinn Eggertsson.
    p. cm. – (Cambridge surveys of economic literature)
ISBN 0–521–34445-X. – ISBN 0–521–34891–9 (pbk.)
1. Institutional economics.   2. Right of property.   I. Title.
II. Series.
HB99.5.T48   1990   89–39485
338.5'01 – dc20   CIP

British Library Cataloguing in Publication Data
Eggertsson, Thráinn
Economic behavior and institutions. – (Cambridge surveys
of economic literature).
1. Economics.   Theories
I. Title
330.1

ISBN 0–521–34445–X hardback
ISBN 0–521–34891–9 paperback

For Anne Cotterill

CONTENTS

Contents

PREFACE

This book grew out of my interest in organizational forms and institutional arrangements and their impact on economic outcomes. Price theory or microeconomics, in its conventional form, treats organizations and institutions the same way as it treats the law of gravity: These factors are implicitly assumed to exist but appear neither as independent nor as dependent variables in the models. Such economy in model making can be eminently reasonable. It enables us to isolate critical relationships and simplifies the use of mathematical tools in the analysis. However, unlike the law of gravity, organizations and institutions are not invariant; they vary with time and location, with political arrangements and structures of property rights, with technologies employed, and with physical qualities of resources, commodities, and services that are exchanged. In fact, production involves not only the physical transformation of inputs into outputs but also the transfer of property rights between the owners of resources, commodities, and labor services. In the transfer of rights, whether within firms or across markets, agents maximize their objective functions subject to the constraints of organizations and institutions.

Once our research questions involve variable organizations and institutions, either as exogenous or endogenous variables, conventional microeconomic analysis becomes a rather blunt instrument. Our traditional tools are not well suited for examining the nature of the firm, the variation in industrial organization, institutional change in economic history, the organization of exchange in formal markets and nonmarket settings, or comparative economic systems. It was a logical development, which we have observed in recent years, that economics departments at various major universities gradually would give relatively low priority to fields of study that deal with organizations and institutions – fields such as economic history, comparative economic studies, the economics of growth and development, and various economic policy areas. This trend in priorities was also reflected in leading journals of economics. One could say that the structure of the economic system itself and of its parts was no longer a central focus of inquiry.

In 1984, I set out to investigate whether my demand for institutional analysis had created its own supply, whether the thesis of institution-free economics had created its antithesis. My working rule was to limit the study to contributions that did not alter the core of the economic approach, particularly the rational-choice model, and to seek a new synthesis of neoclassical and institutional economics. Neoinstitutional Economics is the term I use.

The renewal of a scientific discipline usually does not originate at the center, and I found what I was looking for in various outlying branches of economics. Tremendously interesting ideas were being developed and discussed in subfields within economic history, the theory of the firm, and industrial organization; in the new field of law and economics; and by political scientists who employed the rational-choice model. These contributions had in common the introduction of transaction costs to the analysis. The modern use of the concept of transaction costs originates in two articles by Ronald H. Coase, "The Nature of the Firm" (1937) and "The Problem of Social Cost" (1960).[1] In looking back on these classic articles, Coase (1988) has summarized his contribution in these words:

---

1. Coase, Ronald H. (1937). "The Nature of the Firm." *Economica*, New Series *16* (No. 4): 386–405; idem (1960). "The Problem of Social Cost." *Journal of Law and Economics 3* (No. 1, October): 1–44.

Transaction costs were used in the one case to show
that if they are not included in the analysis, the firm has
no purpose, while in the other I showed, as I thought,
that if transaction costs were not introduced into the
analysis, for the range of problems considered, the law
had no purpose.[2]

The economic approach suggests that, in the absence of transaction costs, their self-interest would always guide the members
of society to contract for the establishment of political structures
and systems of property rights that maximize the national wealth.
In this instance, the study of political processes is of little interest
for the student of economic systems. However, this generalization
is not valid if we introduce transaction costs into the analysis of
political exchange. The rational-choice model is now consistent
with structures of property rights that fail to maximize the national
wealth and may even bring economic decline, which we can in-
terpret as organizational failures due to transaction costs.

As I see it, there are several levels of analysis in Neoinstitutional
Economics, depending on which variables are treated as endogenous. At the first level, the structure of property rights and forms
of organization are explicitly modeled but are treated as exogenous, and the emphasis is on their impact on economic outcomes.
At the second level, the organization of exchange is endogenized,
but the fundamental structure of property rights remains exogenous. Exchange within firms, across formal markets, and in nonmarket situations is organized by means of contracts that constrain
economic agents. For instance, the firm is defined as a network of
contracts. At the third level, attempts are made to endogenize
both social and political rules and the structure of political institutions by introducing the concept of transaction costs.

My book is organized on the basis of these three levels of analysis. Its intended contribution is to bring together heterogeneous
work by scholars in various fields in order to suggest a new research

2. P. 34 in Coase, Ronald H. (1988). "The Nature of the Firm: Influence." *Journal of Law, Economics, and Organization 4* (No. 1, Spring): 33–47.

program, a new approach to the study of economics systems, which at the same time is essentially a generalization or extension of microeconomics. Most of the work I discuss is new; Neoinstitutional Economics as a unified research program took shape in the 1980s. I hope the book will convey a sense of the tremendous potential I see in the new approach that I predict will one day be referred to as economics.

The main contributors to neoinstitutional analysis usually operate at only one of the three levels of analysis that I have described, except for Douglass North. North's vision that the economic approach, augmented by transaction costs and property rights, is a general tool for the study of society at all levels has inspired this book. In fact, the turning point in my thinking was the chance discovery of one of his articles. He responded swiftly and generously to a letter from me and invited me to join his political economy group at Washington University in St. Louis for one semester. The one visit became three, lasting four semesters, and North's continuing support literally made it possible for me to write this book. My debt to Washington University is great. I have been a visiting professor in the Economics Department, a visiting fellow of the Center in Political Economy, and a research associate of the Center for the Study of American Business. Of numerous friends at Washington University I would especially like to thank Wilhelm Neuefeind, Murray Weidenbaum, and my friends and benefactors Lee and Alexandra Benham, who followed my work closely with sound advice, critique, and encouragement and helped me establish important contacts with leading contributors to Neoinstitutional Economics, which included a memorable evening with Ronald Coase in Chicago.

Many of the scholars cited in this book have provided me with unpublished papers and manuscripts and read chapters relating to their work. I would especially like to mention Armen A. Alchian, Yoram Barzel, Robert Bates, Louis De Alessi, Arthur Denzau, Stefano Fenoaltea, Barry C. Field, Eirik Furubotn, and Jack Hirshleifer in the United States; Anthony Scott in Canada; and Bruno

Frey in Switzerland. I thank the Norwegian School of Economics and Business Administration, which provided me with an office one summer, and Rögnvaldur Hannesson, who read several chapters of my manuscript. I also thank Bo Gustafsson in Uppsala for commenting on my manuscript, and Johan Myhrman at the Stockholm School of Economics for both reading my manuscript and using it in one of his courses. At the University of Iceland I have received useful suggestions from Thorvaldur Gylfason and from Thórólfur Matthíasson, who carefully read the manuscript at one stage in its development. Gudmundur Ólafsson gave valuable help with the indexes. The participants in the Economics Workshop of the University of Iceland made useful suggestions. None of these people is responsible for my mistakes.

I thank the University of Iceland for financial support, including a grant from the University Research Fund. My thanks go also to three anonymous referees who were employed by my publisher, and to the excellent staff of Cambridge University Press in the United States. I mention especially Colin Day, who was editorial director at Cambridge when I made my initial contact with CUP and who supported my project from the beginning.

Reykjavík, June 1989

Part I

Introduction to the theory

1

Generalizing Neoclassical Economics: new tools and concepts

1.1. Neoinstitutional Economics and the theory of production and exchange

We are concerned in this book with recent attempts to extend and generalize the theory of price and apply it to economic and political institutions. Our focus is on a certain propensity in human nature, which Adam Smith pointed out – "the propensity to truck, barter, and exchange one thing for another" – and on the consequences of these activities for the use of scarce resources and the creation of wealth.[1]

The economic outcomes of production depend in an important way on the social and political rules that govern economic activity

---

1. Adam Smith, in Chapter 2 of *The Wealth of Nations* (1776), argues that it is this human propensity to exchange that gives rise to the division of labor. Smith, Adam (1776). *An Inquiry into the Nature and Cause of the Wealth of Nations.* [Reprint ed. R. H. Campbell and A. S. Skinner. Oxford: Oxford University Press, 1976.] Buchanan (1964) takes up this point from Smith and suggests that economists should place the theory of markets and not the theory of resource allocation at center stage. "Economists 'should' concentrate their attention on a particular form of human activity, and upon the various institutional arrangements that arise as a result of this form of activity. Man's behavior in the market relationship, reflecting the propensity to truck and to barter, and the manifold variations in structure that this relationship can take; these are the proper subjects for the economist's study." Pp. 313–314 in Buchanan, James M. (1964). "What Should Economists Do?" *Southern Economic Journal 30* (No. 3, January): 213–22.

and society in general. In his pioneering contribution to economics, Adam Smith sought to demonstrate how one specific set of rules contributes more to the wealth of nations than any other. The structure that Adam Smith recommended was one whereby individuals have exclusive private rights to economic assets.

In the more than 200 years following Adam Smith's contribution, the mainstream of research in economics has involved primarily an examination of a single set of idealized rules governing market exchange. In spite of this simplification, the approach has been fruitful: In terms of both analytical power and empirical relevance it overshadows all other theoretical systems in economics and the social sciences. The theory of price (microeconomic theory) has provided valuable insights into the fundamental nature of exchange and resource allocation in decentralized markets and also tools that enable us to predict how equilibrium outcomes are affected by changes in the constraints that individual decision makers face.[2]

However, the rate of return on traditional microeconomic analysis has diminished in recent decades. For some time now, the major implications of the basic model have been well understood, whereas the theory, without significant modifications, is unsuitable for examining a variety of important questions. Even when theoretical tools were available, the traditional model and the cumulative research tradition did not encourage certain lines of investigation. We can point to three areas of inquiry that until recently have been largely neglected by economists of the neoclassical school:

1. How do alternative sets of social rules (property rights) and economic organizations affect behavior, allocation of resources, and equilibrium outcomes?
2. Why does the form of economic organization differ from one type of economic activity to another, even within the same legal framework? In general, what is

---

2. For an introduction to the theory of price, see, for example, Hirshleifer, Jack (1988). *Price Theory and Applications*, 4th ed. Englewood Cliffs: Prentice-Hall.

the economic logic of various contractual agreements, such as the firm, that are used for organizing production and exchange?

3. What is the economic logic behind the fundamental social and political rules that govern production and exchange, and how do these rules change?

Although it must be admitted that neoclassical economists at various times have touched on all three issues, usually the examination has been ephemeral, neither contributing new theoretical concepts nor generating sustained research programs. Since the late 1960s, however, a good number of neoclassical economists have become interested in the structure of economic organization. A new research program has evolved that is aimed at generalizing microeconomic theory while retaining all the essential elements of the economic approach – *stable preferences,* the *rational-choice model,* and *equilibria.*

Lakatos (1970) divides a research program into two components: the program's invariable *hard core* and its variable *protective belt.*[3] A modification of a research program takes the form of readjusting the protective belt, but an alteration of elements in the core represents a switch over to a new research program (paradigm). Stable preference, rational choice, and equilibrium structures of interaction constitute the hard core of the microeconomic paradigm, which all this century has been the dominating research program in economics. Knudsen (1986) identifies the following three elements of the protective belt of neoclassical economics:[4]

1. Specification of the type of situational constraint the agent faces;

3. See, Lakatos, Imre (1970). "Falsification and the Methodology of Scientific Research Programs." In Lakatos and Musgrave, eds. *Criticism and the Growth of Knowledge.* Cambridge: Cambridge University Press.
4. Knudsen, Christian (1986). "Normal Science as a Process of Creative Destruction: From a Microeconomic to a Neo-institutional Research Program." Paper presented at the *International Symposium on Property Rights, Organizational Forms and Economic Behavior.* Lund: The Swedish Collegium for Advanced Study in the Social Sciences.

2. Specification of the type of information the agents have about their situation;
3. Specification of the type of interaction that is studied.[5]

The new approach constitutes a modification of the protective belt of neoclassical economics, primarily, as we shall see, by introducing information and transaction costs and the constraints of property rights. This line of inquiry has no generally accepted name, although such labels as the Property Rights School, Transaction Costs Economics, the New Economic History, the New Industrial Organization, the New Comparative Economic Systems, or Law and Economics are often used to refer to various contributions in this area. We shall refer to the new approach as *Neoinstitutional Economics* in order to emphasize the link with traditional microeconomics and separate our approach from recent contributions by institutional economists who reject elements of the hard core of neoclassical economics, such as the rational-choice model. We refer to this alternative paradigm as the *New Institutional Economics*. There have been outstanding contributions to the New Institutional Economics, especially by Oliver Williamson, whose work, which lies close to the neoclassical tradition, will be discussed in later chapters.[6]

Neoinstitutional Economics (NIE) is still at an exploratory stage: Definitions and terminology are not fully agreed on, and the use of mathematical models is less pronounced than in recent work in microeconomic theory, but there is stronger emphasis on empirical testing. Yet, in spite of certain differences in approach, common strands can be found in the work of contributors to the NIE.

First, the authors tend to make explicit attempts to model the constraints of rules and contracts that govern exchange, and the idealized structure of property rights in the neoclassical model is used primarily as a benchmark.

5. Knudsen (1986), p. 10.
6. See, for example, Williamson, Oliver E. (1974). *Markets and Hierarchies*. New York: Free Press; idem (1985a). *The Economic Institutions of Capitalism: Firms, Markets, Relational Contracting*. New York: Free Press.

Second, the neoclassical assumptions of full information and costless exchange have been relaxed, and the consequences of positive *transaction costs* are examined.

Third, the usual assumption that valuable commodities have only two dimensions – price and quantity – has been eased, and the implications for economic outcomes and economic organization of qualitative variations in goods and services are investigated.

Finally, it should be noted that NIE has benefited greatly from the work of economists who, although usually not considered as belonging to this school, have strived to generalize economic theory. For example, this is true of the pioneering contributions of George J. Stigler to the economics of information, regulation, and industrial organization; Kelvin Lancaster's work on the quality dimension of commodities; and Gary S. Becker's prolific contributions to the theory of human capital and to the allocation of time, and his applications of the economic approach to exchange outside price-making markets, such as his economics of the family. Most of this work will get only indirect mention here.

1.2. Neoinstitutional Economics and the rational-choice model

The rational-choice model, with its emphasis on individual agents who maximize an objective function subject to constraints, is central to the NIE. The task of the theorist is seen as specifying both the decision maker's objective function and his or her opportunity set. However, the NIE has done away with the old dichotomy in neoclassical theory of assuming utility maximization by households and profit maximization by firms.[7]

The neoclassical simplification of personifying the firm and assuming that it maximizes profits made sense in the context of unrestricted market exchange, full information, and fully defined private property rights. In this environment, selfish utility-maximization by agents within the firm is constrained by survival

---

7. P. 66 in De Alessi, Louis (1983a). "Property Rights, Transaction Costs, and X-Efficiency: An Essay in Economic Theory." *American Economic Review 73*, (No. 1, March): 64–81.

considerations, as *competition* eliminates inefficient firms and forces survivors to operate on their least-cost curves and maximize profits. Admittedly, owners of competitive firms may prefer to trade consumption on the job for monetary profits, but the implications of such behavior for equilibrium outcomes are of limited interest, given the strict assumptions of the model.

Furthermore, full information and zero transaction costs eliminate all forms of shirking. For example, a monopolistic firm that is run by hired agents is not constrained by competition in the same way as a competitive firm, but, if we assume that the owners of a monopolistic firm contract with hired agents to maximize profits, the agents have no choice but to honor their contracts because the full enforcement of contracts is costless to the owners. These constraints on behavior are eased when positive transaction costs are introduced, and attention is now drawn to the discretion of all parties to a contract – workers, managers, owners, buyers, and sellers.[8]

The theoretical tools of neoclassical economics, particularly the assumption of rational choice, have always been the subject of much debate. Critics have argued that individuals tend to have unstable preferences, that they do not observe the principle of transitivity in their choices, and that people are not calculators who work at lightning speed through the complete set of data relevant to their decisions.[9]

8. In an early contribution to the neoinstitutional theory of the firm, Alchian and Demsetz emphasized that the key to survival for a business organization was how well it overcame the problem of shirking in team production. See Alchian, A., and Demsetz, Harold (1972). "Production, Information Costs, and Economic Organization." *American Economic Review 62* (December): 777–795.

9. The critics include both the new and the old institutionalists. Thorstein Veblen, writing in 1898, ridiculed the theoretical concept of economic man: "The hedonistic conception of man is that of a lightning calculator of pleasures and pains, who oscillates like a homogeneous globule of desire of happiness under the impulse of stimuli that shift him about the area, but leave him intact. . . . Self-imposed in elemental space, he spins symmetrically about his own spiritual axis until the parallelogram of forces bears down upon him, whereupon he follows the line of the resultant. When the force of the impact is spent, he comes to rest, a self-contained globule of desire as before." Pp. 73–74 in Veblen,

A school of thought, which we refer to as the New Institution-alists, has rejected the postulate of optimization and replaced it with Herbert Simon's concept of *satisficing* or other behavioral axioms.[10] According to Simon, man's rationality is bounded, and individuals use a satisficing strategy – that is, they seek to attain an aspiration level. The satisficing model describes a process lead-ing to a decision: People initiate a search when they fall short of their aspirations, and they also revise their targets. One implication of Simon's theory is that the behavior of a rational individual cannot be deducted from the objective environment; a knowledge of his or her mental processes is needed.

The satisficing model represents a rejection of the "hard core" of the neoclassical research program, to use the terminology of Imre Lakatos. De Alessi (1983) argues that the addition of the constraints of property rights and transaction costs to the neo-classical framework offers a richer, more powerful set of testable implications than does the replacement of maximization with sa-tisficing behavior. Although the satisficing model may offer a more realistically descriptive set of axioms, it yields fewer, less clearly specified implications.[11]

Only time can tell which research program will be more fruitful,

Thorstein (1919). "Why Is Economics Not an Evolutionary Science?" In his *The Place of Science in Modern Civilization*. New York: B. W. Huebsch, pp. 56–81.

10. Simon, Herbert (1957). *Models of Man*. New York: Wiley. A recent compar-ison of psychological and economic models of man by a psychologist and an economist is found in Stoebe, Wolfgang, and Frey, Bruno S. (1980). "In De-fense of Economic Man: Towards an Integration of Economics and Psychol-ogy." *Schweizerische Zeitschrift für Volksvirtschaft und Statistik 116* (No. 2, June): 119–148. The authors argue that the underlying models of human be-havior in economics and psychology, although developed in isolation, are very similar. However, psychology makes an effort to consider the subjectively perceived benefits and costs of alternative activities, whereas economics stresses the role of constraints.

11. De Alessi (1983a) [op. cit., note 7], p. 72. De Alessi's criticism was directed particularly at the work of Leibenstein, who responded to the criticism. See Leibenstein, Harvey (1983). "Property Rights and X-Efficiency: Comment." *American Economic Review 73* (No. 4, September): 831–842, and a rejoinder by De Alessi (1983b). "Reply." Ibid.: 843–845.

Neoinstitutional Economics or the New Institutional Economics; or, perhaps, both approaches will be productive but in separate lines of inquiry. The critical issue for institutional economics is to rise above methodological criticism and advance a workable research agenda. This is where the old American institutionalists, led by John R. Commons, failed. According to Ronald Coase (1984), the work of American institutionalists "led to nothing. . . . Without a theory, they had nothing to pass on except a mass of descriptive material waiting for a theory. . . . So if modern institutionalists have antecedents, it is not what went immediately before."[12]

1.3. Wealth maximization and positive economics: a search for criteria

A fair segment of the NIE literature is normative in nature and reflects a search for socially optimal structures of exchange. Many economists have attempted to derive the optimal structure of rules or property rights in the context of externality problems (spillover effects) such as pollution. For example, Buchanan and Stubblebine (1962), in their famous paper on externalities, state as their basic ethical axiom that the individual has an inviolable right to the status quo.[13] No changes in property rights are justifiable unless they result from voluntary exchange, and those who lose valuable rights should receive full compensation for their losses. Therefore, owners of a factory that emits pollutants should

12. See p. 230 in Coase, Ronald H. (1984). "The New Institutional Economics." *Journal of Theoretical and Institutional Economics 140* (No. 1): 229–231. This viewpoint is generally accepted by modern institutionalists. For example, see Williamson, O. E. (1985b). "Reflection on the New Institutional Economics," *Journal for Theoretical and Institutional Economics 141* (No. 1): 187–195. Incidentally, Williamson (1985b) provides a concise summary of the field which we refer to as the New Institutional Economics, and a comparable, lucid account of Neoinstitutional Economics is found in North, Douglass C. (1986). "The New Institutional Economics." *Journal of Institutional and Theoretical Economics 142* (No. 1): 230–237. Note that North and Williamson use the same name to refer to two distinct paradigms.

13. Buchanan, J. M., and Stubblebine, W. Craig (1962). "Externality." *Economica 29* (November): 371–384.

be compensated for all costs imposed on them by a new "Clean Air Act."[14]

Other economists have set the maximization of utility or the maximization of wealth as their norm, but both approaches involve severe measurement problems. Utility is inherently unmeasurable. Wealth can be measured relatively easily in a well-functioning market system, and, theoretically, we can conceive of an omniscient economist selecting, from the set of all possible rules structures, the structure that maximizes wealth. The optimal set of rules, then, is the one that directs resources into uses generating the most wealth; alternatively, when the rules are optimal, resources are in their most highly valued use.

It is important to realize in this context – that is, the context of neoclassical economics – that value is defined in terms of ability and willingness to pay for a marginal unit of a commodity, and depends indirectly on the ownership of rights and wealth distribution.[15] The value of a miracle drug to a patient dying of cancer is fifty dollars, if that is all she is able and willing to pay for it. If this same person wins a million dollars in a lottery and is willing to allocate that amount to saving her life, she now values the drug at one million dollars. In general, the market value of a commodity is equal to the value of the marginal unit to the marginal buyer.

---

14. Buchanan (1959) tries to reconcile this approach and positive economics, but his success is limited. "The political economist is concerned with discovering 'what people want.' The content of his efforts may be reduced to very simple terms. This may be summed up in the familiar statement: *There exist mutual gains from trade.* His task is that of locating possible flaws in the existing social structure and in presenting possible 'improvements.' His specific hypothesis is that *mutual gains* do, in fact, exist as a result of possible changes (trades). This hypothesis is tested by the behavior of private people in response to the suggested alternatives." (p. 137) Buchanan's advocacy of the unanimity test, "appropriately modified," does indeed represent a value judgment. This is not denying his important point that "the economist can never say that one social situation is more 'efficient' than another. This judgment is beyond his range of competence." (pp. 137–138) Buchanan, James M. (1959). "Positive Economics, Welfare Economics, and Political Economy." *Journal of Law and Economics 2* (October): 124–138.

15. See Demsetz, Harold (1972). "Wealth Distribution and the Ownership of Rights." *Journal of Legal Studies 1* (No. 2, June): 13–28.

Our treatise is not concerned with a search for optimal institutions, organizations, and rules. We limit ourselves to studies in positive economics and focus on the economic effects associated with alternative structures. Having said this, we still need a criterion for comparing economic outcomes, and, for comparing the consequences of alternative sets of property rights, we usually have to resort to the neoclassical concepts of value and wealth. Outcomes are measured in terms of a monetary unit and may involve comparisons of labor productivity, capital intensity of production techniques, output prices, the extent of wealth-maximizing price discrimination, expenditures on research and development, operating expenses, and the proportion of current income devoted to wages rather than investments. However, under certain circumstances, physical measures of inputs, outputs, and natural resources can be used to compare economic outcomes. For example, when comparing the consequences of different ownership structures, we can measure the timing and extent of exploitation of pasturelands, fisheries, hunting grounds, or forests; the extent of managerial discretion (e.g., nepotism in hiring); the quality of services and variety of output; the extent of internal monitoring rules; and the ratio of administrative to other personnel.[16]

Ultimately, we are interested in the impact of various structures of property rights on the wealth of nations. It is recognized that a whole range of rule structures is consistent with each general type of economic system – for example, with private property and market exchange or state property and central management. Rational individuals will compete not only to maximize their utility within a given set of rules, but also to seek to change the rules and achieve more favorable outcomes than was possible under the old regime. In equilibrium, the marginal yield on a unit of expenditure and effort in each area is equal. A reduction in the cost

16. See De Alessi, Louis (1983c). "The Role of Property Rights and Transaction Costs: A New Perspective in Economic Theory." *Social Science Journal 20* (No. 3, July): 59–70; idem (1980). "The Economics of Property Rights: A Review of the Evidence." *Research in Law and Economics 2*: 1–47.

of seeking changes in the structure of property rights will upset an existing equilibrium and lead to a new set of rules and a new distribution of wealth.

Theoretically, only one set of rules will maximize the wealth of a nation. It can be argued that, in the absence of transaction costs, eventually such a set of rules will evolve. Although a shift from a relatively inefficient structure of rights to a more efficient set will involve losers as well as winners, the gains are greater than the losses. Therefore, the winners will compensate the losers and still be better off than before. Yet in the real world, high costs of negotiating and enforcing such agreements prohibit them: Seldom do winners voluntarily compensate losers.

North and Thomas (1973), in their pioneering attempt to explain economic growth in terms of property rights structures, used the following words to explain the nature of the dilemma:

> Economic growth will occur if property rights make it worthwhile to undertake socially productive activity. The creating, specifying and enacting of such property rights are costly. . . . As the potential grows for private gains to exceed transaction costs, efforts will be made to establish such property rights. Governments take over the protection and enforcement of property rights because they can do it at a lower cost than private volunteer groups. However, the fiscal needs of government may induce the protection of certain property rights which hinder rather than promote growth; therefore we have no guarantee that productive institutional arrangements will emerge.[17]

1.4. The cost of transacting and the allocation of resources

The emphasis in the NIE on the costs of transacting derives from Ronald H. Coase's articles on the firm and on social cost.[18]

17. P. 8 in North, Douglass C., and Thomas, Robert Paul (1973). *The Rise of the Western World: A New Economic History*. Cambridge: Cambridge University Press.
18. Coase, Ronald H. (1937). "The Nature of the Firm." *Economica 4* (Novem-

The transaction-costs approach was also inspired by the contributions of Stigler and others to the economics of information.[19] Recent research suggests that the cost of contracting and other transaction costs have profound implications for the allocation of resources and the structure of economic organization. It is primarily the addition to the neoclassical framework of positive costs of transacting that distinguishes Neoinstitutional Economics from traditional microeconomics and changes the agenda for research: The cost of transacting makes the assignment of ownership rights paramount, introduces the question of economic organization, and makes the structure of political institutions a key to the understanding of economic growth.

What, then, are transaction costs? In general terms, transaction costs are the costs that arise when individuals exchange ownership rights to economic assets and enforce their exclusive rights. A clearcut definition of transaction costs does not exist, but neither are the costs of production in the neoclassical model well defined. Matthews (1986) offers the following definition: "The fundamental idea of transaction costs is that they consist of the cost of arranging a contract ex ante and monitoring and enforcing it ex post, as opposed to production costs, which are the costs of executing a contract."[20] Transaction costs are opportunity costs, just like other costs in economic theory, and there are both fixed and variable transaction costs.[21]

The tardy introduction of transaction costs into economic theory

ber): 386–405; idem (1960). "The Problem of Social Cost." *Journal of Law and Economics 3* (No. 1): 1–44.

19. Stigler, George J. (1961). "The Economics of Information." *Journal of Political Economy 69* (June): 213–215. Also of importance are Hayek's early contributions where he emphasizes that, compared to centrally managed systems, a major advantage of the market system is how effectively it economizes on the cost of information. Hayek, Friedrich A. (1937). "Economics and Knowledge." *Economica* (February): 33–54; and Hayek, Friedrich A. (1945). "The Use of Knowledge in Society." *American Economic Review* (September): 519–530.

20. P. 906 in Matthews, R. C. O. (1986). "The Economics of Institutions and the Sources of Growth." *Economic Journal 96* (December): 903–910.

21. For various definitions of transaction costs, see Dahlman, Carl J. (1979). "The Problem of Externality." *Journal of Legal Studies 22* (No. 1): 141–162.

is related to the fact that, until recently, most economic theories and models assumed full information, and transaction costs are in one way or another associated with the cost of acquiring information about exchange. But the concepts of information costs and transaction costs are not identical. A lonely person on a desert island will encounter information costs as he goes about his "home production," but an isolated individual does not engage in exchange and therefore will have no transaction costs. When information is costly, various activities related to the exchange of property rights between individuals give rise to transaction costs. These activities include:

1. The search for information about the distribution of price and quality of commodities and labor inputs, and the search for potential buyers and sellers and for relevant information about their behavior and circumstances
2. The bargaining that is needed to find the true position of buyers and sellers when prices are endogenous
3. The making of contracts
4. The monitoring of contractual partners to see whether they abide by the terms of the contract
5. The enforcement of a contract and the collection of damages when partners fail to observe their contractual obligations
6. The protection of property rights against third-party encroachment – for example, protection against pirates or even against the government in the case of illegitimate trade

It is difficult to imagine a state of full information, a world of costless information, but the activities listed above would be either unnecessary or costless in such an environment. Consider the enforcement of contracts: Rational individuals in a full-information environment would not allocate resources to the enforcement of contractual rights. Potential opportunistic behavior by one's partners in exchange would be known in advance along with potential reactions by the state, outcomes of the judicial process, all possible coalitions of the interested parties, and so on. All individuals would be able to trace out the consequences of cheating and stealing, and outcomes of transactions would be certain.

Let us return to the world of costly information and see how various factors can bring about changes in the costs of transacting. Note first that high transaction costs can limit or prevent otherwise advantageous exchange, such as when trade is threatened by a third party (a band of pirates).[22] When a state introduces and enforces the rule of law in a lawless area, it thereby lowers transaction costs and stimulates trade. When it prohibits trade in certain commodities – for example, heroin or antigovernment literature – it raises the cost of exchanging the restricted goods, perhaps to a point where trade is sharply reduced or abandoned altogether. Historically, the state has lowered transaction costs by establishing and maintaining standards of measurement and by introducing and maintaining stable money, because rapid inflation, particularly variable and unpredictable inflation, increases the cost of transacting.

The impact of technical change on transaction costs is ambiguous. On the one hand, technical change can help to lower transaction costs by introducing, for example, new and effective methods of measurement, but, on the other hand, technical change is associated with more complex commodities, and hence higher transaction costs. Technical change provides an opportunity to design new structures of economic organization that lower the costs of contracting, but the little systematic empirical evidence that exists suggests that the net effect of technical change has been to increase the cost of transacting in advanced industrial economies.

North and Wallis (1986) attempt to measure the changing size of the transaction sector in the U.S. economy between 1870 and 1970. The authors provide estimates for "the total amount of re-

22. North (1968) documents how reduced piracy increased productivity in ocean shipping. North, Douglass C. (1968). "Sources of Productivity Change in Ocean Shipping, 1600–1850." *Journal of Political Economy* 76 (September/October): 953–970.

sources used by firms that sell transaction services in the market, as well as measuring the resources devoted to transacting within firms that produce other goods and services." In the private sector, industries that provide transaction services include wholesale and retail trade (but not transportation), finance, insurance, and real estate. Those occupations outside government, which are related primarily to the facilitation, coordination, or monitoring of exchange, are owners, managers, and proprietors (coordination); clerical workers (processing of information); foremen and inspectors (coordination and monitoring of labor inputs); and police and guards (protection of property). The authors find that the *resource use* of the private and public transaction sectors, measured as a share of GNP, grew from roughly one quarter of GNP in 1870 to over one half of GNP in 1970. Note that their measure includes only specialized transaction resources that are bought or hired and excludes various transaction costs borne by individuals – for example, waiting in lines or investing in search in the factor or commodity markets.[23]

In Chapter 7, Section 7.5, we present arguments to the effect that money is essentially a device designed to lower transaction costs. If these arguments are correct, it is not surprising that no role for money has been found in Walrasian general equilibrium models, because they are based on the assumption of zero transaction costs. When information is costless, individuals are able to trace in their minds all economic outcomes, both present and future. In a model with a finite time horizon, trade patterns and outcomes for all *n* periods are anticipated in period 0 and final

---

23. North, Douglass C., and Wallis, John J. (1986). "Measuring the Transaction Sector in the American Economy, 1870–1970." In *Long-Term Factors in American Economic Growth*, Vol. 51 of *The Income and Wealth Series*, Stanley L. Engerman and Robert E. Gallman, eds. Chicago: University of Chicago Press. North and Wallis are not able to conclude from their study that the *total* output of transaction services has either grown or shrunk. Further, even if the level of transaction costs, measured as a share of GNP, were to increase, transaction costs per unit of commodities could fall with rising productivity of inputs.

settlements can be made at the outset; therefore, the transfer of commodities does not require a two-way flow of money and commodities.[24]

The status of monopolies would be much different in a full-information world than in the world we know, although this is generally not recognized in models that ignore transaction costs. In fact, the distortive effects of monopolies on the allocation of resources would disappear.[25]

One of the well-known outcomes of neoclassical economics is that the introduction of monopolistic practices in a competitive market involves greater losses for buyers than gains for sellers. If the cost of collective action were zero, rational buyers would combine and bribe monopolists to follow the pricing policies of competitive firms. Alternatively, the monopolist might on her own accord select the same output as a competitive industry, but also appropriate the entire consumers' surplus by following a policy of perfect price discrimination, using the demand line to charge different prices for each unit of output. Price discrimination would be easy because the monopolist could, at no cost, establish the true marginal values of her commodity for each customer and also detect attempts by customers to buy for the purpose of reselling. But the cost to the buyers of combining and refusing to deal with the monopolist also would be zero. Finally, the role assumed by the state would influence the outcome. Is it legal to combine against a monopolist? Does the monopolist have the right to act as a perfect discriminator?

The celebrated welfare properties of a free-market system are derived from general equilibrium models assuming full informa-

---

24. P. 3 in Goodhart, C. A. E. (1975). *Money, Information and Uncertainty*. London: Macmillan.
25. This point has been made by Demsetz. See pp. 43–47 in Demsetz, Harold (1980). *Economic, Political, and Legal Dimensions of Competition*. Amsterdam: North-Holland. Demsetz concludes that the deadweight allocation loss, which is associated with monopoly, reappears when we introduce positive transaction costs. But he protests the habit of economists to evaluate real outcomes in terms of models with zero transaction costs as if the costs of exchange were some avoidable, unnecessary evil. The question of transaction costs and efficiency is examined in Section 1.5.

tion. These models show that an unfettered market system tends to gravitate toward an equilibrium where all opportunities for mutually advantageous exchanges between individuals have been used. In equilibrium, no exchange can take place that makes someone better off without at the same time making at least one individual worse off: Given the initial distribution of wealth, the allocation of resources is shown to be (Pareto) optimal.

Critics, going back to Arthur C. Pigou, have argued that there are significant exceptions to this optimal outcome, which are caused by the problem of externalities or spillovers.[26] Production and exchange often confer benefits and impose costs upon individuals without involving them in voluntary exchange, and this fact makes social costs and benefits diverge from private costs and benefits. If such spillover costs and benefits are ignored, the allocation of resources is suboptimal by the neoclassical criterion. But Ronald Coase (1960), in his article on "The Problem of Social Cost," demonstrated that, given the usual neoclassical assumptions of zero transaction costs, the critics were wrong. No matter how the rights to the various resources are distributed initially, the resources will always end up in their highest valued use, and rational agents will always take spillover costs and benefits into account. The problem of social cost disappears.[27]

Coase's theorem is best illustrated with the help of an example. When the cost of collective action and other transaction costs are zero, people living in the neighborhood of a factory that is free to pollute the atmosphere will combine to offer a bribe to the entrepreneur for reducing the emission of pollutants. The maximum bribe

26. Pigou, A. C. (1932). *The Economics of Welfare*, 4th ed. London: Macmillan.

27. In Chapter 4, Section 4.4, we discuss how the *allocation of resources* may change with the legal position, when the price system works without cost, even though the assignment of rights will not affect the *Pareto efficiency* of the economy. A continuing debate surrounds Coase's 1960 article. "No year passes without several articles appearing in the most respected journals refuting the [Coase] theorem and a corresponding number reaffirming it." P. 53 in Veljanovski, Cento G. (1982). "The Coase Theorems and the Economic Theory of Markets and Law." *Kyklos 35* (No. 1): 53–74. This article provides a good summary of arguments by Coase's critics.

offered by the neighborhood will equal the sum of the value of clean air to all the individuals who are affected by the pollution. The offer increases the entrepreneur's *opportunity cost* of polluting, and his or her decision whether to limit or stop the emission depends on the loss of net revenue from doing so relative to the proposed bribe. This assumes, of course, that under the existing system of property rights the factory is not liable for the pollution it causes.

Alternatively, if the *residents* have a right to clean air in the neighborhood, the factory could offer them payments for the right to pollute. If we again assume that the transaction cost of making such agreements is zero, the outcome will once more depend on the relative valuations of air as a resource by the households and by the factory, and the problem of social cost as usually defined in the literature will not arise.

The reader should be clear about the meaning of the terms "social cost" or "inefficient spillovers" in the literature. Consider the case of a Western chemical firm that locates a factory in a poor Third World country in order to take advantage of the low opportunity cost of polluting in that area. The factory emits poisonous fumes that every month kill several individuals in a neighboring village. Assume that the highly profitable output is sold on international markets and that the annual income of the local families is only a few hundred dollars a year. It is conceivable that the total wealth of the families around the factory is only a small fraction of the cost to the firm of limiting the pollution. If that were the case, we would say that the resources had found their highest valued use and that the problem of social cost was not present.[28]

1.5 Transaction costs and efficiency

As was stated in the previous section, there is a theoretical tradition in economics dating back to Arthur C. Pigou, early in the century, which examines *inefficiencies* in the allocation of re-

---

28. But note that unrestricted exchange and zero transactions costs would turn the world into a single market and equalize the price or opportunity cost of polluting.

sources for various areas of economic life. It is a central characteristic of *welfare economics* that economic outcomes derived from the basic neoclassical model are used as a criterion of efficiency. Outcomes that deviate from outcomes in models based on fully defined exclusive rights and costless transactions are called "inefficient."

This practice of comparing the ideal and the actual has drawn protests from several economists, including Harold Demsetz (1969):

> The view that now pervades much public policy
> economics implicitly presents the relevant choice as
> between an ideal norm and an existing "imperfect"
> institutional arrangement. This *nirvana* approach differs
> considerably from a *comparative institution* approach in
> which the relevant choice is between alternative real
> institutional arrangements.[29]

According to Demsetz (1969), words like "nonoptimal," "inefficient," and "over-" or "underutilization" are misleading and ambiguous unless the outcome that they describe can be improved upon. "A relevant notion of efficiency must refer to scarcity and people as they are, not as they could be." Demsetz provides the following quotation from Arrow (1962) to demonstrate how even the most distinguished economists sometimes make careless use of the terminology of welfare economics:

> In an ideal socialist economy, the reward for invention
> would be completely separated from any charge to the
> users of information. In a free enterprise economy,
> inventive activity is supported by using the invention to
> create property rights; precisely to the extent that it is
> successful, there is an underutilization of the
> information.[30]

29. P. 1 in Demsetz, Harold (1969). "Information and Efficiency: Another Viewpoint." *Journal of Law and Economics 12* (No. 1): 1–22.
30. Ibid., p. 11. See pp. 614–615 in Arrow, Kenneth J. (1962). "Economic Welfare and the Allocation of Resources for Invention." In Universities-National Bu-

Demsetz concludes that "modern analysis has yet to describe inefficiency in a world where indivisibilities are present and knowledge is costly to produce."[31] We can add a further point. In the basic neoclassical model, which assumes zero transaction costs, there is no logical rationale for contractual arrangements such as various types of firms or even money. The logic of such arrangements becomes apparent when transaction costs are added to the model. We will argue in later chapters that, ceteris paribus, various contractual arrangements are designed to economize on transaction costs, and transaction costs reflect the scarcity of information. If this basic insight of the NIE is correct, it is not clear how economic outcomes in a world of full information can be used as a yardstick of efficiency in real-world situations.

Staten and Umbeck (1986) take this line of argument a step further in a provocative essay.[32] If efficiency is defined as Pareto efficiency, they argue, then it is logically impossible to derive inefficient solutions from microeconomic models that use the behavioral postulate of constrained maximization. According to the traditional definition of efficiency in neoclassical economics, a resource is used efficiently when it has been allocated to the user who has the highest value for it as measured by the user's willingness and ability to pay. Efficient outcomes result logically from the *assumptions* of microeconomic models whereby individuals are seen as maximizing utility functions subject to constraints. Pareto efficiency is reached when all transactions that are mutually advantageous have been completed, and when, by definition, agents complete all advantageous transactions, given the model's constraints.

The point is illustrated in Figure 1.1, which shows the marginal

reau Committee for Economic Research. *The Rate and Direction of Inventive Activity*. Princeton: Princeton University Press.

31. Demsetz (1969) [op. cit., note 29], p. 19.
32. Staten, Mike, and Umbeck, John (1986). "Economic Inefficiency of Law: A Logical and Empirical Impossibility." Working paper, Department of Economics, University of Delaware, and Department of Economics, Purdue University. The remainder of the section draws on this paper.

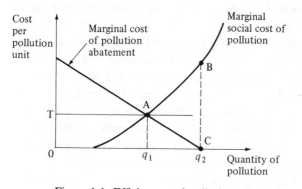

Figure 1.1. Efficiency and pollution abatement.

value to the owners of a factory of the right to pollute (the value of not having to clean up), and the aggregate marginal cost of pollution to the members of a neighboring community. When the factory is free to pollute, the owners make no effort to limit pollution and emit pollutants until point q_2 is reached, where the marginal value of pollution to producers is zero, the aggregate marginal cost of pollution to the community is BC, and the excessive social cost of pollution equals the area ABC. The outcome is said to be inefficient according to the Pareto criterion: The equality between social benefits and costs at the margin does not hold, and the air around the factory is not allocated to uses of highest value.

Staten and Umbeck (1986) emphasize that it is logically impossible to derive a gap comparable to BC in a microeconomic model. Figure 1.1 shows that, in the range of q_1 to q_2, pollution causes more harm to the community than it costs the factory to clean up. Why then don't those who suffer from pollution pay (bribe) the factory to limit the pollution to q_1? The answer must be that one or more constraints are missing from the model, for example, a transaction cost such as the cost of collective action or a legal restraint: The model is misspecified. *The equilibrium outcome in a microeconomic model is Pareto efficient by definition.*

Cheung (1974), in his important article, "A Theory of Price

Control," makes the same point but in passing and without developing it further:

> The lack of a theory to explain legislative action must be my chief defense for using the term "dissipation," which implies economic waste. Yet in a world where each and every individual is asserted to behave consistently with the postulate of constrained maximization, economic inefficiency presents a contradiction in terms. Even outright mistakes are traceable to constraints of some type. The world is efficient, if the model describing it sufficiently specifies the gains and costs of making it so. Such specification, however, is not always essential for the derivation of refutable implications.[33]

Where do we stand, then, with respect to efficiency? First, a comparison of two models both yielding Pareto-efficient outcomes (e.g., when one of the models assumes zero transaction costs) tells us primarily that different constraints yield different equilibrium outcomes, but the exercise does not represent a theoretical demonstration of the existence of a Pareto-type inefficiency. Second, attempts to measure empirically whether Pareto's marginal conditions hold are impractical. The concept of value, defined as the maximum amount of one good that an individual is willing and able to give up for another good, is a theoretical construct that is not observable. And even if measurement were possible, which it is not, a measured discrepancy between social and private benefits and costs at the margin would simply suggest that the assumption of constrained optimization is an unrealistic way to characterize human behavior.

Third, microeconomic models *can* be used to derive testable propositions about human behavior under alternative sets of constraints. For example, the model in Figure 1.1 can be used to predict the effects of a government tax of OT on each unit of

---

33. P. 71 in Cheung, Steven N. S. (1974). "A Theory of Price Control." *Journal of Law and Economics* (April): 53–71.

pollution. If the tax is introduced by the government, then the predictions of the model can also be tested. Similarly, we can theorize about the effects of changes in the laws and regulations, for example, governing the West German trade sector. A prediction that the market price to consumers of certain products will fall, if restrictions on direct exchange between factories and households are removed, can be tested once such changes have been introduced. However, microeconomic theory cannot be used to prove that changes in the constraints facing economic agents will bring benefits net of costs to society.

The question of welfare effects is taken up again (but from a different viewpoint) in Chapter 4, Section 4.3. There we discuss whether the introduction of private property into a sector of an economy where exclusive rights did not exist before will unambiguously increase social welfare if the new arrangement results in an outward move of the economy's frontier of production possibilities.

1.6. The quality dimensions of goods and the cost of measurement

One of the consequences of relaxing the full-information assumption of the basic micro model is to draw attention to the multiple qualitative dimensions of most goods. In a full-information world, all margins of a commodity can be measured and priced without cost, and it is therefore understandable that standard economic theory has, until recently, ignored multiple qualitative dimensions.

In his text on microeconomic theory, Edmond Malinvaud recognizes that nearly all goods possess a number of qualitative margins. Malinvaud suggests that this problem may be bypassed by treating as different goods all versions of the same product that have different qualitative margins:

> In actual fact, many products show a more or less immense range of qualities. . . . However, the concept of a commodity can be adapted to this diversity among products of the same kind. Two different qualities of the same product or service may in fact be represented

by two different commodities. Of course the number of
goods then becomes much greater than that of products
and services. But there is no reason why *l* [the number
of commodities] should not be very large.[34]

This solution is in many ways analogous to the treatment of
uncertainty by Arrow, Debreu, and others who assume that individuals know all conceivable states of the world and associate a
probability with each element in the set of all possible states.[35] It
has been demonstrated that once these assumptions are made,
uncertainty can be incorporated into the neoclassical model without substantially affecting the traditional equilibrium outcomes.
However, because these models do not take into account transaction costs, the introduction, in this fashion, of uncertainty (and
quality variations) does not suggest any role for contractual arrangements, such as the firm. But NIE is concerned with the ways
in which uncertainty about qualitative dimensions of goods and,
more generally, about the behavior of agents affects the organization of production and exchange.

The problem of measurement is a pervasive phenomenon. The
cost of measuring a valuable dimension of a good can be so high that
the cost of measurement exceeds the benefits. In many instances,
such a margin carries a zero price if the composite good is traded. It
is also possible that the cost of measurement is lower to one party of
an exchange than to the other, and that the differential creates an
incentive to design market practices whereby measurement is assigned to the party who has a special advantage in measurement.[36]

The qualitative attributes of commodities tend to grow more
complex with specialization in production and technical change.

---

34. P. 6, Malinvaud, Edmond (1972). *Lectures on Microeconomic Theory*. Amsterdam: North-Holland Publishing.
35. The introduction of uncertainty complicates the definition of a commodity in
modern microeconomic theory even more than the recognition of quality variations. "*The complete characterization of a commodity must specify the states
in which it is available*. In other words, the commodities we shall now be
discussing must be 'contingent,' that is, their existence must be related to the
realization of certain events." Ibid., p. 275.
36. The relationship between market practices and the cost of measurement is
discussed in various parts of this book, particularly in Chapter 7, Section 7.2.

Consider the purchase of an automobile with its hundreds of qualitative margins. The measurement problem involves finding out both the potential dimensions of various makes of cars and the exact condition of a particular (perhaps used) vehicle. Or, take the example of word processing on a personal computer. You are told by a friend that this technique could save you much time, but you really don't know what attributes good word processing programs have or should have, and you know even less about personal computers and their qualitative margins. How does all this affect the organization of exchange and the allocation of resources?

One of the major propositions of NIE is that measurement costs systematically influence the structure of contracts and the organization of markets and of economic institutions in general: When measurement costs rise, economic forces (competition) are likely to work toward new arrangements that lower the cost of measurement (transaction costs).

High measurement costs often invite regulation by the state – for example, the regulation of weights and measures and, in the United States, the requirement by some state governments that dealers in used cars provide all buyers with "free" warranties, which is comparable to selling compulsory insurance to all buyers. Many economists suspect that regulation by the state is often motivated by considerations of redistribution rather than a desire to lower costs, and they also argue that when the state genuinely seeks to lower measurement costs, the effects can be quite the opposite because new types of transaction costs and self-serving agents get in the way. All this may be true in some instances and not in others. Few would doubt that governmental efforts to supply universal standards of weights and measures have often sharply lowered measurement costs. Yet it is probably true that in providing this service the state has at times been motivated by a desire to increase the tax base of the economy by lowering the cost of measuring assets, outputs, and inputs for tax purposes. Redistribution and an increase in net output need not always be mutually exclusive![37]

---

37. See North (1981). Chapter 3, "A Neoclassical Theory of the State." In his *Structure and Change in Economic History*. New York: W. W. Norton; idem

In sum, our interest in qualitative margins of goods and in the cost of measuring them does not reflect an irrational impulse to confound neat economic models that bypass these issues. Rather, we see the cost of establishing qualitative differences in goods and services as a key to a better understanding of the variety of economic organization, ranging from the organization of markets for used cars in America to the arrangements that govern exchange between the Soviet central planner and his plant manager.

1.7. Transaction costs and equilibrium outcomes

According to the rational-choice model, individuals *optimize*, given their fixed preferences, various constraints, and a choice set. A rational individual optimizes by selecting from the choice set those elements that maximize his or her welfare (or objective function). The investigator seeks to model how an optimizing individual reacts to a change in one or more constraints and how such reactions by many individuals lead to new *equilibrium outcomes* of the competitive process. We should note that in real life the restrictions (the constraints) on the choice set are almost infinite and include, for example, the pull of gravity. In order to keep formal models manageable, it is customary whenever possible to specify only constraints that are of theoretical interest to the investigator.

The distinction between optimization and equilibrium outcomes in economic models can be illustrated with an example taken from the theory of the firm. In standard price theory, the firm or its owner is treated as an agent who maximizes profits. If the firm operates in a competitive market, its choices are constrained by the price of inputs and outputs and the available production technology. In this environment, optimization involves the choice of a technology, a combination of inputs that minimizes the cost of production, and finally the selection of a level of output that maximizes profits – namely a level at which marginal cost equals the

(1984). "Government and the Cost of Exchange in History." *Journal of Economic History 44* (No. 2, June): 255–264.

exogenous price of the output. It is a fundamental characteristic of the neoclassical model of competition that individual firms do not compete directly but adjust to changes in exogenous parameters. For example, a change in the price of the output leads each firm to revise its optimization decision – that is, readjust the use of inputs and the level of output – and consider whether to enter or leave an industry.

The system of interaction between agents in the Walrasian general equilibrium model has been labeled *parametric interaction*. Parametric interaction is found in formal models with both complete and incomplete information. However, strategic interaction is also consistent with the rational-choice model. Strategic interaction is said to be indirect when the agents cannot contact each other and make contracts. This process leads to the Nash type of equilibrium. Strategic interaction can also be direct. Then individuals can contact each other and form coalitions, and the sequence of their optimizing decisions typically leads to equilibrium outcomes referred to as the *core*.[38]

An equilibrium outcome is reached when the process of readjustment is completed and there are no further changes in the constraints. The system is then in a state of rest where no individual wishes or is able to make further adjustments. It is important to realize that the well-known long-run equilibrium outcome of a competitive industry – where each firm operates on the lowest point of the average cost curve for a factory of an optimum size, where each firm receives only the normal rate of return on its capital, where returns are equalized across all industries – is not explicitly sought by individual firms. It is rather an unintended outcome of a sequence of decisions by firms that adjust to changes in their constraints.

The NIE attempts to generalize the economic approach and apply it to new areas. These extensions include the following: First, new constraints have been explicitly added, the most important

38. See Johansen, Leif (1981). "Interaction in Economic Theory." *Economie Appliquée 34* (Nos. 2–3): 229–267.

being the structure of property rights and transaction costs. Thus fortified, the economic approach has been used to analyze traditional market exchange; exchange within organizations, such as firms, bureaucracies, and legislative assemblies; and exchange in alternative economic systems. Already this work has led to a better understanding of how even relatively small changes in the assignment of private property rights can significantly affect human behavior. In terms of formal theories, the focus is here on the effects of changes in constraints on *equilibrium outcomes*.

Second, attempts have also been made to explain or endogenize the organization of markets and the structure of contracts. Economic organizations, such as the firm, are modeled as a network of contracts. Competition among organizational forms leads to *equilibrium contracts*.

Finally, social and political institutions are also seen as the outcome of exchange between individual agents. Competition for survival among institutions leads to *equilibrium institutions*. Neoinstitutional economists have just begun to model social and political institutions and attempt to derive testable propositions. This area represents the frontier of research in the field.[39]

Adding transaction costs and variations in the structure of property rights to the neoclassical model enriches it but at the cost of making the analysis more complex. In general, once we step outside the simple micro model with its two dimensions of price and quantity and seek to model adjustments at several margins, it may literally become impossible to make a priori positive statements about human behavior in specific situations. A suburban supermarket may find it profitable to offer a "free" parking lot and let the marginal cost of the parking lot be reflected in the price of the commodities at the store, whereas a comparable store in a downtown area may prefer to expend resources to limit parking to

---

39. North (1981) argues that a successful theory of institutional change will require not only a theory of the state and a theory of demographic change but also a theory of ideological behavior and a theory of technical change. So far there has been limited success in endogenizing some of these factors. See North (1981) [op. cit., note 37], Chapter 6.

customers only or to charge for parking space by the hour. Cheung (1974) has emphasized the same point in the context of price controls:

> If certain outcomes are to be attributed to the control, the constraints specified must conform essentially to those in real practice. Given the usual complexity of any effective price control, and that one control usually differs from another, it is highly unlikely that the actual constraints can be guessed correctly. Furthermore, the use of imaginary constraints will easily lead to *ad hoc* theorizing. . . . The central problem in interpreting the effects of price control is therefore the one common to all empirical economic inquiry. On the one hand the specification of constraints requires an investigation of the real-world situation; on the other the investigation itself must be guided or restricted by some theoretical framework.[40]

There is little doubt that the success of Neoinstitutional Economics will depend on finding the appropriate blend of theorizing and empirical work. The current state of affairs is well summarized by R. C. O. Matthews (1986) in his Presidential Address to the Royal Economic Society:

> Theory has made an indispensable contribution in recent times to advances of understanding in this area. But it seems to me that in the economics of institutions theory is now outstripping empirical research to an excessive extent. No doubt the same could be said of other fields in economics, but there is a particular point about this one. Theoretical modelling may or may not be more difficult in this field than in others, but empirical work is confronted by a special difficulty. Because economic institutions are complex, they do not lend themselves easily to quantitative measurement. Even in the respects in which they do, the data very

40. Cheung (1974) [op. cit., note 33], pp. 55–56.

often are not routinely collected by national statistical offices. As a result, the statistical approach which has become the bread and butter of applied economics is not straightforwardly applicable. Examples of it do exist, the literature on the economics of slavery being perhaps the most fully developed – not surprisingly because slavery is an institution that is sharply defined. But to a large extent the empirical literature has consisted of case-studies which are interesting but not necessarily representative, together with a certain amount on legal court cases, which are almost certainly *not* representative. Is this the *best* we can do? There is a challenge here on the empirical side to economists to see what is the best way forward.[41]

41. Matthews, R. C. O. (1986) [op. cit., note 20], p. 917. To Matthews's list of important empirical work, we might add studies of institutions and contractual arrangements in the areas of industrial organization, natural resources, and agriculture.

2

Property rights, agency, and economic organization

2.1. Property rights and their dimensions

Most goods can be useful, or otherwise give satisfaction to individuals, in several ways. A walking stick can be used for support when walking or to beat an unpleasant neighbor. Potatoes can be eaten baked or used for making alcohol in a basement distillery. A gun can be used for hunting or holding up banks. A site can be used for the construction of a home or a small factory. We refer to the rights of individuals to use resources as *property rights*. A system of property rights is "a method of assigning to particular individuals the 'authority' to select, for specific goods, any use from an unprohibited class of uses."[1] The concept of

1. Alchian, Armen A. (1965) "Some Economics of Property Rights." *Il Politico* *30* (No. 4): 816–829. (Originally published in 1961 by the Rand Corporation.) Reprinted in idem (1977). *Economic Forces at Work* (see p. 130 for the quote). Indianapolis: Liberty Press. The revival of the property rights approach is associated with Alchian's article, and also with Coase's article on social cost (see Chapter 1, this volume), and a paper by Guido Calabresi. "Some Thoughts on Risk Distribution and the Law of Torts." *Yale Law Journal 70* (No. 4, March): 499–553. Important early contributions were also made by Harold Demsetz. See, for example, Demsetz, Harold (1964). "The Exchange and Enforcement of Property Rights." *Journal of Law and Economics 3* (October): 1–44. It is generally accepted that Karl Marx was the first social scientist to have a theory of property rights. "While it is true that many social scientists, including Adam Smith, appreciated the importance of property rights, Marx was the first to assert that the specification of property rights can be explained as responses to social problems that find their source in scarcity, and that property rights struc-

property rights, as used in NIE, is a broad concept.[2] In terms of law, it is wider than the legal concept of property rights, and it also includes social norms, as Alchian (1977) has emphasized:

> The rights of individuals to the use of resources (i.e., property rights) in any society are to be construed as supported by the force of etiquette, social custom, ostracism, and formal legally enacted laws supported by the states' power of violence of punishment. Many of the constraints on the use of what we call private property involve the force of etiquette and social ostracism. The level of noise, the kind of clothes we wear, our intrusion on other people's privacy are restricted not merely by laws backed by police force, but by social acceptance, reciprocity, and voluntary social ostracism for violators of accepted codes of conduct.[3]

It is common to distinguish three categories of property rights: First, there are the rights to use an asset – user rights – which define the potential uses of an asset that are legitimate for an individual, including the right to transform physically or even destroy an asset. We should note that restrictions of rights that shrink the set of permissible uses will lower the economic value of an asset if highly valued uses are excluded. Second, there is the right to earn income from an asset and contract over the terms with other individuals. Third, there is the right to transfer permanently

tures affect economic behavior in specific and predictable ways." Pp. 383–384 in Pejovich, Steve (1982). "Karl Marx, Property Rights School and the Process of Social Change." *Kyklos 35* (No. 3): 383–397.
2. Furubotn and Pejovich (1972) survey the state of the new property rights approach as of the early 1970s. Their well-known survey contains almost no references prior to 1960, and it makes clear that the property rights research program took off in the early 1960s. De Alessi (1980) provides an excellent update with a special emphasis on empirical results. See Furubotn, Eirik G., and Pejovich, Svetozar (1972). "Property Rights and Economic Theory: A Survey of Recent Literature." *Journal of Economic Literature 10* (December): 1137–1162; and De Alessi, Louis (1980). "The Economics of Property Rights: A Review of the Evidence." *Research in Law and Economics*: 1–47.
3. Alchian (1977) [op. cit., note 1], pp. 129–130.

to another party ownership rights over an asset – that is, to alienate or sell an asset.

The set of rights facing Yugoslav workers in the socialist self-management sector is a good example of the many ways in which the three types of rights can blend. The rights structure in Yugoslavia has changed frequently, but the essential feature of the Yugoslav model is that the workers in an enterprise have a restricted right to use its capital assets to generate income but are required to maintain the value of the assets. Usually the allocation of the firm's net income has been regulated by the government. The economic consequences of this arrangement have given rise to a thriving subbranch within economics.[4]

The enforcement of property rights involves excluding others from the use of scarce resources. Exclusive ownership calls for costly measurement and delineation of assets and enforcement of ownership rights. The value of exclusive ownership rights depends, ceteris paribus, on the cost of enforcing those rights – that is, the cost of excluding others, which ultimately depends on coercion. The enforcement of exclusive rights is usually undertaken by both individual owners and the state. Enforcement by the state of ownership rights increases the value of privately owned assets and constitutes one of the cornerstones of market exchange. In areas where the state does not help to enforce contracts or even outright prohibits possession and exchange (e.g., of heroin), high transaction costs usually limit or even prevent exchange.[5]

The cost of enforcing exclusive rights is reduced when the public generally entertains social norms that coincide with the basic structure of rights that the state seeks to uphold. The disintegration of social norms can have important economic consequences. For ex-

4. For example, see Furubotn, Eirik G., and Pejovich, Svetozar (1970). "Property Rights and the Behavior of the Firm in a Socialist State: The Example of Yugoslavia." *Zeitschrift für Nationalökonomie 30* (Nos. 3–4): 431–454.
5. Note that outright prohibition by the state of certain forms of exchange may either lower or raise prices, depending on how demand is affected, how well the ban is enforced, how law-abiding suppliers are, etc. However, economic theory predicts that the quantity traded will fall.

ample, owners of buildings in high crime areas have been known to abandon them when high enforcement costs have reduced the net value of their property to zero.

In general, high transaction costs can limit the enforcement of exclusive property rights even by powerful states. When appropriate social norms are missing, individuals may establish structures of property rights that rival those of the state, particularly in activities where the enforcement of state rules is relatively costly. The Mafia in Italy and the United States is a notorious example of this. From an economic viewpoint, illegitimate property rights are just as consequential as legitimate ones, and the behavior of gangs such as the Mafia resembles the behavior of the state in many ways. The gangs seek to monopolize legitimate and illegitimate industries, such as the disposal of toxic waste or the trade in narcotics, and even tax their "subjects" – for example, by asking owners of restaurants and nightclubs for protection fees. These antistate structures usually hide in the shadow of high transaction costs (sometimes with the help of corrupt or frightened agents of the state) and invite civil war when they come out into the open, unless the state capitulates without a fight. When antistate elements take over the state itself, former criminals become political leaders and their organization becomes a legitimate state.

Exclusive rights can be held by individuals, which is *private ownership*, or by the state (i.e., by those who control it), which is *state ownership*. Related to state ownership is *communal ownership*, whereby a community controls access to a resource by excluding outsiders and regulating its use by insiders. Finally, when ownership is common, no one holds exclusive rights. *Common ownership* or *open access* can be due to prohibitive transaction costs of establishing and enforcing exclusive rights over a resource relative to its value or to a refusal by the state to legitimize and enforce contracts in a particular area. Although this elementary classification of ownership rights has generated a number of interesting hypotheses – for example, regarding the utilization of common resources – the study of comparative economic institutions usually requires more detailed specification of rights. Several basic ownership forms coexist in all economies: For example, in a Western industrial state, we can find common fishing grounds, private pharmaceutical companies, and state-run railways. Furthermore, property rights are nearly always restricted or partitioned in some sense, for instance, by means of regulations governing fishing seasons and fishing gear or the marketing of medicinal drugs.

The concept of state ownership is particularly ambiguous. In a democratic society, state property may have some of the characteristics of common property; for instance, the citizens usually do not have the right to sell their *individual* titles to public property, whereas under dictatorship, state ownership can approach the system of private property with the economy resembling a huge corporation.

Some forms of communal property are often found in primitive societies, and the high seas are usually common property. The Russian Revolution of 1917 made the question of state property an important issue in the modern world, although the phenomenon is well known in history. Under a Soviet-type system of state ownership, the transaction costs of valuing productive assets is relatively high, particularly if they are to be valued in terms of the preferences of millions of households. In practice, the allocation of resources in such systems is in part based on planners' preferences.

The existence of markets for productive assets is the most important feature of a market exchange system based on private property, capitalism. The market price of a productive asset signals the opportunity cost of using the resource in production, also taking into account potential future uses. Relative to other arrangements, the market provides this critical information at low cost. The market value of a means of production is derived from the demand for goods and services by final users, but its value depends also on the distribution of wealth and the detailed structure of private property rights.

2.2. **Attenuation and partitioning of property rights**

When the *state* imposes some limits on exclusive rights, it is customary to refer to these restrictions as the *attenuation* of property rights. Property rights are said to be unattenuated when restrictions on individual rights to use, to earn income from, and to exchange assets are absent, except that the individual does not have the right to cause *physical* damage to the resources of others. According to this definition, a limit on how fast you can drive your car attenuates your user rights, but a ban on using your car to drive over people or drive into shop windows does not. However, the state does not protect the market value of property rights in an unattenuated world: Although you have no right to put fire to the factory of a competitor, you have the full right to bankrupt him by importing a substitute product from Singapore.

The concept of attenuation is somewhat more ambiguous than it appears at first glance, because of *spillover effects* which often arise when an individual exercises his or her rights. Consider the case of a factory that uses a dirty production process and spoils the air for a neighboring community. It can be argued that a regulation that prohibits the use of this particular technology attenuates owners' rights at the factory, but a regulation that permits use of the technology with impunity attenuates the rights of individuals in the neighboring community. May it be, then, that the concept of unattenuated private rights is logically untenable? Conceptually, our problem arises because property rights over a valuable resource – the rights to the air over the factory and the neighborhood – have not been *delineated*. In fact, the dispute between the factory and the community involves a struggle over access to a common property resource. Once ownership over the atmosphere is established, the problem disappears.

Implicit in the basic neoclassical model are two assumptions: that all valuable rights, including the right to airwaves, the space around us, and sunrays, are privately held; and also that these rights are unattenuated by the state.[6] If we add the assumption of

6. Note that this assumption leaves no role for the state except that of a voluntary

full information, valuable rights will always find their highest valued use as Coase (1960) demonstrated.

In the real world, we often find that rights to valuable resources are not fully delineated. There are several reasons for this, which include a weak state, high measurement costs relative to the value of an asset, rapid economic change, and struggle over the distribution of wealth. For example, the introduction of new mechanical devices, such as the automobile, copy machines, computers, or videotapes, often causes uncertainty as to property rights and leaves valuable rights in the public domain. Considerable time may pass, often involving costly disputes, before the state firmly establishes property rights in these areas.

Property rights to a resource are often *partitioned*. Taking the example of land, Alchian describes the partitioning of property rights in these terms:

> By this I refer to the fact that at the same time several people may each possess some portion of the rights to use the land. A may possess the right to grow wheat on it. B may possess the right to walk across it. C may possess the right to dump ashes and smoke on it. D may possess the right to fly an airplane over it. E may have the right to subject it to vibrations consequent to the use of some neighboring equipment. And each of these rights may be transferable. In sum, private property rights to various partitioned uses of land are "owned" by different persons.[7]

According to Coase's theorem, the initial partitioning of property rights does not matter for the allocation of resources (ignoring wealth effects) when all rights are freely transferable and the cost of transacting is zero: After the initial partitioning of rights by the

organization that enforces property rights. Its taxes do not attenuate the right to income but constitute a voluntary payment for protective services.

7. Alchian (1977) [op. cit., note 1], pp. 132–133. Note that taxes are often involuntary and represent a partitioning of rights. Very high taxes can remove any value to the formal owner from a set of rights, with the result that a rational person no longer asserts any claim to those rights.

state, the rights are reaggregated through voluntary transactions by individual owners into clusters that maximize the total value of the resources. But when transaction costs are introduced, the role of the state can have a crucial effect on resource allocation. Negotiation costs and other transaction costs may block the reassignment of rights, and the initial partitioning of property rights by the state may have important consequences for the output of an economy as conventionally measured (GNP). The state has also been known to prohibit certain clusters of property rights (some rights are not marketable).

The property rights approach draws attention to the fact that subtle changes in the content of property rights can change the macroperformance of an economic system and lead to economic growth or stagnation. Any redefinition of the structure of property rights by the state has wealth effects involving both winners and losers, and the property rights approach is not complete without a theory of the state. We discuss the role of the state in Chapter 3 and in the last section of the book, which deals with endogenous property rights.

2.3. The theory of agency and its applications

The theory of agency is a branch of the economics of transaction costs.[8] Although the theory is most commonly used to analyze hierarchial relationships, it has a general application to all forms of exchange. An *agency relationship* is established when a principal delegates some rights – for example, user rights over a resource – to an agent who is bound by a (formal or informal)

---

8. The Jensen and Meckling (1976) article is already a classic reference on agency costs. See Jensen, Michael C., and Meckling, William H. (1976). "Theory of the Firm: Managerial Behavior, Agency Costs and Ownership Structure." *Journal of Financial Economics 3* (No. 4, October): 305–360. Pioneering contributions were made by Spence, Michael, and Zeckhauser, R. (1971). "Insurance, Information and Individual Action." *American Economic Review 61* (No. 2, May): 380–387; and Ross, Stephen A. (1973). "The Economic Theory of Agency: The Principal's Problem." *American Economic Review 62* (May): 134–139. This section also draws on Moe, Terry M. (1984). "The New Economics of Organization." *American Journal of Political Science 28* (No. 4): 739–777.

contract to represent the principal's interests in return for payment of some kind. There are countless examples of agency relationships: For example, landlords and tenants, shareholders and managers of corporations, workers and managers of worker-managed firms, patients and physicians, voters and elected representatives in a democracy, administrators in a Soviet-type economy and plant managers.

Note that each individual in a hierarchical structure, except at the ultimate levels, is simultaneously a principal and an agent when rights are transferred down the organizational ladder. As the interests (utility functions) of principals and agents do not coincide, agents are likely to make suboptimal decisions from the principal's viewpoint unless they are effectively constrained.

In an agency relationship, the agent usually has more information than the principal (because it costs him relatively less to acquire) about the details of individual tasks assigned to him and, of course, about his own actions, abilities, and preferences. Information is distributed *asymmetrically* between the two. Agents often take advantage of the high costs of measuring their characteristics and performance and of enforcing a contract and engage in *shirking* or *opportunistic behavior*.

Jensen (1983) makes the point that there exist two valuable but almost separate agency literatures. He refers to one as the *principal–agent literature* (generally mathematical and nonempirically oriented) and the other as the *positive theory of agency* (less mathematical and more empirically oriented):

> The principal–agent literature has generally concentrated on modeling the effects of three factors on contracts between parties interacting in the hierarchical fashion suggested by the term principal–agent: (1) the structure of the preferences of the parties to the contracts, (2) the nature of uncertainty, and (3) the information structure in the environment. Attention is generally focused on risk sharing and the form of the optimal contract between principal and agent, and on welfare comparisons of the equilibrium contracting

solutions in the presence of information costs vis-à-vis the solutions in the absence of such costs.

The positive agency literature has generally concentrated on modeling the effects of additional aspects of the contracting environment and the technology of monitoring and bonding on the form of the contracts and organizations that survive. Capital intensity, degree of specialization of assets, information costs, capital markets, and internal and external labor markets are examples of factors in the contracting environment that interact with the costs of various monitoring and bonding practices to determine the contractual forms.[9]

Neoinstitutional Economics is primarily concerned with the positive agency literature, which "proceeds on the implicit assumption that the variables emphasized in the principal–agent literature are relatively unimportant in understanding the observed phenomenon when compared with richer specifications of information costs, other aspects of the environment, and the monitoring and bonding technology.[10]

Opportunistic behavior imposes costs on the principal who finds it in his or her interest to monitor an agent and structure the contract in a way that reduces the *agency cost*. A net reduction in agency costs can sometimes be achieved by designing contracts where the interests of principal and agent overlap – for example, by sharing profits – or by the introduction of accounting systems to monitor agents. Contracts often include terms that delineate permissible behavior by agents (which risks tying the agents' hands when some contingency arises). Also, agents may find it to their advantage to offer the principal some collateral as a security against opportunistic behavior by them (referred to as *bonding*).

The marginal rate of return on resources invested to constrain

9. Pp. 334–335 in Jensen, Michael C. (1983). "Organization Theory and Methodology." *Accounting Review 58* (No. 2, April): 319–339.
10. Ibid., p. 335.

agents falls after a point, and in most cases it does not pay to try to eliminate all opportunistic behavior. Therefore, the performance of an agent is seldom measured in its entirety, and measurement takes place only at margins where measurement costs are relatively low. For example, in Soviet-type systems there is reliance on relatively unsophisticated "success indicators."

Nove (1977) provides an excellent discussion of the success indicator problem in the Soviet Union.[11] The problem arises because of the cost to Soviet planners of defining and measuring the output supplied by their production units:

> There is . . . the question of expressing the desired total output target in some way: tons, square meters, length, thousands of units, or pairs, kilowatt-hours, etc. . . . The difficulty arises from the fact that no measure is adequate, whenever there is any sort of product *mix*. . . . The literature on distortions due to plans being expressed in tons goes back at least twenty years. . . . Long ago *Krokodil* published a cartoon showing an enormous nail hanging in a large workshop: "the month's plan fulfilled," said the director, pointing to the nail. In tons, of course. It is notorious that Soviet sheet steel has been heavy and thick, for this sort of reason. Sheet glass was too heavy when it was planned in tons, and paper too thick.[12]

Why cling to tons? Nove suggests two reasons. First, it makes the planning of outputs relatively cheap. Second, in many cases there is no obvious alternative which reduces the costs of agency:

> Take the two examples of sheet steel and plate glass. If the measure were not in tons but in square metres, i.e. in terms of area, the temptation would be to make them thin even if they ought to be heavier. . . . Of course, ideally the plan should specify the "right quantities,"

11. See pp. 87–99 in Nove, Alec (1977). *The Soviet Economy*. London: George Allen & Unwin.
12. Ibid., pp. 93–94.

weights and sizes of all glass, metal goods, sheet steel, nails, etc.. . . . But the problem arises precisely from the impossibility of doing this. This is just what is meant by saying that the center does not and cannot know in detail what needs doing.[13]

Some opportunistic behavior by agents is presumably present in equilibrium contracts of most hierarchical relationships, a residual that remains after the principal has taken advantage of all profitable opportunities to limit shirking. The total cost of agency to the principal is the sum of the investments made in limiting shirking plus the costs associated with remaining or residual shirking.[14] In this context, it is important to note that the net income foregone by the principal due to agency costs is defined in terms of costless enforcement of contracts, a hypothetical state.

The high cost of directly measuring behavior and attributes and the necessary reliance on measurement by proxy (years of schooling, reputation, persuasive rhetoric, letters of recommendation, "success indicators") can give rise to *moral hazard* and *adverse selection*.

The concept of adverse selection can be illustrated by considering the case of employers who hire only workers with college degrees but measure no other correlates of productivity. New applicants are selected at random from applicants with college degrees and paid the average salary for all college graduates in the labor force. Assume further that other employers in the same labor market measure several correlates of productivity (education, age, work habits, work experience, reputation) when they hire workers. In this environment, employers who limit their measurement of the quality of applicants to years of formal education will experience adverse selection because, predictably, their firms will be sought out by individuals from the lower half of the productivity distribution of college graduates.

Moral hazard arises in the enforcement of contracts when the

13. Ibid., p. 95.
14. Jensen and Meckling (1976) [op. cit., note 8], p. 308.

performance of an agent (or any party to a contract) is too costly to be observed as a whole and is measured at only one or a few margins. This may induce an agent to neglect various aspects of his or her assignments and concentrate on performing well in the measured dimensions – for example, by coming to work on time, writing good reports, or filling a weight or volume quota with little regard for product quality.

Competition can in various ways reduce the agency costs of principals and raise the cost to agents of opportunistic behavior. The case of the modern corporation is a classic example of this phenomenon. Berle and Means (1932), in their influential work, *The Modern Corporation and Private Property*, drew attention to the high cost to shareholders of monitoring corporate managers, and for decades their viewpoint dominated the discussion. But recently, economists have emphasized how competition in various markets can lower the agency costs of the modern corporation: for example, competition in the market for managers and also competition for investment funds, which, in turn, causes the relative value of shares in poorly managed firms to fall on the stock market. Managers of inefficient corporations also face threats of attempted takeover by other firms and the possibility of being expelled. These issues are discussed in Chapters 5 and 6.

Finally, we note that, even when agents are loyal and do not shirk, principals are still faced with the task of coordinating their activities, which is yet another cost of transacting.

2.4. Property rights and contracting

The transfer of property rights over consumer goods and services or productive assets, either temporarily or permanently, is accomplished by means of a contract which stipulates the terms of the exchange. The concept of a contract is central to Neoinstitutional Economics. The contractual terms specify what rights are being transferred and on what terms. When the transfer of rights is temporary (renting or leasing), it is customary (e.g., in labor contracts) to state how the resource is to be treated. In the case of a permanent transfer of rights, it is customary to define certain qualitative dimensions and assign liabilities for substandard quality. If payments are spread over a long period of time, the appropriate actions in case of default are implicitly or explicitly part of the contract.

Therefore, contracts have a number of dimensions – that is, a structure – as Steven Cheung, a founder of the new contractual approach has emphasized:

> Combining resources of several owners for production involves partial or outright transfers of property rights through a contract. A contract for the partial transfer of rights, such as leasing or hiring, embodies a *structure*. The stipulations, or terms, which constitute the structure of the contract are, as a rule, designed to specify (a) the distribution of income among the participants, and (b) the conditions of resource use. Under transferable rights, these stipulations are consistent with, or determined by, competition in the market place. . . . The choice of contracts is determined by transaction costs, natural (economic) risks, and legal (political) arrangements. However, the familiar market prices are but one among many of the contractual terms (indeed, in share contracts, prices are not explicitly specified).[15]

The structure of a contract depends on the legal system, social customs, and the technical attributes of the assets involved in the exchange. The more detailed the legal framework and the stronger the ties of custom and social control, the less specific are the written contracts. The state, by using its police power and the courts, assists private individuals in enforcing legitimate contracts and thus lowers the costs of exchange, particularly when the state uses its power to enforce contracts in a *systematic and predictable manner*. The

15. P. 50, Cheung, Steven, N. S. (1970). "The Structure of a Contract and the Theory of a Non-exclusive Resource." *Journal of Law and Economics 13* (No. 1, April): 49–70. See also idem (1969b). "Transaction Costs, Risk Aversion, and the Choice of Contractual Arrangements." *Journal of Law and Economics 12* (No. 1, April): 23–42.

state also lowers the costs of contracting when it provides a system of standard weights and measures.[16]

The extent to which a contract stipulates the various dimensions, when the rights to an asset are exchanged, depends on costs and benefits at the margin, as does all individual behavior according to the rational-choice model. When the costs of contracting are high, several dimensions may not be included in the contract and can later become a source of dispute. This is likely to happen when unexpected developments raise the value of an asset at an unstipulated margin – for example, when copper reserves are discovered in the earth below agricultural land.

It is important to note that mutually beneficial exchange and contracting are not necessarily excluded when the choice set of individuals is exceedingly restricted, such as in the case of slaves. For example, in a society that legitimizes slavery, both slaves and their masters could conceivably improve their position by entering into a contract that stipulated less shirking by the slaves in return for better treatment by the master. Contracting for manumission is another example.

Economic agents are innovative and seek new contractual forms that lower the cost of exchange. The introduction of new contractual forms may be compared to technical innovations in production: The impact in both instances is often to expand the frontier of an economy's production possibilities. However, the set of legitimate contractual arrangements is defined by the state, which defines the fundamental rules of the game.

In the previous chapter, we introduced the concept of *equilibrium outcomes*. In the analysis of equilibrium outcomes resulting from individual optimizing decisions, the structure of economic organization was taken as given. The next step is to endogenize the structure of economic organization or the logic of contractual arrangements. In Part III of this book, we discuss attempts to

---

16. Douglass North has paid particular attention to the role of the state in affecting the costs of contracting. For example, see North, Douglass C. (1981). *Structure and Change in Economic History*. New York: W. W. Norton.

model the logic of contractual arrangements. According to our paradigm, we visualize a competition among all known (and permissible) contractual forms in which the arrangements that minimize all costs survive. Changes in exogenous variables, such as the legal structure, measurement technology, or production processes, can affect the equilibrium structure of contracts, and changes in economic organization affect equilibrium outcomes in both production and distribution.

2.5. Competition and the costs of alternative economic organizations

In society, goods and services are usually not produced in isolation because owners of assets find it profitable to join with other owners and share their resources in production. For example, landlords join with laborers in the use of land and labor services for producing agricultural commodities. Such cooperation involves formal or informal contracts.[17] In one type of contracting, owners of inputs delegate to a central agent, for some period of time, specific rights to direct their assets in production in return for a payment. The economic organization which results is the classic entrepreneurial firm.[18]

In Neoinstitutional Economics, the firm is defined as a web or *nexus of contracts*.[19] Within the firm, the continuous pricing of outputs has been suspended and the inputs are *managed* by the central agent. Contracts are also used in exchange across markets where outputs are measured and priced. But these two forms of contracting overlap frequently, as we discuss below, which suggests that the definition of the firm in NIE is not clear-cut. In fact, the

---

17. Cheung, Steven N. S. (1968). "Private Property Rights and Sharecropping." *Journal of Political Economy 76* (No. 6, December): 1107–1122; idem (1969a). *The Theory of Share Tenancy*. Chicago: University of Chicago Press.

18. Alchian and Demsetz (1972) modeled the organization of various types of firms in terms of contractual relationships. Their pioneering contribution is already somewhat dated. Alchian, Armen A., and Demsetz, Harold (1972). "Production, Information Costs, and Economic Organization." *American Economic Review 62* (December): 777–795.

19. This definition was first used by Jensen and Meckling (1976).

dichotomy of the firm versus the market is unlikely to be a helpful instrument in our search for better understanding of exchange. Rather than attempting some final definition of what constitutes a firm, we could more fruitfully analyze the various contractual forms and seek to discover both their determining factors and their consequences for equilibrium outcomes.

In the classic entrepreneurial firm, a central agent makes a series of bilateral rental contracts with owners of cooperating inputs. The central agent also makes bilateral contracts with the buyers of the firm's output. Contracts with input owners are set in the factor market and contracts with buyers in the product market. As the firm expands, three related developments are noted: Factor markets replace product markets; the allocative role of price signals diminishes relative to administrative decisions; and measurement by proxy becomes more common.[20] This process has been carried furthest in the classic Soviet-type economy which can be characterized as a huge firm where most of the product markets have been internalized, except the market for consumer goods. This point has been made, for example, by Wiles (1977):

> The single enterprise is identified with the state. Its
> Board of Directors is the Cabinet (or maybe the
> Politbureau). Its treasurer is the Minister of Finance.
> The profits of its branches, rather misleadingly called
> enterprises, go automatically to this Minister; they are
> decentrally retained by grace and favor only. . . . There
> is not even any distinction between managers and civil
> servants. There is only one career structure, with total
> transferability of pension rights, seniority, etc.[21]

20. Cheung, Steven N. S. (1983). "The Contractual Nature of the Firm." *Journal of Law Economics 26* (April): 1–21.
21. P. 39 in Wiles, Peter J. D. (1977). *Economic Institutions Compared.* Oxford: Basil Blackwell. Eggertsson (1984) discusses the logic of the Soviet National Firm in terms of Neoinstitutional Economics. Eggertsson, Thráinn (1984). "A Neoinstitutional Model of the Soviet Political and Economic System." Photocopy. St. Louis: Department of Economics, Washington University.

This approach to analyzing the organization of the firm suggests interesting questions, which were stated by Ronald Coase (1937) in his seminal article, "The Nature of the Firm."[22] For example: Why doesn't the firm, when subjected to the forces of competition, break up into its elements, the individual owners of resources? Or alternatively, why doesn't the firm grow until it has swallowed the market or perhaps the whole economy? What factors determine the size of the firm? These and other questions regarding the nature of the firm are examined in Chapter 6. Let us now examine two contractual alternatives to the classic firm.[23]

One alternative to the firm is for the consumer of a product to negotiate across markets separately with several owners of inputs and price each of their contributions to the final commodity. The factor market has now been eliminated, and price signals dominate. In most cases the transaction costs of direct contracting between consumers and input owners are likely to be relatively high, if the product and the production technology are at all complex. To measure and price components of final products such as cameras, radios, and alarm clocks requires a great deal of knowledge, which is costly to acquire for the typical consumer. Even in the case of relatively simply products (Adam Smith's pins), the consumer is required to be familiar with the relevant production technology, and the transaction costs of dealing with several input owners are likely to be high. So also are the costs of enforcing a multitude of contracts and ensuring that input owners supply the designated quality of each component.

In lines of production where the division of labor brings substantial gains in productivity, contracts of this type tend to be relatively costly and not competitive with other arrangements. However, in limited cases specialist buyers may still negotiate with input owners for components. This is known, for example, in the automotive industry, where the purchase of components from very

22. Coase, Ronald C. (1937). "The Nature of the Firm." *Economica 4* (November): 386–405.
23. The following discussion draws on Cheung (1983), op. cit., note 20.

small producers, including unitary firms, has been used to relieve bottlenecks at times when the output demand peaks and strains plant capacity.

As a second alternative to the classical firm, contracting could take the form that input owners bypass a central agent, negotiate among themselves, and price each other's outputs, while one input owner contracts with the consumer over the final product. This structure is relatively ineffective when it is costly to measure individual contributions, such as in the following illuminating example, from Cheung (1983), of making flashlights in Hong Kong:

> When the flashlights are being electroplated or anodized, one worker monitors the tank of chemicals, another rotates the article in the solution, and a third rinses them as they are handed to him on a hanger. The relative contribution of each worker is thus difficult to separate.[24]

Therefore they are paid wages, says Professor Cheung, whereas workers who insert switches are paid by the piece because their contributions are relatively easy to isolate and measure.

Contracts that eliminate the central agent and arrange to measure and price directly the contribution of individual inputs are not uncommon. Cheung (1983), again drawing on the economy of Hong Kong, gives an example of this arrangement from the market for hardwood floors: A consumer who is interested in hardwood floors for his home negotiates with a general contractor who subcontracts with a hardwood-floor contractor who, in turn, finds a subcontractor and provides him with wood; and finally the sub-subcontractor contracts with workers who lay the floor, and pays them by the square-foot laid. Why do arrangements of this kind come about, and why do they survive? In the case of the hardwood-floor business, Cheung (1983) has several suggestions: Output quantity and quality are easily measured, the productivity of the workers who lay the floors is very variable (hence a wage system would

24. Ibid., p. 15.

have relatively high measurement costs), and the place of work is not at fixed locations (making monitoring by a central agent more costly).[25]

Finally, in the context of the cost of alternative economic organizations, note that organizations are designed not only to reduce shirking and opportunistic behavior, but also to facilitate coordination, and coordination is yet another costly activity that is required because information is scarce.

We are now ready to summarize the argument: Cooperative production involves various contractual structures. Some contracts correspond to the traditional definition of the firm, but in other instances the web of contracts among input owners does not match conventional conceptions of the firm.

For instance, Cheung (1983) wonders why usually a big department store is considered to be one firm, whereas a shopping center is seen as a constellation of many firms:

> Consider . . . the case of a big department store bearing only one name but consisting in fact of separate sellers, each leasing a space under one roof, paying a rent to one central agent, and governed by a set of rules on the line of products each can sell and his hours of operations. That would seem to represent a single firm. However, *exactly* the same arrangements are found in most shopping centers, except that the shops bear various names. Why should that matter in determining firm size? Of course, some names are worth more than others, as is evident in the case of franchises, but it is also true that a single corporation may establish a number of subsidiaries, each bearing a different name for a different business.
>
> The truth is that according to one's view a "firm" may be as small as a contractual relationship between two input owners or, if the chain of contracts is allowed

25. Ibid., p. 11.

to spread, as big as the whole economy. . . . Thus it is
futile to press the issue of what is or is not a firm.[26]

NIE is concerned primarily with the economic logic of contractual arrangements, why one contractual form dominates another. In an important way, the answer seems to depend on transaction costs, as we shall discuss in Chapters 6 and 7.

In a full-information economy – where there are no transaction costs, where economic outcomes are known in advance, and where all contracts are fully enforced – the structure of contracts is indeterminate. However, in a world of uncertainty, costly measurement, and incomplete enforcement, economic outcomes may vary, depending on which type of contract is chosen to organize production or exchange. Consider the choice of contractual form by landlords and the owners of labor services. Let us assume that the choice is between several contractual forms, such as lump-sum rental agreements (with or without stipulations designed to preserve the quality of the land), various forms of output sharing, piece-rate contracts, and wage contracts. When transaction costs are positive, each contract structure is associated with different allocation of resources, different distribution of wealth, and different rates of depreciation of the physical asset. If several types of contracts *coexist* in a competitive market that is in equilibrium, we expect that the various contracts are associated with equivalent net gains for equivalent inputs, but not *necessarily* with equivalent outcomes in terms of allocation and depreciation of the assets. Note that in this context "net gains" are measured subjectively and depend, in part, on the resource owner's taste for risk and on the risk associated with different types of contracts.[27]

Central to Neoinstitutional Economics is the concept of *competition among contractual arrangements*. Let us explain this notion by continuing the above example of contracting in agriculture. Our

26. Ibid., pp. 17–18.
27. The question of transaction costs and contractual arrangements in agriculture is addressed in Chapter 7, Section 7.4.

landlords all produce crop A on their land. The plant they grow requires little care; it is planted and harvested once a year, and thus negligence and maltreatment of the plant affect only this year's crop. The landlords have made wage contracts with the workers who attend the fields, plant, and harvest. The net rate of return on the capital supplied by the landlords is 5 percent per annum.

Assume now there is a strong increase in the market demand for an alternative crop, B. Crop B is the yield of a plant that bears fruit four years after the fields are sown and then annually for the next ten years. The plant is delicate and requires constant care. By switching to crop B but keeping the wage system, the landlords can raise the rate of return on their investments from 5 to 8 percent. However, if they also introduce a particular form of an output-sharing contract, the annual rate of return will be 15 percent.

The landlords gradually switch from crop A to crop B as they become convinced that the price increase is not a temporary phenomenon, but for a while they continue wage contracts as they are not familiar with the advantages of output sharing. As the supply of B increases, its price and the rate of return on land in this use begin to fall and the yield differential between crop B and crop A gradually disappears. Rather than watching the yield on B fall, a landlord who has a taste for risky ventures begins to experiment with output sharing contracts that give good results. She is able to overcome an initial aversion to a new system and attract the required labor by offering higher net pay than other landlords, while earning more herself. The landlord's demonstration of the advantages of output sharing is a public good which her competitors eventually take advantage of, and soon several of them have introduced the new system.

However, the high rate of return on output sharing is a temporary phenomenon. As more landlords introduce the arrangement, output expands, and the price of B continues to fall. Those producers of B who still use the wage system find now that the yield on their land is no longer competitive. Soon they are losing money, and the forces of competition compel them to introduce output sharing or find alternative uses for their land.

This hypothetical example suggests that changes in contractual form may often be a long process, particularly when there is a lack of experience with arrangements that would be best suited to a new situation. Once a successful experiment has been made, the forces of competition establish new *equilibrium contracts*. It is also reasonable to expect that a community that has a very long experience with stable technology and a stable range of relative prices has settled on contractual forms that minimize costs for each branch of production, given the state of knowledge about contractual arrangements and the basic structure of property rights.

2.6. The filter of competition

We have just sketched, with the help of a hypothetical example, how changes in the environment (exogenous changes) can lead to the selection of a new contractual form and the demise of previous arrangements. In a competitive market, contractual forms that give rise to positive profits survive, and other forms of organization go under. This notion of an "environmental adaption by the economic system" comes from Armen Alchian's (1950) seminal article, "Uncertainty, Evolution and Economic Theory."[28]

Alchian suggested, as an alternative approach to modeling economic processes, that we begin by assuming complete uncertainty and irrational behavior and then add elements of foresight and motivation – exactly the reverse of the traditional approach. In this way, he sought to show that even given extreme assumptions about uncertainty and unmotivated behavior, "chance does not imply undirected, random allocation of resources" in a market system.[29]

By stating the *minimal conditions* in a competitive process for the selection of the most cost-effective of all known organizational forms, Alchian appealed equally to those who accept and those who reject the rational-choice model. His article is regarded highly

28. Alchian, Armen A. (1950). "Uncertainty, Evolution and Economic Theory." *Journal of Political Economy 58* (No. 3, June): 211–221. It is reprinted in idem (1977). *Economic Forces at Work*. Indianapolis: Liberty Press.
29. Alchian (1977) [op. cit., note 28], p. 23.

by economists of both the New Institutional and Neoinstitutional schools, as Moe (1984) has pointed out:

> In a fundamental sense, Alchian's theory of economic organizations is different from those of Coase or Simon. He disavows an explicit model of individual choice . . . and . . . offers a system-level explanation of organizational emergence, structure, and survival that is largely independent of decision making at the micro level. . . . Yet it is precisely this independence of a distinct model of choice that ultimately renders it compatible with the individualistic theories of both Coase and Simon. . . .
>
> Whether individuals optimize under uncertainty or satisfice under the more limiting conditions of bounded rationality . . . , Alchian's logic of natural selection, when grafted onto either approach, provides a powerful means of deriving and integrating expectations about individuals, organizations and systems. The result in either case is an approach that gains in scope and coherence, and that does so by remaining true to its underlying model of individual choice.[30]

Systematic knowledge of human behavior in a world of uncertainty and incomplete information is fragmentary. Alchian suggested that in this context, rational behavior may call for *modes of behavior* rather than adjustments in terms of the marginal conditions of optimization in traditional economics. The individual is often hampered by imperfect foresight and, even when optimality is definable, he or she may be unable to "solve complex problems containing a host of variables."[31] The rational individual may react to uncertainty by adhering strictly to custom and conventional behavior that in the past had been associated with success. A trial-

---

30. Moe (1984) [op. cit., note 8], pp. 746–747. We add to this the fact that Alchian himself relies on the rational-choice model and the generalized neoclassical approach in his other work. See, for example, the volume of his selected works (Alchian, 1977, op. cit., note 28).
31. Alchian (1977), p. 17.

and-error approach may also be sought, although trial and error can often turn into a life-or-death experiment. The point is, however, that a competitive market selects those contracts that generate positive profits, whatever the individual's approach, although not necessarily maximum profits as defined in a full-information model.

Thus, in a world of uncertainty and high transaction costs, it is likely that most people replace the marginal conditions of economics by modes of behavior, except for risk-seeking entrepreneurial individuals who are prone to make bold experiments in spite of limited information. Such entrepreneurial types are often labeled reckless adventurers when they fail, but are admired and imitated when they succeed. Imitative behavior is quite common, and incompetent imitators may even stumble on a new formula that works better than any prior arrangements.

In many instances, particularly when the cost of information is low, people adjust to changes in the environment by using cost–benefit calculations that represent marginal costs and benefits fairly well. Alchian argued that "the greater the uncertainties of the world, the greater is the possibility that profits would go to venturesome and lucky rather than logical, careful, fact-gathering individuals."[32] However, Alchian's basic point is that even when adjustment to the environment is some random process, "chance does not imply undirected, random allocation of resources" in a market economy because of a selection process that uses realized profits as a criterion.

This important insight is sometimes misunderstood. For example, the notion of a *filter of competition* is not a normative concept. It does not imply that the winners in economic life are necessarily stronger, more intelligent, morally superior, or more deserving than the losers. The filter-of-competition concept is a positive statement, although Alchian did not formulate it as a testable hypothesis.

Also note that the ability to adjust successfully to changes in the

32. Ibid., p. 20.

environment is not distributed evenly among individuals. We can list several reasons why this is so: Physical and mental prowess vary; not all individuals face the same supply curve of information or the same budget constraint; and some individuals have the power to alter the existing structure of property rights in order to minimize their personal cost of unexpected exogenous changes: Imports can be restricted, the sale of new products banned, and new contractual forms declared illegal.

Economic theorists sometimes like to play God and model optimal contracts in a world of full information. Alchian has made the point that such optimal organization may not be introduced even when it is profitable to do so. "What really counts is the various actions actually tried, for it is from these that 'success' is selected, not from some set of perfect actions."[33] But the economist's tools of analysis are still useful, if not to predict actual contracts, then to suggest the direction of change in contractual arrangements in response to exogenous changes. Alchian's fundamental insight remains profound.

33. Ibid., p. 33.

3

Explaining the rules

3.1. Positive theories of the state

Positive theories of the state hold a central role in Neoinstitutional Economics because the state sets and enforces the fundamental rules that govern exchange. The enforcement of property rights depends on power, and economies of scale in the use of violence frequently give a single agent – the state – a monopoly over the legitimate use of violence. But the relationship between property rights and political structures is complex, and exclusive property rights are consistent with a range of alternative power structures. Consider the following three arrangements:

1. A community where there are no legislative or judicial bodies, no enforcement agencies, and no common rules
2. A society where there are common rules that specify exclusive rights, a law-making body, courts of law, but no police force or army and hence private enforcement of law
3. A community where the state sets the rules, arbitrates in disputes, and enforces exclusive rights

We would be surprised to find case 1, the private enforcement of *private rules*, in communities where productive assets such as land are scarce, where people live together in groups, practice the division of labor, and trade among themselves. In order to protect private property under case 1, a large share of the resources of each household would have to be allocated to the private protection of life, limb, and nonhuman assets and to efforts at forming coalitions with other individuals. It is difficult to visualize political equilibrium in this setting. Such communities are likely to drift either toward chaos and disintegration, or toward the concentration of power and the formation of a state.

Case 2, the private enforcement of public rules, is known in history and is found, for example, in Iceland during the Commonwealth, which lasted from 930 to 1262.[1] The political system of Iceland during this period included a constitution, a legislative assembly, and a system of courts, but the government was without an executive branch, and there was no police force or military.

The private enforcement of property rights can be costly for individuals who need to defend their rights against a powerful and ruthless adversary. In the Icelandic Commonwealth, individuals sought support to help enforce their rights (or to violate the rights of others) not only from their extended family and friends but also from powerful opponents of the adversaries.

In case 3, the state defines the basic structure of property rights, arbitrates in disputes, and enforces the rules. By providing order at a relatively low cost, the state expands the community's frontier of production possibilities. In its earlier or more primitive versions, the state is often associated with a single individual or a family who supplies public order, defense, and various amenities in return for the right to tax. The relationship between the ruler and his or her subjects can be thought of in terms of a contract, and the concepts of transaction costs and agency can be used to analyze the structure of the contract.

---

1. David Friedman has made the case that the structure of property rights in the Icelandic Commonwealth was relatively effective even when compared with public enforcement of law in other societies. See Friedman, David (1979). "Private Creation and Enforcement of Law: A Historical Case." *Journal of Legal Studies 8* (No. 2): 399–415. The case of the Icelandic Commonwealth is taken up in some detail in Chapter 9 (this volume): Property Rights in Stateless Societies.

The power of the sovereign is limited by agency costs and constrained by competition.[2] If the sovereign supplies public order and other services at exorbitant prices, his or her behavior is likely to draw offers of more favorable terms of taxation from power brokers inside or outside the state. The capacity to tax is also limited by the problems of agency and measurement costs. In order to collect revenue, the tax base must be identified and measured, and taxes levied and collected. The sovereign must rely on a large number of agents to accomplish this task, and a rational ruler will seek arrangements that minimize agency costs.

If rulers did not face positive transaction costs in the collection of taxes, they would prefer a structure of property rights that maximizes the tax base. When transaction costs are high, as North (1981) has emphasized, it is frequently in the interest of rulers to design structures of property rights that are inconsistent with rapid economic growth. The agency problems of the Soviet leaders may be a recent example of this dilemma. For years it has been observed in the Soviet Union and abroad that various adjustments in the structure of the country's property rights could bring substantial gains in the net output of the Soviet economy. This is apparently recognized by the leaders of the Communist Party, the country's power elite, but no substantial changes in the structure of property rights have been made. One explanation of this apparent paradox is that the rulers are trapped in an agency problem.[3] Most of the suggested changes in property rights involve decentralization of economic power – that is, more power to the agents of the state – which the rulers fear will lead to rising agency costs and loss of control.

2. See North, Douglass C. (1981). *Structure and Change in Economic History.* New York: W. W. Norton. Especially Chapter 3: "A Neoclassical Theory of the State."
3. For example, this point is made in Moore, John H. (1981). "Agency Costs, Technological Change, and Soviet Central Planning." *Journal of Law and Economics 24* (October): 189–214. These issues are discussed in Chapter 10 (this volume): The State in Neoinstitutional Economics.

3.2. **Information costs and political processes**

In political theory or welfare economics, modern democracy is often analyzed in terms of contractual relations among equals. The social contract is designed to provide efficient property rights, ensure adequate supply of public goods, which the free market cannot supply, and arrange for the provision of merit goods such as aid to the sick, elderly, and indigent.[4] The formula, one man–one vote, is supposed to protect the majority of citizens from being subjugated by a minority. A "bill of rights" defining "inviolable human rights" and constitutional stipulations that make it costly for the majority to change such rules are intended to protect minorities against the tyranny of a majority. The vision follows logically from full-information models of political processes in democracies.

In recent years, the evolution of the cost-of-information perspective in economics has inspired economists and political scientists to examine the implications of information costs for political exchange in democracies. We now understand better than before how small groups can wield power in excess of their relative voting strength and thus change the structure of property rights to their advantage, perhaps at the expense of the majority of voters.

How can small groups in a democracy abuse the majority? One explanation hinges both on the unequal distribution of costs and benefits that can result from marginal changes in the structure of property rights, and on the asymmetrical distribution of information between the gainers and losers from such changes.[5]

---

4. A discussion of the allocative and distribution functions of governments is found, for example, in Musgrave, Richard A., and Musgrave, Peggy M. (1976). *Public Finance in Theory and Practice*. New York: McGraw Hill. See Chapter 1, "Fiscal Functions: An Overview." These authors identify three fiscal functions: Along with allocation and distribution, the state is responsible for economic stability.

5. This insight is associated with Stigler's work on the economics of information and the economics of regulation. See Stigler, George J. (1961). "The Economics of Information." *Journal of Political Economy 69* (June, No. 3): 213–225. Stigler, George J., and Friedland, Claire (1962). "What Can Regulators Regulate? The Case of Electricity." *Journal of Law and Economics 5* (No. 1): 1–16; and Stigler, George J. (1971). "The Economic Theory of Regulation." *Bell Journal of Eco-*

This line of reasoning is perhaps best understood with the help of a hypothetical example. Imagine that shoemakers in the country of Pedestria feel threatened by the imports of inexpensive, high-quality shoes from Southern Europe and Asia. At risk are substantial capital losses by the owners of noncompetitive shoe factories and costly depreciation of human capital for workers who have invested in training that is specific to the domestic shoe industry. Large amounts, ranging from thousands to millions of dollars, are at stake for many of the individuals concerned. These losses can be prevented by changing the property rights of importers and consumers – for example, by levying high tariffs on imported shoes, imposing strict quotas on them, or forbidding shoe imports altogether. Measures to limit the availability of inexpensive imported shoes are at the expense of consumers as a whole, but the burden is divided relatively evenly among a large number of people – say, 60 million households.

Assume that the present value of the loss to consumers from the restrictions on imports is on average fifty dollars per household, if the measures are permanent. The rational household would then be willing to invest a maximum of fifty dollars to ensure a free flow of imported shoes, but the typical household may not even know how much is at stake, and the information costs of finding out can be high. Before it decides to act, the household must try to establish what the real plans of the Pedestrian shoe industry are, evaluate arguments put forward, and then calculate costs and benefits. If the industry claims that imported shoes are defective or dangerous or that foreign producers constitute a political threat to Pedestria (e.g., because a devastated domestic shoe industry would be unable to produce boots for the country's armed forces if a large-scale war broke out, closing all foreign trade channels), such claims must be evaluated. The evaluation of arguments for

nomics and Management Science 2 (No. 3): 3–21. Stigler's approach changed the way in which economists thought about regulation, and it also had general application for the analysis of political processes in a democracy. We return to a discussion and evaluation of models involving endogenous property rights in the fourth section of this book.

trade restrictions can be costly, not to mention if the products in question are not footwear but more complex commodities such as pharmaceuticals, cars, or electronic equipment. A compassionate consumer might want to consider whether predictions of dire consequences of free trade for the workers in the shoe industry are accurate, and ideally, the rational household must evaluate how, in the long run, import restrictions are likely to affect pricing policies and efficiency in the domestic industry.

To continue the example, assume that the consumer discovers, after investing in information, that import restrictions are undesirable and will cost her about fifty dollars. If the search costs have already been incurred, they are sunk at this point, and the consumer is ready to contribute a maximum of fifty dollars toward a lobbying campaign to prevent import restrictions. If all households are informed and pool the funds, and are willing to invest in this endeavor, fifty dollars on the average, then the 60 million households have 3 billion dollars at their disposal – a handsome sum. However, not all households would be aware of the potential damage of restrictions. Therefore, the initial sum would be less than 3 billion dollars, and some of the funds would be used to inform other consumers of the problem. Finally, it would pay the consumers to pool their resources in a joint effort if there were substantial economies of scale in collecting information and lobbying bureaucrats and elected representatives.

3.3. **The logic of collective action and the free-rider problem**

The potential economic and political might of (nearly) all consumers of shoes in a democracy is obviously enormous if they pool their resources, but there is an obvious obstacle to such a cooperative effort: the cost of collective action and particularly the free-rider problem.[6]

Consider what is likely to happen if an enterprising individual sought to take advantage of economies of scale in information

---

6. The classic reference for the free-rider problem is Olson, Mancur (1965). *The Logic of Collective Action*. Cambridge, Mass.: Harvard University Press.

gathering and lobbying and offered, at a price well below fifty dollars, to sell consumers protection against restrictions on the import of inexpensive foreign shoes. The manager of such an operation would soon realize that the services of free trade are a public good and that the costs of dividing up public goods and selling them to the public are prohibitive. Any consumer who refuses to pay for the services of our entrepreneur stands to gain from free trade in imported shoes just as much as those who paid to uphold it. Individuals cannot be singled out and restricted to buy only domestic shoes because such discrimination conflicts with constitutional rights in most democracies, and, more importantly, the cost of enforcing the discrimination would be unacceptably high. The rational consumer will realize that her contribution has no perceptible impact on a nationwide lobbying effort, and also, if the lobbying is successful, she will stand to gain, whether she contributes or not. But, if all consumers think like this, no one will mount a campaign against the protectionists.[7] In simple terms,

---

7. The problem of free riding is related to the prisoners' dilemma in game theory. The prisoners' dilemma arises when two conditions are present: (1) The actions and welfare of individuals are interdependent; and (2) the individuals cannot communicate with each other, or, more precisely, cannot make binding agreements. The dilemma can be illustrated with the example of two prisoners who are accused of plotting together against the government and are kept in separate cells. The evidence against them is limited, and each is offered freedom if he or she testifies against the other prisoner, who will then get the death sentence. If both prisoners testify against each other, both will receive a heavy sentence, and if neither talks they will get away with a light fine. Each prisoner will contemplate the actions of the other. If the other prisoner talks, the outcome for oneself's not talking is the death sentence whereas talking brings a heavy sentence. If the other prisoner refuses to cooperate with the state, then not talking brings a light fine whereas betrayal is rewarded with freedom. In this situation it appears rational for each prisoner to testify against his or her former colleague. When both testify, both receive heavy sentences. The two maximize their joint welfare by not testifying, and that is what the model predicts would happen if the prisoners could discuss their plans (and make enforceable agreements).

Consumers who contemplate whether or not to support an antiprotectionism campaign are in a similar situation as the prisoners in the example above. Each consumer may find that lack of information about the behavior of other con-

this is the nature of the free-rider problem, the great scourge of collective action.

In sum, three factors combine to limit political actions by our consumers in defense of the free flow of shoes across national borders: the high costs of obtaining reliable information about the relevant facts, the free-rider problem, and the relatively small sum that is at stake for the average individual. Turning to the domestic shoe industry, we find that, in contrast to the situation for consumers, the relevant information is available to each firm at a relatively low cost; there is more at stake on average for each individual; and fewer individuals are involved, thus lowering the cost of overcoming the free-rider problem.

We will return to the free-rider problem later in this book, particularly in Chapter 9, but note here that one way around the free-rider problem is to let the state raise the cost to individuals who refuse to join groups, pay membership dues, and, generally, refuse to participate in collective action. For example, the right to work in certain professions, industries, or factories can be tied to membership in a union or professional association. Business groups that have lobbying as a primary aim are common, and sometimes a refusal to join may involve direct costs for the uncooperative parties. Furthermore, it is possible that a firm that has a large share of the market may have incentives to act alone and invest in restrictive legislation.[8]

As we have noted, there are many reasons why the struggle between the general public and small, well-organized pressure groups tends to be one-sided. In fact, one might be inclined to conclude from the arguments presented above that the impossibility of free international trade is a foregone conclusion. But various factors work against special interest groups and limit their effectiveness, including laws against bribery, rules regulating the behavior of lobbyists, and public spiritedness of civil servants and

sumers, and the high costs of finding out and making binding agreements make not donating to the campaign the rational choice.

8. See Olson (1965) [op. cit., note 6] for an elaboration of these points.

legislators. Conflict of interest among well-organized pressure groups can also reduce their influence – in our hypothetical example, conflict between domestic manufacturers and importers of shoes.

3.4. The concept of equilibrium political institutions

Exchange and production in modern societies take place within a framework of rules that are socially and politically determined and enforced. Therefore, the allocation of resources is affected by changes in the rules structure (by the reassignment of property rights) and, at one remove, by changes in social and political institutions.

In democratic societies, fundamental changes in property rights are usually brought about through some voting procedure, either directly through a popular vote or indirectly through the voting by elected representatives. In either case, the outcome of voting is usually governed by the so-called majority rule. In the postwar period, the nature of outcomes that flow from majority-rule voting has been given exhaustive examination by economists and political scientists. The pioneering contribution was made by Arrow (1951), who contributed the "impossibility theorem" and defined the research program in this area for the next twenty-five years.[9]

The literature on voting soon came to the following conclusion: Assume we have a body of agents with predetermined and stable preferences who are faced with a choice between the elements in a set of alternatives. The choice is made on the basis of majority-rule voting. Then it can be demonstrated that the outcome depends not on preferences but on the sequence of votes: how and in what order the elements are compared. Almost any outcome is possible, depending on the sequence of votes; in other words, there is no equilibrium outcome of the electoral system if the agents are free

9. Arrow, Kenneth J. (1951). *Social Choice and Individual Values.* New York: Wiley. The discussion below is based on Shepsle, Kenneth A., and Weingast, Barry (1983). "Rational Choice Explanations of Social Facts." Working paper. St. Louis: Washington University.

to manipulate the sequence of votes.[10] Formal political theory also led to the conclusion that voting coalitions tend to be unstable solutions to vote-trading and logrolling.[11]

These findings of formal political theory were at odds with empirical and descriptive studies that did not reveal evidence of the disequilibrium that the theory associated with majority rule. It is interesting to note that formal political theory was strongly influenced by contemporary microeconomics and its emphasis on rational choice and equilibrium. Furthermore, the behavioral revolution in political science, just like the field of economics, paid almost no attention to the structure of institutions and their restraining influence on behavior. This is now changing. In recent years, the influence of the property rights approach in economics has extended also to political science and given rise to what some call the new institutionalism or the new political economy, an area in which politics and economics overlap. We consider the new approach to be an integral part of the NIE.

Recently critics have argued that the "pure majority-rule model" is without an empirical counterpart in legislative assemblies or other rule-making bodies. They claim that, in fact, voting and decision making are controlled by elaborate procedures that yield

10. Equilibrium outcomes are possible if someone is given monopoly power over the agenda, that is to say, the power to control the sequence of votes. Voters could influence the outcomes by bribing the person who controls the agenda. If transaction costs are zero, the final outcome is independent of the person given control over the agenda, but this need not be so when transaction costs are positive. The genesis of the agenda control literature is usually identified as Romer, Thomas, and Rosenthal, Howard (1979). "Bureaucrats Versus Voters: On the Political Economy of Resource Allocation by Direct Democracy." *Quarterly Journal of Economics 93* (No. 4, November): 563–587.

11. These findings are presented in Shepsle, Kenneth A. (1983). "Institutional Equilibrium and Equilibrium Institutions." Working Paper No. 82. St. Louis: Center for the Study of American Business, Washington University. For formal proofs, see, for instance, McKelvey, R. D. (1976). "Intransitivities in Multidimensional Voting Models and Some Implications for Agenda Control." *Journal of Economic Theory 12* (No. 3): 472–482; and Cohen, Linda, and Matthews, Steven (1980). "Constrained Plot Equilibria, Directional Equilibria and Global Cycling Sets." *Review of Economic Studies 47* (No. 5, October): 975–986.

equilibrium outcomes. For example, Shepsle (1983) points to the 600-plus pages of *Deschler's Procedures of the U.S. House of Representatives*. The new institutionalists agree that there may be no equilibrium outcomes associated with unrestricted voting among alternatives in an institution-free environment, but they maintain that in the real world there are institutional arrangements that tend to yield stable outcomes.

What are these institutional arrangements? Shepsle and Weingast (1981) refer to *structure-induced equilibrium*.[12] Essentially the argument is as follows: The institutional structure of rule-making bodies contains various building blocks that constrain behavior to result in stable outcomes. The choice process does not involve all agents voting among all possible alternatives. Rather, the set of decision makers is partitioned, for example, into committees, and the set of alternatives is divided into jurisdictions. Some mechanism assigns agents to committees – for example, self-selection (the method used in the U.S. Congress) – and committees are given exclusive property rights over specific jurisdictions. In the U.S. Congress, committees often can close the door on changes in their jurisdiction by not proposing any bill. Their *ex post* power in conference committees enables them to enforce this restriction and also gives them substantially a monopoly of agenda control for making changes. At the least, the support of all committees for changes in matters under their jurisdiction is almost always required for a bill to have a chance of passage through each house.[13]

---

12. Shepsle, Kenneth A., and Weingast Barry, R. (1981). "Structure-Induced Equilibrium and Legislative Choice." *Public Choice* 37 (No. 3): 503–519.
13. In their 1981 paper, Shepsle and Weingast (1981) explain the power of committees primarily in terms of their role as "gatekeepers" or agenda setters in their respective jurisdictions. In a recent paper, Shepsle and Weingast (1987) modify their position by emphasizing the ex post sources of committee power: "Committees, as agency setters in their respective jurisdictions, are able to enforce many of their policy wishes not only because they originate bills but also because they get a second chance after their chamber has worked its will. This occurs at the conference stage in which the two chambers of a bicameral legislature resolve differences between versions of a bill." P. 85 in Shepsle, Kenneth A., and Weingast, Barry R. (1987). "The Institutional Foundations

According to this arrangement, agents have given up considerable power in many areas in return for disproportionate power in jurisdictions of special interest. The delegation of authority to committees suggests the existence of an agency relationship and a need for a system of monitoring by the parent body. In fact, the monitoring of committees takes many forms. Institutional leaders may have confidants on each committee and also monitor reactions of legislators, lobbyists, constituents, and presidents to the work of the committees. Moreover, the output of committees, bills passed onto the floor for deliberations and voting, must survive the amendment process. Procedural rules are designed to control outcomes when bills are handled by the whole legislative body or one of its chambers. These are rules, for instance, relating to the types of amendments that are allowed and the sequence in which alternatives are compared. Furthermore, strong reactions by constituents of legislators who are not on a committee provide credible evidence that something needs to be done about the committee's work. If enough legislators have such complaints, one would expect action to be possible or anticipatory reaction by the committee to avoid the control measures that might be taken.

Institutional arrangements, such as the division of decision makers into committees and the assignment of property rights over specific jurisdictions to members of committees, modify the traditional conclusions of the public-choice literature. Public choices over social preferences are no longer cyclical, and no longer is almost any outcome possible depending on the sequence of votes.

But this line of reasoning raises another problem.[14] Let us define *institutions* as sets of rules governing interpersonal relations, noting that we are talking about formal political and organizational practices. Assume that agents have certain expectations ex ante about the link between institutional structure and outcomes of social

of Committee Power." *American Political Science Review 81* (No. 1, March): 85–104.

14. The following discussion is based on Shepsle (1983) [op. cit., note 11], p. 9.

choices. Then given the agents' preferences for outcomes, there is derived demand for institutions. If institutions are somehow chosen as we want to argue, then we are back to the disequilibrium outcomes of majority-rule voting, and the choice among institutions will not lead to stable or equilibrium institutions. And it does not help to argue that the choice of institutions is prescribed by higher rules, written or unwritten constitutions, because this only pushes the argument one step back, requiring us to predict unstable constitutions.

Just as in the case of voting outcomes, empirical observations tell us that the institutional structures in democratic countries are relatively stable, that they tend to be equilibrium institutions. Shepsle (1983) has tried to solve this dilemma and explain in terms of the rational-choice model why institutional structures tend to be stable.

Shepsle's first point is that the structure of political institutions and the outcomes associated with them reflect the interests of those in power: Economic power breeds political power. Individuals who try to enhance their power by altering political institutions may expect costly retaliations if their efforts are unsuccessful. Ex ante it is often uncertain whether attempts to change political institutions will succeed, for example, because agents may find strategic advantage in not revealing their preferences before the final vote. These uncertainties may in part account for institutional stability.

Second, political institutions are designed to facilitate cooperation among decision makers, or that is one of their functions. In exchanges between politicians, transaction costs tend to be high, as are the costs of exchange among criminals or sovereign nations, because there is no powerful third party that helps to enforce contracts in these areas, unlike the situation in the marketplace. Therefore, self-enforcement of contracts is relatively important in political exchanges. In repeat-play dealings, a good reputation is valuable to a dealer, and a reputation for reneging on promises can be costly. But self-enforcement of contracts is an ineffectual arrangement in many situations, particularly in multilateral exchanges where it is costly to discover who is cheating whom, where there is room for free riding, and where it is not clear who should bear the cost of punishing agents for opportunistic behavior.

With all this in mind, Shepsle (1983) argues that political institutions are ex ante agreements about cooperation among politicians. According to this view, institutions can be seen as a capital structure designed to produce a flow of stable policy outcomes, and institutional change is a form of investment. One of the costs of institutional change is the uncertainty about which outcomes the new regime will produce. Uncertainty implies that a given structure may ex ante be associated with a *set* of structure-induced equilibrium points. Ex post this uncertainty is gradually reduced as the operational qualities of a new institutional structure become known.

Finally, Shepsle (1983) argues that this uncertainty about the impact of structural change on equilibrium outcomes is enough reason to stabilize institutions and prevent continuous institutional change. He maintains, thus, that the calculations of agents in decisions involving policy choices are qualitatively different from calculations regarding institutional change.

The new approach to political organizations is analogous to the studies of the nature of economic organizations which we introduced in the previous chapter. For example, the committee system in the U.S. Congress and agenda control are seen as a rational structure just like the modern corporation. In a similar vein, Weingast (1984) has argued that a priori it is unreasonable to assume that the employees of the U.S. federal bureaucracy are agents out of control because it is in the interest of their immediate principals, the members of Congress, and of course their ultimate principals, the voters, to develop an institutional structure that limits agency costs.[15] Weingast concludes that such a system is indeed in place:

15. Weingast, Barry R. (1984). "The Congressional-Bureaucratic System: A Principal–Agent Perspective." *Public Choice 44* (No. 1): 147–192. See also idem (1983). "Bureaucratic Discretion or Congressional Control? Regulating Policymaking by the Federal Trade Commission." *Journal of Political Economy 91* (October, No. 5): 766–800.

It is an equilibrium political institution, which the players either cannot change or do not seek to change.

This system involves specialized Congressional committees, public hearings, and monitoring of bureaucratic behavior by members of the public who report back to their representatives. In terms of the Weingast model, this system of control is more cost-effective than direct monitoring of the bureaucracy by members of Congress and their staff, which used to be the traditional view of how bureaucrats were controlled.

McCubbins and Schwartz (1984) come to the same conclusion as Weingast (1984).[16] They refer to direct, centralized monitoring of the executive branch by the legislature as *police-patrol oversight*, and argue that scholars, who complain that the U.S. Congress has neglected its oversight responsibilities, fail to recognize another decentralized, incentive-based control mechanism, which they refer to as *fire-alarm oversight*.

The application of the economics of property rights, transaction costs, and agency to political institutions is on the verge of transforming our understanding of American political institutions. There is reason to believe that the new approach will also provide valuable insights, theorems, hypotheses, and empirical findings, not only for modern American institutions but also for institutions across time and space.

3.5. Ideology and the rational-choice model

In our discussion of the logic of collective action and the free-rider problem, it was mentioned that the economic approach has not been successful in explaining certain group actions. Gordon Tullock's (1971) economic theory of revolution is a good illustration of the limits of the purely economic approach when applied to group behavior in situations where there are incentives for free

16. McCubbins, Mathew D., and Schwartz, Thomas (1984). "Congressional Oversight Overlooked: Police Patrols Versus Fire Alarms." *American Journal of Political Science 2* (No. 1, February): 165–179.

riding.[17] Tullock bases his theory on rational-choice assumptions and comes up with essentially a theory of nonrevolution which is well suited to explain why revolutions are relatively infrequent, even in states ruled by tyrants.

Economic man is unlikely to take part in popular uprisings where his marginal contribution to the success of the revolution is technically zero, where his personal economic gains are nil or negative, but where his chances of being killed or wounded are substantial. If we leave out situations where society imposes severe costs on those who refuse to take part, participation under such circumstances can be explained only in terms of a commitment to moral values, to an ideology.

Tastes have traditionally been exogenous variables in economic theories, and little is known in the other social sciences about the formation of ideologies and why they change. Nonetheless, ideologically motivated behavior is formally consistent with the rational-choice model and the economic approach. Individuals are then seen as having a taste for ideology, and a trait such as honesty is assumed to be substitutable at the margin for other goods, except when a moral value is given infinite weight in the preference function.[18]

Experiments, for example, where wallets are left in public places for passers-by to find, suggest that "honest behavior" is more frequent when small values are at stake, which indicates a downward-sloping demand curve for rectitude. But this is not the whole story, because a serious problem arises in the analysis of institutional change when ideological beliefs appear to be unstable – when individuals at one time point support a given structure of property rights and at another point risk their lives tearing it down.

North (1981) has argued that modifications of social values – that is, changing ideologies – are a major factor in institutional

---

17. Tullock, Gordon (1971). "The Paradox of Revolution." *Public Choice 9* (Fall): 89–99.
18. The discussion of ideology below draws on Chapter 5, "Ideology and the Free Rider Problem," in North, Douglass C. (1981). *Structure and Change in Economic History.* New York: W. W. Norton.

change, and the NIE is incomplete without a theory of ideology. In the long run, widespread respect for the law, for the rights of fellow citizens, for the state, and for the authority of the ruler is essential for the preservation of any society. The stock of social values is a form of capital which the rulers can augment by investing in propaganda, for example, through the school system. Without a supportive ideology, the cost to the power elite of monitoring the citizens, and the cost to the citizens of monitoring each other, would approach infinity. A society where everybody behaves solely in an egotistical and cold-blooded fashion is not viable.

When social change is related to changes in ideological behavior, we are concerned whether the behavioral change is due only to a change in the opportunity cost of respecting law and order (a move along the demand curve) or whether it reflects new values (a shift in the demand curve). There is no doubt that institutional change in general, and ideological behavior in particular, represent one of the most important, and most difficult, frontiers of research in the NIE.

3.6. Can we explain the rules?

Several scholars have raised doubts about the validity of the economic approach for analyzing the fundamental rules that govern exchange in society. We end this chapter by considering briefly some of these objections.

First, it is often argued that economic analysis has little to offer in terms of testable hypotheses, except when behavior is constrained by competition and represents adjustments to exogenous parameters. Social rules are determined in the political arena, and political behavior typically involves strategic interactions and interdependence rather than adjustments to fixed parameters. The simplifying assumptions of the economic approach yield useful hypotheses when applied to big groups, because the law of large numbers cancels out erratic individual behavior; but the economic analysis of politics often involves small groups, and economists have had limited success in developing empirically relevant models of the behavior of oligopolists, in spite of theoretical advances in game theory.

There is certainly truth to this argument, and we do not want to minimize the theoretical difficulties of dealing with strategic behavior. Yet, in the past, there has been a tendency to underestimate the constraints on behavior that competitive forces impose. To take an extreme example, even Joseph Stalin must have been constrained by competition and agency considerations, as indicated by the dictator's survival for a large number of years.[19] The NIE looks for competitive constraints in unexpected places. For example, in the theory of the firm it is now understood that heads of large corporations are constrained by competition in the market for managers, the market for loanable funds, and the market for corporate takeovers, even though they are not directly controlled by diffuse shareholders. Similarly, various constraints on behavior in the political arena have been brought to our attention. It was mentioned above how the behavior of federal bureaucrats is constrained by the committee system in Congress and monitored by the public. Other scholars have, for example, studied electoral control of incumbent performance in office, and so on.

Another criticism, which is related to our previous section, is that the economic approach is said to fail to take account of non-economic motivation, a particularly serious omission when analyzing political institutions. This criticism is partly based on a misunderstanding. It has already been stated that the choice of arguments for individual preference functions is primarily a practical issue of selecting the terms that yield the greatest theoretical insights and predictive power. A problem arises when social values change, because the NIE does not have a workable theory of ideology. This deficiency is recognized by many scholars of the NIE, such as North (1981).

Still another criticism of the NIE is that wealth or utility max-

19. Incidentally, we are not aware of attempts to analyze formally the dynamics of Stalin's grip of power and control over his agents for more than a quarter century.

imization is not a general law of behavior, but rather behavior sanctioned by rules only for special occasions – competitive markets.[20] We are not sure whether this will be a serious stumbling block for the NIE. Observations that seem to suggest that individual behavior in certain areas is inconsistent with the rational-choice model are often mistaken because the evaluation is made in terms of full information. What appears as a casual approach to decision making – for example, consistent with Simon's principle of "satisficing" – can be explained in terms of maximization and rational choice when transaction costs are taken into account.[21] In situations pervaded by uncertainty, optimization as defined in the full-information model is probably not carried out by the typical individual.[22] But we believe that such situations can often be modeled in terms of rational choice and competitive constraints to derive useful insights and hypotheses, at least compared to other available theoretical paradigms.

It is important to note in this context that the economic approach is essentially tautological and accommodates all sets of values we care to include and all possible constraints. It breaks down only when tastes fluctuate at random or when people make regularly inconsistent choices. Furthermore, the rational-choice model is not a useful scientific tool unless the specification of the preference function is explicit enough to enable the theorist to derive falsifiable propositions.

20. Field, Alexander J. (1979). "On the Explanation of Rules Using Rational Choice Models." *Journal of Economic Issues 13* (No. 1): 49–72.
21. A presentation of the satisficing approach is found in Simon, Herbert A. (1957). *Models of Man*. New York: Wiley; idem (1978). "Rationality as Process and as Product of Thought." *American Economic Review 68* (May): 1–16. A defense of the rational-choice model and the economic approach is found in De Alessi, Louis (1983a). "Property Rights, Transaction Costs, and X-Efficiency: An Essay in Economic Theory." *American Economic Review 73* (March, No. 1): 64–81. See also a response by Leibenstein, Harvey (1983). "Property Rights and X-Efficiency: Comment." *American Economic Review 73* (September, No. 4): 831–842, and a rejoinder by De Alessi (1983b). "Reply," Ibid.: 843–845.
22. This point is discussed in Alchian, Armen A. (1950). "Uncertainty, Evolution, and Economic Theory." *Journal of Political Economy 58* (No. 3, June): 211–221. See our Chapter 2, Section 2.6.

The final criticism of the NIE, which we report here, is the argument that it is unreasonable to seek to explain social rules in terms of relative prices.[23] Rules are designed to reduce uncertainty, and much of their usefulness is minimized or lost if they fluctuate freely with changes in prices. Also, such extreme institutional instability is inconsistent with the empirical evidence. There is no reason to believe that two countries with similar endowments and technologies will have similar structures of property rights. Political authorities do not change the rules each time relative prices change in an attempt to maximize wealth net of enforcement costs, because frequent changes in the rules would cause chaos and be counterproductive.

Here several points are in order. First, the NIE does not say that the structure of property rights depends only on technologies and endowments. The nature of the state, the governmental structure of a country, is a critical determinant of the rules structure, and, in turn, the political system of a country is a complex phenomenon that depends on a country's proximity to neighboring powers, its history of invasions and foreign occupations, the evolution of religious and cultural ideas, and a host of other variables. The detailed nature of the causal relationships among these factors is well beyond our understanding. For example, it is not likely that the NIE, using the economic approach, will in the near future give a detailed explanation of why the Soviet Union developed its current political and economic system. But the economic approach can be useful in modeling the choice set of Soviet rulers, and how it is constrained by technologies, endowments, agency costs, and competition. Furthermore, the approach may enable us to predict how rational rulers adjust property rights to changes in these constraints, or at least forecast the direction of change.

Second, not all price changes make it efficient from a purely

---

23. See Field (1979) [op. cit., note 20], and also Field, Alexander J. (1981). "The Problem with Neoclassical Institutional Economics: A Critique with Special Reference to the North/Thomas Model of Pre-1500 Europe." *Explorations in Economic History* 18 (No. 2): 174–198.

economic viewpoint to change the structure of property rights when transaction costs are positive. A change in the rules that govern exchange is an investment, and often it is worth changing the rules only when there is to be a lasting change in relative prices – for example, when technological change permanently lowers the cost of information.

In sum, the basic structure of property rights is determined by the state and reflects the preferences and constraints of those who control the state. All choices made by individuals and groups who control the state are constrained by the requirement to maintain power, but the ultimate impact of institutional change on power relationships is often shrouded in uncertainty. Therefore, institutional changes that in traditional neoclassical models appear to be consistent with wealth maximization are often seen as disadvantageous by the power elite because the changes are likely to raise the cost of agency or even threaten an outright loss of control.

In other words, there are various ways of explaining the relative stability of the structure of property rights without discarding the rational-choice model. Indeed, property rights, far from being dangerously flexible, often lag behind changes in the environment and act as brakes on economic development and growth. It is the analysis of such crippling inflexibility that perhaps constitutes the most interesting task ahead for the NIE.

Part II

Property rights and economic outcomes

4

The economics of exclusive rights

4.1. Introduction

In this chapter we contrast the economics of exclusive and nonexclusive ownership of resources and examine the consequences of alternative sets of social rules. Section 4.2 introduces the economics of the common pool, and explains how competition among users of common property can result in a dissipation of the potential rental income from the common asset.[1] Examples from U.S. economic history are used to explain the concept of de facto common property.

In Section 4.3, we examine the costs of assigning and enforcing exclusive rights. In fact, the establishment of exclusive rights uses up resources just as does competition for a nonexclusive asset. The transfer of public timberland to private ownership in the Pacific Northwest during the late 1800s and early 1900s is taken as an example of a relatively costly privatization process. The section ends with a demonstration (in terms of a general equilibrium model) of our inability to make positive statements about the impact on aggregate welfare of the establishment of exclusive property rights, even when the change leads to an increase in net output. The reason is that the impact depends on the true nature of

---

1. The term *common property* (or open access) should not be confused with communal property. See our discussion in Chapter 2, Section 2.1.

individual utility functions which we do not know and cannot measure.

Section 4.4 takes the discussion beyond the dichotomy of exclusive or nonexclusive rights and examines, in light of Coase's theorem, the interplay between transaction costs and conflicting uses of resources. A verbal discussion and a simple general equilibrium model (an Edgeworth box) is used to illustrate Coase's theorem, the implications of high transaction costs, and the economic consequences of alternative legal rules. Changes in the law governing liability for work-related accidents in nineteenth-century Britain, and other examples, are used to explain how economic outcomes can vary with alternative assignments of property rights. We emphasize that it is not self-evident that rules and rulings by the state will be designed to maximize the aggregate utility or wealth of a community.

In the final section, 4.5, we examine how restrictions imposed by the state on the terms of contracts between individuals – for example, price ceilings or price floors – affect economic outcomes. It is argued that such measures can place real income in the public domain (as common property) and lead to costly competition and to new forms of organizing production and exchange. Rationing by waiting is discussed as an alternative to the price mechanism. However, buyers and sellers have an incentive, given the new constraints, to minimize the dissipation of nonexclusive income. The extraordinary history of rent controls in Hong Kong is used to illustrate these issues.

4.2. Common property

With the exception of the perfectly defined and enforced private property rights of the basic neoclassical model, economists have paid more attention to common property and its consequences for the allocation of resources than to any other structure of rights. For example, the economics of the "common pool" are at the center of fisheries economics, which is an important branch of applied microeconomics.[2] There exists, therefore, a well-developed corpus of theory dealing with the consequences of nonexclusive ownership.

The economic consequences of using common inputs in production can be illustrated with a simple graphic model. In the model of Figure 4.1, which originates with Gordon (1954), exclusively owned input and common inputs are used in combination: for example, common fishing grounds and private fishing boats, gear, and labor; or privately owned cattle and common pasture land. It is assumed that there are only two factors of production, *homogeneous* labor and a common natural resource in fixed supply, such as a piece of land or a fishery. The opportunity cost of applying labor to the natural resource is determined by the (exogenous) market wage in alternative activities, W^0. The diagram shows how the values of the average and marginal products of labor fall as more units of labor are applied to the fixed natural resource, R^0.[3]

Let us examine more carefully what happens when *one more unit* of labor is added to R^0. The contribution to total output by the new labor unit, L_i, can be viewed as twofold. As all the labor units are of the same quality, unit L_i produces Q/L_N, where Q is the value of total output and L_N the total number of homogeneous labor units. Second, the addition of L_i has the effect of *reducing* the average product of existing (intramarginal) labor units – as indicated by the slope of the *VAP* curve. The value-of-marginal-

2. The pioneering contribution to the economics of common resources in the fishery was made by the Danish economist Jens Warming. Warming's insights were independently discovered some forty years later by the Canadian economist H. Scott Gordon. Warming, Jens (1911). "Om 'Grundrente' af Fiskegrunde." *Nationalökonomisk Tidsskrift*: 495–506; Warming, Jens (1931). "Aalgaardsretten." *Nationalökonomisk Tidsskrift*: 151–162. See also Andersen, P. (1983). " 'On Rent of Fishing Grounds': A Translation of Jens Warming's 1911 Article, with an Introduction." *History of Political Economy 15* (Fall, No. 3): 391–396; and Gordon, H. S. (1954). "The Economic Theory of a Common Property Resource: The Fishery." *Journal of Political Economy 62* (April): 124–142.
3. The discussion that follows draws on Cheung's important 1970 article. Cheung, Steven N. S. (1970). "The Structure of a Contract and the Theory of a Nonexclusive Resource." *Journal of Law and Economics 13* (April): 49–70.

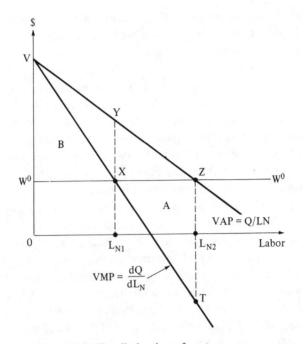

Figure 4.1. The dissipation of rent.

product curve, *VMP*, summarizes the two effects just mentioned, and gives the net addition to total output that results when a marginal unit of labor, L_i, is added to R^0, the fixed natural resource.

If R^0 is privately owned, the two effects of adding labor to the fixed resource are both taken into account. For example, if R^0 is owned by a private firm that hires labor at the fixed wage rate, W^0, the firm will employ L_{N1} units of labor because this level of operations maximizes the rental income from R^0, represented by the triangle B in Figure 4.1. Note that the rent-maximizing outcome can prevail even when R^0 is common property, provided the resource is used by only one decision unit and there is no threat of entry by others.

The equilibrium outcome is different when there are no exclusive rights to R^0 and the resource is utilized by more than one independent decision unit. Under these circumstances, each unit, L_1, takes account only of its own output, Q/L_N, and pays no attention to the cost it imposes on the other units.[4] These external costs can be illustrated with the help of Figure 4.1. Imagine that there is an infinitesimal increase in the labor input at L_{N1}. The output of the marginal unit is shown by $L_{N1}Y$, the fall in productivity of the intramarginal units is equal to XY, and the net increase in output is $L_{N1}Y - XY = L_{N1}X$.

If each decision unit ignores the costs it imposes on others, new labor units will enter until $VAP = W^0$ and $L = L_{N2}$. At this point the remuneration of each decision unit (VAP) is equal to its marginal opportunity cost, W^0, and crowding reduces the rent from the common natural resource, R^0, to zero: The net income from the resource is *dissipated* through the interplay of competitive forces. In Figure 4.1, the level of dissipation in equilibrium is measured by the triangle A (XZT), which is equal to the maximum rent that R^0 can yield, the triangle B (XVW^0). It is clear from the diagram that the net addition to output by labor units ($L_{N2} - L_{N1}$) is less than their potential contribution in alternative activities, which is measured by the market wage, W^0. In Figure 4.1 the last labor units that are added to R^0 contribute a negative marginal product. This outcome can be found, for example, in a fishery where the entry of fishermen continues after the total catch has started to fall. However, a negative marginal product is a possible but not a necessary outcome of this model.

Note that the model shows only the equilibrium outcome associated with nonexclusive ownership in R^0 (an outcome whereby average product equals marginal opportunity cost for the private

4. This assumes that high transaction costs prevent the decision units from making contractual agreements to maximize the joint rental income from the resource. Cheung (1970) [op. cit., note 2] argues that the contracting approach to the problem of social cost leads to new and fruitful questions: "Why do market contracts not exist for certain effects of actions? Because of the absence of exclusive rights, or because transaction costs are prohibitive? Why do exclusive rights not exist for certain actions? Because of the legal institutions or because policing costs are prohibitive? Why do some conceivably more efficient stipulations not exist in the structure of a contract? And what implications for resource allocation and income distribution can we deduce from all this?" (p. 58)

inputs), but it does not analyze the process of adjustment by the labor units in terms of the usual marginal conditions of optimization. Cheung (1970) has modeled this process, using a diagram comparable to Figure 4.1. In Cheung's model, the decision units enter in sequence. The first firm, F_1, maximizes the rent from R^0 by extending its use of labor (the owner's labor and/or hired labor) until the value of the marginal product of labor, VMP_1 and the exogenous market wage, W^0, are equal.

The second firm, F_2, maximizes its share of the *remaining rent* by equating the value of the marginal product of its labor units, VMP_2, with W^0. However, when the second firm enters, VMP_1 shifts to the left, and F_1 readjusts its level of operations and *reduces the use of labor*. Firms F_1 and F_2 share the·rent equally, but the total rent is now smaller than when F_1 was the only user of R^0. The process of entry continues until the equilibrium outcome of Figure 4.1 is reached at a level of utilization where $VAP = W^0$ – although the individual firms make adjustments in terms of their VMP and not VAP.[5]

Cheung's model, which is analogous to Cournot's duopoly solution, implies that in equilibrium the number of entrants (decision units, firms) will approach infinity. Cheung (1970) emphasizes that this unrealistic outcome of his model depends on its simplifying assumptions: If the private inputs are not homogeneous and their comparative advantage in using R^0 varies, if there are economies of scale (e.g., in boat or gear size or distance of travel to the fishery) or if there are cost barriers to entry, then the number of entrants is finite.

The simple model of Figure 4.1 provides a striking indication of how the definition and enforcement of property rights, or the lack thereof, can affect economic outcomes. The model suggests that the rent from resource, R^0, is fully dissipated when R^0 is common property, and that the output of the economy is reduced by an amount equal to the rent, and, further, compared to exclusive

5. Cheung (1970) provides graphic and algebraic versions of this model. See pp. 61–63.

ownership, that more units of the privately owned input are employed, with the net contribution of the last units being less than their opportunity cost. We defer to later chapters the interesting question why the state or the individuals directly concerned tolerate these outcomes.

The discussion above was concerned solely with how *intensively* R^0 is used under alternative structures of property rights, but in reality optimal resource use involves adjustments at several margins: the choice of product, technology, input investments, time shape of the output flow, and so on. The choice at these various margins depends in part on the cost of defining and policing exclusivity and the costs of negotiating and enforcing contracts, a process that in turn depends on the physical attributes of the resources and the institutional environment. Therefore, rent dissipation may set in even before active competition begins among the users of common property. For example, in the absence of exclusive rights farmers may prefer to use a piece of land for grazing cattle rather than planting fruit trees if the costs of policing investment in fruit trees is relatively high, even though orchards are more profitable than cattle if the policing costs are not counted.[6]

When exclusive rights are not fully defined – for example, because regulation by government is incomplete – resources can become de facto common property, but this need not be immediately obvious. Libecap and Johnson (1980) argue that "the chronic overgrazing on the Navajo Reservation is the result of the policies of the Interior Department and the Navajo Tribal Council."[7] According to Libecap and Johnson, rules laid down by these bodies have led to the preponderance of small herds of sheep and have restricted the consolidation of grazing lands, which in turn have increased the cost of negotiating and maintaining property rights (e.g., the cost of enforcing the authorized stocking levels) and

6. Ibid., pp. 52–54.
7. P. 69 in Libecap, Gary D., and Johnson, Ronald N. (1980). "Legislating Commons: The Navajo Tribal Council and the Navajo Range." *Economic Inquiry* 18 (January): 69–86.

have prevented gains from economies of scale. Individual property rights are limited in various ways. Each family is given user rights to a small plot of land which is informally specified, and unanimous agreement from neighboring users is required for fencing. In short, "the cumulative effect of the Tribal Council's policies has been essentially to legislate a common property condition for the range."[8] The economic outcome of this arrangement has been to erode the land, lower net income per sheep (or parcel of land), and force many Navajo to leave their traditional employment of sheep raising and accept wage work or welfare. And the property rights structure that has produced this outcome was, according to Libecap and Johnson, initially designed to preserve the pastoral culture of the Navajo.

Examples of de facto common property abound. When fishermen are given exclusive rights to patches of the ocean, they do not obtain control over migratory stocks of fish that migrate between the territorial waters of sovereign states. The fish stocks are still de facto common property. The structure of property rights to federal oil land in the United States during the early years of the twentieth century is another example.[9] Although subsurface oil formations are often thousands of acres in size, individuals could acquire only up to twenty acres of land for oil explorations.[10] This arrangement meant that property rights to oil were in fact assigned only upon extraction, and the outcome that resulted was rent dissipation on a large scale – reflecting choices of input investments, time profiles of production, and other factors:

> Excessive wells were dug along property lines to drain
> oil from neighboring acres; extracted oil was placed
> in surface storage (open reservoirs as well as steel tanks),

8. Ibid., p. 83.
9. Libecap, Gary D. (1984). "The Political Allocation of Mineral Rights: a Reevaluation of Teapot Dome." *Journal of Economic History 44* (June): 381–391.
10. "Prior to 1909 property rights to federal oil land were assigned under the placer mining law. Under this law individuals could claim 20 acres of land for oil exploration, and upon discovery of oil could secure title at $2.50 per acre." Ibid., p. 383.

where it was subject to evaporation, fire, and spoilage; and rapid extraction rates reduced total oil recovery as subsurface pressures, necessary for naturally expelling subsurface oil, were prematurely depleted.[11]

These adjustments at various margins were associated with the dissipation of rental values, and Libecap (1984) suggests that large figures were involved:

> In 1910 in California estimates of oil losses from fire and evaporation ranged from . . . 5 to 11 percent of the state's production. In 1914 the Director of the Bureau of Mines estimated losses from excessive drilling at $50,000,000 when the value of total U.S. production was $214,000,000. The FOCB [Federal Oil Conservation Board] in 1926 estimated recovery rates of only 20 to 25 percent with competitive extraction, while 85 to 90 percent was possible under certain circumstances with controlled extraction.[12]

In modern societies it is unusual to find valuable assets as pure common property. Typically we find only elements of common property and various forms of government regulation. The traditional neoclassical analysis of common resources suggests that dissipation can be controlled by regulating one or a few margins, for example, through a tax on effort or output. However, Neoinstitutional Economics emphasizes that dissipation usually can take place at any of several margins, and control at one margin is unlikely to produce the desired results. Cheung (1970) points out that, in situations where the right to contract exists, it is usual that private contracts for the use of natural resources contain a large number of stipulations that are intended to control behavior at several margins.[13] Similarly, effective regulation will usually require a complex structure of rules. We return to this point in Section 4.5.

---

11. Ibid., p. 383.
12. Ibid., pp. 383–384.
13. Cheung (1970), op. cit., note 3.

4.3. The cost of producing property rights

In the model of resource utilization of the previous section, the gains from establishing exclusive rights to a valuable resource, R^0, were measured by the triangle B (in Fig. 4.1). This elementary presentation ignores the costs both to the state and to private individuals of establishing exclusive rights. It is important to realize that the costs of the resources that are diverted to the "production" of property rights are often substantial.[14] "The worth of perfectly defined and enforced rights is represented by the net present value of the rents and individuals would be willing to spend up to that amount to obtain these rights. If the rents can be obtained for less than this amount, net rents will be positive and society's output will be greater."[15]

For example, consider the process whereby the state transfers ownership of land to private holders. A massive exit by government from land ownership took place in North America in the previous century, and "the nineteenth-century disposal into private hands of the entire American public domain from the Ohio to the Pacific was surely the most breathtaking of these events. And the alienation of Canadian lands in all the colonies and the North-west Territory was almost as dramatic."[16] The rules for disposing of federal land varied. Land was "awarded to squatters, sold, granted to encourage production of certain goods and services or given to those willing to make certain investments in the land."[17]

The policies followed by the U.S. government in assigning private ownership to public land often limited the allowable size of

14. "Establishing and producing property rights is very much a productive activity towards which resources can be devoted." P. 165 in Anderson, Terry L., and Hill, Peter J. (1975). "The Evolution of Property Rights: A Study of the American West." *Journal of Law and Economics 18* (No. 1, April): 163–179.

15. P. 440 in Anderson, Terry L., and Hill, Peter J. (1983). "Privatizing the Commons: An Improvement?" *Southern Economic Journal 50* (No. 2, October): 438–450.

16. P. 559 in Scott, Anthony (1983). "Property Rights and Property Wrongs." *Canadian Journal of Economics 16* (No. 4): 555–573.

17. Anderson and Hill (1983) [op. cit., note 15], p. 447.

holdings and required the investment of unnecessary resources in the land in order to claim it. The process for qualifying for ownership under such rules can dissipate the potential rent from the land. Anderson and Hill (1983) point out that, in certain game-theoretic situations (e.g., the prisoners' dilemma), the expenditure of resources on the qualifying process may even exceed the rent.[18] However, it is important to note that investment in privatization can also take the form of an exchange of wealth that does not use up the resources of the economy. This is the case when the rights are acquired in return for existing assets, for example, at an auction or by bribing.

Libecap and Johnson (1979) provide interesting estimates of the costs of the privatization process in the case of U.S. federal policies for the transfer of public timberland to private ownership in the Pacific Northwest during the late 1800s and early 1900s.[19] By the mid-nineteenth century there were extensive economies of scale in lumbering, but the government, wanting to give property rights only to small farmers, insisted on disposing only of small plots limited to 160 acres per claimant.[20] "Plots could be obtained only by bona fide settlers for domestic use under Preemption, Home-

18. The triangles A and B in Figure 4.1 represent two types of potential waste. Triangle A represents the waste associated with overutilization of the resources when it is common property, whereas triangle B represents the maximum amount of resources individuals are willing to spend for acquiring exclusive rights to the resource. Note that the equality of triangles A and B in Figure 4.1 depends on the linearity of the VAP line. If the VAP curve is nonlinear, A can be smaller or larger than B. If A (the measure of dissipation associated with common property) is smaller than B (the maximum potential rent), competition for exclusive rights to the rent may be more costly in resources than the inefficiencies of the common pool. Ibid., p. 441.
19. Libecap, Gary D., and Johnson, Ronald N. (1979). "Property Rights, Nineteenth-Century Federal Timber Policy, and the Conservation Movement." *Journal of Economic History 39* (No. 1, March): 129–142.
20. "Logging operations were highly capital intensive, requiring spur railroad lines and other equipment to handle the huge logs of the virgin forests. Because there were economies of scale in the cutting of timber, efficient logging operations required large tracts of land in excess of that allowed by law." Ibid., p. 130.

stead, and Timber and Stone Laws, and there was no way for lumber companies directly to procure large sections of forested land from the government."[21]

But the lumber companies circumvented federal restrictions on ownership and acquired timberland at high transaction costs. Libecap and Johnson (1979) drew up a simple cost-of-acquisition function for the timber companies:

> Expected gains $= Pr(q) [P - C - q] - [1 - Pr(q)] [C + q]$,
> which becomes
> Expected gains $= Pr(q)P - [C + q]$

Here P is the market price of an acre of land with secure property rights; C is the government price of land; q the expenditure on evasion of federal restrictions; and $Pr(q)$ the probability of successfully obtaining ownership rights with expenditure q on evasion.[22] If it is assumed that competition for valuable forest tracts reduces expected gains to zero, we can write:

$$P[Pr(q)] = (C + q)$$

namely, in equilibrium the cost of claiming each acre of land will equal its expected value.[23] During the period under consideration, P, the market value of forest tracts with secure property rights increased over time, and the expected gains from claiming land, the term $P[Pr(q)]$, also increased.[24] The logic of the model suggests that land was claimed by the lumber companies as soon as the expected gains had risen to match the costs, $C + q$, and that

---

21. Ibid., p. 130.
22. "P is primarily determined by changes in stumpage prices (the value of standing timber) which were rising throughout the period from 1880 to 1915. C . . . the government price of land was either $2.50 or $1.25 depending on the law used, and it did not change." Ibid., p. 132. Note that it is assumed here that the cost of failure does not include imprisonment or a fine.
23. The authors assume diminishing returns to investment in evading the law, which yields, in the equation $P = (C + q)/Pr(q)$, a U-shaped functional relationship between P and q. Libecap and Johnson (1979), p. 133.
24. This need not have been the case if the emphasis on law enforcement and penalties for violating the law had also increased over time.

the tracts were claimed sequentially with the most valuable land claimed first.[25]

The restrictions on the lumber companies' ability to acquire timberland resulted in an elaborate system of evasions. The companies employed agents who located and secured the land by contracting with cruisers who secured desirable plots and with entrymen who staked the claims under federal law and lied as to their intent. Libecap and Johnson (1979) provide empirical estimates of q, the cost of attempts to evade federal restrictions. They estimate that "as many as half of the claims made under all three laws for timberland in the Northwest were illegal."[26] The *direct resource cost* of fraudulent transfers ranged from about 60 percent of P, the market price of land (under the Timber and Stone laws) to nearly 80 percent of P (under the Preemption law). Excluded from these calculations are outright bribes to Land Office officials (transfers) and payments to timber cruisers (also required for legitimate transfers).[27] Libecap and Johnson estimate that the resource cost (rent dissipation) of illegal transfers of timberland in the Northwest in the period from 1881 to 1907 amounted to some $17 million, which is about one third more than the government received for the sale of the land.[28]

Anderson and Hill (1983) contrast federal land policy in the nineteenth century with arrangements prevailing on the American frontier where extralegal institutions evolved for defining and enforcing property rights to land, water, timber, minerals, livestock, and personal property. These improvised structures of rights came

25. The most valuable land, of course, having the highest P. One might expect that much timberland would have been claimed within the law by private individuals (who did not need to invest in fraudulent activities and risk punishment) and then legitimately sold to lumber companies. The evidence suggests that such transactions were insignificant until the 1900s. The authors suggest several explanations for this which are related to the high cost for the companies of dealing with a large number of individuals acting independently and holding land of variable quality at varying locations.
26. Libecap and Johnson (1979) [op. cit., note 19], p. 137.
27. Ibid., p. 136.
28. Ibid., p. 138.

about through the interaction of the users of the resources, the residual claimants, rather than being imposed from the outside by the agents of the state.[29] Anderson and Hill argue that the frontiersmen designed less wasteful processes for assigning property rights to natural resources than the federal government did at a later date. For example, unnecessary investments on the land to determine ownership were usually not required.

Modern examples of rent dissipation associated with the assignment by the state of exclusive rights are numerous. "Just as the Homestead Act generated too many cabins on the American Frontier, exploration requirements on the continental shelf generate an excessive amount of drilling activity. This is particularly true under British and Norwegian rules for drilling in the North Sea."[30]

Expenditures associated with the assignment of property rights are sunk costs and do not affect decisions regarding output once the transfer of rights has taken place, but enforcement costs are variable, repeated in each time period, and incurred by both individual owners and the state. High costs of enforcing rights may render exclusive ownership of a resource economically inviable. For example, consider the costs of enforcing property rights in the resources of the ocean.

After World War II, there was a gradual retreat from the common property doctrine that had prevailed for most of the resources in the oceans.[31] By the end of 1977, a majority of coastal nations had declared exclusive jurisdiction over resources in the ocean, typically extending 200 nautical miles from shore. Enforcement of property rights in these large zones is executed by the individual states and, in the case of fisheries resources, takes the form of excluding or controlling foreign fishermen and regulating domestic ones. For example:

29. Anderson and Hill (1983) [op. cit., note 15], p. 414.
30. Ibid., pp. 448–449.
31. Clarkson (1974) provides an account of the historical development of the law of the seas. Clarkson, Kenneth W. (1974). "International Law, U.S. Seabeds Policy and Ocean Resource Development." *Journal of Law and Economics* *17* (No. 1): 117–142.

The United States government spent approximately $100 million annually on fisheries law enforcement alone following its extension of jurisdiction over marine fisheries. Additional transaction costs (which include the costs of administration, data collection and research) may approach $200 million annually. Potential benefits from fisheries, in the form of economic rent, may range from $200 million to $500 million annually.[32]

The enclosure of the ocean may reduce the waste of the common pool but at the price of high enforcement costs. The costs of enforcement can be lowered not only by new technologies (radar and the airplane) but also by new and more effective forms of regulations and assignments of rights. Typically, fisheries economists have ignored enforcement costs, at least until recently, in their analysis of the consequences of various forms of regulations, such as simple aggregate quotas, gear restrictions, and area and seasonal closures.[33] Anderson and Sutinen (1984) argue that gear restrictions, which usually are thought of as ineffective methods of regulations (since they can increase the cost of production), "may be less costly to enforce than other measures . . . [and] could turn out to be the most efficient method of regulation when enforcement is taken into account."[34]

Can it be claimed that the "production" of private property rights will always increase social welfare, if the resources devoted to the definition and enforcement of exclusive rights have less value

32. See p. 3 in Andersen, Peder, and Sutinen, Jon G. (1984). "The Economics of Fisheries Law Enforcement." In Skog, Göran, ed. *Papers Presented at the First Meeting of the European Association for Law and Economics.* Department of Economics, University of Lund.

33. Scott (1979) discusses these issues and concludes: "A survey of the economic literature of fisheries regulation shows that little of analytical value for the comparison of alternative regulatory techniques has emerged." P. 725 in Scott, Anthony (1979). "Development of Economic Theory on Fisheries Regulation." *Journal of the Fisheries Research Board of Canada 36*: 725–741.

34. Anderson and Sutinen (1984) [op. cit., note 32], p. 9. The case against gear restrictions was made by Crutchfield, J. A. (1961). "An Economic Evaluation of Alternative Methods of Fishery Regulation." *Journal of Law and Economics 4* (No. 1): 131–141.

than the additional output associated with private ownership? Furubotn (1985) examines this question with the help of a general equilibrium model and comparative statics and finds that no positive statements of a general nature can be made about the social welfare effects of privatization.[35] Let us consider these issues in some detail.

A large-scale transfer of common resources to private owners cannot properly be analyzed with the help of a partial equilibrium model, such as the one in Figure 4.1, because the transfer affects not only output but also the distribution of wealth and relative prices. The process of privatization will have several effects: Output per unit of inputs is likely to increase, but factor supplies in direct commodity production are reduced as inputs are diverted to the production of property rights (the definition, acquisition, and enforcement of rights). Let us examine these developments in a simple model of general equilibrium for a market exchange economy with two commodities (Figure 4.2).[36] Our first consideration is whether a change from common ownership to private ownership in some important sector of the economy will cause the production possibilities locus of the economy to shift outward.[37] In Figure 4.2 we assume that output losses due to the use of inputs for the enforcement of exclusive rights are less than the output gains associated with exclusive ownership of the resource, and, therefore, the production possibilities (PP) frontier shifts outward (to the northeast).[38]

35. The discussion that follows is based on Furubotn, Eirik G. (1985). "The Gains from Privatization. A General Equilibrium Perspective." Working paper. University of Texas at Arlington, Department of Economics. Also see Furubotn, Eirik G. (1987). "Privatizing the Commons. Comment and Note." *Southern Economic Journal 54* (No. 1): 219–224.

36. See Furubotn (1985), op. cit., note 35.

37. Note that the costs to individuals of acquiring a common resource are sunk costs which disappear in later periods. In other words, in a multiperiod analysis of the privatization process the output gains from privatization will be greater in later periods than in the initial period when resources are used up in a competition for private rights to the resource.

38. As the production possibilities frontier moves out in consequence of the privatization of some resource, the frontier may change its shape, and it is also

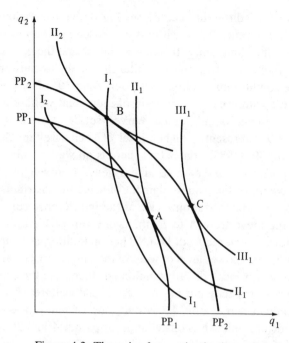

Figure 4.2. The gains from privatization and social welfare.

What general statements can be made about the impact on social welfare when the PP frontier shifts outward following a change in the structure of property rights? If we restrict ourselves to positive economics, the social welfare functions that reflect ethical norms are ruled out, and we are left with the Pareto criterion and the traditional concept of individual indifference curves and their aggregates, community indifference curves (Scitovsky contours).

Let us assume that the resource to be privatized is land. In Figure 4.2, initially, when land is in part common property, the relevant production possibilities contour is PP_1 and the economy is in equilibrium at point A. When this position is given, the existing distribution of individual welfare can be used to derive a consistent

possible (but not shown in Figure 4.2) that the new locus intersects the old locus.

set of community indifference curves, set 1. A move from a lower to a higher indifference curve within set 1 is seen as Pareto improvement for the community. It is now assumed that the granting of exclusive rights to the commons shifts the *PP* locus outward, and the new equilibrium position is at point *B* on PP_2. But point *B* is associated with a new distribution of individual welfare and a new set of community indifference curves, set 2.

Does point *B* represent a higher level of social welfare than point *A*? Furubotn (1985) argues that there is no way, within the confines of positive economics, to give a general answer to this question. If we make the value judgment of using the distribution of welfare prior to privatization (set 1 of the indifference curves) to evaluate the move from *A* to *B*, then, in terms of Figure 4.2, social welfare has been reduced. Point *B* lies on indifference curve I_1 which represents a lower level of welfare than indifference curve II_1 where point *A* is located. Privatization has increased the economy's productive capacity but has reduced social welfare.

But the outcome in Figure 4.2 is only one of many possible outcomes. For example, the constellation of points *A* and *B* and the two sets of indifference curves could be such that a move from *A* to *B* represents an unambiguous *increase* in social welfare. Furthermore, there exists a point on the new *PP* locus, point *C*, which is on indifference curve III_1. Point *C*, therefore, represents a higher level of community welfare than either point *A* or point *B* (*C* is Pareto superior to positions *A* and *B*). If the members of the community could both agree to assign exclusive rights to the commons and arrange that gainers compensate losers, the economy could, technically, move from *A* to *C* and bypass position *B*. Yet, in practice, high transaction costs are likely to prevent extensive contracting between gainers and losers. It is also possible that the government could intervene, using taxes and bounties, to move the economy to position *C*, but such measures require a political consensus, and extensive intervention could affect *incentives* and shift PP_2 *inward*.

In sum, a large-scale transfer of common-property resources to private ownership, or even a relatively modest change in the structure of rights, such as the reassignment of liability in a world of exclusive rights, affects both the productive capacity of the economy and the distribution of wealth, and creates, in a market economy, a new basis for the valuation of commodities. Therefore, from the viewpoint of positive economics, it is impossible to evaluate the impact of changes in property rights on social welfare.

The point is that utility functions are unobservable theoretical constructs that are useful primarily as a basis for predicting empirical regularities in behavior. For measuring and comparing levels of social welfare, it is required that our assumptions about the nature of utility functions be empirically correct, and that there exists some common unit for measuring and aggregating the utility of individuals. For example, if it were empirically true that utility functions were *interdependent* to the extreme degree that an individual's welfare depended entirely on his or her wealth relative to others, the question of whether privatization moved the PP frontier inward or outward would be of no interest, as it is only the distribution of wealth that matters.[39] In short, the impact of changes in property rights on aggregate social welfare depends on the true nature of individual utility functions, which we do not know and cannot measure.

4.4. Conflicting uses and the cost of transacting

In a previous section (4.2), we discussed how the dissipation of rental income is caused by a failure to take account of costly interactions when several decision units apply private inputs to a common resource. In this section, we examine whether costly (or beneficial) spillover effects disappear when exclusive rights replace common ownership. It is concluded that, even under a regime of exclusive ownership, decision makers may fail to allow for costly or beneficial interactions – fail to internalize them – when the costs of transacting are high.

Below we make the following points:

---

39. Furubotn (1985), p. 13.

1. In a model of fully defined and enforced private property rights and *zero transaction costs*, resources will find their highest valued use no matter how the state assigns property rights and liabilities.

2. When the costs of transacting are positive, as they are in the real world, resources need not find their highest valued use as measured by the market rule.[40] Economic outcomes depend on the details of the social and legal systems, and the rule of liability matters.[41]

3. The firm, the market, and the legal system are all costly social arrangements. The social and economic organization affects both the allocation of resources and the costs involved in the allocation process. Certain social arrangements are associated with a greater net output than other arrangements. New legal instruments can affect productivity just as strongly as new techniques of production.

4. The assignment of property rights and liabilities affects the distribution of wealth in society. The structure of property rights reflects the interests, values, and constraints of those who control the state.

Consider the case of a realty firm that unexpectedly discovers that an airport is being planned close to a complex of rental apartments owned by the firm. It is foreseeable that noise from airplanes flying at low altitudes will reduce the market value of the apartments, if such flights are allowed. But according to Coase's theorem, the initial assignment of property rights in the airspace above the apartments, to either the airline or the realty firm, will not

40. We avoid here using the word *efficiency*. See our discussion, in Chapter 1, Section 1.5, of the meaning of efficiency once transaction costs are introduced into economic theory. Efficiency is an unmeasurable characteristic of models. If we assume that agents are rational maximizers, all models yield efficient outcomes – regardless of whether transaction costs are zero or positive. Efficiency is a logical consequence of the assumptions in models assuming maximizing behavior.

41. See Demsetz, Harold (1972). "When Does the Rule of Liability Matter?" *Journal of Legal Studies 1* (No. 1, February): 13–28.

influence the use of that airspace, *provided that the costs of transacting are zero* (or low) and that the parties are free to transfer their rights if they wish.[42]

Coase's reasoning is now familiar. Let us look at the calculations of costs and benefits by the airline that owns and operates the airport. If all rights to the airspace above the apartments rest with the realty firm, the airline must purchase the right to fly over the apartments, and the decision whether to buy this right depends on the usual calculations of marginal costs and benefits. On the other hand, if the airline has an exclusive right to the airspace, the realty firm will offer to pay the airline for not flying over the apartments. The offer of such payments is seen as an implicit cost of making the flights and figures in the decisions of the airline. In other words, the assignment to either party of the rights to the airspace determines only whether the opportunity cost of using the air for flying is an *explicit* or *implicit cost*. Parallel reasoning applies to the cost–benefit calculations of the realty firm.

According to Coase (1960), it is useful to think of inputs as *bundles of rights* rather than physical entities. The right to use the airspace is an input, and its use in any particular activity has an opportunity cost. If this input is used by the airline, the opportunity cost reflects less peace and quiet at the apartments; if it is used by the realty firm, the opportunity cost takes the form of inconvenience for the airline. The assignment of ownership rights over the airspace to either firm does *not* eliminate costly interactions. But

---

42. The theory is implied in Coase (1960) but not stated explicitly. The idea appeared first in Coase's 1959 article about the economics of broadcasting. In a sense, Coase's theorem is a restatement of "Adam Smith's theorem" about the invisible hand, and the "true" Coase's theorem should read: The location of liability matters when the costs of transacting are high. See p. 336 in McCloskey, Donald N. (1985). *The Applied Theory of Price*, 2nd ed. New York: Macmillan; Coase, Ronald N. (1960). "The Problem of Social Cost." *Journal of Law and Economics 3* (No. 1, October): 1–44 [reprinted in Breit, William, and Hochman, Harold, eds. (1968). *Readings in Microeconomics*. New York: Holt, Rinehart & Winston]; and Coase, Ronald N. (1959). "The Federal Communications Commission." *Journal of Law and Economics 2* (No. 1, October): 1–40.

when the costs of transacting are low these costly interactions are *internalized*: The opportunity cost of the airspace is included in the calculations of both parties, and the airspace will find its use of highest value, provided there are no legal restrictions on the transfer of these rights.[43] The equilibrium solution may involve noisy flights, but the costs arising from the noise are no different from the costs of other inputs used in producing flights, such as the cost of fuel. The noise is not a spillover in the sense of welfare economics, and the joint market value of the assets of the realty firm and the airline are maximized. Finally, we note that equilibrium can be reached through adjustments at a number of margins – for example, by adjusting the number of flights, the time of flights, type of aircraft, and use of noise-abatement equipment or through the soundproofing of housing units and alternative uses of the subadjacent land.

Several authors have argued that examples of the type presented by Coase (1960) in his seminal article correspond to situations of bilateral monopoly rather than competitive markets where prices are exogenously given to traders.[44] The critics would argue that the airline and the realty firm in our example have no good alternatives to trading with each other and cannot rely on any exogenous rules for dividing their joint rent from the airspace. In the jargon of game theory, they are involved in a *bargaining game*, and the final outcome can be a stalemate with the airspace not being assigned to its use of highest value. Whether we agree or not with the critics depends on our definition of the concept *zero transaction costs*. If we take it to mean that all information is available at no cost, then bargaining games cannot exist and all prices are indeed exogenous. However, we believe that scholarly debates over exact definitions of zero transaction costs are not fruitful as they draw attention from

43. The input will be put to a use whereby its opportunity cost is minimized.
44. For example, see Cooter, Robert (1982). "The Cost of Coase." *Journal of Legal Studies 11* (No. 1, January): 1–34; and Veljanovski, Cento G. (1982). "The Coase Theorems, and the Economic Theory of Markets and Law." *Kyklos 35* (No. 1): 66–81.

Coase's main contribution which was to arouse our awareness of the implications of *positive* transaction costs.

When transaction costs are high, the allocation of resources in a market economy can be strongly affected by the assignment of legal rights and the criteria used by the state for settling competing claims. In real life the cost of negotiating with a large number of individuals over the rights to use their airspace – say, for trans-continental flights – is probably greater than the benefits from such agreements. This was recognized by the U.S. Supreme Court in *United States v. Causby*, a case involving a dispute over the use of airspace. The Court first acknowledged: "It is an ancient doctrine that a common-law ownership of land extended to the periphery of the universe: *Cujus est solum ejus est usque ad coelum.*"

Using phrases which concealed the fact that private ownership rights assigned under an "ancient doctrine" were being taken away, the Court went on to say:

> That doctrine has no place in the modern world. The air is a public highway as Congress has declared. Were that not true, every transcontinental flight would subject the operator to countless trespass suits. Common sense revolts at the idea. To recognize such private claims to the airspace would clog these highways, seriously interfere with their control and development in the public interest, and transfer into private ownership that to which only the public has just claim.[45]

Coase's theorem, the implications of high transaction costs, and the economic consequences of legal instruments can be illustrated with the help of a general equilibrium model. This has been done by Haddock and Spiegel (1984), using an Edgeworth box.[46] The following discussion is based on their work.

---

45. *United States v. Causby*, 328 U.S. 256, 261 (1946). Cited on p. 446 in Samuels, Warren J. (1971). "Interrelations Between Legal and Economic Processes." *Journal of Law and Economics 14* (October, No. 2): 435–450.
46. Haddock, David, and Spiegel, Menahem (1984). "Property Rules, Liability Rules, and Inalienability: One View of the Edgeworth Box." In Skog, Göran,

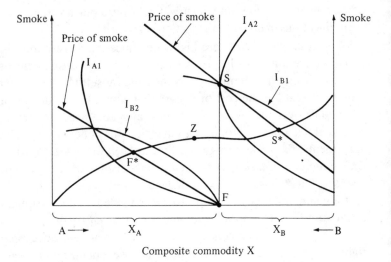

Figure 4.3. The assignment of property rights and economic outcomes in an Edgeworth box.

Figure 4.3 represents a world inhabited by two individuals, A and B, who consume the composite commodity, X. Individual A also consumes cigarette smoke, whereas cigarette smoke is a source of disutility for B. The Edgeworth box in Figure 4.3 is unusual in that it does not have a lid, which is due to our assumption that cigarettes are a free good (imagine that A smokes leaves or herbs, which are found in abundant quantities in nature and need no processing). A's pleasure from additional smoking diminishes after a point and his marginal utility of smoking eventually drops to zero and then becomes negative.

In Figure 4.3, the original entitlements of the composite commodity, X, are X_A and X_B. I_A and I_B are representative indifference curves from the utility functions of each man. For A, a move in a northeasterly direction is a move toward higher levels of utility, but B reaches higher levels of utility by traveling southwest. The

ed. *Papers Presented at the First Meeting of the European Association for Law and Economics*. University of Lund, Department of Economics.

line running through the box horizontally is the *contract curve*, which connects all points of tangency between the indifference curves of A and B. If the two parties trade their original entitlements until all opportunities for gains from trade have been exhausted, and assuming zero transaction costs, the final, equilibrium outcome must lie on the contract curve.[47]

Let us begin by assuming that B has acquired the right to a smokeless environment and A cannot smoke unless he uses some of his X to purchase from B the right to smoke. If the transaction costs of arranging trade between A and B are very high, these costs can outweigh potential gains from trading. If that is the case, the equilibrium outcome is represented by point *F* in the diagram, which corresponds to the original entitlements – and there will be no smoke. The outcome will also be at *F*, even when A and B are ready to trade, if the state rules that the right to clean air is inalienable and enforces that rule.

When the costs of transacting are low, the parties may find it advantageous to trade. If the price of smoke in terms of X is *exogenously* given (and represented by the straight lines with negative slopes in Figure 4.3), then A and B use trade to move from *F* to *F**, which is a point on the contract curve. Outcome *F** represents a higher level of utility for both A and B than outcome *F*: Both A and B move to higher indifference curves (and higher levels of satisfaction).

Next consider what happens when A is given an unlimited right to smoke. In order to maximize his utility, A will increase his smoking until the marginal utility of an additional cigarette falls to zero. In terms of the diagram, A will travel up the vertical line from point *F* until he reaches point *S* where a marginal increase in smoking adds nothing to his utility. When transaction costs are high, point *S* will be the equilibrium outcome, but when trade is possible and prices are exogenous, A and B will trade to point *S** on the contract curve.

---

47. In the terms of neoclassical welfare theory, only points lying on the contract curve are Pareto efficient.

Several important issues can be illustrated with this simple diagram. If the costs of transacting are so high that they prevent trading, the economic outcome will not be on the contract curve. In other words, the outcome is inefficient according to the traditional neoclassical model which abstracts from transaction costs. At either point, *S* or *F*, the two individuals, A and B, can gain from trading and could increase their welfare by moving to points on the contract curve – or so the story goes. But why do we find equilibrium solutions at points such as *S* or *F*? If our model assumes rational choice and maximizing behavior, there are two possible answers: Either we have made a logical error in deriving the equilibrium solution, or the model is misspecified and some important variables have been omitted – for example, the costs of transacting. In the latter case, the inclusion of transaction costs will reveal that, *given the current institutional structure*, points *F* and *S* are indeed Pareto efficient. If the transaction costs are higher than the gains from trade, it is indeed *inefficient* to move from *F* to *F** or *S* to *S** through interpersonal exchange. We emphasize that the institutional structure is taken as given in the neoclassical model of exchange. For instance, our individuals might reach point *F** or *S**, if transaction costs were lowered enough through *institutional change*. Taken in isolation, lower costs would be associated with superior equilibrium outcomes. However, institutional change is usually not without costs that also must be taken into account. Therefore, the gains associated with new outcomes must be related to the costs of institutional change.

As we have seen, A and B will not reach the contract curve through trade when the costs of transacting are high enough. But they can reach the contract curve nonetheless, if the state redefines the bundles of initial rights (or endowments), placing A and B directly on the curve – for example, at *Z*.[48] A reassignment of property rights by the state which moves A and B onto the contract curve, for example, from *F* to *Z*, can bring net social gains, but

---

48. Note that extreme positions, such as unlimited smoking or no smoking, are unlikely to be on the contract curve.

the additional costs to the state of assigning and maintaining the new structure of rights must be taken into account.[49]

According to the strongest version of Coase's theorem, alternative assignments of rights do not affect the allocation of resources, provided that the costs of transacting are zero. But this is strictly true only of profit-maximizing firms that are not bound by financial constraints and are too small to influence relative prices. The assignment of property rights to an individual has a *wealth effect* that influences his or her valuations. This is obvious from Figure 4.3. When the costs of transacting are zero, the outcome is S^* if A has an unlimited right to smoke, and F^* if B has the right to live in a smokeless world.

Finally, consider the case of bilateral monopoly where the price of smoke in terms of commodity X is not given but the parties must try to establish the price by entering into a bargaining game. The outcome of such games is indeterminate. For example, if the initial entitlement is F, and trade is potentially advantageous, we can say only that the outcome will be to the left of the vertical FS line and somewhere inside the lens formed by I_{A1} and I_{B2}. Similarly, if the initial entitlement is S, then the settlement will be to the right of the FS line and inside the lens formed by I_{A2} and I_{B1}. In either case, the outcome can be off the contract curve, owing to unskillful bargaining, although such outcomes are less likely when the parties deal repeatedly with each other.[50]

In the smoke problem above, an equilibrium solution involves some constellation of X_A, X_B, and smoke. In a more realistic model, the equilibrium solution may involve adjustment at several

---

49. Note that if we extend rational behavior and optimization to the state in a theoretical analysis, then the logic of our model requires that the state make all adjustments in the structure of property rights that yield net benefits. Net benefits must be defined in terms of the utility function and constraints of those who control the state.

50. One possible outcome is a stalemate with no trade at all. Also note that the model of Figure 4.3 is, in fact, not appropriate when transaction costs are positive and transactions use up resources. If the Edgeworth box represents all available assets and resources, the effect of trade that involves positive transaction costs is to shrink the box.

margins, and in real life it is not easy to second-guess the adjustments made in a well-functioning market where the cost of transacting is low. Let us imagine that the state is concerned to establish, through regulation and legal remedies, a solution to noise nuisance from low-flying aircraft, which will maximize the joint market value of all the assets involved. For this purpose the airline is given a qualified right to make noisy flights, but there are to be no night flights, and each aircraft is required to use specific noise-abatement equipment, and these rights and duties are inalienable. But equilibrium outcomes in markets where exchange is costless may involve far subtler adjustments than those described above. For example, the outcome might include permission for certain valuable night flights, the insulation against sound of houses near the airport, new uses of the land, and so on.

Yet for practical purposes the comparison of real-world situations with outcomes in models assuming costless exchange can be misleading. The appropriate approach is to compare economic outcomes associated with *practicable social arrangements* and consider whole systems rather than single margins. Coase (1960) illustrates this point with the example of an individual who decides to drive through a red traffic light at a deserted intersection late at night and gets fined for doing so. As our driver did not harm anyone and must pay a fine, her punishment represents a situation in which the private product is less than the social product – if the case is viewed in isolation. Does this imply that we should then leave it to the judgment of each individual whether to stop at a red light? Coase's answer is that "the problem is to devise practical arrangements which will correct defects in one part of the system without causing more serious harm in other parts."[51]

The evaluation of alternative social arrangements is a complex task. For example, consider how the assignment of liability for work-related accidents affects the rate of accidents. Veljanovski (1984) has examined the impact of the Employers' Liability Act

---

51. Coase (1960); reprint in Breit and Hochman, eds. (1968) [op. cit., note 42], p. 449.

of 1880 on the rate of industrial injuries in nineteenth-century Britain.[52] Before the 1880 act, employers were not liable for workers' injuries that resulted from negligent behavior by foremen and supervisors, but the new law made the employers responsible for their agents.

How did the 1880 act affect the *rate of industrial accidents* in Britain? *Theoretically*, it is possible to think of several answers. For example, if work injuries are exogenous random events, the assignment of liability does not affect the frequency and nature of accidents. If the rate of injuries is a function of investments in safer technologies, the assignment of liability does not affect the rate of accidents or the workers' net pay *if the costs of transacting are low*. The reasoning is as follows: When the cost of injuries is carried by the *workers*, they will offer to work for less at workplaces that have invested in safety. When the cost of accidents falls on the employer, he or she has an incentive to lower the total wage bill by investing in safety. Also, the workers' pay, net of injury costs, is the same whether they or the employer is legally responsible for the accidents.

The rate of injuries also depends on the willingness of individuals to show care and follow safety regulations, and the assignment of liability may affect their incentive to do so. The workers in a firm could contract with each other and with foremen and supervisors over the "production of safety." But, because of free riding, the enforcement of multilateral contracts specifying care and attention to the safety of others is likely to be costly.[53] The enforcement problems must be seen in the context of the contractual nature of the firm (which we discuss in Chapter 7).

---

52. Veljanovski, Cento G. (1984). "The Impact of the Employers' Liability Act 1880." In Skog, Göran, ed. (1984). *Papers Presented at the First Meeting of the European Association for Law and Economics*. University of Lund, Department of Economics.
53. The situation is a classic case of the prisoners' dilemma. When enforcement costs are high, each worker may find that his or her best option is to avoid the costs of showing care, regardless of whether other workers are careless or cautious.

In Neoinstitutional Economics the classical firm is defined as a nexus of contracts where several input owners make bilateral contracts with a central agent, rather than with each other, in order to minimize transaction costs and maximize the joint value of their assets. It is quite possible that cost minimization also demands that the workers contract with the central monitor, rather than with each other, to enforce a certain level of caution in the workplace. If that is the case, the next question is whether the cost of enforcing such safety contracts is strongly dependent on the assignment of liability for work-related accidents. If the employer is not liable in court for his or her agents, can the safety contract be enforced at relatively low costs through competition in the marketplace? When enforcement is through competition, the cost to an employer of not living up to his or her part of the contract is a bad reputation and a high wage bill because a special premium on wages would be required to entice employees to work for a firm that does not offer an effective safety contract.

How did the Employers' Liability Act of 1880 affect the rate of industrial accidents in the United Kingdom? Veljanovski (1984) has examined the rates of fatal and nonfatal injuries in British coal mines before and after the 1880 act. He found (1) that in the second half of the nineteenth century there was a *secular downward trend* in the rate of accidents per 1000 workers, and (2) that a regression analysis associated a *slight increase* both in fatal and nonfatal injuries with the 1880 act. The regression findings are not conclusive, but they suggest the complexity of the situation.[54]

Finally, this leads us to a theme that is common in the literature on law and economics: How efficient or inefficient is the legal system? We have already discussed various difficulties associated with the concept of efficiency, particularly in models that include transaction costs. In the law-and-economics literature, a law is efficient if it guides resources to their most valuable uses, and value is determined by the consumers' willingness to pay.[55] This discus-

---

54. Veljanovski (1984) [op. cit., note 52], pp. 139–144.
55. "The terms 'value' and 'efficiency' are technical terms. 'Efficiency' means ex-

sion usually ignores the cost to the state of changing the structure of property rights and also the possibility that the state maximizes some other variable than the *value* variable of neoclassical economics. The analysis usually takes the form of comparing the value of an asset (or the joint value of a set of assets) under alternative legal structures.

A number of economists, mainly in the United States, have argued that the structure of Anglo-Saxon Common Law is consistent with economic efficiency as defined above. Posner (1977) is the classic reference and provides an excellent survey of this work. Posner, citing numerous examples, argues that in Common Law the assignment of rights over resources is left to the market when the costs of transacting are low, whereas the assignment is handled by state intervention when transaction costs are high. In this way, it is assured that resources find their most productive use. For example:

> The landowner's right to repel a physical intrusion in the form of engine sparks is only a qualified right. The intruder can defeat it by showing that his land use, which is incompatible with the injured landowner's, is more valuable. But if my neighbor parks his car in my garage, I have a right to eject him as a trespasser no matter how convincingly he can demonstrate to a court that the use of my garage to park his car is more valuable than my use of it.
>
> The different treatment of the cases has an economic justification. The market is a more efficient method of determining the optimum use of land than legal proceedings. If my neighbor thinks his use of my garage would be more productive than mine, he should have

ploiting economic resources in such a way that 'value' – human satisfaction *as measured by aggregate consumer willingness to pay* for goods and services – is maximized. Willingness to pay, the basis of the efficiency and value concepts, is a function of many things, including the distribution of income and wealth."
P. 10 in Posner, Richard A. (1977). *Economic Analysis of Law*, 2nd ed. Boston: Little, Brown.

no trouble persuading me to rent it to him. But if he merely *claims* that he can use my garage more productively, he thrusts on the courts a difficult evidentiary question: which of us would really be willing to pay more for the use of the garage? In the spark case, negotiations in advance may be infeasible because of the number of landowners potentially affected, so if the courts want to encourage the most productive use of land, they cannot avoid comparing the values of the competing uses.[56]

When high transaction costs make allocation through the market a costly solution, the state can choose among several forms of intervention to guide resources to their highest valued uses.[57] One approach is to allocate exclusive rights directly. This solution may require partitioning among individual owners the rights to a resource and placing restrictions on the later transfer of these rights.[58] In other circumstances, it may be more appropriate to alter the structure of property rights in a way that lowers transaction costs and encourages market exchange – for example, by enforcing exclusive rights to the commons or introducing individual marketable quotas in ocean fisheries.

56. Ibid., pp. 39–40.
57. "It is time that we inquired more closely into the sources of high transaction costs. The factor usually stressed by economists is a large number of parties to a transaction. . . . [But it should not] be assumed that fewness of parties to a transaction is a sufficient condition of low transaction costs. If there are significant elements of bilateral monopoly in a two-party transaction – i.e., if neither party has good alternatives to dealing with the other – the transaction costs may be quite high. . . . The costs of transacting are highest where elements of bilateral monopoly coincide with a large number of parties to the transaction – a quite possible conjunction. For example, if homeowners have a right to be free from pollution the factory that wishes to acquire the right to pollute must acquire it from every homeowner." Ibid., p. 45. To this we add that transaction costs also vary with characteristics of assets and resources and with types of contracts.
58. For this approach to work, the legal system must be flexible enough to reassign rights and liabilities swiftly when circumstances change, for example, because of technological innovations.

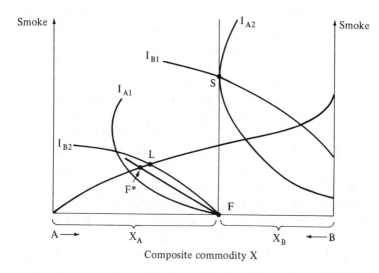

Figure 4.4. Compensation through the legal system and welfare.

When rights are not traded in the market but transferred by the state, their price is set by the courts and other agents of the state. Technically this price can be negative, zero, comparable to the price that would prevail if voluntary exchange were possible, and so on. When rights are taken involuntarily from an owner, either by the state or by another individual, the courts often seek to determine a rate of compensation for the victim that makes him "whole." Theoretically, this is equivalent to putting the victim back on his indifference curve. Haddock and Spiegel (1984) make it clear that in this form of exchange the "seller" (i.e., the victim) is deprived of all gains from trade.[59]

Their point is illustrated in Figure 4.4. Assume that the state has given individual B the right to clean air, and the initial entitlement is *F*. Let A partly appropriate B's entitlement by smoking and establish outcome *S*. If the penalty that the state imposes on A for depriving B of his right to a smokeless envi-

---

59. Haddock and Spiegel (1984) [op. cit., note 46], p. 61.

ronment is only to restore B to his original indifference curve, I_{B2}, by compensating him with commodity X, then A will reduce smoking and compensate with X until point L is reached. Note that outcome L is on the contract curve. Alternatively, the state could make A pay a price for smoking that corresponds to the hypothetical market price of smoke in terms of X. The outcome for A is now point F^*. Both solutions, L and F^*, are Pareto efficient, but they lead to different levels of satisfaction for A and B. In this simple example, the state can favor B without sacrificing efficiency in the Pareto sense.

It is clear that the state can profoundly affect the allocation of resources. The individuals who control the state, whether it is a democratic state or not, have their own utility functions and separate interests from the subjects or constituents at large. Therefore, it is not self-evident that rules and rulings by the state are designed to maximize the aggregate utility or wealth of the community. This question is taken up in the book's last section.

4.5. Restrictions on the right to contract and dissipation of nonexclusive income

In this section, we discuss how restrictions imposed by the state on the terms of contracts, for example, through price ceilings or price floors, affect economic outcomes. We make the following points:

1. Effective limits on contractual terms, such as price restrictions, do not cause a disequilibrium but lead to a new equilibrium.
2. Controls often give rise to new forms of organizing exchange that supplement or replace the price mechanism.
3. The new arrangements are likely to result in higher transaction costs than those incurred under allocation by price because they are chosen only when the price mechanism is suppressed.

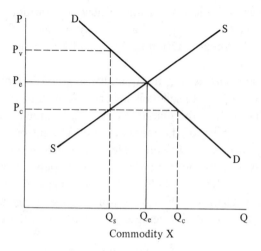

Figure 4.5. Price ceiling in a competitive market.

4. Controls may lead to adjustments in the form of using or producing goods.
5. When limits are imposed on contracts, buyers and sellers have an incentive to make those adjustments that minimize the potential loss in value that the controls can cause, or, in the words of Cheung (1974), *minimize the dissipation of nonexclusive income.*[60]

Restrictions imposed by the state on the terms of contract can take many forms. We begin by examining the implications of *price ceilings*. Figure 4.5 gives a conventional presentation of the impact of a price ceiling, P_c, on the economic outcome in a competitive market. At P_c, which is below the equilibrium price, P_e, there is *excess demand* for commodity X equal to $(Q_c - Q_s)$, but note that

---

60. The discussion in this section is based on pioneering contributions to Neoin-stitutional Economics by Yoram Barzel and Steven Cheung. Barzel, Yoram (1974). "A Theory of Rationing by Waiting." *Journal of Law and Economics 17* (No. 1, April): 73–95; and Cheung, Steven N. S. (1974). "A Theory of Price Control." *Journal of Law and Economics 17* (No. 1, April): 53–71.

the diagram gives no indication of how a new equilibrium is established.[61] The new rationing mechanism may be based on, for example, physical strength, rationing by friendship, skin color, coupons, or waiting.[62]

But the diagram tells us that the quantity supplied is reduced from Q_e to Q_s when price to sellers is lowered from P_e to P_c, and that P_v, the value of X to the marginal buyer, is greater than P_c, the money price he pays for the marginal unit. The introduction of a price ceiling, unsupported by other measures (such as rationing by coupons), has, in part, put commodity X in the public domain – as indicated by the differential $(P_v - P_c)$ – and has given rise to a new exchange mechanism. The way in which property rights are reestablished will, other things being equal, depend on the costs of transacting.

Rationing by waiting is frequently used to restore equilibrium, particularly in consumer markets. It is an exchange mechanism based on the first-come–first-served principle. Each buyer can typically purchase only a limited amount of the commodity and is sometimes forbidden to reenter the queue in a given time period or resell the commodity. Provided $P_c > 0$, each buyer pays a twofold price: a money price, P_c; and a waiting price, $(P_v - P_c)$. It is clear from Figure 4.5 that the new arrangement has resulted in a higher (total) price to the buyer than the old equilibrium price: $P_c + (P_v - P_c) > P_e$.[63]

---

61. "Demand and supply schedules are conceptual tools which restrict the maximum quantities of a good [that] individuals are willing to buy or sell at varying prices. With all the underlying qualifications, we are able to arrive at situations where the observed prices and quantities are said to be determined and where these in turn determine income distribution and resource allocation. As a corollary, specified changes in demand and supply conditions will lead to implied changes in the transacted prices and quantities. But as they stand, these conceptual tools are not equipped to handle a situation where the price they are designed to determine is controlled." Cheung (1974) [op., cit., note 60], p. 54.
62. Ibid., p. 54.
63. This conclusion must be qualified. The old market curve is strictly no longer valid because not all individuals transfer waiting prices into money prices at

Let us assume that commodity X is distributed free of charge by the government ($P_c = 0$), and each buyer can only have k units of the commodity and is fully informed about the required waiting time. Barzel (1974) has demonstrated that demand is still finite under these circumstances, the equilibrium waiting time per unit of X is a negative function of the size of individual quotas, k, and, given k, that the equilibrium waiting time is inversely related to the total supply of X. And there are other striking parallels with the price system: When the money price is zero, the value of X to the marginal buyer is equal to his waiting cost, and, at the margin, the consumers' surplus is zero. Also, the waiting time is determined by the marginal buyer and is equal for all buyers in the queue.

It is sometimes argued that rationing by waiting, rather than by price, benefits the poor because their cost of waiting (the opportunity cost of their time) is lower than for the rich. Barzel (1974) explores this issue by examining who will stand in line when $P_e > P_c$. To simplify, he assumes that utility functions are identical, that time costs (wages) are proportional to total income (the sum of wages and unearned income), and that there is an effective ban on resale. Barzel shows that the composition of the queue depends on the ratio of the income elasticity to the price elasticity for the commodity. Namely, the higher the income elasticity relative to the price elasticity, the larger is the proportion of rich people in the queue.[64]

For example, if the income elasticity of demand for tickets to the opera is high and the price elasticity of demand low (as there are only imperfect substitutes available), then, according to Barzel's model, subsidizing opera tickets is likely to benefit the rich more than the poor. But if we relax the assumptions of identical utility functions and fixed proportions between time costs and total income, then the subsidies will favor individuals with strong tastes

the same rate. However, this refinement can be ignored for our purposes. Barzel (1974) [op. cit., note 60], p. 84.
64. Ibid., p. 88.

for opera and, in a given income group, people with a low ratio of wage income to total income.

And finally, a word about the queue as a social institution. *Queuing* is a method of establishing property rights to a commodity by waiting. The control of this process is usually in the hands of buyers and sellers and requires a high degree of *voluntary compliance* by the competing individuals with the rules of the queue. When the stakes are high, the temptation to jump the queue may become so strong that rationing by waiting is no longer a viable mechanism of exchange. For example, a price floor, P_f, which makes it possible for producers to sell their commodity at a price above the old equilibrium price ($P_f > P_e$), usually involves large stakes for each firm. As the quantity supplied at P_f exceeds the quantity demanded, the right to sell at P_f must be assigned somehow, but usually this is not done by queuing. Barzel (1974) argues that high costs of enforcing the rules of the queue is the reason why waiting is uncommon when commercial sellers are involved – for example, when import quotas are allocated among firms.[65]

Rationing by waiting is only one of many possible adjustments when the state puts limits on the terms of a contract. For example, when the government of Iceland forbids the purchase of new fishing vessels in order to protect the country's fishing grounds, owners have existing vessels sawed in half and lengthened in order to substitute a bigger boat for an additional boat. Cheung (1974) generalizes this tendency in the following proposition:

> When the right to receive income is partly or fully taken away from a contracting party, the diverted income will tend to dissipate unless the right to it is exclusively assigned to another individual. The dissipation of non-exclusive income will occur either through a change in the form of using or producing the good, or through a change in contractual behavior, resulting in a rise in the cost of forming and enforcing contracts, or through a combination of the two.[66]

65. Ibid., p. 92.
66. Cheung (1974) [op. cit., note 60], p. 58.

In his 1974 article, Cheung applies this proposition to price and rent controls. Individuals who are constrained by price regulations often resort to illicit payments (rather than waiting) to restore equilibrium. Illicit transactions are relatively costly, but they are often nearly impossible to prevent. For example, in the case of rent controls, a tenant can offer to buy a broken chair from a landlord at an exorbitant price, where the excess price margin on the chair is roughly equal to the present value of the difference between market clearing price, P_e, and the controlled price, P_c.[67]

Price controls can also lead to adjustments in production and the reallocation of existing assets. When faced with effective price ceilings, producers can alter *qualitative dimensions* of their products by using inferior inputs or by economizing at various margins in the case of composite commodities. For example, in the case of housing, rent controls often result in the withdrawal of maintenance services or separate prices for services that formerly were included in the rent.

Cheung (1974, 1975, 1976) has analyzed the extraordinary history of rent controls in Hong Kong, which at times have had side effects strong enough to rock the colony's economy, and he demonstrates how a regime of rent controls can create perverse incentives for urban renewal.[68] The history of rent control shows that it is not enough to control only the price terms of the rental contract if the state wants to provide tenants with housing at a price below the equilibrium market price. For one, landlords who are subject to controls have a strong incentive to evict tenants and seek new ones who are willing to pay the market-clearing price through an illegal lump-sum entrance fee. In order to neutralize these incentives, rent control laws and regulations usually strictly limit the landlords' right to vacate their property, but such strictures can seriously conflict with urban renewal. Landlords are therefore

67. Ibid., p. 63.
68. Cheung, Steven N. S. (1975). "Roofs or Stars: The Stated Intents and Actual Effects of Rent Ordinance." *Economic Inquiry* 13 (March): 1–21; (1976). "Rent Control and Housing Reconstruction: The Postwar Experience of Prewar Premises in Hong Kong." *Journal of Law and Economics* 19 (No. 1): 27–53.

often allowed to vacate their buildings for the purposes of demolition and reconstruction. However, if landlords are always free to evict tenants when they plan to renew their property, they have under rent control a perverse incentive to tear down relatively new structures and rebuild them, if there is a wide gap between the free-market price and the controlled price. The reason is that the new tenants will pay an illegal lump sum equal to the present value of the difference between the market price and the control price, a side payment that is now a part of the expected return on investment in reconstruction.[69]

Cheung (1976) reports how in 1967 several factors coincided in the Hong Kong housing market to make for an economic disaster: Inflation had widened the gap between the regulated rent and the free market rent; a new building code had been introduced that allowed taller residential structures than before; and a license to evict and rebuild could be obtained relatively easily if applications were filed before a certain time limit. The landlords responded to all these incentives, and, according to Cheung, filed in the following two-year period applications to demolish about *one third* of all residential buildings in Hong Kong. A colossal building boom was set in motion which, before long, ended with an economic collapse involving the colony's whole economy. In fact, the effects of rent controls can be as devastating as aerial bombardment.

In an earlier paper, Cheung (1974) theorizes that adjustments made by buyers and sellers in response to controls will tend to

---

69. Tenants could counter the landlord's incentive to reconstruct by offering him bribes high enough to make demolition and reconstruction financially unattractive. Therefore, if the costs of negotiating and enforcing such agreements were zero, rent controls would not affect the rate of reconstruction. Cheung gives several reasons why these transaction costs were high in the Hong Kong housing market. For example, as most tenements had a large number of apartments and the subletting by tenants of rooms within an apartment was common, the problem of free riding by individual tenants, who refused to pay their share of the bribe, hoping to enjoy the benefits anyway, was likely to arise. Such problems of collective action do not arise when a prospective tenant attempts to bribe his way into an apartment. Cheung (1975) [op. cit., note 68], pp. 12–14.

minimize the potential net loss of value that can follow when the state limits the terms of contracts, or in his words, minimize the dissipation of nonexclusive income. Cheung offers the following proposition:

> Given the existence of non-exclusive income and its tendency to dissipate, each and every party involved will seek to minimize the dissipation subject to constraints. This will be done either through seeking alternatives in using or producing the good so that the decline in resource value is the lowest, or through forming alternative contractual arrangements to govern the use of production of the good with the least rise in transaction costs, or through the least costly combination of the two procedures.[70]

Cheung's argument runs as follows: When the state fixes a price, P_c, below the market-clearing level, P_e, real income is left in the public domain (as common property), unless the authorities also assign exclusive rights to it, perhaps, through a system of ration coupons.[71] Competition for nonexclusive income leads to its dissipation – for example, through the time costs of waiting – unless individuals seek alternative arrangements to minimize this loss of value. In the case of rent controls of residential housing, the landlord's alternatives may include the following: (1) the use of the rental unit for his or her own family; (2) various forms of illegal side payments; (3) demolition and reconstruction; and (4) the conversion of the tenement into, for example, an (unregulated) warehouse.

Optimizing landlords will select arrangements that minimize their losses from the rent control and maximize the return on their assets, given the new constraints. Potential users of the housing services will compete, and, subject to the new constraints, the resource will go to the highest bidder. Finally, other things being

70. Cheung (1974) [op. cit., note 60], p. 61.
71. In the long run, the state must also guarantee the continued supply of the commodity at P_c.

equal, those contractual arrangements will be preferred that involve the lowest costs of transacting. It follows that the final economic outcome is one that minimizes the dissipation of unassigned income, subject to the relevant constraints. The concept of constrained minimization of the dissipation of nonexclusive income is, in spite of its cumbersome name, an important addition to economics and has general applications in models assuming positive transaction costs.

5

The ownership structure of firms and economic outcomes

5.1. Introduction

In Chapter 5 we study how the ownership structure of the firm affects economic outcomes. Continuing the discussion begun in Chapter 2, we see the firm as a nexus of contracts involving in various ways the owners of inputs and the buyers of commodities. An examination of the economic logic of these contractual arrangements and their relation to the costs of transacting is reserved for Chapter 6.

We begin this chapter with a digression on property rights and production functions and go on to look at some major types of firms that are found in modern market economies. These include not only privately owned firms, which often are subject to various forms of government regulations and restrictions on the right to contract, but also "political firms," that is, firms owned by the state.

5.2. Rights, incentives, and production functions

Why do we expect that the economic outcomes of productive activities organized within firms depend on the internal rules of the firms and, more generally, on the external structure of property rights? In answer to this question, Jensen and Meckling (1979) have argued that production functions depend on the structure of property rights just as they depend on the state of technology.[1] They define the firm as a network of contracts specifying the rewards and costs that arise out of the cooperation of individuals in production. The prevailing set of penalties and rewards affects the behavior of rational agents and hence the output of the firm.

More formally this can be summarized as:

$$Q = F_R(L, K, M, C: T)$$

where Q, output, is a function of labor, capital services, and material inputs (L, K, and M, respectively).[2] T is a vector representing technology and the state of knowledge relevant to production. F is the set of all production functions that can be partitioned according to systems of property rights. F_R is a production function that corresponds to property rights structure R. Jensen and Meckling refer to R as defining the external rules of the game for the firm, spelling out what contractual arrangements are legal or illegal, what the penalties are for illegitimate behavior, and when and to what extent the state uses its police power to enforce contractual arrangements. The definition of R also involves social mores.

The external rules of the game delimit, C, the *internal rules* of the game available for the firm to choose from, given the state of knowledge. In other words, the term C represents a generalized index describing the choice set of organizational form (comparable to the technological choice set of neoclassical production theory), and it can include "such parameters as partnership or corporate form, ... the degree of decentralization, ... whether to own or lease equipment, ... the nature of compensation plans."[3]

Jensen and Meckling attempt to show by their reformation of

---

1. Jensen, Michael C., and Meckling, William H. (1979). "Rights and Production Functions: An Application to Labor-Managed Firms and Codetermination." *Journal of Business 52* (No. 4): 469–506. In neoclassical economics, a production function describes the outer boundaries of the set of outputs available to a firm (or maximum output) for given quantities of inputs and a given technology of production.
2. Ibid., p. 471.
3. Ibid., p. 471.

the production function how the structure of property rights affects individual behavior and output by influencing the range of internal rules of the game available to the firm – or rather by affecting the costs of using alternative contractual arrangements. For example, when a contractual arrangement is illegal, the costs of using it are usually very high, but even when an arrangement is legal, it may be of little advantage if the state chooses not to use its police power to help enforce such contracts or lacks the power to do so. Let us look closer at the Jensen–Meckling model using as an illustration the case of Ethiopian farmers as reported in the *New York Times*.[4]

The Ethiopian revolution of 1975 and the Marxist–Leninist government of Mengistu Maile Mariam radically changed R, the structure of property rights in the country's agriculture. Farmland, formerly largely owned by feudal overlords, was divided into plots and allocated to farmers, with the government in effect becoming the landlord. The new structure of property rights leaves Ethiopian farmers with a rather small set of legitimate contractual arrangements, C, to choose from. For example, they are not allowed to own the land or contract long-term leases, nor can they, when things go well, expand the size of their plots beyond narrow limits set by the state. The farmers are not permitted to contract to sell their output at market-clearing prices but are forced to sell at lower prices fixed by the state. Also, the state has discouraged the storing of grain as a hedge against hard times ("speculation") and the hiring of farm laborers.

How has this property rights structure, R, affected productivity in Ethiopian agriculture? Economic theory suggests, for example, that the restrictions on private property rights listed above are likely to dull the farmers' incentives to invest in the long-term improvement of the land they cultivate. When exclusive ownership rights by individual farmers are restricted and long-term leases not allowed, the farmers are unlikely to allocate resources to various potentially lucrative investment projects because their rights to yields accruing in future periods are uncertain.

4. May 23, 1985.

Other aspects of the property rights structure in Ethiopia can also affect the productivity of agricultural land. For example, fixing prices of agricultural products below the equilibrium level makes forms of economic activity other than farming (at state prices) more attractive. The cost of leisure has also fallen, and farmers may reduce their work effort if the substitution effect is stronger than the income effect.

In short, the new structure of property rights does not seem to support output expansion in the agricultural sector. In fact, the *New York Times* quotes development specialists as saying that the new structure of property rights, along with drought and a civil war, explains why millions of people were dying of starvation in Ethiopia in 1985.

Note that there are two sets of effects involved in our Ethiopian example. First, the new (external) structure of property rights rules out certain (internal) forms of agricultural organizations, such as large-scale capitalistic farms, which, in turn, puts technology and production functions associated with such organizational forms off limits to the farmers. Second, the new rules have changed relative prices and have altered the allocative decisions of the farmers that can be interpreted as adjustments in terms of a given production function. Both factors affect economic outcomes. This suggests that the Jensen–Meckling modification of the production function concept does fully capture the interaction between property rights structures and economic outcomes.

Consider another example. Some retail distribution chains, such as vendors of fast food, have found it more profitable to use franchise arrangements rather than hire managers to run local outlets. It has been argued that this arrangement is advantageous because it lowers monitoring costs and helps to protect the value of specialized investment in brand names.[5] Holders of franchises are

5. See p. 16 in De Alessi, Louis (1980). "The Economics of Property Rights: A Review of the Evidence." *Research in Law and Economics 2*: 1–47. De Alessi's paper is the best available survey of empirical work relating to the economic consequences of alternative structures of property rights. However, with few

expected to monitor output quality carefully because they are residual claimants (i.e., have a right to the net income of the operation), but in addition the parent firm often provides most of the nonlabor inputs and makes periodic inspections of local premises in order to further enforce quality and protect the brand-name capital of the chain.

Shelton (1967) has compared the accounts of retail outlets where a hired manager replaced a franchise arrangement or vice versa, thus holding constant most of the relevant variables except the management contract. He found that outlets operated by managers who are residual claimants are more profitable than outlets run by hired managers, even when the latter receive bonuses for profitable operations of up to 30 percent of their salaries.[6]

What does this finding tell us about the production function for fast food? Imagine that franchise arrangements were made illegal and effectively removed from the *C* set (because an illegal arrangement would become too costly to operate), and let us assume that we would observe a fall in productivity in firms affected by the law. What does such a drop in productivity imply? Does it mean that the firms now operate on a new production function for fast food? Let us follow the argument above, and say that productivity has fallen because the managers have fewer incentives than before to monitor carefully the quality of nonlabor and labor inputs. If statistical tests of production functions measured the quantity and *quality* of inputs directly, instead of measuring them by proxies (hours of work, years of education, pounds of meat), *no change* would be registered in the production functions themselves. But the quality of inputs is seldom measured directly, especially in the case of labor services, because of high measurement costs. Hence the banishment of franchising would be registered as a shift in the statistical production functions of the affected firms.

exceptions, De Alessi's survey covers only structures of rights and contractual arrangements found in North America.

6. Shelton, John (1967). "Allocative Efficiency v. 'X-Efficiency': Comment." *American Economic Review 57* (No. 5): 1252–1258.

We might try to get around this dilemma by modeling the monitoring of quality and, more generally, the enforcement of contracts as a production process. If franchise arrangements are made illegal, it is then equivalent to banishing an efficient technology of monitoring and shifting the firm over to a new production function for monitoring. But note that the problem with production functions, which Jensen and Meckling (1979) are trying to solve, arises from the fact that the quality of inputs varies with the incentives offered to their owners; for instance, the quality of the labor factor varies with relative prices. The production functions of neoclassical economics are better suited to handle chemical and engineering processes than human interaction, such as agency relationships.

Consider next a change in R, which involves an increase in the cost of enforcing property rights – for example, because of a growing climate of violence or less police protection by the state. If fast-food outlets now require the services of two armed guards, then it would represent a new production function for making and distributing hamburgers – independent of all problems of measuring quality.

Finally, consider changes in the external rules, R, that outlaw certain types of information systems and thus raise the cost of information and coordination – for example, if decentralized producers were deprived of the price signals of unrestricted market exchange and instead had to depend on information from a regional planning board. In this instance, we would also register a shift in production functions even if we somehow could measure all quantitative and qualitative dimensions of labor, capital, and material inputs.

5.3. The open corporation and agency costs

Demsetz (1980) refers to the hypothetical economic system of neoclassical economics as the *decentralized model*. According to the usual implicit and explicit assumptions of the decentralized model, the cost of information is zero; private property rights are fully defined and enforced at zero cost; and the state stays in the background, upholding the institutions of market exchange. Economic outcomes derived from this model are found in the standard textbook: For any underlying distribution of resources, wealth is maximized; output is valued by consumers who take indirectly into account the value of leisure and other extra-market activities; income distribution depends on wages and the prices of nonhuman inputs which equal the value of marginal products; and economic resources always find their highest-valued uses.[7]

When transaction costs are added to the decentralized model, we have, according to Demsetz, a *laissez-faire economy*, a term we shall use below. The laissez-faire model is used to analyze the implications of competition when the cost of transacting is positive.

In a laissez-faire economy, the state does not restrict private ownership rights, but because of information costs, ownership rights are often less than fully defined or enforced. Laissez-faire competition, reacting to these costs, reveals itself in ways not readily understood in terms of the decentralized model.[8] Demsetz (1980) assumes that in the laissez-faire model "the use of payments to influence the behavior of others is neither prohibited nor frowned upon."[9] Also, "the laissez-faire filtering process, using the *profit test*, selects some of these business organizations for survival and rejects others."[10]

The laissez-faire model can be used not only to analyze the structure of economic organizations and their associated outcomes, but also to explain various market phenomena. For example, search costs imply that in equilibrium the price of a homogeneous good may vary in the same market. If search costs are given, the theory implies also that the standard deviation of prices will be smaller for high-priced goods than low-priced goods (the benefits are greater and the search lasts longer when we are collecting information about prices in the market for high-priced goods).[11]

7. Demsetz, Harold (1980). *Economic, Political, and Legal Dimensions of Competition*. Amsterdam: North-Holland.
8. Ibid., p. 22.
9. Ibid., p. 21.
10. Ibid., p. 25.
11. Ibid., p. 49.

Let us now look at the *open corporation* in terms of the laissez-faire model.

The corporate form dominates industrial production in contemporary capitalistic market economies and stands in sharp contrast to the traditional owner-managed firm which often is implicit in economic theories. The modern corporation is associated with a number of contractual arrangements, such as limited liability, specialization in ownership and management, and organized stock exchanges. These arrangements seem to have evolved in order to take advantage of modern technology, which often requires capital-intensive operations on a large scale. The economic logic of the corporate form is discussed in the next chapter, but at present we are concerned with the agency costs that result from the separation of ownership and management in the corporation.

Berle and Means (1932), in *The Modern Corporation and Private Property*, initiated the modern debate about the problems of agency costs, which the corporate form seems to invite.[12] Restated in modern terminology, the argument advanced by Berle and Means was that the transaction costs to shareholders of monitoring management tend to be high relative to the benefits, particularly when ownership is dispersed and the cost of collective action high. They concluded, on theoretical rather than empirical grounds, that professional corporate managers tend to be agents out of control.

The Berle–Means thesis had a profound impact on economists and social philosophers. Corporate managers were seen as being their own masters and, as they did not bear the full wealth consequences of their actions, likely to allocate resources to uses that were not aimed at maximizing the firm's present value. Economic outcomes of production organized in corporations would reflect

---

12. Berle, Adolf A., and Means, Gardner C. (1932). *The Modern Corporation and Private Property*. New York: Macmillan. Berle and Means did not use the term "agency costs."

excessive consumption on the job, shirking, corporate goals other than profit maximization, and limited incentives to introduce and adapt new technologies unless the new technique satisfied some personal goals of the managerial class.

Since the early 1960s, economists of the property rights school have given the Berle–Means thesis a thorough examination. Pioneering contributions were made by Manne in articles such as "Mergers and the Market for Corporate Control" (1965).[13] The agency problem of the corporation was formalized in a paper by Jensen and Meckling, "Theory of the Firm: Managerial Behavior, Agency Costs and Ownership Structure" (1976), one of the most cited articles in the economics and social science literature.[14] The authors describe the "motivation" of their paper in the following words:

> In this paper we draw on recent progress in the theory of (1) property rights, (2) agency, and (3) finance to develop a theory of ownership structure for the firm. In addition to tying together elements of the theory of each of these three areas, our analysis casts new light on and has implications for a variety of issues in the professional and popular literature such as the definition of the firm, the "separation of ownership and control," the "social responsibility" of business, the definition of a "corporate objective function," the determination of an optimal capital structure, the specification of the content of credit agreements, the theory of organizations, and the supply side of the completeness of markets problem.[15]

13. Manne, H. G. (1965). "Mergers and the Market for Corporate Control." *Journal of Political Economy 73* (April): 110–120; see also idem (1962). "The 'Higher Criticism' of the Modern Corporation." *Columbia Law Review 62* (March): 399–432.
14. Jensen, Michael C., and Meckling, William H. (1976). "Theory of the Firm: Managerial Behavior, Agency Costs and Ownership Structure." *Journal of Financial Economics 3* (No. 4, October): 305–360.
15. Ibid., pp. 305–306.

A good overview of the new economics of the corporation is found in a special issue of the *Journal of Law and Economics*,[16] but a complete economic theory of the corporate form along with corroborating empirical evidence has yet to emerge. In more recent theoretical applications of Neoinstitutional Economics to the corporation, it is usually assumed that the firm operates in a laissez-faire economy as defined above.This implies that in the long run, compensation for the *same quality* of managerial services is roughly equal in all firms. Similarly, the rate of return on invested funds is roughly the same in long-run equilibrium after allowing for variations in risk, uncertainty, and the cost of monitoring investments.

Jensen and Meckling (1976) have demonstrated theoretically that an owner-manager, who shares the ownership of a firm with nonmanaging stockholders, does not run the firm with an intent to maximize its value, compared either to the manager's decisions if he or she were the sole owner of the firm, or to a hypothetical world where the monitoring costs of outside owners are zero. Hypothetical worlds are not relevant alternatives, but this finding raises the question how firms with nonmanaging owners can compete with owner-managed firms with no outside owners – a question that is deferred to the next chapter. At this point, we are concerned with the extent of serious agency problems in firms with outside owners. But note that agency costs are real costs, and, theoretically, opportunistic behavior and noncompliance with contracts will persist in equilibrium, if the marginal cost of monitoring agents falls short of marginal benefits before full enforcement of contractual agreements has been reached.

It is a central point of the new approach to the corporation that there are forces in a laissez-faire economy that constrain opportunistic behavior by managers and limit the agency problem: *competition in capital markets* tends to equalize in the long run the expected net rates of return on investments (after taking into account all the nonpecuniary factors that may be involved). The

16. Vol. 26, No. 2 (June 1983).

performance of an open corporation is continuously evaluated in capital markets, and an abnormal fall or rise in the stock prices of a particular firm is a relatively reliable and inexpensive signal to dispersed stockholders that reveals information about the quality of management and the commercial success of their corporation. *Competition in the market for managers* tends to equalize total pay (including fringe benefits and on-the-job consumption) for managers of the same quality, but the mix of on-the-job consumption and financial rewards may vary. Demsetz (1983) argues that there will be more on-the-job consumption in firms where the owners' monitoring costs are high, and people with strong tastes for on-the-job-consumption will seek out such firms. Finally, *competition among management teams* in the market for corporate take-overs weeds out inefficient management by means of mergers or tender bids, and the threat of such actions constrains others.

Along with the forces of competition, various *contractual devices* work to constrain opportunistic behavior. Jensen and Meckling (1976) mention several monitoring and other control activities. These include auditing by the auditing committee of the board of directors, formal control systems, budget restrictions, and incentive compensation systems whereby managers are, for example, paid partly with common stocks in their corporation, linking the managers' total pay directly to the performance of the firm.[17] Jensen and Meckling (1976) also point out that the owner-manager could expend resources to guarantee to the outside equity holders that he will limit his shirking:

> We call these expenditures "bonding costs," and they would take such forms as contractual guarantees to have the financial accounts audited by a public accountant, explicit bonding against malfeasance on the part of the manager, and contractual limitations on the manager's decision making power (which impose costs on the firm because they limit his ability to take full advantage of

17. Jensen and Meckling (1976) [op. cit., note 14], p. 323.

some profitable opportunities as well as limiting his
ability to harm the stockholders while making himself
better off).[18]

So far no one has thought of a direct test or measure of the
agency costs of corporate organizations relative to other business
organizations. But there exists a substantial body of empirical evidence, mostly studies since 1975, dealing with the market for corporate managers and the market for corporate control. The
findings suggest that competition in these markets effectively lowers agency costs and raises the value of the firm as measured by
its share prices.

One line of research has investigated the relationship between
the various forms of management compensation and the market
value of the corporation, as measured by its stock prices. The
evidence suggests that various compensation programs have lowered agency costs and have raised the value of the firm. For instance, eleven empirical studies dealing with "Management
Compensation and the Managerial Labor Market" are found in a
special issue of the *Journal of Accounting and Economics* [vol. 7,
(Nos. 1–3), 1985]. As an example of the findings presented there,
Murphy, and Coughlan and Schmidt, report a positive relationship
between the annual compensation of executives and current year
stock prices. Coughlan and Schmidt, in their article, and Benston,
in his article, report a negative correlation between stock prices
and subsequent turnover of executives – which suggests that the
job tenure of managers depends on their performance. Also, Teh-
ranian and Waegelein report (1) that the announcement of executive compensation plans that reward managers for performance
raises stock prices at the time of announcement, and (2) that corporations that reward their executives for performance based on
the current year have unexpectedly high earnings in the eleven-
month period after adopting the plan.

We should note that statistical relationships between compensation programs and the value of the firm are often consistent with

18. Ibid., p. 325.

more than one hypothesis. For example, compensation systems that link the pay of managers directly to the performance of their firm can be associated with higher stock prices and higher annual earnings for two reasons: either because these pay systems create new incentives for the managers or because such plans are typically introduced when managers expect favorable developments on the basis of information that the stock market does not have until the plans signal it. But on balance, the statistical evidence seems to support the notion that various contractual arrangements and market forces work to align the interests of shareholders and professional managers.

Jensen and Ruback (1983) review empirical studies that examine the effects of competition in the market for corporate control.[19] The important question here is whether competition for the control of corporations, which is manifested in mergers, tender offers, leveraged buy-outs, proxy offerings, and other complex phenomena, works to reduce agency costs and increase the value of the firm. Jensen and Ruback find ample evidence that the shareholders of firms that are taken over gain substantially through abnormal increases in stock prices (defined as deviations from a regression line) which follow take-overs, and this gain is on top of the purchase premia received by those stockholders who surrender their shares in a take-over. The "abnormal" increase in stock prices averaged from 8 to 30 percent, depending on the form of take-over. Jensen and Ruback (1983) also conclude from their survey of the empirical evidence that (1) in take-overs the shares of bidding companies gain little or nothing in value; (2) the gains in share prices that result from mergers are not due to the creation of monopoly power in product markets; and (3) in the case of unsuccessful take-overs there is an abnormal decline in the stock prices of both bidders and targets – except in the case of proxy fights when stock prices increase.[20] Jensen and Ruback regard the value of shares in finan-

---

19. Jensen, Michael C., and Ruback, Richard S. (1983). "The Market for Corporate Control: The Scientific Evidence." *Journal of Financial Economics 11* (Nos. 1–4): 5–50.
20. By the word "bidders" Jensen and Rubeck are referring to companies trying

cial markets as an unbiased estimate of the present value of the firm. They recognize that take-overs involve substantial transaction costs – fees of managers, lawyers, economists, and financial consultants – but conclude that the costs are small relative to the gains, and that take-overs seem to weed out inefficient management and add to society's net wealth.

The reader must be warned that a recent rush of studies, following Jensen and Ruback (1983), has provided mixed evidence on the economic consequences of take-overs. The bidding for the shares of a target firm constitutes an increase in demand and should raise the price of the target's shares. The controversy centers on whether take-overs increase the *joint value* of the shares of bidders and targets. Note also that there is no reason to believe that *all* take-overs increase net wealth.[21]

5.4. Various forms of business organization: corporations, partnerships, proprietorships, financial mutuals, and nonprofit organizations

Although the open corporation plays a dominant role in the nonfinancial sector of modern industrial economies, other forms of business organization, such as the closed corporation, the partnership, the proprietorship, the financial mutual, and the nonprofit organization, also thrive in the same general economic environment. In order to survive in a laissez-faire economy, a business organization must supply goods at prices comparable to or lower than those of other forms of organization *and still cover costs*. The question of why different forms of business organization survive side by side in a laissez-faire economy is postponed until

to purchase another company, the "target." *Proxy contests* involve the pooling of voting rights of shareholders in an attempt to gain controlling seats on the board of directors. The other forms of takeovers are *mergers*, which involve direct negotiations between managers of bidding and targeted firms, and *tender offers*, where shareholders are approached directly and offered a higher price for their shares than their value on the stock exchange.

21. See Cook, Richard E. (1987). "What the Economics Literature Has To Say About Takeovers." Working Paper No. 106. St. Louis: Center for the Study of American Business, Washington University.

the next chapter. In this section we briefly examine economic outcomes associated with these various organizational forms.

In the property-rights literature, firms are usually classified in terms of contractual arrangements that govern the ownership of their residual income. A firm's residual income is the sum that remains when those with fixed-payoff contracts have been paid. The basic rationale for classifying firms in terms of the structure of residual claims is to focus attention on the extent to which chief decision makers in the firm bear the wealth consequences of their actions. Also, the rules governing the structure and transferability of residual claims can give rise to a conflict between output maximization by the firm and utility maximization by the owners, as we shall see.

We have already noted that in the open corporation, residual claims can be owned by outsiders who have no managerial duties but ultimately control the firm, at least formally. This arrangement has given rise to various agency problems as well as arrangements to reduce the cost of agency. A very important aspect of the open corporation is the ability of each individual owner to trade his or her residual claims – that is, the shares – freely and at low transaction costs.

Fama and Jensen (1985) have analyzed how the ability to trade shares at low costs affects investment decisions.[22] The following example illustrates their viewpoint: Let us assume that the managers of an open corporation have decided to invest in a project with payoffs far in the future. It has been calculated correctly that this project is one that will maximize the present (market) value of the firm, when the market rate of interest is used to calculate net worth. A shareholder who strongly values current consumption relative to future consumption, one whose *marginal rate of time preferences is high* relative to the market rate of interest, may find that the stream of payoffs associated with the project in question does not match her preferred pattern of consumption. But in the

22. Fama, Eugene F., and Jensen, Michael C. (1985). "Organizational Forms and Investment Decisions." *Journal of Financial Economics 14* (No. 1): 101–119.

case of an open corporation, this shareholder has no incentive to block the proposed project, since it maximizes the market value of her shares, and, furthermore, she can trade the shares at low transaction costs and substitute them for other financial assets of equal value but with a more satisfactory payoff pattern.[23] In other words, there is no conflict between the owner's self-interest and investments that maximize the market value of the firm.

The shareholders of a closed corporation are usually the firm's leading decision makers or individuals favored by those who manage the firm (relatives, acquaintances, etc.). With owners managing the company, agency costs are reduced from what they are when professional managers are employed. Agency costs are further reduced in partnerships and proprietorships, where usually all residual claimants are also chief decision makers in the firm and bear the wealth consequences of their actions. But as agency costs go down when the extent of outside ownership is reduced, other problems may appear. Fama and Jensen (1985) argue that in closed corporations, partnerships, and proprietorships, conflict may arise between utility maximization by the owners and the maximization of the market value of their firms. For example, assume that the owners of a partnership invest all their investable funds in the firm, and there is no outside financing available because of agency problems. An investment option that would maximize the present value of the firm (using the market rate of interest) might provide owners who value current consumption highly with an unsatisfactory earnings stream. One option, which the impatient owners of our partnership might have, is to sell the firm (sell the rights to the particular production function that they possess) to other individuals whose marginal rate of time preferences is relatively low (e.g., this could be true of younger entrepreneurs). However, even if potential buyers could be found, which is not self-evident, high transaction costs might block the sale of the firm. If the owners

23. The discussion assumes the existence of freely functioning capital markets, including a stock market, which can be found only in a handful of countries around the world.

are not able to sell (or borrow against) their residual claims (except by incurring very high transaction costs), investment options that maximize the market value of the partnership are foregone.

The analysis of Fama and Jensen (1985) suggests then that in the absence of effective markets for the residual claims of closed corporations, partnerships, and proprietorships, there is a tendency to "underinvest" according to the "market-value decision rule." In other words, the relative advantage of these forms of business organization does not lie in long-term risky investments on a large scale. Although Fama and Jensen (1985) examine only optimal investment rules for different types of business organizations, they assert that other management decisions – for example, financial, dividend, insurance, accounting, and market policies – also depend on the nature of a firm's residual claims. But the work on endogenizing these variables has just begun, and the empirical evidence is limited.

Mutuals are organizations found primarily in financial activities. For example, there are mutual investment funds, savings and loan associations, and insurance mutuals. The striking characteristic of the mutuals is that their customers are also residual claimants – for example, depositors in savings and loan associations, and policyholders in mutual insurance companies. The residual claims of mutuals are usually issued in direct proportion to the amounts of deposits or policies, up to a limit. The residual claims are redeemable when the customer withdraws his business, but they cannot be bought and sold.[24]

Mutuals are not managed by their owners, nor are their professional managers constrained by a competitive market for residual claims. Therefore, economic outcomes should involve relatively extensive shirking and opportunistic behavior by management. Nicols (1967, 1972) has provided evidence that supports this contention. Nicols compared stock and mutual savings and loan associations, and found that the mutuals had higher cost functions, slower growth rates (and, hence, were losing their market share),

24. De Alessi, Louis (1980) [op. cit., note 5], pp. 17–18.

less risky portfolios, less activity in marketing, managers who served longer in office, a larger staff, and chief executive officers who had a greater tendency to employ relatives.[25] With the evidence against the mutuals being so negative, one may ask how do they survive at all. This question comes up in Chapter 6, but, in the meantime, we suggest three possible answers: (1) that this form of organization indeed will not survive; (2) that government regulation gives it an effective protection; or (3) that high agency costs of a certain type are more than matched by relative advantages in other areas.

The problem of shirking should be greatest in private nonprofit organizations where there are no residual claimants. Donations are a major source of finance for these organizations, and management is constrained primarily by the need to preserve the goodwill of current and future donors. Donors do not seek a financial return on their contributions, but they usually want to support only a certain type of activity and can be expected to withdraw their support on receiving evidence of fraud or serious inefficiency by management.[26]

Frech (1976) has compared three types of organization – stock companies, mutuals, and nonprofits – which are all engaged in the same task, that of processing Medicare claims for the U.S. Social Security Administration, in order to determine whether charges are allowable, and that of paying the claimants.[27] Frech found that he could rank these three types of firms according to their level of productivity as measured by costs per processed claim (with the claims measured in dollar units), average processing time, and errors per $1000 of claims processed. Processing costs were highest

25. Nicols, Alfred (1967). "Stocks Versus Mutual Savings and Loan Associations: Some Evidence of Differences in Behavior." *American Economic Review 57* (May): 337–347; idem (1972). *Management and Control in the Mutual Savings and Loan Association.* Lexington, Mass.: Lexington Books.
26. Fama, Eugene F., and Jensen, Michael C. (1983). "Agency Problems and Residual Claims." *Journal of Law and Economics 26* (June): 327–349.
27. Frech, Harry E. III (1976). "The Property Rights Theory of the Firm: Empirical Results from a Natural Experiment." *Journal of Political Economy 84* (February): 143–152. Cited in De Alessi (1980) [op. cit., note 5], pp. 18–19.

for nonprofits and lowest for the stock companies. The same ranking was observed for processing time and errors, although the difference between mutuals and nonprofits was not statistically significant.[28] It is important to note that the three forms of organization would not have survived side by side in a laissez-faire market. In this instance, each firm had been granted property rights in processing claims in a specific territory by the government and was compensated on a "reasonable cost" basis.

5.5. Regulated firms and economic outcomes

The new property-rights literature and Neoinstitutional Economics have made important contributions to the economics of regulation. The emphasis on the firm as a complex structure of contracts designed by maximizing agents who take into consideration risk, transaction costs, and competitive forces has increased general awareness of unintended side effects of government regulation. Also, the realization that changes in property rights usually involve both winners and losers, plus the application of the concepts of information and transaction costs to political processes have given rise to the interest-group model of regulation. This approach now coexists with the public-interest theory of regulation.

It is generally agreed that in the past 100 years or so, Western governments have increasingly restricted the property rights of owners of inputs, particularly nonlabor inputs, and increased the role of the state in economic activity. In many cases the rights of labor and consumers have been enhanced, and in other cases the structure of rights has been changed to benefit one occupation or industry at the expense of another. The economic consequences of these changes have been to redistribute wealth and possibly to lower gross national products and growth rates as conventionally measured.[29]

---

28. De Alessi (1980) finds some of Frech's test procedure troublesome, but "the general results he reports seem strong enough to withstand more rigorous empirical evaluation." See p. 19.
29. Note that the sacrifice of marketable products for cleaner air may show up in

These changes are rather imprecisely referred to as *regulation*. Nowhere has the trend toward regulation been documented and analyzed more carefully than in the United States, but the evidence suggests that generalizations tend to be unreliable in this area and judgments should be made on the basis of individual cases. For example, economists have drawn attention to instances where regulation of industry has had consequences other than those intended by policymakers and regulators, often because of unexpected side effects.

Consider the case of a monopoly, either a natural monopoly or a firm granted monopoly power by the state, which would earn a rate of return well above the opportunity cost of capital – unless it is subjected to profit restrictions by the state. Economists have shown that such profit restrictions can have unintended side effects. First consider the so-called Averch–Johnson effect, which suggests that a constrained firm may select a *more capital-intensive technology* than an unconstrained firm does.[30] If the firm can borrow at a rate below the allowed rate of return on its capital, it may pay to swell the firm's capital base until the rate of return has fallen to the permissible level. In fact, the *outside owners* of a regulated monopoly are indifferent as to whether the gap between the unconstrained rate and the allowed rate of return on capital is closed by lowering output prices, by taxes, or by inflating costs. However, as Alchian and Kessel (1962) have pointed out, professional managers will prefer to close the gap by inflating certain costs that increase their on-the-job consumption.[31] De Alessi's (1980) survey of the empirical literature finds both support for the Averch–John-

a lower GNP: The value of clean air is not directly registered in the national accounts. Of course, such a drop in GNP tells us nothing about what has happened to the welfare of the community.

30. Averch, H., and Johnson, L. L. (1962). "Behavior of the Firm under Regulatory Constraints." *American Economic Review 52* (December): 1053–1069.

31. Alchian, Armen A., and Kessel, Reuben A. (1962). "Competition, Monopoly and the Pursuit of Money." In National Bureau of Economic Research, *Aspects of Labor Economics*. Princeton: Princeton University Press.

son thesis and evidence of more on-the-job consumption in regulated monopolies than in other comparable firms.[32]

The regulation of the U.S. oil industry, introduced in 1973 in response to the OPEC oil embargo, has come under close scrutiny:

> Originally adopted as a part of a 90-day economy-wide emergency measure to stop a rise in inflation in 1971, oil price controls were eventually embodied in well-targeted legislation designed to deal with the emergence of the Arab oil embargo in the winter of 1973–1974. These "temporary" controls far outlived the emergencies that gave them birth and lasted just six and one-half months short of a full decade. Over this period, the nation's petroleum markets were subjected to no fewer than six different regulatory agencies and seven distinct price control regimes, each successively more complicated and pervasive.[33]

Kalt (1981, 1983) shows that the effects of the measures were to discourage domestic oil production, encourage imports of foreign oil, and prop up world oil prices.[34] The policy makers who introduced the new regulations of the oil industry claimed that their aim was to limit inflation in the United States, secure adequate supplies of oil at as low a cost as possible, and avoid windfall gains in the U.S. oil industry. None of these objectives was reached, partly owing to a failure to understand the interaction of market forces and complex regulations, and partly because of the strong influence on regulators by special-interest groups.

In Neoinstitutional Economics, it is emphasized that most goods and services have a large number of valuable dimensions. If a

---

32. De Alessi (1980) [op. cit., note 5], pp. 19–27.
33. Pp. 87–89 in Kalt, Joseph P. (1983). "The Creation, Growth, and Entrenchment of Special Interests in Oil Price Policy." In Noll, Roger G., and Owen, Bruce M., eds. *The Political Economy of Deregulation: Interest Groups in the Regulatory Process*. Washington, D.C.: American Enterprise Institute.
34. Kalt, Joseph P. (1981). *The Economics and Politics of Oil Price Regulation*. Cambridge, Mass.: MIT Press.

regulator controls only one margin, firms are likely to make countervailing adjustments on other unregulated margins. A persistent regulator may then attempt to expand his control to several additional margins, but such efforts often involve high transaction costs and success is not guaranteed. Kalt (1983) describes in these words the process that is sometimes initiated by well-intended regulations:

> Regulations adopted to address a specific and fairly well defined problem create unintended economic distortions. These resulting problems are addressed with further stop-gap regulations. The cycle repeats itself; and at each stage there are economic winners and losers as regulation alters prices, costs, contracts, supplies, and demands. Affected parties that are well organized and well endowed financially are coalesced and inevitably influence the growing patchwork of regulation. The end result is a system that, in its overall design, accords with no one's conception of sound economic policy for the country but has a well-entrenched special interest residing in each of its component parts.[35]

Regulation of the U.S. airline industry provides a good example of the need to control not one but several margins in order to restrain competition. Before the airline deregulation of 1978, the Civil Aeronautics Board (CAB) regulated airline fares and routes in the United States. The airlines reacted by introducing competition at various unregulated margins such as competition in flight-schedule frequency. The CAB responded to these adjustments at unregulated margins by attempting to regulate them also, "even to the point of writing regulations that defined the size of a coach class seat and the amount of meat that could be lawfully served on a sandwich."[36]

35. Kalt (1983) [op. cit., note 33], p. 98.
36. P. 156 in Noll, Roger G., and Owen, Bruce M. (1983b). "Conclusions: Economics, Politics, and Deregulation." In Noll and Owen, eds. (1983a) [op. cit., note 33], pp. 155–162. See also Kahn, Alfred E. (1983). "Deregulation and Vested Interests: The Case of Airlines." In ibid., pp. 132–151.

We have so far talked about regulatory efforts that failed to reach the desired goals or involved harmful, unintended side effects. But sometimes regulations are initiated outright by special-interest groups, or special interest may capture the regulatory process. The high cost of information and collective action can make such behavior possible in a democracy. Part of the strategy for minority interest groups is then to spread false information about the costs and benefits of the regulatory measures. For example, it is commonly argued that the absence of regulations will bring one or more of the following: *destructive competition* (among airlines, in the stock market), the *elimination of desirable cross-subsidies* (no more service to small communities by airlines or trucking), *excessive risk and harm to consumers* (electrocution of users if terminal telephone equipment is supplied by others than a national monopoly).

The literature on regulation sometimes gives the impression that all regulation is stupid, corrupt, or both. This conclusion should be avoided. First, the word *regulation* is perhaps not a very helpful term. Any specification by the state of the structure of property rights is, in a sense, regulation. Goldberg (1976) makes the case that the distinction between private and public rules is not clear, particularly when transactions involve a long-run contractual relationship:

> In this sense, all transactions, however well defined they might appear, are nested in a complex pattern of contractual jurisdictions which, taken together, establish the rights, obligations, and ultimately the transaction costs of the respective parties. We can view the problem of designing (and adjusting) the complex pattern of restrictions through two convenient fictions. On the one hand, we can envision people "choosing" the rules in which their behavior is to be embedded. On the other hand, we can view all authority as reposing in a central government which then decentralizes decision making to lower level governments and to private individuals who can write "private legislation" in the form of private

contracts. If we ignore the normative overtones of these two approaches (admittedly not an easy task), they are not so terribly different. In both cases we are really saying that the line between private and public rules (restrictions) is blurred, and that to achieve desirable results society will have to erect a set of barriers or restrictions (transaction costs) to channel behavior; this set of barriers will establish a complex admixture of public and private jurisdictions.[37]

In fact, much of the critical literature on regulation examines recent changes in property rights that seem to transfer wealth from one group to another at the cost of reduction in overall output as valued in the market. But history reveals periods when the structure of property rights (and regulation) has been both supportive of economic growth and a hindrance to growth. These issues are discussed in the last section of this book.

Second, the case against regulation may have been overstated because many critics have compared outcomes in regulated industries with ideal states derived from the neoclassical model and thus made themselves guilty of the Nirvana fallacy, as Demsetz would say. Goldberg (1976) makes a strong case along these lines.[38] The paradigmatic transaction of the neoclassical model is a discrete transaction conveying a well-defined object, and the exchange is often cloaked in anonymity. But there is another important class of transactions that projects exchange into the future and involves long-term contracts and ongoing relationships. Goldberg (1976) uses the example of a university that negotiates a food-service contract with a private firm. The task of specifying and enforcing contractual agreements at all relevant margins – for example, regarding price, quality, or reasonable profits – is clearly enormous,

37. Pp. 52–53 in Goldberg, Victor P. (1976). "Toward an Expanded Economic Theory of Contract." *Journal of Economic Issues 10* (No. 1, March): 45–61.
38. Goldberg, Victor P. (1976). "Regulation and Administered Contracts." *Bell Journal of Economics 7* (No. 2): 426–441.

and the outcome may have seemingly perverse characteristics comparable to outcomes in regulated industries.

Complex long-term transactions often involve specialized investment by one or both sides to an exchange, as we shall discuss in the next chapter in connection with the contractual nature of the firm. If transactions are terminated prematurely, the owner of a specialized asset will suffer a capital loss. Government regulation is, at least potentially, a method to induce specialized investments and encourage long-term contracts. In the absence of government regulation, private individuals use other methods to protect their specialized investments. For example, to avoid a holdup by his supplier, a private businessman may resort to stockpiling or insurance, rely on multiple suppliers or standby capacity, or even attempt vertical integration with the supplier. Goldberg (1976) does not deny that government regulation has often been used to profit special-interest groups, and that it has often produced unintended perverse results, but he insists that regulation should be evaluated in terms of practicable alternative arrangements.

5.6. Political firms

In the twentieth century, the share of resources that is allocated by political firms has grown rapidly in the Western world. The term "political firm" is taken from De Alessi and is used here to denote any organization owned by a local or national political unit that employs labor services and material inputs to produce commodities. We are concerned here only with political firms that operate in a capitalistic market environment.

Do economic outcomes of political firms differ systematically from the outcomes of privately owned firms? Before we attempt to answer this question, it is important to note that the contractual nature of political firms varies greatly and the associated variation in the structure of costs and rewards suggests variable economic outcomes. Yet, political firms have one thing in common: The general public is their ultimate *collective* owner. Furthermore, individual citizens usually have no direct claim on the residual income of political firms (although positive or negative residuals may affect them indirectly through lower or higher taxes), and they cannot transfer their ownership rights (and duties) except by leaving the political unit.[39]

We should also note that many political firms have as their explicit goal *not* to sell their output at a price that covers costs. There are several explanations for this behavior. In the case of a *pure public good*, the cost of transferring and enforcing exclusive rights to *individual units* of the commodity is so high as to make the marketing of each unit impractical (e.g., selling units of defense or flood control to single buyers). Therefore, the production of pure public goods is usually financed by taxation. Another reason is that those who control the state prefer to see higher levels of consumption of certain goods, so-called *merit goods*, than would result if the goods were sold for profit in private market exchange. For example, the opera houses of Scandinavia cover only about 15 percent of costs through ticket sales, and the balance is made up mostly by the government. But in other cases, political firms often earn profits, and sometimes very large profits: Consider state liquor stores or the state oil company of Norway.

Whatever the outcome of the operations of a political firm, the individual voter usually does not have much control over his or her agents. For example, a citizen owner of a local public transit company, one badly run and heavily subsidized, does not have many options to escape her responsibility for a negative residual that eventually will be passed on to her as higher taxes. The owner has the choice of either leaving the community and seeking another place to live where public organizations and political firms are more to her liking, or attempting to influence the operations of the firm through the political process. The costs of either alternative, leaving or collective action, are often high relative to the benefits. For instance, high property taxes will be reflected in property values

39. Neither are the residual claims of political firms transferable in the market, nor do political firms buy back their "shares."

and hence in the sale price of the assets of property owners who sell their property and leave.

When the ownership of a firm, whether public or private, is dispersed, the incentive for each owner to monitor the managers is limited. But in the case of private firms, an individual can specialize in ownership of firms operating in lines of production of which he or she is knowledgeable. Such consolidation is impossible in the case of political firms: Each voter is a part owner of all the political firms in the community.

In certain cases, it can be particularly expensive to monitor the operations of political firms – for example, when it is official policy not to cover costs or when information about inputs and outputs is kept a state secret (defense, intelligence services). In other cases, the output of public organizations is particularly difficult to measure (Departments of State and Commerce). Sometimes no market prices exist for the output of these organizations (although usually prices exist for the inputs or their close substitutes), and, if the output is unique, comparisons with cost conditions in private firms are difficult.

When information costs are high and the citizen owners have weak incentives for monitoring political firms, there is a strong case for specialized monitoring by state agents (such as the General Accounting Office or Congressional committees). Also, contracts can be written to limit opportunistic behavior, and the constraints of competition are not entirely absent (although devices such as lifetime tenure, which are common in political firms, seem to weaken competitive forces).

Empirical comparisons of economic outcomes of political firms and private firms can be difficult when political firms operate in other lines of production and have goals different from those of private firms. But several authors have sought to compare economic outcomes of private firms and political firms when both produce the same easily marketable output. For example, in the United States a whole range of studies has compared the economic performance of private and municipal electric utilities. Others have examined public versus private transit systems, private and public hospitals, and fire prevention services that are either government operated or provided by the government but supplied on contract by private firms. Refuse collection has been subjected to similar tests. Davies has compared private and public interstate air carriers and private and public banks in Australia. These and other studies have been carefully reviewed by De Alessi (1980) and seem to provide consistent evidence of lower productivity in political firms than private ones. The studies reviewed by De Alessi suggest that the management of political firms not only has a limited incentive to cut costs but also is less likely than the management of private firms to invest in a price strategy that maximizes the value of their firm.[40] In most instances, such as refuse collection, it is reasonable to assume that relatively high costs are not an explicit goal sought by the polity that owns these public organizations. But there are situations in which high costs, holding quality constant, can represent an independent goal. This is sometimes the case when a locally operated project receives federal funds, and local voters and politicians correctly associate more federal funds – and higher costs – with more employment and higher local incomes.

The evidence just presented raises an interesting question. If it is correct that political firms tend to be high-cost producers, why then do polities decide to establish political firms in those lines of production that can be served *equally well* by private firms? Several answers can be suggested. A *taste* for political firms (ideology) is one possible explanation. Another explanation may be that reliable information about the relative cost disadvantages of political firms is not available to voters and their representatives. A third possibility is that political firms are in part intended as a mechanism for transferring wealth – for example, by providing pleasant places of employment for favored or needy individuals.

Finally, we should note that public goods need not be produced by political firms. Technically, the state can provide these commodities to the public and have private firms produce them on

40. De Alessi (1980) [op. cit., note 5], pp. 33–40.

contract, but in practice this may be difficult to arrange when the output in question is hard to measure (foreign policy) or when the arrangement can have dangerous consequences for the polity (when defense is contracted out to a private army). In such circumstances the state has an incentive to reduce transaction costs through vertical integration – by internalizing these activities. Exchange by the state with private firms is clearly less risky when the contract involves not defense but army boots or uniforms. The case of military equipment is more ambiguous. Although governments have tried to introduce monitors on the production sites of private contractors, examples of flagrant opportunistic behavior by defense contractors abound. It is not clear how much such behavior would be reduced if military equipment were produced by government-owned firms or how costs and the ability to innovate would be affected.[41]

41. De Alessi, Louis (1982). "On the Nature and Consequences of Private and Public Enterprise." *Minnesota Law Review 67* (No. 1, October): 191–209.

Part III

Explaining economic organization

6

The contractual nature of the firm

6.1. Introduction

Adam Smith began his *Wealth of Nations* with an examination of the internal works of a pin factory, but he soon turned his attention to other things: the coordination of a market system and the economics of growth and development. For more than a century and a half following the publication of Smith's masterpiece, the nature and internal organization of the firm received little attention in mainstream economic theory. At the same time the firm grew in size and complexity. McNulty (1984) describes how preoccupation with certain themes – with the macroeconomic distribution of income among rent, wages, and interest, or the logic of the competitive model and decentralized allocation of resources – pushed aside issues related to the firm and its internal organization:[1]

> The marginalist revolution and the development of
> neoclassical price theory, while producing a theory of
> the firm which was lacking in the earlier classical
> analysis, nonetheless failed to provide a full rationale
> for the firm's role in the economic system. Indeed, in its

---

1. McNulty, Paul J. (1984). "On the Nature and Theory of Economic Organization: The Role of the Firm Reconsidered." *History of Political Economy 16* (2): 233–253.

157

single-minded emphasis on choice in factor substitution, it reduced the firm, conceptually and analytically, to a set or series of actual or potential exchange relationships not unlike those of the market itself. Its incorporation of the firm fully into the market nexus, thereby perhaps obscuring some of the fundamental differences between these two institutions, was undoubtedly one of the principal reasons why the neoclassical paradigm left unasked the fundamental questions not raised until Coase's pathbreaking analysis appeared several decades later.[2]

In the first half of the twentieth century, the competitive firm of neoclassical theory was modeled as an entity that faced parametric prices, substituted land, labor, and capital to minimize costs, and adjusted its output until marginal cost was equal to price. No attempts were made to answer questions about the basic nature of the firm: For example, does the firm complement or substitute for the market, and why does the organization of the firm vary so greatly?

In Chapter 2, we discussed how Ronald Coase's famous article of 1937, "The Nature of the Firm," belatedly fathered an important research program dealing with the organization of the firm and using the theoretical tools of neoclassical economics. The new theory of the firm is still young and rapidly evolving. The leading contributors tend to present their ideas in nontechnical fashion – that is to say, their use of diagrams and mathematical models is limited. Also, the major scholars in this area have not standardized their vocabulary and defined their terms carefully, which sometimes makes it difficult to see whether we are dealing with overlapping or competing theories. We have chosen here not to survey separately the contributions of each of the leading figures in this area, such as Alchian, Barzel, Coase, Demsetz, Furubotn, Jensen, Meckling, and Williamson.[3] Rather, we try to summarize the general thrust of their analysis as simply and concisely as possible.

---

2. McNulty (1984) [op. cit., note 1], p. 245.
3. See, for example, Alchian, Armen A. (1965). "The Basis of Some Recent

6.2. The firm: What is it?

When analyzing the nature of the firm, the new literature tends to emphasize two aspects: A firm involves a set of long-term contracts between input owners, and a firm replaces the product market with a factor market where price signals play a relatively small role (as output is not measured continuously and sold for a price) and, typically, hierarchical relationships are substituted for market exchange. For example, the owner of a labor input *contracts* with an entrepreneur for a monthly salary and in return transfers certain user rights over his labor resource to the entrepreneur. The labor resource does not respond to price signals once such *long-term contracts* have been made. Rather, it is *managed.* The chief characteristic of long-term contracts is that they limit responses to future events by the parties – for example, with respect to price, quantity, and quality. Therefore, a series of spot-market exchanges is not comparable to a contractual relationship.

Economists who study the nature of the firm have sought primarily to explain variations in the type of contracts that the owners of inputs make. In Demsetz's laissez-faire economy, discussed in the previous chapter, only contractual forms that minimize costs

Advances in the Theory of Management of the Firm." *Journal of Industrial Economics 14*: 30–41; idem (1984). "Specificity, Specialization, and Coalitions." *Journal of Institutional and Theoretical Economics 140* (No. 1): 34–39; Klein, Benjamin, Crawford, Robert G., and Alchian, Armen A. (1978). "Vertical Integration, Appropriable Rents, and the Competitive Contracting Process." *Journal of Law and Economics 21* (No. 2): 297–326; Barzel, Yoram (1984a). "The Entrepreneur's Reward for Self-Policing." *Economic Inquiry 25* (No. 1): 103–116; Alchian, Armen A., and Demsetz, Harold (1972). "Production, Information Costs, and Economic Organization." *American Economic Review 62* (December, No. 5): 777–795; Demsetz, Harold (1983). "The Structure of Ownership and the Theory of the Firm." *Journal of Law and Economics 26* (June): 375–393; Furubotn, Eirik G. (1985). "Codetermination, Productivity Gains, and the Economics of the Firm." *Oxford Economic Papers 37* (No. 1): 22–39; Jensen, Michael C., and Meckling, William H. (1976). "Theory of the Firm: Managerial Behavior, Agency Costs, and Capital Structure." *Journal of Financial Economics 3* (No. 4, October): 305–360; Williamson, Oliver E. (1975). *Markets and Hierarchies: Analysis and Antitrust Implications.* New York: Free Press; idem (1985). *The Economic Institutions of Capitalism: Firms, Markets, Relational Contracting.* New York: Free Press.

(or maximize the joint net output of the inputs) survive in the long run: The equilibrium contractual structure is an endogenous outcome of a maximizing process. The analysis of contractual behavior, the way in which contracts are designed to lower transaction costs, can become quite complex. Sometimes contractual terms are used to create joint incentives in order to make contracts partly self-regulating. In other instances, the contractual structure is designed to protect input owners who have made investments specific to a joint effort and fear "holdups" by other agents.

But all these complicated issues have little to do with the one-person or *unitary firm* as McNulty (1984) has emphasized. In a unitary firm, the same individual owns all the inputs used to produce an output. The owner-manager of a unitary firm contracts to buy her inputs and sell her outputs, but the internal organization of the firm is not characterized by contractual relations. Furthermore, the unitary firm not only is a substitute for the product market (by bringing various inputs together), but also complements the market by responding to price signals from the market or, in many cases, by setting its own prices. The firm and the market are components of an interactive system:

> The unitary firm – whether . . . [an] elderly gentleman with his pushcart, a consulting economist, an independent middleman or artist – cannot properly be viewed as "a system of relationships," as Coase conceptualizes the firm; it is not formed to monitor "team" production, the reason given by Alchian & Demsetz for the existence of firms; and its internal operation does not involve "collective" action, as in Arrow's scheme. Yet to the extent which it exists, it plays a fundamental economic role no less than its larger and more diverse counterparts, aspects of which cannot be performed by the market.[4]

4. McNulty (1984) [op. cit., note 1], pp. 245–246. The models of the firm that McNulty refers to are found in Coase, R. H. (1937). "The Nature of the Firm"; Alchian, Armen A., and Demsetz, Harold (1977). "Production, Information

The simple structure of the unitary firm is well suited to clarify certain aspects of the firm that sometimes are forgotten when we examine more complex organizations. The owner-manager of a unitary firm performs functions that are required for market production but can be carried out only within the firm: He or she must discover and produce commodities that have valuable dimensions. Usually, commodities have several value dimensions related to *form, location, and time.*[5] McNulty (1984) emphasizes that "the qualitative dimensions of goods . . . can be traded and priced, but not determined and changed, within the network of market relationships" (p. 248). Even the homogeneous quality of goods in the basic competitive model must somehow be determined.

It is the entrepreneur who searches and experiments in a world of costly information, attempting to discover and produce commodities that have valuable dimensions. Profits are the entrepreneur's reward for a successful search. Even the most elementary of entrepreneurs, the newsboy, will fail if he is not successful in discovering valuable margins. The newsboy's activities are successful when he offers an interesting newspaper at the right place and time – possibly combined with pleasant appearance and manners. Also, the newsboy must communicate information about his product to potential customers.[6]

Costs, and Economic Organization." *American Economic Review 62* (No. 5, December): 211–221; and Arrow, Kenneth J. (1974). *The Limits of Organization.* New York: W. W. Norton.

5. The literature on monopolistic competition had important things to say about product quality, which now are largely forgotten: See, for example, Chamberlin, Edward H. (1953). "The Product as an Economic Variable." *Quarterly Journal of Economics 67* (February, No. 1): 1–29. Lancaster has added variable quality margins to the modern theory of demand. He assumes that utility is derived from qualitative attributes of commodities that cannot be bought independently of the commodities. See Lancaster, Kelvin J. (1966). "A New Approach to Consumer Theory." *Journal of Political Economy 74* (No. 2, April): 132–157. Finally, Becker bridges the gap between the firm and the household by modeling the consumer as a *producer* of his or her own utility or satisfaction, using as input both purchased and homemade goods and being constrained by time. See Becker, Gary S. (1965). "A Theory of the Allocation of Time." *Economic Journal 75* (September): 494–517.

6. This example is taken from McNulty (1984) [op. cit., note 1], p. 249.

The firm is a production unit that does not consume or use all of its output and is economically viable because of the gains in productivity from specialization. The entrepreneur, who searches for valuable combinations of inputs, may contract with other owners of inputs and form a coalition of producers, but the search for profitable lines of production in an uncertain world is central to his or her other activities.

6.3. Coalitions of resource owners

The unitary firm of the newsboy, the vendor of roasted chestnuts, the solitary lawyer, dentist, or farmer is a relatively unimportant form of economic organization in modern industrial societies. Most sectors of the economy are dominated by larger firms – coalitions of resource owners.[7] Why do coalitions of input owners produce commodities at lower cost, in many instances, than a series of unitary firms? This was the question originally asked by Coase (1937) in his inquiry into the nature of the firm.[8]

Cheung (1983) has restated Coase's central argument: In a laissez-faire economy, there are two ways in which a consumer can acquire a composite commodity through exchange – assuming specialization in production of the commodity's individual components. The customer can either negotiate with a large number of unitary firms for each component and their assemblage, or contract with a representative of a coalition of resource owners, a central

---

7. Cheung (1983) has emphasized that *firm size* depends on the form of contract chosen by input owners to accomplish any given task: "If an apple orchard owner contracts with a beekeeper to pollinate his fruits, is the result one firm or two firms? This question has no clear answer. The contract may involve a hive-rental contract, a wage contract, a contract sharing the apple yield, or, in principle, some combination of these and still other arrangements. . . . Most economists would probably opt for only one firm if the beekeeper is hired on a wage contract but for two if the hives are rented. Does it make sense to say that the number of firms, hence firm size, depends on the chosen form of contract?" (pp. 16–17) Cheung concludes that it really does not matter for the purposes of economic analysis how we define the firm. Our concern should be with the logic of alternative contractual forms and economic outcomes that different contracts foster. Cheung, Steven N. S. (1983). "The Contractual Nature of the Firm." *Journal of Law and Economics* 26 (April): 1–21.

8. This topic was introduced in Chapter 2.

agent, for the complete commodity. The choice between the two alternatives depends on which set of contractual arrangements supplies the commodity at a lower cost.

We should note, however, that the structure of contracts *within the coalition* can take many forms in a market economy. Williamson (1980) discusses, for example, the following arrangements:[9]

1. "A merchant-coordinator ... supplies the raw materials, owns the work-in-process inventories, and makes contracts with the individual entrepreneurs, each of whom performs one of the basic operations at his home using his equipment." This corresponds to the *putting-out system* of the early stages of Western industrialization.

2. The *federated mode* where work "stations are ... located ... side by side in a common facility. Intermediated product is transferred across stages according to contract. So as to avoid the need for supervision or continuous coordination, buffer inventories are introduced at each station." Each station then makes bilateral contracts with predecessor and successor stations in the production chain.

3. The *inside contracting mode* where a capitalist provides floor space and machinery, raw material and working capital, and the sale of the final product. But the task of coordinating the production process is delegated to inside contractors, who hire and supervise their own employees.

4. The *authority relation*, which corresponds to the basic capitalistic firm and is characterized by hierarchical relationships.

In addition one can think of various forms of communal ownership.

In most cases it would be costly for a consumer to contract with a number of unitary firms for the purchase of a composite com-

---

9. Pp. 14–17 in Williamson, Oliver E. (1980). "The Organization of Work: A Comparative Institutional Assessment." *Journal of Economic Behavior and Organization 1* (March): 5–38.

modity. The transactions may require costly expert knowledge of components and the repeated measurement and valuation of the output of a large number of individuals.[10] Therefore, the cost to the consumer of establishing the price of various components is likely to be high, if the production of the commodity is organized through the price mechanism. As an alternative, production can be organized within a firm where a central agent makes bilateral, long-term contracts with each of the input owners and sells the final product to the buyers. The choice of contractual form depends on the relative cost of contracting under each arrangement. In his pioneering contribution to this literature, Coase (1937) states that "the distinguishing mark of the firm is the supersession of the price mechanism" (p. 334). "The main reason why it is profitable to establish a firm would seem to be that there is a cost of using the price mechanism" (p. 336). And, "a firm is likely therefore to emerge in those cases where a very short term contract would be unsatisfactory."[11]

When a coalition of resource owners replaces a set of unitary firms, one type of transaction costs is substituted for another: The costs of transacting across markets are reduced as *one* transaction replaces a *set* of transactions, but a new type of cost emerges, the transaction cost of forming and maintaining a coalition of producers – often referred to, in the literature, as agency costs. The transaction costs of agency are reflected in the final price of the commodity to the buyer.

In their pioneering contribution, Alchian and Demsetz (1972) offer a somewhat different explanation from that of Coase, for the advantages of coalitions of input owners.[12] The *joint output* of a team can be greater than the sum of individual contributions made

---

10. In certain circumstances, however, it is possible that unitary firms would specialize in selling expert knowledge about components to consumers.
11. P. 337 in Coase, Ronald H. (1937). "The Nature of the Firm." *Economica 16*, new series (November): 386–405, reprinted in Stigler, George J., and Boulding, Kenneth E., eds. (1952). *Readings in Price Theory*, pp. 331–351. Chicago: Richard D. Irwin. The page numbers above are from *Readings*.
12. Alchian and Demsetz (1972), op. cit., note 3.

in isolation. But the problem with teamwork is that an individual often can reduce her effort without a proportional reduction in her income, because it is not feasible to measure the marginal product of each team member (although the output of the whole team can be measured at a relatively low cost). This creates perverse incentives to shirk (as each individual does not bear the full wealth consequences of her shirking), and causes accumulating rounds of shirking which can even lead to the dissolution of the team. In order to prevent this type of free riding, the members of the coalition employ a central agent and give her the right to hire, fire, and monitor team members. But who will monitor the monitor? This problem is solved by giving the central agent a claim on the firm's residual income. Alchian and Demsetz's important early contribution has been criticized on the grounds that it is easy to conceive of successful coalitions of input owners where there are no *direct technical gains* in productivity associated with teamwork and where the above argument does not hold. In later contributions, Alchian has emphasized firm-specific assets and the role of long-term contracts in protecting specialized investments. This is discussed below.

The substitution of one form of contracting for another continues until, at the margin, costs equal benefits. Formally, we can say that a firm, which may have begun as a unitary firm, will expand until the marginal benefits of internalizing an additional activity (reduction in the cost of transacting across markets) is equal to the marginal costs of internalizing an additional activity (the increase in internal agency costs). This applies equally to decisions involving larger output of the same commodity, vertical integration of the production process, expansion into new lines of production, and integration of a number of identical factories. Transaction costs also affect the feasibility of external financing, which in turn limits the size of the firm.

6.4. **The entrepreneurial function and measurement costs**

The joint value of a team that cooperates in production depends on the way in which team members are rewarded and how they are monitored. Production involves both relatively routine tasks and exploratory activities that are partly subject to chance. Below we argue that, ceteris paribus, "the person whose contribution to the common effort is the most difficult to measure will assume the position of entrepreneur, employing and supervising the other persons."[13]

Economic agents operate in an environment where information is costly and outcomes are affected by chance. They collect information and draw samples from the set of potential ventures, potential team members, and potential contractual forms and contract with individuals outside the coalition, such as buyers of output and sellers of input. We refer to these activities as the *entrepreneurial function*.[14]

Barzel (1987a) has analyzed the role of the entrepreneur in terms of his concept of *measurement costs*. He argues that the high cost of measuring entrepreneurial activities is a critical factor in explaining the contractual nature of the *entrepreneurial firm*. The measurement cost is high because the entrepreneur engages in complex activities often involving outsiders; and, more importantly, the outcome of the entrepreneur's activities partly depends on chance, and the cost of isolating and measuring the stochastic element is often very high. How costly it is to measure the random factor depends on the nature of the project.

Barzel (1985) presents a model of two agents who cooperate in production. He assumes that their working time is the only input, and that one of the agents is a residual claimant who divides his time between working and supervising the employee. The output of the employee increases with supervision but at a declining rate. It is also assumed that the two individuals seek to maximize the value of their joint output. Let us assume that the value of the output is maximized when individual A is the residual claimant-

13. P. 103 in Barzel, Yoram (1987a). "The Entrepreneur's Reward for Self-Policing." *Economic Inquiry* 25: 103–116. The discussion in this section abstracts from contractual problems associated with firm-specific investment, which are examined in the following section.
14. See Alchian (1984) [op. cit., note 3], pp. 35–36.

monitor and individual B is the employee. Barzel uses his model to show that the two roles will be reversed if the market wage of B, the employee, increases beyond a certain point. (The increase is exogenous and represents a higher value of marginal product for B.) Why does B become the employer? The main reason is the following: Because of the decreasing returns from supervision, the *net gains* from supervising an employee will become zero before all shirking has been eliminated. Hence, the output of a supervised worker is less what it would be if she were her own boss and devoted the same amount of time to production. When the value of the contribution of an agent (and her wage) has become very high, output maximization demands, ceteris paribus, that she monitor herself by becoming a residual claimant. Once an individual takes over as the residual claimant, output maximization also demands that she be assigned nonroutine tasks which are hard to measure.[15]

In terms of agency theory, we can say that information about entrepreneurial activities has an asymmetrical distribution that gives strategic advantages to the entrepreneur over other members of the coalition. This can give rise to serious moral hazard problems unless the entrepreneur is effectively constrained by some contractual arrangement. Self-monitoring appears as an efficient solution to this measurement problem: In the classical firm, entrepreneurs are constrained by their claims on the residual value of the joint venture.

The performance of the coalition's (the firm's) other inputs can typically be measured or estimated indirectly by means of various proxies at a relatively low cost.[16] The owners of these inputs tend to make fixed-income contracts (stipulating wages or rent), or contracts involving incentive payoffs tied to a specified measure of performance, and receive remuneration that is at least equal to

---

15. See Barzel (1987a) [op. cit., note 13], pp. 104–110.
16. When it is relatively cheap to directly measure and value the marginal product of an input, its owner is, ceteris paribus, more likely to make some form of a piece-rate contract, and the arrangement may resemble that of a unitary firm.

the pay available in the best alternative employment of their resource. Each input owner makes a bilateral contract with the entrepreneur-residual claimant, who is given the right to change the members of the coalition because the task of getting together an efficient team is a trial-and-error process.

The value of the coalition depends on the entrepreneur's skills, effort, and luck in discovering commodities with valuable characteristics; assembling efficient teams; finding appropriate contractual arrangements; and enforcing contracts. By having a claim on the residual, the entrepreneur reaps all the benefits of raising the value of the coalition and bears all the cost when the value of the fixed-income contracts exceeds the value of the coalition (except when the risk of loss is borne entirely by outside financiers).[17] The central agent has an obvious incentive to enforce the fixed-income contracts of the other input owners – who themselves also have an interest in the contracts being enforced. Yet measurement costs usually make the full enforcement of contracts not worthwhile.

Extensive shirking can reduce the value of a productive coalition and lead to its dissolution. This imposes losses upon individuals who stand to gain from joining in a successful coalition. If remuneration is flexible and shirking leads to reduction in pay for a *group* of inputs within the coalition – assuming that group performance can be measured more cheaply than individual performance – then the input owners may find themselves in an unsatisfactory situation. Namely, they would prefer higher incomes and less shirking, but collective action to control free riding by group members is prevented by high costs. The prospect of shirking creates an

17. Payment only in the case of success is a familiar contractual arrangement: For example, real estate agents usually are rewarded only when they make a sale. Note that in a competitive market the expectation of a positive residual is necessary to motivate entrepreneurial activities: The residual is not an income that in equilibrium is competed away. In addition, the rewards of an entrepreneur in a competitive market may include an element of rent if she has unique abilities for search or monitoring. Finally, note that this theory of returns to entrepreneurship cannot be successfully integrated into neoclassical economics without dropping the assumption of full information.

incentive to design contractual arrangements to overcome the free-riding problem. An entrepreneur-monitor, who has a claim on the residual, represents a classic solution to free riding by the members of productive coalitions.

The high cost of isolating the personal contribution of the entrepreneur and the difficulties of constraining her behavior in a stochastic environment have implications for the financing of entrepreneurial ventures. Barzel (1987a) argues that, because of the measurement problem, the rate of return on a businesswoman's search for a profitable venture is an *endogenous variable*: The expected rate of return on her search depends on the extent (and method) of outside financing. Outside observers will find it difficult to measure the behavior of an entrepreneur in search of profitable opportunities: to measure his diligence and whether he substitutes projects with a low probability of a high yield (and a high probability of failure) for projects with a high probability of a more modest return and higher expected yield. If an entrepreneur shares the gains when a project is successful but not the financial losses in case of failure, he has an incentive to seek out risky projects with a small chance of a very large return. When measurement costs are high, then "the smaller the businessman's contribution to financing, the lower the expected return on the project."[18] This suggests that the search for profitable opportunities will tend to be self-financed by the entrepreneur (as "the mere act of collaboration implies a fall in the venture's expected return"), although that will depend on the line of activity in question: "In general, self-financing may give way to market financing at a juncture where measuring the product becomes easier."[19]

18. Barzel (1987a) [op. cit., note 13], p. 113.
19. Ibid., p. 113. All this suggests that relatively wealthy individuals tend to become entrepreneurs. In neoclassical economics the entrepreneurial function is commonly explained in terms of *risk aversion*. This tradition is associated with Frank Knight. Barzel (1987a) demonstrates that the transaction-costs and moral-hazard explanation of the entrepreneurial function does not depend on the risk-aversion argument. Barzel (1987b) documents that Knight (1921), in his *Risk, Uncertainty and Profit*, was fully aware of the measurement and moral hazard problem and its implications for the entrepreneur's contractual status

Alchian and Woodward (1987) refer to assets and investments as being *plastic* when some technological or physical attributes make it costly to monitor an agent who manages the resources. In these situations it is difficult for outside observers to second-guess whether an administrator of resources is trying to maximize the joint value of a cooperative effort or bias the outcome toward her personal interest:

> We conjecture as further illustrations that enterprises with "intellectual research and capital," e.g. fashion designers, professional service firms such as engineering, law and architecture, computer software creation, are especially plastic and susceptible to moral hazard. In contrast, industries with less plastic resources are railroads, utility services, airlines, petroleum refining (but not exploration), and other activities involving much in a way of "hard" resources.[20]

6.5. Aspects of coalitions: specific investments, appropriable quasi-rents, unique resources, and dependence

In this section we deal with three concepts that recently have gained importance in the new literature on contracting and the firm: *appropriable quasi-rents, unique resources,* and *dependence.*[21]

within the firm. Later in his book, Knight dropped this line of reasoning and presented his famous argument that the entrepreneur is less risk-averse than the other input owners and assumes, therefore, the bulk of the risk associated with their joint effort along with the role of a residual claimant. Knight borrowed the term "moral hazard" from the insurance literature but apparently himself coined the term "residual claimant." Barzel, Yoram (1987b). "Knight's Moral Hazard Theory of Organization." *Economic Inquiry 25* (No. 1): 117–120; Knight, Frank H. (1921). *Risk, Uncertainty and Profit.* Boston: Houghton Mifflin. See also LeRoy, Stephen F., and Singell, Larry D., Jr. (1987). "Knight on Risk and Uncertainty." *Journal of Political Economy 95* (No. 2, April): 394–406.

20. P. 117 in Alchian, Armen A., and Woodward, Susan (1987). "Reflections on the Theory of the Firm." *Journal of Institutional and Theoretical Economics 143* (No. 1): 110–136.

21. The discussion below is based on Klein, Crawford, and Alchian (1978), op.

The strategic relationships associated with quasi-rents and a small number of traders, and the importance of long-term contracts in this context were given a pioneering treatment by Oliver Williamson. Williamson has developed his own terminology and uses a modified version of the rational-choice model, *bounded rationality* (see our discussion of this concept in Chapter 1). Williamson's contributions have left a strong mark on the new theory of the firm, and several of his terms have become common usage: for example, *markets and hierarchies* (actually the name of his famous 1975 book), *opportunistic behavior* (breach of contract involving strategic manipulation of information), and *hostages* (property pledged by one side to a contract to protect the interest of the other side).[22]

Quasi-rents arise as the result of *specialized investments*. Once committed, specialized resources cannot be transferred to alternative uses without a loss in value. Investments can be specific to a country, an occupation, or an industry, and they can also be firm specific. The trial-and-error process of discovering valuable margins of commodities and finding successful teams is a specific investment. In the words of Alchian (1984), "Part of the value of a successful team is the value of having assembled a successful team – that is, the avoidance of future costs of *searching for* a successful team." Hence, the market values of the individual resources involved in a firm sum to less than the market value of their joint product.[23] Investment in human capital and physical goods can be either specific or general.[24] When a factor of production receives

cit., note 3; Alchian (1984), op. cit., note 3; and Alchian and Woodward (1987), op. cit., note 20.

22. For example, see Williamson, Oliver E. (1975); op. cit., note 3; idem (1985), op. cit., note 3; idem (1983b). "Credible Commitments: Using Hostages To Support Exchange." *American Economic Review* 73 (September): pp. 519–549.

23. Alchian (1984) [op. cit., note 3], p. 35. See also Alchian and Woodward (1987) [op. cit., note 20], p. 7.

24. Gary S. Becker's theoretical analysis of investment in human capital with its concepts of general training and specific training is one of the cornerstones of the theories discussed below. Becker, Gary S. (1964). *Human Capital: A The-*

a quasi-rent, the resource's reward in its current use is higher than in the best alternative employment. In other words, the quasi-rent corresponds to the difference between current earnings and earnings in the best alternative employment, which implies that the quasi-rent of an input can be expropriated without causing its owner to withdraw the resource from its current use.[25]

The quasi-rent accruing to specific investment can be appropriated in many ways. It can be confiscated by illegal means, for example, by gangsters who operate protection rackets, or legitimately by the owners of inputs on which the specific asset is *dependent*. There are two ways in which a specialized resource can become dependent on cooperating inputs. First, when it is costly to find substitutes for cooperating inputs or, in our terminology, when they are *unique*, the withdrawal of an input, for which there are only more costly or inferior substitutes, reduces the value of a specific investment. For example, consider the resignation of a headwaiter who is a star attraction in a restaurant; the cancellation of a rental agreement, which forces a retail store to leave a location where it has become a landmark; the decision by a winner of the Nobel Prize for chemistry to leave a small private college for one of the big California universities. The second type of dependence is rooted in asymmetrical information, high measurement costs, and opportunistic behavior. When it is costly to measure performance and prevent shirking or sabotage by a cooperating input, the value of a specialized asset is at risk – even when the cooperating input has close substitutes. For example, think of an unskilled worker in a bottling plant who does not screen dirty bottles, thereby damaging the bottler's reputation and reducing the value of her specialized capital assets.[26]

It follows, therefore, that when specific investments depend on

oretical and Empirical Analysis with Special Reference to Education. New York: National Bureau of Economic Research.

25. Note that quasi-rent is associated with *investments*, but economic rent or pure rent is derived from *rare and valuable qualities of nature*, such as rich agricultural land, oil fields, unusual talent or beauty.

26. Alchian (1984) [op. cit., note 3], pp. 36–38.

other inputs, they are vulnerable to attempts to expropriate their quasi-rents. If the cooperating inputs have close substitutes, the bargaining strength of their owners depends on how much shirking, opportunism, and sabotage they can muster without bearing the full cost of such actions, whereas the bargaining strength of owners of unique inputs depends on how much their withdrawal affects the value of the specific resource. Finally, it is important to note that resources can be *interdependent*: Input A can be both unique to input B and dependent on B – implying, of course, that the dependence is mutual.

In order to understand better the issue of dependence, imagine a factory located in an arid region where a single well is the only source of water, and water is a vital input for the factory. For some but not all owners of the other inputs used in production at the factory, the well is a unique resource on which they depend. Unskilled workers and generalists can find new, equally valuable jobs without engaging in costly search. The factory also leases a computer which can easily be rented to other firms at no loss in value to its owner. In fact, Alchian (1984) argues that the owners of inputs whose wealth is unaffected by the fortunes of the firm where their inputs are employed cannot, in a meaningful economic sense, be members of the team or coalition that constitutes the firm.

But entrepreneurs at the factory, who have invested in a search for valuable commodities and successful teams, the owners of firm-specific capital goods, and those who have invested in firm-specific skills – all are vulnerable to threats by the owner of the well to raise the price of water and appropriate their quasi-rents.

In general, a worker who invests in firm-specific human capital risks expropriation of the returns. Once the investment is made, the worker is at the mercy of the firm's central agent who can refuse to raise his wage to match the newly acquired skills, unless some arrangements are made to constrain the central agent. In fact, it might seem logical that the central agent (or, more generally, the residual claimants, whoever they are) should bear the cost of investment in firm-specific human capital and also collect the return. However, in this case the worker might attempt to appropriate the return on his specific skills by threatening to leave the firm unless his wage is increased. One solution to this dilemma is some form of sharing between the two parties of the costs and benefits of investment in firm-specific human capital. Using the terminology of Oliver Williamson, we could say that the sharing arrangement is comparable to the exchange of hostages.[27]

Also note that dependence is often mutual: In our example, the factory may be the only potential large-scale user of the well, and, without the purchases of water by the factory, the well is of little or no value to its owner.

When individuals calculate the net expected return on specialized investments, they discount the yield by the probability that the quasi-rent will be appropriated. Even a small probability of appropriation can make the present value of a potentially profitable project negative, and this gives investors an incentive to take various measures to protect their quasi-rents prior to the commitment of their resources to specialized uses. The owners of assets, on which specialized investments depend, also have an incentive to offer investors some guarantee that their quasi-rents will not be appropriated. The protective measures and guarantees can be of two kinds.[28]

First, the owner of a specialized resource can reduce her dependence on other inputs by becoming their owner. In our example, the entrepreneur will not build her factory at this location unless she first can acquire the well. Alchian (1984) makes the point that strongly interdependent assets of a firm (except human capital) tend to be owned in common, and the firm can therefore be defined as a *cluster of interdependent assets*.

The other way to protect quasi-rents is through long-term contracts (or equivalent unwritten rules) designed to *constrain the set*

27. The modern version of this line of reasoning was developed by Gary Becker (1964), op. cit., note 24.
28. The third possibility is some kind of protection of quasi-rents by the state. As the discussion is still based on Demsetz's laissez-faire economy, we do not examine possible roles for the state.

of future options of input owners who are strategically placed to appropriate quasi-rents. For example, the owner of the well may try to lure the factory to his region by offering a long-term contract specifying the future price of water and guaranteeing steady supplies. In general, those who stand to benefit indirectly from investments by others in specialized assets have an incentive to make contractual guarantees to potential investors that their quasi-rent will not be appropriated.

In recent years, the concepts of specific investments, quasi-rents, and dependence have been used to analyze the logic of various contractual structures. Some of this work is reported below. We note at this point that long-term contracts designed to protect quasi-rents tend to make prices less flexible than indicated by standard price theory. Neoclassical economists have been reluctant to deal with rigid prices and wages as the phenomenon does not fit their theoretical framework, and have therefore had little to say about important empirical issues, such as the nature of unemployment. Hopefully, the new theory of contracts will provide valuable tools to deal with these important issues.

6.6. The structure of firms in laissez-faire markets: competing forms of organization

Why do we find a variety of business organizations in modern market economies?[29] Partly the answer is found in an unequal treatment by the state of firms, industries, and economic

---

29. In this section we draw on many sources but particularly the following: Fama, Eugene F., and Jensen, Michael C. (1983a). "Agency Problems and Residual Claims." *Journal of Law and Economics 26* (June): 327–349; idem (1983b). "Separation of Ownership and Control." *Journal of Law and Economics 26* (June): 301–325; idem (1985). "Organizational Forms and Investment Decisions." *Journal of Financial Economics 14* (No. 1): 101–119; Williamson, Oliver E. (1983a). "Organizational Form, Residual Claimants, and Corporate Control." *Journal of Law and Economics 22* (No. 2): 233–261; Klein, Benjamin (1983). "Contracting Costs and Residual Claims: The Separation of Ownership and Control." *Journal of Law and Economics 26* (No. 2, June): 367–374; Demsetz, Harold (1983). "The Structure of Ownership and the Theory of the Firm." *Journal of Law and Economics 26* (No. 2, June): 375–393.

sectors, for example, with respect to taxes and subsidies. If we leave this important explanation aside, there are reasons to believe that even in a laissez-faire economy various forms of economic organization will survive side by side. It is to this issue that we now turn.

Usually, entrepreneurs have a choice of several ways to organize production with respect to technologies and contractual structures. But in a laissez-faire economy the choice of organizational form is constrained by the criterion of profitability: Survival depends on finding arrangements that enable the firm to supply commodities at comparable or lower prices than its competitors and still cover costs. In his 1937 article on the nature of the firm, Coase argued that the equilibrium size of an economic organization is indeterminate when the cost of transacting is zero. Clearly, transaction costs must be an important variable in explaining the variation in economic organization. An examination of modern economic organizations – for example, proprietorships, partnerships, mutuals, open and closed corporations, nonprofits – should reveal why each organizational form is best suited to deal with the type of transaction costs that a particular kind and scale of production involves.

However, the reader is reminded that the world around us is not Demsetz's laissez-faire economy. Forms of organization may survive because they receive privileges from the state, such as favorable tax treatments. In other instances, an organizational form is laid down in law, for example, when all commercial banks are required to be limited liability corporations. Sometimes an organization may survive in spite of an inappropriate structure because it is cushioned from the forces of competition by the rent received for a unique resource (a singularly brilliant owner-manager, ownership of a valuable natural resource used as input). Also, the competitive survival process takes time. The following theories of equilibrium organizations for alternative lines of production should be seen not as a precise description of reality but as theoretical models representing general tendencies.

Attempts to analyze the relative advantages of alternative structures must focus on factors that contribute to the lowering of costs.

But once we lift the traditional assumptions of full information and introduce uncertainty and transaction costs (Demsetz's laissez-faire model), cost minimization becomes a complex multidimensional problem. The costs to be minimized now include the cost of coordination and the cost of enforcing contracts.

Consider briefly various aspects of cost minimization by firms in a laissez-faire economy. First, there are the economies of large-scale operations (due to technological factors) which in some lines of production lower the cost per unit of output. These gains can be analyzed in terms of the traditional full-information model and have been given much theoretical and empirical examination in neoclassical economics. Second, asymmetrical information, measurement costs, and different utility functions of individuals who cooperate in production can give rise to agency costs that depend in part on the structure of contractual arrangements. For example, vertical relations between production units often involve high transaction costs which sometimes can be lowered by vertical integration. Third, in many large organizations production processes, which are potentially advantageous, cause firm-specific information to accumulate at dispersed points within the firm. This dispersion and concentration of information can make it advantageous to delegate the right to initiate and carry out decisions to specialized managers, and also has implications for the design of effective monitoring systems. Fourth, the cost of collecting information and coordinating production increases as an organization becomes larger and more complex. These costs can sometimes be lowered when a large organization is divided into several semiautonomous units. Fifth, economic enterprises often involve an uninsurable risk. The assignment of risk bearing and residual claims among those affiliated with an organization affects incentives and economic outcomes. Some authors even consider the contracts that specify residual claims to be the key to our understanding of economic organization. Sixth, firm-specific human capital gives rise to a whole range of unique agency problems. Firm-specific physical capital goods tend to be owned in common to avoid attempts to appropriate firm-specific quasi-rent, or long-term contracts are used to constrain potential appropriators. Both of these options are limited in the case of human capital: The sale of human capital is illegal, and many types of long-term contracts that constrain future options of owners of human capital (e.g., requiring them to stay with the firm) are also against the law. Therefore, the special nature of human capital gives rise to attempts to lower transaction costs by means of particular types of formal and informal contracts.

Let us now examine six common forms of economic organization in advanced capitalistic economies and try to explain the relative advantage of each type in terms of the considerations listed above.

6.6.1. Proprietorships

A proprietorship is a business venture where one person is both the residual claimant and the firm's ultimate decision maker. The owner-manager bears the full wealth effects of his or her decisions so there is no *common ownership problem* in proprietorships. Furthermore, agency problems arising from the *separation of ownership and control* are avoided. These are the main advantages of this form of business organization. But there can be several disadvantages. For example, proprietorships can run up against the *horizon problem* and the *diversification problem*.

The horizon problem arises because of a conflict between the timing of net income flows from investments that the owner makes in the firm and her desired pattern of consumption. When the proprietor's time preferences reflect more impatience than is implied by the market rate of interest, some investments in the firm that are profitable by the market criterion (and maximize the market value of the firm) may be unacceptable to her. The horizon problem is likely to become more pronounced when returns accrue beyond the horizon of retirement. The proprietor could solve this problem by borrowing from individuals who are ready to lend at the market rate of interest or by reorganizing as an open corporation. She could then invest the proceeds from such transactions in a portfolio with a satisfactory yield pattern.[30]

30. Fama and Jensen (1985) [op. cit., note 29], pp. 103–106.

But outside financing of investments in proprietorships can be impractical or very costly. It can be difficult for outside observers who have invested in a proprietorship to judge whether the owner-manager seeks to bias outcomes in his own favor. Also the market value of a proprietorship often depends strongly on the owner's human capital, and the firm's resale value is therefore low when the owner retires from the business. When this is the case, neither the proprietor nor outside investors have an incentive to make long-term investments in the firm toward the end of the owner's career.

The diversification problem arises because proprietors often have to invest a large share of their human and physical wealth in their firms, and, according to portfolio theory, the cost of risk bearing for risk-averse individuals can be reduced by investing in several projects yielding income flows that do not have a strong positive correlation. This implies that the cost of risk bearing in a proprietary firm that depends on the owner's human capital and internal financing is relatively high – compared to investors with more diversified portfolios – and suggests, ceteris paribus, that the proprietor may avoid risky investments that, according to the market rule, would increase the value of the firm.

In sum, proprietorships tend to be constrained by the owner's wealth because of the high transaction costs of external finance, and this form of organization is not suited for activities where the economies of large-scale operations are important. The relative advantage of proprietorships is found in care-intensive, small-scale activities where there are high returns to careful monitoring (e.g., of output quality) by the owner-manager and where the cost of monitoring by outsiders is particularly high.

6.6.2. Partnerships

With few exceptions our analysis of proprietorships applies also to partnerships. By pooling resources of several individuals, *partners*, it is possible to ease the financial constraint of proprietorships and take some advantage of economies of scale in production. Partnerships can also provide an opportunity to lower the cost of risk bearing as each owner can now invest a smaller share of his or her wealth in the firm. A reduction in the cost of risk bearing can also be achieved by diversifying the commodities produced by the firm.

But partnerships are not free from the common-ownership problem. Usually, the partners are both the firm's residual claimants and its major decision makers, but the incentive advantages of combining both functions diminish as the number of partners increases. Although the partners as a team bear the full wealth effects of their actions, each individual does not; an individual partner's share in the wealth consequences of his or her actions is $1/N$, if we assume there are N equal partners.[31] Partnerships are rarely large organizations with a great number of partners, except in the case of *professional partnerships* to which we now turn.

In professional partnerships the most important asset that the partners bring to the firm is their own human capital rather than financial capital. Nonhuman capital tends to be a relatively unimportant share of total assets in these firms: The physical resources of proprietorships are mostly general rather than firm specific (consider the office space and equipment of law firms, accounting firms, and medical clinics), and the transaction costs of outside financing of investment in general resources are relatively low.

The advantages of a very large professional firm, say, a law firm, over a firm of small or medium size must rest on some economies of scale – for example, in supplying on-the-job training to young professionals or building a reputation and communicating it to potential customers. In general, the agency costs of professional partnerships are, ceteris paribus, directly related to the number of

---

31. The common ownership problem is further accentuated by the fact that, at common law, each party is individually (jointly and separably) responsible for all debts incurred by the partnership. If the $1/N$ share exceeds the net worth of the other partner, then the remaining more wealthy partner must pay the negative residual. Thus a partner may, even without a fellow partner skipping town, be legally responsible for all the wealth consequences of the partnership, if they are negative.

partners. Agency problems are mitigated in various ways: Newcomers must go through a period of apprenticeship before they become full partners; commonly, an internal committee of partners monitors performance and renegotiates individual shares periodically; the monitoring problem is made easier by the fact that professionals tend to work in small teams, and the performance of a team is usually highly visible; and, finally, the value of a professional's human capital depends on his or her reputation, and mistakes hurt reputations. In order to protect their own human capital, the members of a professional team have a strong incentive to monitor and prevent malpractice by team members.

In sum, large professional partnerships must face relatively costly agency problems that are, in successful firms, countered by the benefits of large-scale operations. But the economies of scale may vary by *type* of professional firm (law, accounting, advertising, health), the *task*, and the *client* (divorce cases, corporate taxation cases). These details have received limited attention in the literature.

6.6.3. The closed corporation

Contracts specifying residual claims in closed corporations are less restrictive than residual contracts of proprietorships and partnerships. In closed corporations the shareholders are usually "insiders" (managers) or people who have special relations to the owner-managers, such as friends and relatives, whereas in partnerships the residual claim is usually restricted solely to owner-managers. By limiting the choice of shareholders to mutually agreeable and socially related individuals, the agency problems associated with the separation of ownership and control do not rise with full force in the closed corporation. Residual claimants of closed corporations have *limited liability*, which lowers their cost of risk bearing (shifting it to outside debtors), but these organizations do not enjoy fully the benefits of allowing individuals to specialize in either risk bearing or management. And as the number of owner-managers increases, so does the common property problem.

Shares in closed corporations are neither evaluated nor traded in organized financial markets, as the residual contract restricts the transfer of shares. As the firm is not evaluated on a stock market, the transaction costs of terminating ownership in a closed corporation by selling one's shares can be high. This may affect investment decisions, as we argued above, and discourage owners of closed corporations from investments that would increase the firm's market value. Note that the concept "market value" is used here in a theoretical sense. By it we refer to the present value of the firm's flow of net income as priced in a perfect capital market and assuming that the property rights to the income streams can be transferred at no cost or loss in value. Fama and Jensen (1983a, 1983b, 1985), on which we base much of this discussion of the logic of business organization, emphasize that investments in proprietorships, partnerships, and closed corporations are not, as a general principle, based on the market rule:

> The proprietorships, partnerships and closed corporations observed in small scale production and service activities take a more direct approach to controlling agency problems in the decision process. The residual claims of these organizations are implicitly or explicitly restricted to decision agents. This restriction avoids costs of controlling agency problems between decision agents and residual claimants, but at the cost of inefficiency in residual risk bearing, and a tendency towards underinvestment. As a result proprietorships, partnerships and closed corporations will not generally follow the market value decision rule. . . . These organizations survive in the face of such inefficiencies when the agency costs that are avoided by restricting residual claims to decision agents exceed the higher costs induced by foregone investments and inefficiency in residual risk bearing.[32]

On the other hand, Fama and Jensen argue that "decision rules for open corporations, financial mutuals and nonprofits can be

---

32. Fama and Jensen (1985), p. 118.

modeled with the market value rule popular in the financial economics literature."[33] We will consider each of these forms in turn.

6.6.4. The open corporation

The open corporation dominates large-scale production in the advanced industrial countries. The relative advantage of this form of organization lies in the structure of residual claims, which encourages large-scale risky investments. The common stocks of the open corporation, the least restricted residual claims in general use, minimize the potential conflict between *utility maximization by owners* (shareholders) and maximization of the *market value of the firm*. When the shares receive an unbiased evaluation and are traded at low cost in the stock market, corporate owners can trade shares for other financial claims in order to match the time pattern of cash flows with their preferred pattern of consumption. Therefore, the owners' primary concern is with the maximization of share values.[34] Note that *limited liability* is a key factor in lowering the cost of trading shares. If liability were unlimited, the financial status of share owners would become a central concern at the time of transfer and sharply raise the cost of transacting, and an anonymous exchange of shares would not be possible. It is limited liability that guarantees continued existence of the firm despite ownership changes and "enables more complete capitalization of anticipated future results into current corporate stock values and managerial decisions."[35]

A further advantage of the open corporation is that shareholders are able to *diversify* their portfolios by holding any number of shares in one or more corporations along with other financial in-

---

33. Ibid., p. 117.
34. "When common stock prices reflect relevant available information and when common stocks are traded without transaction costs in a perfectly competitive capital market, the consumption streams that a stockholder can realize in future periods are constrained only by current wealth. The interests of stockholders are then served by investment decisions that maximize the current market value of their wealth. Market value, of course, reflects all costs, including the agency costs in the decision process." Ibid., p. 117.
35. Alchian (1984) [op. cit., note 3], p. 42.

struments. By diversifying their assets, the owners lower the cost of risk bearing, which makes risky ventures more attractive to them and gives a competitive edge to the corporate form in production requiring large-scale risky investments.

The open corporation enables individuals to specialize in risk bearing, on the one hand, and in management on the other. With the separation of these two functions, the set of top managers is no longer restricted to wealthy individuals who are willing to take risk. The specialization of the risk-bearing function has given rise to an effective market for residual claims that continuously evaluates the firm and, by implication, the performance of the agent-managers. Similarly, the separation of the decision-making and risk-bearing functions has led to the development of a market for professional managers that constrains the behavior of agent-managers.

But the open corporation is not without problems. When the firm becomes very large in order to take advantage of economies of scale, the cost of coordination is likely to rise, even if all the members of a corporate team have identical utility functions and do not shirk. Furthermore, a conflict of interest between outside owners and inside professional managers constitutes a new set of problems that perhaps represents the major disadvantage of the corporate form.

Fama and Jensen (1983a, 1983b) argue that all organizations where the risk-bearing function and the decision function have been separated are characterized by a *diffuse system of control* at *all* levels of the hierarchy. In fact, a diffuse system of control is found in all organizations where rights are *delegated* – for example, by a proprietor to his or her agents. The point of Fama and Jensen's argument, as we understand it, is that, with outside ownership, control is applied at all levels of an organization, *also at the top of the hierarchy*.

Fama and Jensen divide the decision function in the firm into four components: initiation of proposals, ratification, implementation, and control. They then aggregate initiation and implementation into *decision management*, and ratification and control into *decision control.*[36] Fama and Jensen argue that the functions of decision management and decision control are always separate in organizations in which the owners have specialized in risk bearing. It is possible that the same person may be engaged both in management and control but then in two separate areas within the firm.[37]

The authors also put forward the interesting hypothesis that the *structure of the board of management* of an organization will reflect the *type of moral hazard* facing the outside residual claimants. In the case of open corporations, opportunistic behavior by managers is constrained to a considerable degree by the capital market and by the market for professional managers. Therefore, the tendency in corporate boards of management is to emphasize the evaluation of proposals rather than to concentrate on controlling managerial transgressions. The board members are often inside and outside experts at project evaluation.

Williamson (1983a) has emphasized how the invention of new forms of organization has transformed the structure of the corporation. Until the early 1930s, U.S. corporations were organized around the so-called U-form, a unitary structure that divided the firm by function – such as finance, marketing, manufacturing, and the like. As the corporation grew in size, so did various problems of decision control. The response was the invention of the modern multidivisional structure, the M-form, which introduced "semiautomatic operating divisions (mainly profit centers organized along product, brand, or geographic lines)."[38] Strategic decision management and control were separated from operating decisions and assigned to a *general office.*[39] The transformation from the U-form

---

36. Fama and Jensen (1983b) [op. cit., note 29], pp. 303–304.
37. "The central complementary hypotheses about the relations between the risk-bearing and decision processes of organizations [are that] (1) separation of residual risk bearing from decision management leads to decision systems that separate decision management from decision control; [and] (2) combination of decision management and decision control in a few agents leads to residual claims that are largely restricted to these agents." Ibid., p. 304.
38. Williamson (1983a) [op. cit., note 29], p. 352.
39. Ibid., p. 353.

to the M-form spans the period from around 1930 to 1960 and was described by Alfred D. Chandler (1962) in his *Strategy and Structure*.[40] Williamson (1983a) points out that the M-form was introduced in two corporations, DuPont and General Motors, where residual-claimant status and management were still joined, which suggests that the introduction of the M-form was in response to rising costs of both coordination and internal agency problems as the firms became very large rather than an answer to a growing conflict of interest between inside managers and outside owners.[41] Finally, Williamson explains the surge of corporate conglomeration in the mid-1960s as a result of the mastery of the M-form by corporate leaders: Once in place and its advantages fully understood, the M-form gave rise to an even larger equilibrium size of the firm.

6.6.5. The financial mutual

The *customers* of financial mutuals are also the residual claimants, which makes this form of organization unusual. For example, the policy holders of mutual insurance companies, the shareholders of mutual funds, and depositors of mutual savings banks hold residual claims that are redeemable on demand at a price set according to a prespecified rule. Fama and Jensen (1983a, 1983b) argue that redeemable residual claims are a relatively low-cost mechanism for diffuse control, making the mutual a viable organization: The withdrawal of resources by residual claimants is a form of partial take-over or liquidation by the claimholders.

Mutuals are organizations with specialized managers who are not risk bearers in the firm. Redeemable claims can be seen as an inexpensive, effective control mechanism, but only if it is possible to liquidate the assets of the organization at a relatively low cost when the residual claimants withdraw their resources. According

---

40. Chandler, Alfred D., Jr. (1962). *Strategy and Structure: Chapters in the History of the Industrial Enterprise.* Cambridge, Mass.: MIT Press. See also Williamson, Oliver E. (1981). "The Modern Corporation: Origins, Evolution, Attributes." *Journal of Economic Literature 19* (December): 1537–1568.
41. Williamson (1983a) [op. cit., note 29], p. 357.

to this view, the assets of mutuals must not be firm specific and their sale must not involve high transaction costs. This requirement suggests that redeemable claims are a suitable control mechanism for organizations that specialize in holding financial assets. Within the set of all financial organizations, according to the Fama–Jensen thesis, "relative to mutuals, corporate financial organizations should be more involved in business activities other than the management of financial assets, and these business activities should involve relatively more nonfinancial assets that can only be varied with large costs."[42] But given these limits on the portfolio of mutuals, the residual claimants can agree on the maximum wealth or market value rule for decisions.[43]

Finally, Fama and Jensen (1983b) argue that, owing to the relatively efficient diffuse control mechanism of financial mutuals, residual claimants have limited interest in using the board of managers for decision control: "The role of the board, especially in the less complex mutuals, is largely limited to monitoring agency problems against which redemption of residual claims offers little protection, for example, fraud or outright theft of assets by internal agents."[44]

Alchian and Woodward (1987) expand the definition of mutual organizations to include nursing homes, country clubs, and other social clubs as well as financial mutuals, and give an interpretation different from that of Fama and Jensen regarding the economic logic of these organizations.[45] According to Alchian and Wood-

---

42. Fama and Jensen (1983a) [op. cit., note 29], p. 340. The authors provide empirical evidence that supports this contention.
43. Fama and Jensen (1985), op. cit., note 29. There is no secondary market for the residual claims of mutual organizations because of the price rule used to redeem claims. Note that "common stockholders of open corporations forego the direct control rights inherent in redeemable residual claims, but active capital markets for common stock make them more appropriate as residual claims in activities that involve large amounts of assets that are difficult to price, have high transaction costs, and are more efficiently owned within the organization than rented." (pp. 114–115)
44. Fama and Jensen (1983b) [op. cit., note 29], p. 318.
45. Alchian and Woodward (1987) [op. cit., note 20], pp. 132–134.

ward: "Mutuality enables the members to (a) prevent outside eq-
uityholders from expropriating value by lowering the quality of
service, and (b) preserve for incumbents any gains from admitting
new members."[46] They argue that the members of social clubs are
interdependent resources, that "the members have 'specific capital'
in one another, and that specific capital could be expropriated by
an independent owner." But "if people could be costlessly inter-
changed in social relationships, no expropriable social value would
exist, just as in firms where employees have perfect substitutes."[47]

6.6.6. Nonprofit organizations

Private nonprofit organizations, which finance their activities partly through donations, will survive in a laissez-faire economy if they can offer their commodity at a lower price than other
organizations and still cover costs – in this instance, with revenues
from both donations and sales. In order to enlist donations, nonprofits must specialize in the production of merit goods, that is,
commodities that some individuals would like to see others consume more of (classical music vs. popular music or educational
programs vs. automobiles fall in this category).

In nonprofit organizations there are no residual claims, as this
would amount to claiming a share of the donations. The absence
of residual claimants avoids agency problems between donors and
residual claimants but not between donors and decision managers.
Fama and Jensen (1983b) argue that potential agency problems
between donors and managers are alleviated by a strong presence
of donors on the board of nonprofit organizations.[48] Fama and
Jensen (1985) argue that investment decisions by nonprofits may
quite well be efficient on the market criterion: Provided that donors
have diversified portfolios, they will favor those capital projects
that have the highest market value, as they minimize the market
value of donations needed for a given nonprofit activity.[49]

46. Ibid., p. 133.
47. Ibid., p. 134.
48. Fama and Jensen (1983b) [op. cit., note 29], p. 319.
49. Fama and Jensen (1985) [op. cit., note 29], pp. 115–117.

6.7. A graphic model of the choice of organizational form

Fama and Jensen (1985) provide a graphic model of the choice of organizational form, which summarizes many of the basic notions that underlie the discussion in this and the previous chapter. Following Jensen and Meckling (1979), they assume that for any business venture there is a set of production functions, one function for each type of contractual arrangement. Let us assume that individual A holds the property rights to venture V. If A invests in V in time period 1 (t_1) he will reap the return in time period 2 (t_2). It is assumed there are only two periods, and A can choose from only two forms of organizations: The venture can be organized as a proprietorship financed entirely from the proprietor's wealth or as an open corporation. The corresponding production or transformation functions are $F(K; P)$ and $F(K; O)$ where K represents the amount of resources invested, P stands for proprietorship, and O for open corporation. The functions map how current resources can be transformed into future resources through investment in venture V.

In Figure 6.1 we examine the choices available to A by considering transformation function $F(K; P)$, ignoring for the moment his opportunity to organize the venture as an open corporation (to sell shares in the venture). Individual A has resources equal to K at his disposal in period t_1 and his object is to maximize his utility or welfare from these resources. The basic question he faces is how to divide his current resources, K, between consumption and investment in the current period, t_1. The answer depends on his investment opportunities and his preferences for current versus future consumption.

Individual A has two investment opportunities: He can invest in venture V, where the payoff is represented by $F(K; P)$, or he can buy securities in open corporations on the outside capital market, where the market rate of return is r. The transformation function for investments in securities is represented in Figure 6.1 by a straight line whose slope is equal to $-(1 + r)$.

The optimal division of consumption between t_1 and t_2 depends on A's utility function and more specifically on his time prefer-

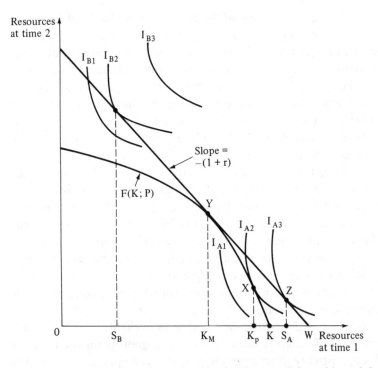

Figure 6.1. Transformation function for a proprietorship and the optimal level of investment.

ences. In Figure 6.1, each I_A curve shows combinations of resources consumed in t_1 and t_2, which give A the same level of satisfaction. The slopes of the indifference curves represent A's marginal rate of time preferences. Let us assume that A is relatively impatient, putting relatively little value on consumption in t_2. Given these constraints, A reaches his highest obtainable level of satisfaction at point X, which is a point of tangency between indifference curve I_{A2} and $F(K; P)$. Point X corresponds to investment in V equal to K_pK and consumption in t_1 equal to OK_p. Consumption in t_2 can be read off the vertical axis.

But A's high marginal rate of time preference, implied by the slope of his indifference curve at X, causes a problem: The commitment of only $K_p K$ to venture V represents an underinvestment in the venture according to the market rule, given r, the market rate of return. According to the market rule, investment in V should be carried to a point where the internal rate of return is equal to the market rate of return, which occurs in point Y. In Figure 6.1, $K_M K$ is the level of investment that maximizes the present market value of the venture, which is equal to $K_M W$.

Let us now assume that A can find another individual, B, who also has resources equal to K at her disposal in t_1, but B is not as impatient as A; her opportunity cost of postponing consumption in t_1 is less. This is indicated by relatively flat indifference curves, I_B. We also assume that A can sell B the *property rights* to venture V without the transformation function $F(K; P)$ shifting inward.[50] The net value to B of the rights to production function $F(K; P)$ is equal to KW. B would invest resources equal to $K_M K$ in venture V, buy securities equal to $S_B K_M$, and use OS_B for personal consumption in t_1.

After his sale of the rights to V, A's current resources have increased from OK to $OK + KW$, and his utility-maximizing point is now in Z on indifference curve I_{A3}, which represents a higher level of satisfaction than point X on I_{A2}. A would now buy securities for $S_A W$ and consume OS_A in $t = 1$.

But it is possible that A could find no B-type proprietor who is ready to purchase venture V. A might then consider organizing the venture as an open corporation, as illustrated in Figure 6.2. Different organizations involve different costs and different pay-offs. In Figure 6.2, it is assumed that the nature of V is such that the venture is most effectively organized as a proprietorship, which causes $F(K; O)$ to lie below $F(K; P)$. The maximum market value of the rights to V is relatively low when the venture is organized as an open corporation. In Figure 6.2, the value of $F(K; O)$ is equal to KW_o, which is less than KW_p, the value of $F(K; P)$ to a proprietor of type B. Fama and Jensen (1984) refer to the differ-

---

50. Such a shift might be expected, for example, if $F(K; P)$ depended on A's unique human capital.

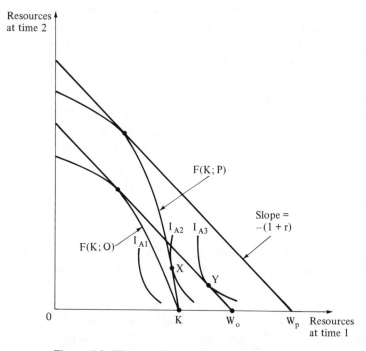

Figure 6.2. The cost of agency and transformation functions for a proprietorship and an open corporation.

ence $(KW_p - KW_o)$ as the gross agency costs of an open corporation compared to a proprietorship.

Finally note that in Figure 6.2, A could still increase his welfare by selling the rights to V to a corporation for KW_o. A's new optimal point is now Y on indifference curve I_{A3}.

7

The logic of economic organization

7.1. Introduction

In Chapter 6, we studied the economics of organizational forms in the firm. The firm was broadly defined as a nexus of contracts, but the interlocking webs of contractual relations made it impractical to nail down a more precise definition. Our subject thus became the economics of contracts. In Chapter 7, we go beyond questions relating to the nature of the firm and apply transaction-costs analysis to various organizational forms and market practices. The coverage is not exhaustive. Rather it serves as an illustration of Neoinstitutional Economics in action. We hope to demonstrate, through our examples, that the relative economic advantage of alternative contractual forms is rooted in transaction costs and cannot be explained in terms of frictionless neoclassical economics.

The topic of endogenous social and political institutions is reserved for the fourth and last part of the book. In the present chapter, the community's legal framework and social conventions are taken as given, and in most cases the framework is Demsetz's laissez-faire economy: the neoclassical competitive market plus transaction costs.

In Section 7.2, we begin our exploration of market practices by looking at the problem of measuring the *quality* of goods and services. Various market arrangements are seen as ways of mini-

193

mizing measuring costs and lowering the effective price to buyers. The examples are drawn mostly from the market for consumer goods, but the basic analysis applies to all types of exchange. In this section various important concepts are introduced such as *search goods* versus *experience goods, investment in reputation,* and *excessive measurement.* One of our conclusions is that it can be economically advantageous in certain circumstances to avoid excessive measurement by suppressing information.

Section 7.3 examines the costs of enforcing contracts in the labor market. The problem of enforcing the extreme condition of slavery is used as an illustrative example where we ask, in particular, When is slavery more productive than other forms of organization in the labor market? Also, when do we expect the ownership of human capital to be more valuable to the slave, who embodies it, than to the master, a situation which, according to Coase's law, implies that people will tend to possess their own human capital?

Section 7.4 deals with contractual arrangements in agriculture. First we examine the puzzle of the open-field system which persisted in European agriculture for centuries, although the system, when viewed through neoclassical spectacles, seemed to involve unnecessary costs. We present three competing explanations of the open-field system. In each case the solution hinges on a missing market, missing due to high transaction costs. Next we take up another long-standing puzzle, the alleged inefficiency of share-cropping and search for the economic rationale of share contracts. The section ends with an examination of the contractual mix in agriculture and a review of empirical studies primarily emphasizing the U.S. experience.

In terms of the pure neoclassical model, the use of money is a costly practice that does not make economic sense, and attempts to explain the existence of money in economic terms have relied on the concept of transaction costs. The chapter's last section, 7.5, looks at monetary arrangements and systems of exchange. The economics of *token money* are presented in terms of the concepts of experience goods and investment in reputation. One conclusion is that several parallel exchange systems exist within the same economy because individuals and exchanges are heterogeneous with respect to transaction costs.

7.2. Market practices, measurement, and quality variation of products

It is usually more costly to measure qualitative attributes of a commodity or a service than to measure its price. According to Neoinstitutional Economics, the costs of measuring quality give rise to various market practices that are designed to lower these measuring costs and minimize the final cost to buyers of commodities. In this section we introduce studies that examine the *economic logic of various market practices*, mostly in markets for consumer goods (although the approach has a general application). In many instances market practices evolve in response to various constraints imposed on exchange by the state, but our discussion is based on the laissez-faire model and does not consider these cases.

Nelson (1970), in a pioneering contribution, has made a distinction between *search goods* and *experience goods*.[1] According to Nelson's definition, the quality of search goods can be established by inspection prior to purchase whereas the quality of pure experience goods can be measured only by using the product. Brands of canned tuna fish are examples of experience goods, whereas women's dresses are typical of search goods. In practice, a buyer can measure the qualitative dimensions of most commodities through either search or experience, but the preferred way of establishing quality depends on the relative costs of the alternative methods of measurement. When the quality of a commodity is variable, the measurement of quality is costly for buyers and often also for sellers. In this context, the relative measurement costs of sellers and buyers are an important factor for explaining the organization of markets.

The concept of experience quality suggests that incentives for supplying experience goods of high quality may be lacking in mar-

---

1. Nelson, Phillip (1970). "Information and Consumer Behavior." *Journal of Political Economy 78* (No. 2, March/April): 311–329.

kets where sellers have little to gain by *investing in reputation*. Hence low-quality commodities may drive high-quality commodities out of the market. This is the message of Akerlof's famous "lemon model."[2] The issues involved can be illustrated with a simple model that is based on Klein and Leffler (1981).[3]

Let us assume there is a discreet range of quality for commodity X: minimum quality, q_{min}, and high quality, q_{high}. High-quality units of X are produced at a higher cost than minimum-quality units, as we can see from the relative positions of the marginal and average cost curves in Figure 7.1. It is easy to establish analytically the equilibrium price and output for high- and minimum-quality X, if we ignore the costs of measurement.

In a competitive industry with a free entry, the long-run equilibrium output for a representative firm that produces the lower grade of commodity X is established where average unit cost is at a minimum (assuming a factory of an optimal size), namely at output level Q_0 in Figure 7.1. The corresponding equilibrium price for $X{:}q_{min}$ is P_0. Similarly, the equilibrium output of a representative producer of $X{:}q_{high}$ is Q_1, and she faces an exogenous market price, P_1.

However, these classic results need not hold when the cost of measuring quality is introduced. Consider the situation where the cost to a buyer of establishing the quality of commodity X prior to purchase and consumption is very high whereas the attributes of X can be established at no extra cost by using the product.

2. Akerlof, G. (1970). "The Market for 'Lemons': Quality Uncertainty and the Market Mechanism." *Quarterly Journal of Economics 84* (August): 488–500. Consider, for example, the unorganized market for used automobiles operated through the classified advertising columns of newspapers in a big city. Akerlof's analysis suggests that only cars of lowest quality would be put on this market.
3. See p. 620 in Klein, Benjamin, and Leffler, Keith B. (1981). "The Role of Market Forces in Assuring Contractual Performance." *Journal of Political Economy 89* (No. 4, August): 615–641. The discussion below is based also on Holler, Manfred J. (1984). "Quality Enforcement by the Invisible Hand of Prices and Costs." In Skog, Göran, ed. *Papers Presented at the First Meeting of the European Association for Law and Economics.* Lund: Lund University, Department of Economics, pp. 76–88.

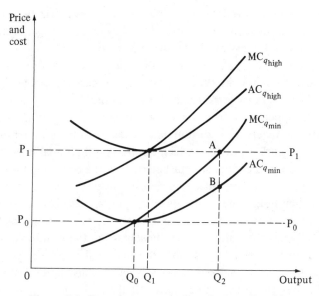

Figure 7.1. Experience goods: how low quality drives out high quality.

Assume also that producers (sellers) can control the quality of X at no cost to themselves. In other words, information is distributed asymmetrically between buyers and sellers, which can give rise to moral hazard.[4] Imagine that the basic neoclassical outcomes, (P_0, Q_0) and (P_1, Q_1), have been established and enforced by the state through severe punishments of sellers who market low-quality X disguised as high-quality X. The state decides now to stop enforcing quality in the market for X, and the opportunity arises for a producer of minimum-quality X to market her product as high-quality X.

The profit-maximizing output level for a counterfeit producer of $X: q_{high}$ is Q_2, and she would make pure profits equal to $Q_2(A - B)$ by selling each unit at price P_1 [with $(A - B)$ being the difference between price and average unit cost at Q_2]. How-

---

4. See our discussion of moral hazard in Chapter 2, Section 2.3.

ever, this scheme would work only in the short run or until buyers had learned through experience that they were being cheated. From then on buyers would refuse to pay price P_1 for any X, and consequently the high-quality version of the commodity would disappear from the market as high-quality cars disappear from impersonal markets in Akerlof's (1970) example.

The disappearance from the market of X:q_{high} creates an incentive for producers and consumers to design contractual arrangements and market practices which ensure that high-quality X (and other experience goods) are marketed. This can be brought about, for example, if sellers make specialized investments that pay off only if they honor the terms specifying quality in their contracts with buyers. For this arrangement to work, the buyers must be aware of such commitments (or "hostages" in the terminology of Williamson),[5] which implies that the marginal cost to buyers of measuring such specialized or nonsalvageable investments should be less than the prospective gains: "If the consumer estimate of the initial sunk expenditure made by the firm is greater than the consumer estimate of the firm's possible short-run cheating gain, then a price premium on future sales sufficient to prevent cheating is estimated to exist."[6]

The capital serving as collateral must lose value if the firm cheats. These expenditures need not give the consumer any direct utility, but, when circumstances permit, "the competitive process forces the firm-specific capital investments to take the form of assets which provide the greatest direct service value to consumers."[7] Also note that the supply of quality goods can be ensured by various non-market solutions, such as vertical integration or enforcement of quality by the state through regulation and the courts.

Nelson (1974) suggests that the advertising of experience goods serves two primary functions for the rational buyer, and neither

5. Williamson, Oliver E. (1983). "Credible Commitments: Using Hostages to Support Exchange." *American Economic Review 73* (No. 4, September): 519–540.
6. Klein and Leffler (1981) [op. cit., note 3], p. 631.
7. Ibid., p. 626.

of these functions is the provision of direct information about the experience quality of commodities that are advertised.[8]

First, advertising "relates brand to function" and provides information about the basic uses of a product. The prospective buyer is informed that product Y is a headache medicine and not a washing powder. Nelson argues that the incentives in unregulated market exchange usually ensure that this type of information is relatively free of bias because in most cases it relates to the search quality of commodities. For example, a prospective buyer can establish at relatively low cost prior to purchase whether a commodity is a vacuum cleaner or a photographic camera, and it is irrational to try to deceive him or her on this point through false advertising.

Second, the volume of advertising relating to the experience quality of a commodity is a signal to buyers that shows the extent of committed investment by the seller. According to Nelson, what matters most to a rational buyer is not what advertising says about quality, but simply that the brand advertises and invests in nonsalvageable capital. If it is assumed that tastes cannot be changed through advertising, then voluminous and expensive advertising of a brand suggests that the producer is committed to quality. This conclusion is further supported by the argument that firms that are particularly efficient producers of quality (i.e., can supply the highest utility per dollar of cost of a commodity) have the greatest incentive to advertise experience goods.

In the case of search goods where quality is established most efficiently prior to purchase, advertising is likely to contain more reliable information about quality than is found in the advertising of quality goods (or experience quality). The seller is now con-

---

8. Nelson, Phillip (1974). "Advertising as Information." *Journal of Political Economy 82* (No. 4, July/August): 729–754. Note that in his analysis Nelson does not attempt to examine "advertising's impact on a consumer's utility function, holding information constant." In other words, he does not look into the idea whether advertising changes people's tastes. "The change-in-taste idea cannot be effectively tested because no real theory about taste changes has been developed." (p. 752)

strained by the buyer's ability to establish quality (e.g., the style of a dress) by inspection prior to purchase. Nelson (1974) uses his model to predict, for example, the way in which advertising/sales ratios will differ by industry and how the choice of advertising media will vary by industry and finds support for his hypotheses.

In general, investments in reputation, brand name, or goodwill can all be classified as hostages, and the same is true of investment in human and physical capital that is specific to the production of a quality brand. Start-up investments of this kind can bar opportunistic entrepreneurs from entering with the intent of appropriating the quasi-rents of established sellers of quality by marketing counterfeit products.

The problem of enforcing quality arises also in trade between firms – for example, when a producer deals with a distributor and the latter undertakes to supply some of the quality dimensions of the commodity. The provision of quality at the distribution stage can involve demonstration services, maintenance, and the provision of showrooms with all types of a brand. Shirking by retailers can dissipate the quasi-rent of producers, reduce the value of a respected brand name, and remove incentives for producing high-quality commodities. One solution to this dilemma is the vertical integration of firms. It has also been suggested that various market practices, such as resale price maintenance, the tying of the sale of two or more commodities, and the granting of sole distribution rights in a territory, are often designed to create incentives at the distribution stage to maintain quality standards.[9]

Market practices are affected not only by the cost of measuring experience quality but also by the cost of measuring search quality. According to our working hypothesis, only those market practices survive that minimize the effective price to the buyers, including the cost of measuring quality. Although it may be possible in

---

9. For example, see Leffler, Keith B. (1982). "Ambiguous Change in Product Quality." *American Economic Review* 72 (No. 5, December): 956–967; idem (1985). "Quality Assurance: Manufacturer and Retailer Incentive Compatibility." Working paper. Seattle: University of Washington.

analytical exercises and theoretical models to divide a buyer's total cost of a commodity into measurement cost and production cost, the two cost concepts are virtually inseparable in real life. The cost of measurement enters at various points throughout the process of production and distribution. A producer may spend resources, for example, on standardizing her product in order to lower the measurement costs of marketing it or she may reject an "efficient" technology because it is associated with high measurement costs. Barzel (1982, 1985) has provided valuable insights into the role of measurement costs in the organization of markets.[10] The remainder of this section is based on Barzel's contributions.

When a commodity that has variable quality is traded, the costs of measurement can be substantial. The seller needs to establish the quality level of the good in order to price it, and the buyer may want to measure the product again to verify that it is of the asserted quality. But, other things being equal, only arrangements that minimize the cost of measurement are likely to pass through the filter of competition.

The survival hypothesis implies that measurement will be undertaken by that party to exchange who has easy access to information and lower costs of measurement, provided that incentives to cheat are curbed and trust is established. The survival hypothesis also suggests that, other things being equal, quality will be measured at points in the process of production, exchange, and consumption where it can be done with the least expenditure of resources.

Barzel argues that various market practices and social institutions have emerged because they create disincentives for cheating and free riding, and make it optimal from the individual viewpoint of both buyers and sellers to avoid excessive measurement and accept arrangements that result in a lower effective price to buyers.

---

10. Barzel, Yoram (1982). "Measurement Costs and the Organization of Markets." *Journal of Law and Economics 25* (April): 27–48; idem (1985). "Transaction Costs: Are They Just Costs?" *Journal of Institutional and Theoretical Economics 141* (No. 1): 4–16.

These practices and institutions include warranties, professional certification, share contracts, offers to buy a pig in a poke, state-imposed requirements to withdraw dairy products prior to a certain date, brand names, and limits on advertising by physicians.

In trade with heterogeneous commodities, such as apples, measurement or sorting can often be done more efficiently by sellers than buyers. A seller may enjoy economies of scale in measurement relative to individual buyers, and in situations where one seller deals with many buyers, the seller will sort each item only once whereas the buyers will sort each item at least once. Sorting by buyers can therefore give rise to excessive measurement.

Consider the following arrangement which is designed to avoid excessive measurement.[11] A merchant sorts his apples into several categories, each carrying a different price according to the quality of the apples, but within each category are apples of varying quality. Therefore, the value of some of the apples is greater than their price, and the value of others is less than their price. The choice of the buyers is constrained: They are not allowed to choose apples from within each class (the apples are sold in sealed containers). Finally, the degree of sorting is such that this arrangement provides the consumers with apples of various average levels of quality at the lowest possible cost to them (including their own measurement costs), and the cost of providing finer sorting (and less variability in quality) than this is greater than the additional satisfaction. Other market practices, such as finer sorting by the seller or sorting by buyers, will then fail to pass the survival test of market competition among sorting arrangements, and our merchant has stumbled on an equilibrium sorting scheme.

Goods and services cannot always be sold in sealed containers, and individual buyers may find it to their advantage to free-ride and try to pick highly valued items when a heterogeneous product is offered at a single price. Rushing or waiting to acquire unpriced quality will result in the dissipation of value – for example, in the case of heterogeneous theater seats, restaurant tables, or hotel

---

11. Barzel (1982) [op. cit., note 10], pp. 28–32.

rooms, which are offered at a single price. In extreme cases, high costs of sorting and unconstrained sorting can make a commodity unmarketable, and under certain circumstances the net output of society can be increased by *limiting the choices of buyers*.

Sorting by seller is a workable arrangement if she can convince the buyer that he is making a random choice from an acceptable distribution. The buyer must not believe that the seller has strong incentives to cheat or that fellow buyers have the opportunity to pick unpriced quality. Various market practices can bring this about. If a buyer observes that a seller has invested in a brand name, in advertising, or in reputation, that her business depends on repeated dealings with customers, that minimum professional standards are enforced by a third party, then he can take these factors to signal an acceptable quality distribution of the goods and services traded. Picking and choosing by buyers can be prevented if a seller suppresses information. Barzel suggests that this is often practiced by dealers of used cars who refuse to give detailed information about the cars in their lots. Information can also be suppressed by selling goods in nontransparent packaging or by forbidding professionals to advertise their individual merits.

Sometimes measurement by buyer can minimize the effective price of a product to a consumer – for example, in the case of many durable consumer goods (experience goods) where measurement is a costless by-product of use. The use of warranties may then be the equilibrium method of measurement. Warranties guarantee the buyer minimum quality and discourage measurement at the point of exchange. When the cost to sellers of detecting opportunistic behavior by the holders of warranties is high, they may no longer be a competitive market practice, but that outcome depends on the cost of other forms of measurement (e.g., at the point of exchange).

7.3. Measurement costs and the organization of labor markets: forced labor

The study of labor markets is a separate branch of economics because of the human factor: Owners of labor services are inseparable from their human capital. Admittedly, the problems of shirking, moral hazard, and, in general, opportunistic behavior are present in all markets, and the owner of any physical input, who rents it out, cares about conditions of use to the extent that they affect the value of the asset. But these problems are particularly acute in the labor market. People's incentive to work for unrelated others tends to be weak, and working conditions are valued even when they do not affect the market value of the worker's human capital.

From a worker's standpoint, the optimal employment package is multidimensional and involves not only a price (e.g., a wage or a share in output), but also working conditions, location, and other factors, and optimizing individuals determine simultaneously their supply of labor and their consumption of commodities, leisure, and conditions of work. Furthermore, the supply of labor to a firm has many dimensions and varies not only with time (e.g., hours of work) but also with intensity and quality of effort. All this suggests that the measurement and enforcement costs of labor contracts can be high, and that the structure of contracts in the labor market is an important determinant of economic outcomes. In this section we do not seek to review the extensive literature on contracts in the labor market but use the special case of slavery to illustrate the implications of positive transaction costs and the measurement problem for the organization of labor markets.

According to Coase's theorem, the ownership of valuable rights to economic assets tends to gravitate toward individuals who value those rights most, irrespective of the initial assignment of entitlements, provided that the exchange of rights is not blocked by high transaction costs or legal restrictions. Now, what does Coase's law suggest about the ownership of human capital? Can human capital be more valuable to someone other than the person who embodies it? If the members of group A are given full property rights over individuals in group B, is the arrangement likely to be Pareto stable in the long run, or will the Bs buy back the rights to their human capital?

Elementary economic reasoning suggests that in the long run

the institution of slavery is inviable economically. The argument runs as follows. The economic value of owning a slave, his market price, is measured by the present value of the slave's output minus the present value of the cost of maintaining him (his productive consumption). As a slave receives only a fraction of his marginal product, enough to cover productive consumption, he has fewer incentives to work hard than if he were to internalize his entire marginal product as free workers do. Therefore, a slave who has the option to buy his freedom could, by working hard, afford the price and possibly also raise his consumption above the physical minimum. This argument assumes (1) that high agency costs make it possible for slaves to engage in opportunistic behavior and control their work effort within limits; (2) that high costs of contracting, such as enforcement costs, do *not* prevent slaves from negotiating their freedom; and (3) that ex-slaves can find work where their pay depends directly on their effort.

But we must also allow for the fact that a master can largely ignore the leisure preferences of his slaves and drive them to work longer hours than free workers would normally choose to work. In order to compensate his former master and improve his own material living standards, a freeman must work as many hours as a slave and/or harder than a slave.

Consider next how this analysis is affected by the introduction of zero monitoring costs, which make it impossible for slaves to shirk on the job.[12] The masters can now ignore the preferences of their slaves for both work intensity and work hours. A slave can still afford to buy his freedom, but he must now work both long hours and intensely, and retain only a small share of his output or enough to cover productive consumption. The net gain to the freeman is equal to the satisfaction of being free, but his consumption and work effort is the same as in slavery. But to gain

12. For a general equilibrium model of a slave economy of the traditional neo-classical variety, see Bergstrom, T. (1971). "On the Existence and Optimality of Competitive Equilibrium for a Slave Economy." *Review of Economic Studies* 38: 23–36.

freedom is clearly a Pareto improvement, and only high costs of contracting for manumission can protect the institution of slavery in the short run. In the long run, market arrangements tend to erode high contracting costs.[13]

Fenoaltea (1984) has suggested that the above analysis neglects the possibility that pain incentives may stimulate higher levels of productivity than ordinary rewards.[14] When the physical integrity of a person is directly threatened, the threat can give rise to anxiety, brute effort, and higher levels of productivity than free workers can hope to reach, or so the argument goes. If we also assume that the fear of defaulting on manumission contracts and being returned to slavery is an imperfect substitute for a direct application of pain incentives, then the initial assignment of rights to human capital matters, even in a Coasian world of zero transaction costs. Hence slavery can be Pareto stable in the long run.

Fenoaltea's argument is illustrated in Figure 7.2.[15] Line GP_s maps the value of output per day as a function of hours worked for a representative pain-driven slave. As the hours of work are increased, a point is reached where the slave's marginal product begins to fall and eventually becomes negative. Line GP_f represents output per day for the same person if he were a freeman and drove himself as hard as he possibly could. The NP_s line shows

13. We have ignored the possibility that slave owners may enjoy economies of scale in production (including household production, such as child care and cooking), which might put freemen at a disadvantage and raise the price of freedom beyond what they could afford. The economies-of-scale argument is valid only if high transaction costs prevent freemen from contracting to set up comparable forms of organization as those of their masters. For a careful discussion of the economics of slavery, see Engerman, Stanley L. (1973). "Some Considerations Relating to Property Rights in Man." *Journal of Economic History 33* (No. 1, March): 43–65; idem (1986). "Slavery and Emancipation in Comparative Perspective: A Look at Some Recent Debates." *Journal of Economic History 46* (No. 2, June): 317–339.
14. Fenoaltea, Stefano (1984). "Slavery and Supervision in Comparative Perspective: A Model." *Journal of Economic History 44* (No. 3, September): 635–668.
15. Figure 7.2 is based on Barzel, Yoram (1977). "An Economic Analysis of Slavery." *Journal of Law and Economics 20* (April): 87–110. See p. 90.

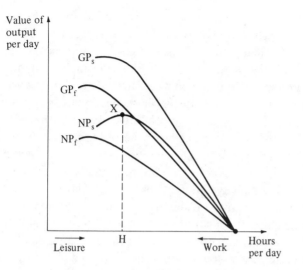

Figure 7.2. The productivity of slaves and freemen.

the slave's net product, which is found by subtracting his maintenance cost (productive consumption) from the gross product. Note that productive consumption is a positive function of the work effort, including the hours of work.

A slave owner will pick point X on the NP_s curve, and thus determine the slave's hours of work and hours of leisure per day. Point X is chosen because it represents the largest net output that the slave can yield. If the master were to rent the slave, he would demand a rent per day equal to XH, assuming that the renter were responsible for the upkeep of the slave. And, if the slave were sold, his price would equal the discounted sum of all the XHs over the remaining workdays of his life.

It is clear from Figure 7.2 that a freeman could not afford his price. His net product is represented by line NP_f, and it is lower than NP_s because he is not driven by pain incentives. As the lines are drawn, the net output of a freeman will always be less than XH, even if he worked more hours than a slave does.

We shall return to the question of pain incentives below, but let us now consider whether unpleasant working conditions could contribute to the long-term viability of slavery in a Coasian model. Superficially, this may appear to be the case. A firm employing free labor in activities that are singularly filthy and unpleasant must pay a compensating differential on wages in order to attract workers, whereas another firm employing slaves need not compensate for the disutility of the employment conditions. Hence, firms using slaves could put firms using wage labor out of business.

However, disagreeable working conditions do not make slavery a Pareto stable organization in the long run, unless there are insurmountable productivity differentials between slaves and free labor due to pain incentives. If the productivity of freemen is the same as the productivity of slaves, slaves could afford to buy their freedom and would prefer to do so. A freeman seeking employment in the disagreeable occupation would have to transfer all his surplus above subsistence to his former master, and, although he would enjoy freedom, there would be no compensation for unpleasant working conditions. In this instance, freemen gain freedom, but there is no improvement in their living standards and conditions of work.

Finally, if we still assume zero monitoring costs, certain restrictions on property rights could make slavery economically viable. A strict ban against manumission gives a competitive edge to firms who use slave labor, as they can limit their labor costs to productive consumption and work their laborers longer and harder than free workers choose to do for a comparable pay. Under these circumstances, the theory of pain incentives is not needed to explain the survival of slavery.[16]

We are now ready to examine more closely how positive transaction costs, including monitoring costs, affect the relative advantage of slavery as a form of productive organization. Our conclusion is that transaction costs tend to reduce the relative advantage of slavery because various agency problems and asso-

16. See Bergstrom (1971), op. cit., note 12.

ciated costs are either particularly severe or unique to the master–slave relationship. Consider the following four cost items:

1. The costs of controlling the consumption of slaves for the purpose of maximizing their productivity. A problem arises here because slaves maximize their utility without due regard for the relationship between consumption and productivity, and may have preferences for commodities, such as alcohol, that can adversely affect their capacity to work.[17]

2. The costs associated with feigned illness and self-inflicted damages, and the costs of preventing such behavior, which is motivated by a desire of unfree labor to reduce the work load.

3. Costs arising from a propensity of slaves to cause intentional damage to outputs and cooperating inputs, a tendency rooted in the anger and ill will of the enslaved and their demand for the leisure that results from breakdowns in production.

4. The costs of monitoring the behavior of slaves and enforcing the condition of slavery in order to prevent uprisings and flights.

The agency problems that arise in the master–slave relationship consume resources and lower the net product that accrues to the owner. Various policing or monitoring costs may wipe out whatever productivity gains are associated with pain incentives, and the use of rewards to enlist more cooperation from the slaves also reduces the owner's net gain. All this could reverse the position of the net product curves of Figure 7.2.

Fenoaltea (1984) theorizes that slavery is a viable form of labor organization only if it is based on pain incentives, and that pain incentives enhance productivity only in some activities and not in others. According to Fenoaltea's thesis, pain and anxiety can create

---

17. See Barzel (1977) [op. cit., note 15] on the "policing of consumption" (pp. 97–98).

brute effort, but anxiety also reduces the quality of work as the harassed worker is clumsy, unimaginative, and ill-willed. Furthermore, production technologies vary with respect to their effort and care intensity. Care-intensive activities tend to be capital intensive, whereas effort-intensive activities are land- (natural resource) intensive. Consequently, the comparative advantages of forced labor are found in effort- and land-intensive activities, where the condition of slavery can be enforced at a relatively low cost, for example, by working the slaves in gangs.

Fenoaltea argues that these conditions are met in various lines of agriculture, mining, stonecutting, and public works that use primitive technologies. The right conditions were present on the slave plantations in the American South whose primary crops, such as corn and cotton, were annual plants "where next year's harvest was unaffected by this year's carelessness,"[18] but this was not the case in ancient Rome, where the vines and the olive trees of the slave plantations were capital- and care-intensive. The spontaneous disappearance of slavery in antiquity has long puzzled and fascinated historians. Fenoaltea has suggested an explanation, namely that the production process on the Roman plantations was capital- and care-intensive, a setting where pain incentives are relatively ineffective and slavery is not a Pareto-stable organization.

In real life, the costs of contracting for manumission tend to be high, for example, because of constraints in the capital market, and it is also common that the economic opportunities open to freemen are relatively restricted by law and custom. When these barriers to exit coincide with an ample supply of slaves and low prices, for example, in the wake of a victorious war, slavery may spill over into care-intensive activities where this form of organization has no general economic advantage. Fenoaltea's (1984) model suggests the following hypotheses regarding the dynamics of slavery:

18. Fenoaltea (1984) [op. cit., note 14], p. 644.

1. Slavery will appear first and disappear last in the effort-intensive sector where pain incentives are appropriate.
2. When slavery spills over into care- and capital-intensive sectors, there will be reliance on ordinary rewards to mitigate problems of agency. In particular, the harshness of treatment will vary inversely with the care- and capital-intensity of an activity.
3. Manumission will be activity specific, with the highest frequency in the most care- and capital-intensive activities.

Fenoaltea offers support for his model by drawing on a wide range of historical examples. However, the experience of slavery is as varied as are the constraints facing different societies. The appropriate structure of property rights can make almost any form of unfree labor viable. In fact, Fenoaltea (1984) cites an interesting example of this diversity. Roman law put strict limits on legal agency, which caused difficulties for big landlords who were required to contract in person with their tenants. But there was a loophole: Slaves were nonpersons under Roman law and seen as an extension of their masters. Therefore, it was legitimate for men of property to use slaves as their agents, a practice that gave rise to the anomaly of slave agents supervising free tenants. In other words, because the structure of property rights effectively limited the right of agency, "an effective substitute for the nonhuman person [the firm] or the legal agent was found in the human non-person [the slave], who was legally but his master's instrument."[19]

Our discussion of the economic logic of slavery would be incomplete without a mention of Domar's well-known 1970 article, "The Causes of Slavery and Serfdom: A Hypothesis."[20] In his article, Domar makes the important point that a necessary condition for using slaves in production is that their marginal product

19. Ibid., p. 657. The bracketed words are added.
20. Domar, Evsey D. (1970). "The Causes of Slavery or Serfdom: A Hypothesis." *Journal of Economic History* 30 (March): 18–32.

be greater than their productive consumption (the cost of subsistence of a slave, in his words). In agrarian societies this condition implies that the ratio of land to labor is high and that population expansion does not put too strong pressure on limited resources. In extreme cases, the land/labor ratio can be so high that the price of land is zero.

The strong version of Domar's hypothesis, which is based on a model that considers only two factors of production, labor and land, runs as follows: "Of the three elements of an agricultural structure relevant here – free land, free peasants, and non-working landowners – any two elements but *never all three can exist simultaneously.*"[21]

Historically, of course, free land has not always given rise to slavery but, on the contrary, has often given the working man a special advantage. Domar recognizes that the agricultural structure found in reality depends on variables that are excluded from his model, namely political variables, and that free land is neither a sufficient nor a necessary condition for the existence of slavery.

When the agency costs of a particular organization seem to be unreasonably high relative to other forms of organization, the transaction-cost approach suggests that we look for constraints or offsetting benefits at some unexpected margin. For example, in our discussion of the open corporation in Chapter 6, it was concluded that competition in the markets for capital and for managers constrained the potentially very high agency costs of open corporations, and also that the corporate form offered special advantages for raising capital on a large scale. In this section, we have taken a look at slavery as a productive organization. As the condition of enslavement suggests severe disincentive and measurement problems, we looked for countervailing benefits and discussed Fenoaltea's hypothesis that the benefits are found in enhancement of productivity which pain incentives can generate in certain types of activity. The last word has not been written about slavery, and we may agree or disagree with Fenoaltea's

21. Ibid., p. 21.

thesis, but it is an important example of the new way of thinking about the logic of economic organization suggested by Neoinstitutional Economics. We now proceed to an examination of contractual relations in agriculture.

7.4. Transaction costs and contractual arrangements in agriculture

In the two previous sections we have applied Neoinstitutional Economics to the market for consumer goods and to the labor market and sought to explain the logic of various market practices in terms of transaction costs. Now we turn our attention to a vast and important subject, contractual arrangements in agriculture.

Various contractual arrangements involving rights to the use of land in agricultural production were, of course, the predominant forms of economic organization in the preindustrial phase of modern economies and still are in most developing countries. As our topic is extensive and the literature voluminous, we limit the discussion to two issues: the survival for centuries of the *open-field system* as the dominating form of organization in agriculture in the Northern European plain, in spite of the apparent inefficiencies of this arrangement; and, similarly, the persistence of *share contracts* at different times and places, an arrangement that many economists since Adam Smith have found inferior to other available forms of organization.

The theoretical debates surrounding the economic logic (or lack thereof) of the open-field system and share contracting are still unresolved, and we shall not seek to settle the disputes here. Rather, we use contributions by various scholars in this area to illustrate how the NIE approaches the study of economic organization. There are three elements to this approach.

First, it is assumed as a *working rule* that low-cost organizations tend to supersede high-cost ones (a point that has characterized the thinking of prominent economists from Marx to Alchian).

Second, when high-cost organizations appear to persist and it seems that reorganization would increase net output, we search for hidden benefits at unexpected margins. Such offsetting benefits may involve a reduction in supervision costs or an increase in output in a related activity when a nexus of contracts ties several activities, or a host of other factors. Costly behavior is also constrained by contractual stipulations. Usually, a contract contains a number of terms in addition to those stipulating price and quantity. A careful examination of the structure of a contract may reveal that it contains terms that constrain wasteful behavior. Finally, if the search for hidden benefits or contractual constraints is in vain, we search for political constraints that block the rearrangement of property rights. It is recognized that the polity may not adopt output-maximizing property rights if the new structure might cause *distributional losses* for those who control the state. And, according to Neoinstitutional Economics, high (transaction) costs of collective action are the principal reason why the members of a community cannot agree on new rules that would increase the community's aggregate output.[22]

With this in mind we are ready for a look at the open-field system.

7.4.1. The open-field system

For a long time the puzzle of the open-field system has fascinated economists, although analytical progress had to wait for the development of transaction-costs analysis.[23] The puzzle relates

---

22. Again, note that the concept of inefficiency becomes useless when the neoclassical model is taken to its logical conclusion and all costs and benefits are accounted for. The cost of collective action is a real, not imaginary, cost. If such costs block a structural change in property rights, it is not correct to talk about inefficient property rights. According to the Pareto criteria, changes must be voluntary, and it follows logically from the assumptions of the neoclassical model that all adjustments where benefits exceed costs will take place. Note that an involuntary change in property rights can lead to a very large increase in total net output for a community, but involuntary changes cannot be evaluated in terms of the neoclassical concept of efficiency and the Pareto criteria.

23. A pioneering application of transaction costs to economic organization in agriculture was made by North and Thomas (1971). North, Douglass C., and Thomas, Robert P. (1971). "The Rise and Fall of the Manorial System: A

to the costs associated with the scattering of the strips cultivated by each household in an open-field village, costs that appeared to be both real and unnecessary.

The organization of the open-field system, which dominated agriculture in Northern Europe through the Middle Ages and beyond, was not uniform, but the typical features were the following:[24] The open-field village was a collective form of organization where the basic unit of decision was the family. Each peasant household cultivated a number of unfenced, scattered strips often less than an acre each. The household was subject to detailed central regulations, and after the harvest an open field served as a common field for the herds of the villagers, which were managed jointly.

There is a long tradition for describing open fields as a costly form of organization. Consider the following characterization of the system by McCloskey (1972):

> The scattering of each man's holdings in dozens of small strips had direct costs in waste of time moving from one strip to another and in the disincentive to enterprise created by the spill-over of one man's sloth or malice onto his neighbors' strips. Furthermore, scattered strips implied common grazing on the fallow, with consequent over-use of the land and the spread of animal disease. In turn, common grazing implied the subjugation of each man to communal decisions on when grazing should give way to crops and what crops should be planted, regardless of his land's comparative advantage.[25]

Theoretical Model." *Journal of Economic History 31* (No. 4, December): 777–803.

24. Pp. 1–5 in Fenoaltea, Stefano (1986). "The Economics of the Common Fields: The State of the Debate." A paper prepared for the *International Symposium on Property Rights, Organizational Forms and Economic Behavior*. Uppsala: The Swedish Collegium for Advanced Studies in the Social Sciences. See also new, extended version: idem (1987). "Transaction Costs, Whig History, and the Common Fields." Working paper. Princeton: Institute for Advanced Study.

25. McCloskey, Donald N. (1972). "The Enclosure of Open Fields: Preface to a

McCloskey catalogs these objections in an article that is a preface to his program of extensive research into the enclosure of open fields and its impact on the efficiency of English agriculture in the eighteenth century. Although McCloskey's later work revealed that many of these objections were invalid (e.g., overgrazing was limited by regulation, and labor was not wasted by excessive travel), he did conclude that open fields were indeed inefficient *for the narrow purpose of cultivation.*

The classic open-field system disappeared in England in the early 1800s but survived into the twentieth century on the continent of Europe. In many countries of the Third World, the scattering of strips is still very common and represents to many experts of economic development a regrettable practice for the very poor – the throwing away of food.[26]

Below we look at the work of three economists – McCloskey, Dahlman, and Fenoaltea – who have sought to explain the economic logic of scattering. Each author arrives at a different solution to the puzzle, but their explanations are not mutually exclusive and in each case the answer depends explicitly or implicitly on transaction costs. All three authors reject the possibility that high transaction costs of rearranging property rights to land might explain the persistence of scattering. Through the centuries, they argue, it should have been possible for the owners of land to find opportunities to consolidate their holdings if there were strong incentives to do so, and a series of small steps toward consolidation would have transformed the system. Transaction costs, although

Study of Its Impact on the Efficiency of English Agriculture in the Eighteenth Century." *Journal of Economic History 32* (March): 15–35.

26. "A 1969 survey team of the Asian Development Bank, noting the prevalence of scattering in Japan, Korea, Indonesia, Thailand, Pakistan, and India, argued that 'the basic cause of operational inefficiency on small farms is the poor farm layout. ... A farm of one hectare may be divided into more than a dozen small fields.' " Pp. 11–12 in McCloskey, Donald N. (1986). "The Open Fields of England: Rent, Risk, and the Rate of Interest, 1300–1815." University of Iowa: Departments of Economics and of History. Forthcoming in Galenson, David, ed. *In Search of Historical Economics: Market Behavior in Past Times.* Cambridge: Cambridge University Press.

high in the short run, would not have been an obstacle in the long run. Therefore, the explanation of why cultivators persist in using a costly form of organization and sacrificing agricultural output must be sought in some offsetting benefits.

McCloskey's answer is that scattering represents behavior toward risk: The strips were scattered to insure the farmer against crop failure.[27] By sampling the different types of soil and crops of his village, the individual farmer diversified his portfolio, so to speak. If production was too specialized, then output failure involving a certain crop or a type of soil could bring disaster to his family.

The reader may ask whether the conditions of production within a typical open-field village were variable enough to permit a reduction in the variance of output by scattering. McCloskey, whose research deals mainly with English open fields, claims that the conditions were variable enough. The typical open-field village in England was about two square miles in area, and crops could vary enough over that small area to make it desirable to hold a diverse portfolio of strips, according to his evidence. For example: "The average width of the English hailstorm is two or three hundred yards, cutting a swath of damaged grain through a consolidated holding 300 yards on a side."[28]

A farmer who scatters his strips receives a lower average income than a comparable farmer who consolidates his strips, but scattering reduces the variance of the income. Therefore, a risk-averse farmer can increase his welfare by sacrificing some output (through scattering) in return for more certainty, a smaller likelihood of disastrous crop failure.

27. McCloskey, Donald N. (1986), op. cit., note 26; idem (1975). "The Persistence of English Common Fields," and "The Economics of Enclosure: A Market Analysis." In Parker, W. N., and Jones, E. L., eds. *European Peasants and Their Markets: Essays in Agrarian Economic History*. Princeton: Princeton University Press, pp. 73–119; idem (1976). "English Open Fields as Behavior Toward Risk." In Uselding, Paul, ed. *Research in Economic History*, Vol. 1. Greenwich, Conn.: JAI Press, pp. 124–171.
28. McCloskey (1986) [op. cit., note 26], pp. 48–69.

McCloskey's explanation that the open-field system was a manifestation of behavior toward risk requires that other less expensive methods of insurance were unavailable. High transaction costs must have precluded other forms of insurance. In this context we should note that scattering stabilizes only the output and consumption of *individual households* but not the output of the open-field *village as a whole*. Stabilization could be reached without scattering and *without sacrificing output* by storage and trade among the villagers. Indeed, McCloskey (1986) is aware of this possibility: "The one sort of alternative insurance we can know about is storage of grain."[29]

Was scattering a cheaper way of insuring against disaster than storage of grain? After reviewing the evidence, McCloskey concludes that, although the storage of grain was not unknown, it was generally more expensive than scattering. He also argues that the cost of storage fell dramatically in modern times, primarily due to a fall in the interest rate, but "most of the cost of storage was the interest rate, that is to say the opportunity cost of tying up 6 shillings in a quarter of wheat for a month."[30]

McCloskey derives the marginal cost of storage from the monthly rise in the price of grain in the months following the harvest. With free entry into the storage business, the marginal benefit of storage (the price rise) should in equilibrium equal the marginal cost of storage. McCloskey roughly estimates that English farmers lost about 10 percent of their output by scattering, whereas the costs of storage on an annual basis amounted to one third or more of the harvest.

If the McCloskey thesis is correct, then the costly scattering in the open-field villages of England was a substitute for the even more costly capital and insurance markets at a time when high transaction costs either prevented the development of such markets or strictly limited the gains from trade.[31] In our times the same

29. Ibid., p. 70.
30. Ibid., p. 73.
31. The McCloskey insurance–high-cost-of-storage thesis has been criticized by

argument seems to be consistent with scattering in some of the developing countries. McCloskey also argues that from the sixteenth century, technological progress lowered output variation in English agriculture and thereby reduced the demand for insurance. Part-time work outside agriculture is another way of self-insuring, and such opportunities became more common in the seventeenth and eighteenth centuries.[32]

Dahlman (1980) is another major contributor to the study of open fields.[33] He also appeals to high transaction costs in solving the puzzle of scattering, but the missing market is not for insurance but grazing rights.

Dahlman takes as his premise that there were *economies of scale in grazing*: A single herdsman could in many cases supervise the entire village herd. But there were obstacles in the way of a joint management of the herd if individual holdings were consolidated because consolidation put individual farmers in a strategic position to hold up the entire village by refusing to join in common grazing except on exorbitant terms. The solution to this dilemma was the introduction of scattering, which made independent grazing impossible and removed the strategic advantage of individual households.

The bargaining strength of individual households can be weak even in villages with consolidated plots. The threat of not joining in common grazing is empty when the loss to the noncooperating farmer of not joining is greater than the loss to the rest of the village if he does not join. That situation can arise if the economies

Fenoaltea on theoretical and empirical grounds, and McCloskey has responded. See Fenoaltea, S. (1976). "Risk, Transaction Costs, and the Organization of Medieval Agriculture." *Explorations in Economic History 13* (No. 2, April): 129–151. McCloskey (1977) responded in "Fenoaltea on Open Fields: A Comment." *Explorations in Economic History 14* (No. 4, October): 402–404. Fenoaltea (1977) rejoined with "Fenoaltea on Open Fields: A Reply." *Explorations in Economic History 14* (No. 4, October): 405–410. See also McCloskey (1986), op. cit., note 26.

32. McCloskey (1986), pp. 74–75.
33. Dahlman, C. J. (1980). *The Open Field System and Beyond: A Property Rights Analysis of an Economic Institution.* Cambridge: Cambridge University Press.

of scale in grazing are (nearly) exhausted before the last villagers join with their animals. The gains to the cooperative of having the marginal farmer join are minimal when the economies of scale are exhausted, whereas the costs of grazing to an outsider are high.[34]

A third student of the open fields, Fenoaltea, seeks the logic of scattering in the potentially high transaction costs of managing large farms. Fenoaltea views the open-field village as a large operational unit that combines the advantages of family farming with the economies of large-scale farming. This time the culprit is the high transaction costs in the market for labor service in agriculture. The Fenoaltea thesis also differs from those of McCloskey and Dahlman because for him scattering represents *an outright efficient way of organizing cultivation*.[35]

According to Fenoaltea, the economic logic of the open-field village is best understood if the village is seen as one economic unit. The unit economizes on the cost of supervision, a notorious problem of large-scale farming, by designating the family farm or the peasant household as the basic decision unit. This form of decentralization makes it possible to rely on self-enforcement to a large degree, and on the inexpensive monitoring of small groups of agricultural workers. Various externalities that accompany common ownership and decentralization are then internalized, to a point, through regulation and central management.

The economies of large-scale farming on the European plain depended on the ability of large and diversified farms to move the labor force and other variable inputs around and assign them to work where their marginal product was highest, but the optimal allocation of these resources varied unpredictably, owing to rain, changes in temperatures, and other factors. In Fenoaltea's model, the open-field village reproduced the advantages of the big estate

34. This point has been made by Fenoaltea. See Fenoaltea's (1982) review of Dahlman's (1980) book, in *Speculum 57*: 125–128; and Fenoaltea (1986), op. cit., note 24.

35. See Fenoaltea, 1976, 1977, 1982, and 1986, op. cit., notes 31, 31, 34, and 24, respectively.

by assigning each cultivator, big or small, individual shares, each collection of strips ideally representing the whole range of available quality of land. The individual peasant was then able to make the same marginal adjustments with his variable inputs as the manager of a large estate would do.

A recurrent theme of this section of the book is that economic organizations evolve to economize on transaction costs. Our discussion above gives only a summary account of the sophisticated research and reasoning of McCloskey, Dahlman, and Fenoaltea, but we hope to have made the point that the economic logic of the open-field system can be understood only in terms of transaction costs. The discussion of *institutional change* is reserved for the book's last section, but we might add here a short note on the demise of English open fields. About half of the agricultural land in England was enclosed in 1700, but early in the 1800s nearly all the land had been enclosed. This was accomplished by some 5000 acts of Parliament and at least an equal number of voluntary agreements. The enclosure effort peaked during the sixty years from 1760 to 1820.[36] The three authors agree that the open-field village was no longer a viable economic organization in England at the time of the enclosure movement, whatever had been the system's original advantage. The high costs of rearranging property in land and the enforcement costs, for example, due to fencing, suggest that those who carried the costs expected substantial gain or at least normal return on their investment.

The cost of enclosing has been estimated very roughly to total £2 per acre based on the English price level prior to the inflation of the Napoleonic Wars. Some 14 million acres were enclosed after 1700.[37] "The return to enclosure was high: an expenditure of £2 per acre (ignoring here transfer costs) yielded an increased rent accruing to the landlord of 10 shillings

36. McCloskey (1972), p. 15; idem (1986) [op. cit., notes 25 and 26], p. 8.
37. McCloskey (1972), p. 34.

in each year following, or a rate of return of 25 percent per year."[38]

However, the return on investment in enclosure need not come from an increase in output, as many authors have concluded. The gain may consist of a transfer of wealth to the investor through the seizure of the property rights of others. In the words of one writer: "Enclosure (when all the sophistications are allowed for) was a plain enough case of class robbery."[39] The robbery hypothesis receives support from Allen (1982) in an econometric study of actual inputs and outputs of open and enclosed land in England. Allen concludes that the major consequence of the enclosure of open fields in eighteenth-century England was not to raise agricultural output but to redistribute existing income.[40]

If the transfer-of-wealth explanation is correct, then the costs to the "robbers" of using Parliament and other political institutions to bring about the enclosure, plus the cost of fencing and other enforcement expenditure, must have been less than the costs of alternative ways of transferring wealth between the social groups in question. Alternative ways of transferring wealth might be, for example, regular taxation or a private agreement between the parties on a wealth transfer, both avoiding the deadweight loss of enforcing enclosed fields.

Finally, if we accept that open fields had at one point a relative advantage as an organization but lost that advantage toward the beginning of the eighteenth century or earlier, we need an explanation of what eventually undermined the system. One explanation suggested by Dahlman and Fenoaltea is that technical change and expanding markets strained the decision process in the open-field village. The cost of reaching an agreement among poorly educated peasants on an optimal strategy in the face of technical change

38. Ibid., p. 35.
39. Thompson, E. P. (1963). *The Making of the English Working Class*. New York: Random House, p. 218. Cited in McCloskey (1972), p. 29.
40. Allen, Robert C. (1982). "The Efficiency and Distributional Consequences of Eighteenth Century Enclosures." *Economic Journal 92* (December): 937–953.

became too high and put the open-fields system at a relative disadvantage. The village was replaced by a smaller unit that was better able to adjust to changing times, namely the capitalistic farm.

7.4.2. Sharecropping and the contractual mix in agriculture

Sharecropping or share tenancy is a traditional form of organization in agriculture where a landlord leases his land to a cultivator in return for a share of the crops. The landlord may also provide other inputs, including entrepreneurial expertise, or the tenant may supply all inputs except land.

Sharecropping is another example of the puzzling persistence of seemingly inefficient organizations. Economists have long characterized share contracts as inefficient, inferior to wage contracts and fixed rental contracts. The critics include both Adam Smith and Alfred Marshall, and in our times there are economists who link economic stagnation in Third World countries to the prevalence of share tenancy in their agriculture.[41] In this instance, agricultural communities, which in many cases are very poor, seem to sacrifice food rather than introduce new contractual forms, such as wage labor.

The paradoxical status of share tenancy in conventional analysis is illustrated by the model in Figure 7.3, which shows the alternatives open to a landlord who faces an exogenous rental share, r, and an exogenous wage rate, w. If the landowner decides to hire a laborer at wage rate w (or work the fields himself at an opportunity cost of w dollars per hour), he would maximize his

---

41. A summary of the traditional view of sharecropping is found in Johnson, D. G. (1950). "Resource Allocation Under Share Contracts." *Journal of Political Economy* 58 (No. 1, February): 111–123; and Cheung, S. N. S. (1969a). *The Theory of Share Tenancy*. Chicago: University of Chicago Press. Alfred Marshall's position on sharecropping was ambiguous. McCloskey points out that much of the modern position on sharecropping, which takes account of monitoring costs, is contained in Marshall, Alfred (1920). *Principles of Economics*, 8th ed. London: Macmillan, pp. 644–645. See McCloskey (1985). *The Applied Theory of Price*, 2nd ed. New York: Macmillan, p. 493.

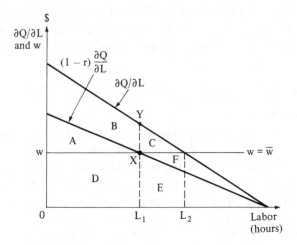

Figure 7.3. The inefficiency of sharecropping in a neoclassical model.

wealth by extending the use of labor (the only variable input in the model) until its marginal cost is equal to the marginal yield. This occurs at L_2 hours of work, where the rent of the land is equal to blocks $[A + B + C]$ in the diagram, and the (explicit or implicit) wage bill equals $[D + E + F]$.

The landlord can also lease the land to a tenant for a share, r, of the output. An optimizing tenant will equalize his costs and benefits at the margin by adding hours of work until the marginal yield of labor, $[(1 - r) \, \partial Q / \partial L]$, is equal to the wage (the tenant's marginal opportunity cost). In Figure 7.3, the equilibrium labor input is now L_1 hours of work, and the reduction in hours from L_2 in the previous case to L_1 corresponds to a fall in output equal to $[(A + B + C + D + E + F) - (A + B + D)] = [C + E + F]$. Note that the tenant's marginal product at L_1 is greater than marginal cost, w, by the amount YX, which suggests that the share contract arrangement violates the neoclassical marginal conditions for efficiency and causes a loss of net output to society equal to triangle C.

It is also noteworthy that the landlord's rental income has fallen from $[A + B + C]$ under self-cultivation or wage contracts to B when share contracts are used, whereas the tenant earns $[A + D]$ for L_1 hours of work, but receives only D for L_1 hours as a wage laborer. Cheung (1968), in a pioneering contribution, has pointed out that the economic outcome which this model associates with sharecropping cannot represent long-run equilibrium.[42] The logic of economics suggests that contracts that generate lower rents per acre than other arrangements will be avoided by landlords. Similarly, the high earnings of share tenants relative to wage workers represent disequilibrium in the labor market. The market for land is also in disequilibrium. A sharecropper has an incentive to continue leasing more land until its marginal product has been driven to zero, because additional land costs the sharecropper nothing but increases his income by $[(1 - r) \, \partial Q/\partial H]$, where H stands for the amount of land leased by the tenant.[43]

Cheung (1968) argues that equilibrium contracts usually have several dimensions, and the puzzle that share tenancy poses for neoclassical economics can be solved by endogenizing the structure of contracts. In his 1968 article, Cheung endogenizes the following structural variables: r, the rental share; H, the quantity of land per tenant; and L, the amount of labor supplied by the tenant. In Cheung's model, the equilibrium values for r, H, and L are such that net incomes of both landlord and tenant are the same under sharecropping as they are under wage contracts.

Cheung's outcome, which is derived with the *assumption of zero transaction costs*, can be explained in terms of our Figure 7.3. If it is assumed that the equilibrium amount of land, H, has already been determined, then Cheung's solution involves that the share tenant makes a contractual obligation to work L_2 hours (rather than L_1 hours as he would prefer), and r, the landlord's rental share, is adjusted (changing the slope of the $[(1 - r) \, \partial Q/\partial L]$ line)

---

42. See Cheung, S. N. S. (1968). "Private Property Rights and Sharecropping." *Journal of Political Economy 76* (No. 6, December): 1107–1122. See also Cheung (1969a), op. cit., note 41.
43. Note that H is assumed to be constant in Figure 7.3.

until triangles *F* and *A* are equal. At that point, the tenant's earnings under a share contract, $[D + E + A]$, are equal to his earnings under a wage contract, $[D + E + F]$. Furthermore, total output is the same under either, and so is the landlord's share in total output. The two contractual forms are also equivalent to a third type, the fixed rental contract where the equilibrium rent equals $[A + B + C]$.

Cheung's model with zero transaction costs suggests that share contracts need be neither irrational nor inefficient, but the demonstration that various types of contracts can give equivalent outcomes *does not explain why one type is preferred to another or provide a theory of contracts*. A theory of contracts must take account of transaction costs. Cheung (1969b) makes this point clear: "The choice of contractual arrangement is made so as to maximize the gain from risk dispersion subject to the constraint of transaction costs."[44]

Let us consider risk first.[45] Variations in the yield of land due to exogenous factors, such as changes in climatic conditions, are a major source of risk and uncertainty for the cultivator. Contractual arrangements cannot remove output fluctuations caused by random exogenous factors, but they can shift the risk of such fluctuations. The risk of output variations is borne by the landowner in the case of wage contracts that guarantee fixed wages, but by the tenant under fixed-rent contracts. Share contracts share the risk.

It has been suggested that a farmer's attitude toward risk depends on how poor he is, and that the choice of contracts is affected by the individual's degree of risk aversion.[46] A very poor farmer

44. P. 25 in Cheung, S. N. S. (1969b). "Transaction Costs, Risk Aversion, and the Choice of Contractual Arrangements." *Journal of Law and Economics 13* (April): 49–70.
45. The discussion in this section draws on an excellent paper by Amid, M. J. (1986). "The Theory of Sharecropping. A Survey." Paper presented at *The International Symposium on Property Rights, Organizational Forms and Economic Behavior*. Uppsala: Swedish Collegium for Advanced Study in the Social Sciences.
46. Ho, S. P. S. (1976). "Uncertainty and the Choice of Tenure Arrangements:

can ill afford to take risk. For example, if his average income is close to physical subsistence, then a reduction in output by, say, one standard deviation in a bad year can bring starvation (assuming that high costs have prevented storage or insurance). A farmer in this position is likely to avoid fixed-rent tenancy. The situation is more complex when we allow for hybrid contracts. For example, a fixed-rent contract can include an insurance clause whereby the landlord forsakes some of his rent in a bad year. Also note that in some situations of high risk and uncertainty, farmers with great entrepreneurial abilities may do better than the average farmer, and prefer fixed-rent contracts in order to take advantage of their abilities.

Higgs (1973) has developed a model where he shows how changes in the level of risk in an agricultural community affect the *relative importance* of contractual forms.[47] Higgs derives an un-ambiguous relation between the rental mix and the level of risk, given the assumption that landlords and tenants always differ in their aversion to risk. For example, when tenants are more risk-averse than landlords, there is, for a community, a direct relation between the level of risk and the frequency of share rental relative to a fixed-payment rental.

But the sharing of risk can be achieved by mixing elements of wage payments and fixed-rental payments in the same contract. Stiglitz (1974) has shown that a mixed contract can provide any sharing of risk that a pure share contract can do. He concludes that risk alone does not explain the existence of sharecropping.[48]

Some critics of Cheung's (1968) model of sharecropping argue that the enforcement costs of ensuring that the tenant works L_2 hours, rather than only L_1 hours, is likely to be very high, and the model therefore unrealistic. But that very point is made by Cheung

Some Hypotheses." *American Journal of Agricultural Economics 58* (No. 1): 88–92.

47. Higgs, Robert (1973). "Race, Tenure, and Resource Allocation in Southern Agriculture, 1910." *Journal of Economic History 33* (March): 149–169.
48. Stiglitz, Joseph E. (1974). "Incentives and Risk Sharing in Sharecropping." *Review of Economic Studies 41* (No. 2): 219–255.

in his original contribution. It must be remembered that the introduction of enforcement costs influences all forms of contracting. For example, Lucas (1979) points out that wage contracts also involve enforcement costs.[49] By assuming increasing marginal cost of supervision as more labor is hired, Lucas formally established the equilibrium condition for the allocation of land between sharecropping and other forms of cultivation.[50] In short, transaction costs are the key variables for explaining the variation in contractual arrangements in agriculture.

7.4.3. Empirical studies of the contractual mix in agriculture

Empirically, the structure of contracts in agriculture is both complex and variable, and several types of contracts are found even on the same farm. This is evident, for example, from data for the United States, where the Census Bureau started as early as 1880 to ask questions in the decennial census about the contractual form under which farms were operated. Alston and Higgs (1982) have surveyed "what has been learned about the contractual mix in Southern agricultural since the Civil War."[51] Their survey

49. Lucas, R. E. B. (1979). "Sharing, Monitoring, and Incentives: Marshallian Misallocation Reassessed." *Journal of Political Economy 87* (No. 3): 501–521.
50. Lucas (1979) compares a mixed economy of both wage and share contracts with an economy of only wage contracts and finds that the former arrangement provides greater social welfare, when the contractual mix is governed by private incentives. Another result from Lucas's model is the derivation that the incidence of share contracts increases with the cost of monitoring wage labor, and with the labor intensity of the crops. Lucas did not carry out empirical tests of his hypotheses, but he suggests that the model may have a general application because sharecropping belongs to "a wider class of enterprises which might be dubbed joint ventures. Other common forms in this class include both piece-rate labor payment and the joint operation of a subsidiary by parent companies." (p. 520)
51. Alston, Lee J., and Higgs, Robert (1982). "Contractual Mix in Southern Agriculture Since the Civil War: Facts, Hypotheses, and Tests." *Journal of Economic History 42* (No. 2, June): 327–353. Their survey provides important evidence of sophisticated analysis of the economics of contracts by economists working in the late nineteenth and early twentieth centuries. In 1924, a government report published by the Department of Agriculture concluded: "The form of the tenant contract is determined largely by the abilities and willingness

makes clear that our ability to predict in detail the overall structure of contracts is quite limited, but some headway has been made in predicting marginal changes in the contractual mix over time and across geographical areas. The most successful explanatory variables are *proxies representing the cost of contracting*.

The theoretical derivation of the details of contractual structures in agriculture and the empirical testing of such theories represent a complex, perhaps unmanageable, affair. Consider the following five points:

1. An optimal contract will allow for the sharing of risk. The formula for risk sharing will depend on the relative risk aversion of the contracting parties, and the degree of risk varies with crops grown, technology used, geographical area, type of soil, and markets for inputs and outputs.

2. The optimal contract depends on the entrepreneurial abilities of the owner of the labor input, and on his ownership of both human and physical capital, which often is subject to financial constraints.

3. The owner of land must consider the probability of premature termination of the contract by the cultivator – for example, during the harvest season, when the demand for labor is high. Various contractual devices can be used to tie the worker to the land, such as withholding wages until after the harvest.

of the respective parties to supply capital, provide supervision and assume risk." Gray, L. C., and others (1924). "Farm Ownership and Tenancy." In *Yearbook 1923*, Washington D.C.: U.S. Department of Agriculture, p. 586. These early insights seem to have disappeared from economic theory as it became increasingly more mathematical, but were rediscovered in the 1960s and 1970s. Alston and Higgs claim that, in spite of technical extensions, our theoretical understanding of contracts in agriculture has not advanced much in the past half-century, and important contributions have involved primarily econometric testing. They support this assertion by citing two doctoral dissertations, one by Enoch Banks (published in 1905), who "emphasized the interrelation between the incidence of risk and the type of contract," and the other by Robert Brooks (published in 1914), who "stressed the interrelation between the cost of supervising labor and the type of contract." Alston and Higgs (1982), p. 332.

4. The party who supplies the land maximizes her wealth both by securing a large flow of net income and by protecting the resource against premature depreciation caused by careless treatment.

5. If other assets such as draft animals, fertilizers, seeds, and farm machinery are supplied by the landlord, the need for supervision is all the greater, yet there may be economies of scale in supervision when many types of assets are supervised. For example, when a landlord supervises both the uses of his land and various other physical assets, the marginal cost of also supervising the labor input can sometimes be low.[52]

This complexity does not prevent us from studying the *impact on the contractual mix of changes in one or a few variables.* Alston and Higgs (1982) report various tests of hypotheses regarding marginal adjustments in the structure of contracts. For example, there is evidence of a positive relation between the value of land and (1) the frequency of wage contracts relative to sharecropper contracts, and (2) the frequency of sharecropper contracts relative to fixed-rent contracts. The explanation, according to Alston and Higgs, is that valuable land is given much supervision, and the additional cost of supervising labor is relatively low. Hence contractual forms that require relatively intensive supervision of labor are favored, and the landlord avoids problems associated with share contracts, which we illustrated in Figure 7.3. As we would expect, the authors report that the opposite holds true when a great proportion of the work stock is held by labor. The proportion held by labor is positively associated with the relative frequency of fixed-rent contracts.

The marginal cost of supervision should increase with the size of the land unit, if the supply of reliable supervisors (such as family members) is inelastic. Alston and Higgs (1982) report evidence of a negative relation between the relative importance of wage contracts and the average size of units of land owned in a district.

---

52. These are some of the points emphasized by Alston and Higgs (1982), and Cheung (1969b), op. cit. notes 51 and 44, respectively.

During the period 1930–1960, wage contracts rapidly replaced tenancy in the Deep South. Alston (1981) reports that mechanization of agriculture was the major determinant of variation in the extent of tenancy in the South, both over time and across ten cotton-growing states.[53] According to his thesis, the introduction of tractors lowered the cost of supervision in many ways and made tenancy contracts relatively unattractive.

> Because it lacks discretion, a machine's performance is comparatively uniform. Once tractor power was adopted, standardization of production was introduced. It became easier to measure labor input when employing the tractor, since the variance of labor's output (e.g., quality of rows plowed) is smaller. By assessing the acreage plowed or measuring the quantity of gasoline consumed by the tractor, a landowner could monitor a combination of tractor and labor inputs more cheaply than he could a combination of animal and labor inputs.[54]

7.5. Money in a system of exchange

In this chapter we have illustrated the transaction-costs approach to economic organization by examining market practices in three areas: the market for consumer goods, the labor market, and the market for agricultural land. We end the chapter by examining the market for money.

Economists are not in consensus on a definition of money, or on its role and uses. In models of the Walras–Hicks–Patinkin tradition, money is an intellectual appendage to the theoretical structures, and even when general equilibrium models incorporate risk (the Arrow/Debreu variety), they give no analytical explanation

53. Alston, Lee J. (1981). "Tenure Choice in Southern Agriculture." *Explorations in Economic History 18* (July): 211–232.
54. P. 324 in Alston, Lee J. (1979). "Costs of Contracting and the Decline of Tenancy in the South, 1930–1960." *Journal of Economic History 39* (No. 1, March): 324–326.

of the existence of money.[55] However, monetary economists have long understood that the usefulness of money in individual exchange depends on the way it economizes on information. In fact, the concept of transaction costs has one of its historical roots in unconventional contributions to monetary theory, some of which are reviewed below.

Economists of earlier periods, contemplating the uses of money, often tried to answer the question by informally analyzing transaction costs under various systems of exchange. The most elementary trade model is the one of unorganized barter.[56] The task of finding a productive role for money in formal economic theory is still incomplete in spite of many valuable insights contributed by economists going back at least to Adam Smith. We can do no more in this section than to sketch a brief outline of the role of money in systems of exchange where transactions are costly.

7.5.1. Definitions

The exchange of rights to economic resources is a universal social phenomenon. In communities of semiautarkic households, the volume exchanged may be small, but even in primitive agri-

55. This point is made, for example, in Ostroy, J. M. (1973). "The Informational Efficiency of Monetary Exchange." *American Economic Review 63* (No. 4): 597–610. Incorporating the concept of the information costs of individual exchange into the standard theory of value is not easy. Ostroy points out that this poses a dilemma: "How to make money appear without making the standard theory disappear?" P. 608.

56. The trials and tribulations of barter exchange are well illustrated by the case of a certain Mademoiselle Zélie, which the British economist W. S. Jevons, writing in the previous century, uses in his treatise on money and the mechanism of exchange. Mademoiselle Zélie, a singer of the Théâtre Lyrique in Paris, gave a concert in the Society Islands while on a professional tour around the world. "In exchange for an air from *Norma* and a few other songs, she . . . [received] three pigs, twenty-three turkeys, forty-four chickens, five thousand cocoa-nuts besides considerable quantities of bananas, lemons and oranges. . . . As Mademoiselle could not consume any considerable portion of the receipts herself, it became necessary in the meantime to feed the pigs and poultry with the fruit." P. 1 in Jevons, W. S. (1910). *Money and the Mechanism of Exchange*, 23rd ed. London: Kegan Paul. Cited in Clower, R. W., ed. (1969). *Monetary Theory*. London: Penguin, p. 25.

cultural societies there is usually some trade. It is hard to conceive of a state that does not tax its subjects, and taxation involves the transfer to the state of scarce resources in return for bona fide citizenship and other rights.

We refer to arrangements that guide the transfer of rights as the *system of exchange*. A system of exchange is made of laws, rules, and conventions, and various instruments to facilitate payments. Most economies contain several parallel systems of exchange. A *means of payment* is a device for completing transactions so that no party has valid claims for further payments.

When the shivering baker meets the hungry tailor in their classic textbook encounter and they swap bread and clothing, bread and clothing serve as the instruments of (final) payment that complete the transfer of rights between them. The baker could also lengthen the *chain of transactions* by selling her bread for rice and then exchange the rice for clothing. In this case the rice is bought by the baker for the purpose of resale and serves as an *indirect link* in the transaction chain. Most systems of exchange are characterized by both direct and indirect flows.

It has been observed in nearly all known societies that certain assets, commodities, or claims appear with great frequency as indirect links in transaction chains. We refer to such assets as *media of exchange*. A medium of exchange that is also a means of (final) payment is referred to as *money*. In fact, rice served for centuries as a principal medium of exchange and money in large parts of Asia.

7.5.2. The services of money

It is appropriate for economists to treat money as yet another valuable commodity and examine the flow of services supplied by the stock of money. Let us begin by stating that the demand for money derives in part from the gains associated with specialization in production. If people did not find it advantageous to specialize in production or if they specialized in both production and consumption, there would be no need for a medium of exchange. However, a medium of exchange also would not be needed, even in a complex exchange economy, if information was costless. In a model where information is free, a sequence of indirect transactions makes no sense because the agents can settle their accounts through *multilateral clearing*. In other words, agent A could transfer commodity X to agent B, and receive in return commodity Y from agent C, who thus pays her debt to B.

Positive information costs limit the gains from trade (even reduce potential gains to zero) and give rise to transaction chains with indirect links. The gains associated with indirect flows are best understood when roundabout methods of exchange are compared with an alternative exchange system, double-coincidence barter. In the example above, the demands of the baker for clothing and the demands of a tailor for bread must coincide in time and place, and indivisible commodities can cause problems.

When the number of commodities equals N, there are $(1/2N)(N-1)$ exchange ratios if each commodity is traded with all the other $N - 1$ commodities. It has often been pointed out that the exchange ratios are reduced to $N - 1$ if one of the commodities is made a unit of account. The resulting reduction in information costs can be compared to the impact on transaction costs when measures of weight, height, or temperature are standardized.[57] However, one can conceive of a unit of account that is not simultaneously one of the means of payment (e.g., the British guinea) or an economy that uses a common unit of account but does not rely on specialized means of payment. Although historical evidence suggests that a generalized means of payment is usually also the most efficient unit of account, we still need an independent explanation of indirect exchange.

Brunner and Meltzer (1971) offer perhaps the best analysis yet of the services of money in an exchange economy. In their model our baker has two alternatives when she seeks to trade some of her bread for clothing. First, in preparation for direct exchange

57. See p. 787 in Brunner, Karl, and Meltzer, Allan H. (1971). "The Uses of Money: Money in the Theory of an Exchange Economy." *American Economic Review 61* (December): 784–805.

she can invest in a search for information by exploring the circumstances of tailors in a given area – studying their tastes, the quality of their clothing, and their need for bread. Or in the language of economics, the baker can attempt to discover the tailors' true demand curves for bread and their true supply curves for clothing.[58] Investment in search uses time and other resources directly, and there are also various waiting costs, such as storage of commodities and delayed gratification of wants.

Second, the baker can add indirect links to her transaction chain and in this fashion reduce transaction costs, acquire information about quality, lower the expected price of clothing in terms of bread, and reduce its variance. Indirect exchange also involves various waiting costs, and, other things equal, the cost of transacting increases directly with the number of links.

Experience tells us that certain commodities tend to appear as indirect links in transaction chains more frequently than do other commodities. A theory seeking to explain the services provided by money must account for this phenomenon. Brunner and Meltzer (1971) offer as an explanation that certain assets or commodities involve relatively low marginal transaction costs, that these costs tend to fall the more often an individual trades an asset, and finally that most individuals face comparable structures of transaction costs (that the costs of transacting commodities are not randomly distributed across individuals). Certain commodities emerge as a specialized medium of exchange when buyers and sellers invest in arrangements that reduce uncertainty and improve their expected price ratios.

The Brunner–Meltzer model does not consider production (except the production of information), and it is assumed that each individual holds an initial endowment of resources. The optimizing individual is now faced with a rather wide range of choices: "His problem is to find the optimal sequence of transactions and the

---

58. If trading posts for each pair of commodities in the economy were established, the baker's search costs would be lowered as she could go directly to the bread–clothing post. See, for example, Clower, ed. (1969) [op. cit., note 56], p. 11.

optimal investment in information while choosing an optimal bundle of goods or consumption plan."[59] The model suggests that several exchange systems may coexist within the same economy.

Niehans (1969, 1971) has also analyzed how money can emerge spontaneously in market exchange, as part of an optimizing process, by extending the basic neoclassical model to include transaction costs that depend on characteristics both of commodities and of traders.[60] Transaction costs are assumed to be proportional to the volume of trade and to enter the model in a similar fashion as would proportional transportation costs. By varying patterns of transaction costs, the Niehans model gives rise to different payments systems, some monetary, others nonmonetary.

For example, consider a medium of exchange that is used in indirect exchange. The model shows that there is always a rate of transaction costs associated with this medium that is high enough to make it efficient to replace indirect exchange by direct barter. In other words, a progressive increase in the transaction costs of monetary exchange will eventually eliminate money. Similarly, a general increase in all transaction costs (for all transactors and all goods) will lower the volume of market exchange and eventually make it optimal for people to consume only their own endowments, and trade will cease. If we go in the other direction and reduce all transaction costs to zero, the model reduces to a special case: the basic neoclassical system. In the neoclassical general equilibrium version of the Niehans model, "the choice between barter and monetary exchange and, in the case of monetary exchange, the choice of medium (or media) of exchange, are matters of economic

59. Brunner, Karl, and Meltzer, Allan H. (1971) [op. cit., note 57], p. 788.
60. Niehans, Jürg (1969). "Money in a Static Theory of Optimal Payment Arrangements." *Journal of Money, Credit and Banking 1* (No. 4, November): 706–726. In the model presented in this paper, consumption is assumed to be given independently of monetary arrangements, but that restrictive assumption is abandoned in a later paper where consumption and monetary arrangements are jointly determined. See Niehans, Jürg (1971). "Money and Barter in General Equilibrium with Transaction Costs." *American Economic Review 61* (No. 5, December): 773–783.

indifference. As a consequence, a neoclassical system is unable to give an explicit analysis of monetization and monetary services."[61]

Niehans (1971) also considers the consequences of reducing transaction costs to zero for one commodity, M. As it now is inefficient to use any other commodity as a medium of exchange, M becomes a general medium of exchange, and direct barter will always be inferior to monetary exchange.

Finally, Niehans (1971) and Brunner–Meltzer (1971) make the interesting point that specialized traders and middlemen are substitutes for decentralized information, and suggest that their role is analytically comparable to that of media of exchange such as money.

7.5.3. Consumer confidence and the brand name of money

Niehans and Brunner–Meltzer do not examine explicitly what characteristics make some assets relatively inexpensive to use as money, but common sense suggests two important considerations, at least in the case of the commodity money: The transaction costs of using a commodity as money tend to be low when its physical characteristics are easily measured, and when there exist for the commodity diverse resale markets with stable expected resale price and low variance.

Clower (1969) argues that a great many commodities have physical characteristics required of a medium of exchange (such as portability, indestructibility, homogeneity, divisibility, and cognizability), and the choice of a general medium of exchange is essentially a social decision. In Clower's own words: "The technical characteristics of commodities chosen to serve as 'money' are of minor economic importance; what matters is the existence of social institutions condoned either by custom or [by] law that enable individuals to trade efficiently *if they follow certain rules* . . . "[62]

Clower does not preclude the spontaneous evolution of general

---

61. Niehans (1971) [op. cit., note 60], p. 780.
62. Clower, R. W., ed. (1969) [op. cit., note 56]. "Introduction." (p. 13)

media of exchange during historical or prehistorical periods, but argues that mature exchange systems everywhere depend on legal and institutional restrictions that raise the cost of using media of exchange other than the sanctioned ones and lower the cost of using authorized instruments of indirect exchange: "The peculiar feature of a money economy is that some commodities . . . are denied a role as potential or actual means of payment. To state the same idea as an aphorism: *Money buys goods, and goods buy money; but goods do not buy goods.*"[63]

Yet the hold over the money market by social convention and the state is less than these words may suggest.[64] The stock of money is a *durable good* that provides a *flow of service* to the consumer. But money differs from most if not all durable goods in that the *quality of money*, the real services rendered, are a function of future supply, as Klein (1974) points out in an important article. An increase in the supply of money that is unanticipated by consumers can sharply reduce the flow of services from their current holdings of money. Similarly, an individual will find that his money provides no services in exchange or as a store of value if other individuals conclude that the asset is worthless. In other words, the quality of a nominal unit of money depends on its resale value. However, the cooling services of a refrigerator are not diminished if the producer increases the supply of her product; only its resale value is lowered.

The user of money adjusts her real money stock until marginal costs equal marginal benefits. The marginal opportunity cost or the price of monetary services is measured by the difference between the nominal rate of interest and the rate of return on the money asset, $(i - r_m)$. The demand for money in real terms is therefore a negative function of $(i - r_m)$. But that is not all. The

63. Clower, R. W. (1967). "A Reconsideration of the Microfoundations of Monetary Theory." *Western Economic Journal* 6 (No. 4, November): 1–9. Reprinted in Clower, ed. (1969), quote from pp. 207–208.
64. The following discussion is based on Klein, Benjamin (1974). "The Competitive Supply of Money." *Journal of Money, Credit and Banking* 6 (No. 4, November): 423–454.

demand for money is also a positive function of β, the user's confidence in the money, and β is negatively related to the variance of the anticipated rate of change of prices in terms of the money. If the user of the money is confident that she can correctly predict price changes in terms of this money, then β has a high value. If several monies are used in the same economic system, and, for each, $(i - r_m)$ has the same value (and the opportunity cost of holding these monies is identical), then high-confidence (high β) monies will drive out low-confidence monies.[65]

Information about the future performance of suppliers of money is costly. Therefore, it is costly to provide and acquire information about the quality of a monetary asset. Confidence can be created by relying on physical supply constraints and by using commodity monies, such as gold, whose supply is limited in nature. Another approach is to guarantee convertibility on demand, and at a fixed exchange rate, of a token money into a commodity and perhaps also hold reserves of the commodity. The deadweight social cost of using a commodity as a medium of exchange is the loss of alternative use, such as the use of gold as dental fillings. Token money usually does not have valuable alternative uses, but the costs of creating consumer confidence in token money can exceed the opportunity cost of using commodity money such as gold.

Token money is a pure case of what we referred to as experience goods in the first section of this chapter: It has no measurable physical characteristics that inform the user about the quality of monetary services it will provide and is not accepted by users unless the supplier makes costly investments in brand-name capital, which is seen as a collateral or a hostage by the consumers. In the case of unbacked fiat money, the potential gains from cheating consumers by overissuing can be very large, which suggests that very large investments in brand-name capital may be required. The

65. Ibid., p. 433. "The value of the brand name of, or consumer confidence in, a money, is therefore assumed to be related to the anticipated *predictability* of the future price level in terms of the money, while the quality of a nominal unit of money is assumed to be related to the anticipated *stability* of the future price level in terms of the money." Ibid., p. 433.

introduction of unbacked fiat money only relatively recently in most countries is not fully understood,[66] but it is not unreasonable to assume that the belated appearance of fiat money is linked to a reduction in the cost of creating consumer confidence.

7.5.4. The competitive supply of money

History records extensive intervention by the state in the money industry. In the case of fiat money, many economists have argued that intervention is necessary because the competitive supply of token money at freely fluctuating exchange rates would lead to an infinite price level and degenerate into commodity money, a literal paper standard.[67]

Klein (1974) has examined these arguments in terms of the concept of brand-name capital. He concludes that a competitive money industry will not degenerate through overissue if certain conditions are met. First, each money brand would have to be easily recognizable by the consumers, and, second, both the firms and the users of money must make the same estimates of the potential gains to the firms of cheating on consumers by overissuing. In equilibrium, the opportunity cost to a firm of not deceiving the consumers by overissuing is equal to the firm's profit stream. In other words, the firm balances the returns on its brand-name capital against the once-for-all gains of dissipating the brand name.[68] If consumers estimate the gains to the firms of cheating to be less than the firms themselves estimate these gains, then overissue and worthless token money may be the outcome.

Hayek (1976) has called for the denationalization of money and the introduction of privately supplied currency. He believes that the self-interest of private producers would lead them to protect their brand names and keep the real value of money more stable

66. Until 1933, the U.S. Government promised to convert on demand its money into gold.
67. This is the viewpoint even of Milton Friedman (1959). *A Program for Monetary Stability*. New York: Fordham University Press, p. 7.
68. Klein (1974) [op. cit., note 64], p. 438.

than the central authorities have done during the previous half century.[69] One way to evaluate Hayek's proposal is to draw lessons from historical experiences with privately issued currency. The cases most often quoted by both proponents and opponents of free banking are the Scottish and American experiences in the eighteenth and nineteenth centuries.[70]

The evidence, for example, from the free banking system in New York State 1838–1863, as reviewed by King (1983), suggests that a private monetary system need not bring disasters as some critics maintain.[71] But it is also important to realize that the New York system was neither "free" nor "unregulated." In New York, private bank notes had to be denominated in dollars; a dollar denominated a particular weight of gold; and all notes were convertible into gold at fixed exchange rates. The government printed and registered the notes, required that circulating notes were bond secured, defined the class of eligible securities, and served as the custodian of the securities. And, the banks were required to hold a minimum amount of specie reserves against circulating notes.[72] We will not attempt here to weigh the pros and cons of private monetary and banking systems, but it is not unreasonable to state that "economists know little about the operation of fully private monetary systems."[73]

69. Hayek, Friedrich A. (1976). *Denationalization of Money*. Hobart Paper. London: The Institute of Economic Affairs.

70. See various essays in Salin, Pascal, ed. (1984). *Currency Competition and Monetary Union*. Martinus Nijhoff Publishers. Note also Stanley Fischer's (1986) review essay dealing with this volume, "Friedman Versus Hayek on Private Money." *Journal of Monetary Economics 17* (No. 3): 433–439.

71. King, Robert G. (1983). "On the Economics of Private Money." *Journal of Monetary Economics 12* (No. 1): 127–158.

72. King (1983) [op. cit., note 71], pp. 142–143. The most common criticism of free banking, gleaned from a review of the free banking episodes in history, is that many issuers of circulating notes tend to fail, often because of their own fraudulent behavior, "so noteholders only obtain a fraction of the face value of their notes." (p. 139) King concludes that the losses to noteholders in the New York system were relatively small. (p. 156)

73. Ibid., p. 128.

7.5.5. *The choice of systems of exchange*

The theoretical question whether money can emerge spontaneously in exchange is separate from theoretical and empirical issues concerning the role of the state in the introduction of monetary organization. Money is an instrument that can lower the ruler's transaction cost of wielding his power. For example, the payment of taxes in money rather than in kind enlarges the opportunity set of the ruler and his cohorts, and money is an efficient unit of account that lowers the cost of measuring the tax base and the subjects' taxes.

The acceptance of token money depends on trust, but trust is related to state power. Early kingdoms were forced to cast their more precious coins out of valuable metals partly because the regimes often were unstable, and domestic coins faced direct competition from foreign coins. With the rise of the modern national state the use of token money became more common. Legal and tax barriers against substitute currency were erected, the level of general taxation was raised, and taxes were payable in government money. Stability and power seem to breed fiat money.[74]

Klein (1974) recognized that the ability of a national state to run down the brand-name capital of its currency by overissuing represents a very large potential tax, which might be valuable in situations such as wartime, when conventional taxation is inviable or too slow. National governments may prefer to hold some of their coercive capital in highly liquid form.[75]

Transaction costs are associated not only with the characteristics of assets and commodities and investments in brand names but also with *characteristics of individuals* and the *social networks* in which the traders operate.[76] A large share of all exchange, even in highly advanced industrial societies, does not depend on a spe-

---

74. P. 10 in Goodhart, C. A. E. (1975). *Money, Information and Uncertainty.* London: Macmillan.
75. Klein (1974) [op. cit., note 64], p. 449.
76. This point is emphasized in Goodhart, C. A. E. (1975) [op. cit., note 74], pp. 5–9.

cialized means of payment. For example, this is generally the case for transactions in the family or within monasteries, where each member of a group has a (socially) defined role specifying his rights and duties.

Goodhart (1975) makes the point that the same is true of transactions within a typical firm where managers direct the use of resources without making payments each time. This argument is somewhat misguided. The employers use money to buy the right, for example, to labor services during a specific block of time. The various tasks of each worker usually are not individually priced and paid for because high measurement costs would make such payments inefficient. The situation is similar to the case of a woman who pays a contractor to build her a home and where the specification of details is left open (within limits) depending on the availability and price of materials and the evolution of the buyer's knowledge about interior designs as she becomes more familiar with available alternatives. It is not correct to say that long-term contracts of this nature do not involve the use of money.

Within limits set by the state, the choice of an exchange system depends in an important way on the cost of acquiring information about a trading partner and the cost of enforcing contracts. Trade between total strangers has a potential for very high transaction costs, and it can proceed only if the two parties trade easily measurable commodities or use specialized media of exchange whose value is independent of the bearer. A trader is reluctant to accept credit instruments of no inherent value in return for commodities unless he has reliable information about the buyer. Knowledge that a buyer has invested in trust within a trading community and will lose his valuable reputation if he fraudulently uses worthless instruments lowers the cost of using credit as a medium of exchange. When the trade network is tight, when information about the worth of fellow traders is cheap, when sanctions are inexpensive to administer, and the cost of losing the confidence of the group is high, a specialized medium of exchange may even be inferior to multilateral barter as an exchange mechanism. In sum, *we usually find several parallel exchange systems within the same economy because individuals and exchanges are heterogeneous with respect to transaction costs.*

Technological innovations have revolutionized payments mechanisms and have lowered the cost of acquiring information about trading partners and their claims. For example, advances in printing technology have made paper money a more reliable means of payment. The development of photography made personal identity cards more dependable and facilitated the use of personal checks as a medium of exchange. Communications technology has lowered the cost of establishing the existence of bank deposits and has made possible the introduction of credit cards, yet another innovation that has lowered the information cost of using bank deposits as money.[77]

In Chapters 6 and 7, we examined the logic of contractual arrangements in various markets by looking, for example, at contracts in the input market that give rise to the firm, at contracts in agriculture, and at contracts for forced labor. The analysis focused on the impact of transaction costs on the structure of contracts, and our assumptions of rational choice and individual utility or wealth maximization led to the conclusion that individuals will seek contractual arrangements that maximize the joint value of their resources subject to constraints imposed by technology, the system of property rights, and transaction costs.

In the last three chapters, we turn our attention to one of these constraints, the structure of property rights, and examine the role of the state in shaping the institutional structure.

---

77. Following Goodhart (1975), we define personal checks as a medium of exchange but not as a means of (final) payment and hence not as money. Checks allow exchange to proceed, but final payment takes the form of a transfer between bank accounts.

Part IV

Explaining property rights

8

The emergence of property rights

8.1. Introduction

The state can affect the net wealth of a community by redefining the structure of property rights, and by providing public goods, such as standardized weights and measures, which reduce the costs of transacting. Neoinstitutional Economics suggests that the rules of the game, which in part are controlled by the state, have a fundamental role in determining whether an economy enters a path of growth and development or stagnation and decline. But why should any government lay down rules that retard the economy? Although little can be said a priori about the utility function of those who control the state, it is unreasonable to assume that, other things being equal, they either prefer or are indifferent to economic decline in their country. This conclusion should be independent of our model of the state, be it one assuming a contract state or a predatory state. For example, a ruler of a predatory state who seeks to maximize her wealth by taxing her subjects, will, other things being equal, attempt to maximize the tax base, the national income. An increase in the national income due to more clearly defined property rights and less dissipation of rent should be welcomed by both subjects and ruler, as it can be used to augment both tax revenues and general living standards.

In terms of the economic approach to institutions, it follows that failure to take advantage of output-enhancing adjustments of property rights must be due to some transaction-cost constraint. In fact, the neoinstitutional approach suggests a macro version of Coase's law: *The economic growth and development of a country are basically unaffected by the type of government it has, if the cost of transacting in both the political and economic spheres is zero. However, when transaction costs are positive, the distribution of political power within a country and the institutional structure of its rule-making institutions are critical factors in economic development.*

In their well-known survey of property rights, Furubotn and Pejovich (1972) emphasize that "a theory of property rights cannot be truly complete without a theory of the state. And, unfortunately, no such theory exists at present."[1]

The authors refer to ongoing research by Buchanan, McKean, Niskanen, Tullock, and North which may fill this gap, and mention especially a 1972 paper by North in which he attempts to use the basic economic model of utility maximization to explain why "the state has frequently traded inefficient property rights (e.g., licence to operate in a closed market) for revenue, and by doing so throttled economic growth."[2]

Although much work has been undertaken in this area since 1972, attempts to model the emergence of property rights and institutional change are still the least developed area of Neoinstitutional Economics. The last section of the book considers recent attempts to endogenize both the set of rules that constrains the choice of individual participants in economic exchange and the rule-making institutions themselves. In Chapter 8 we look at models that seek to explain the emergence of property rights without developing an explicit theory of the state and of political processes. Chapter 9 is concerned with social structures, transaction costs, and property rights in stateless societies and in the inter-

---

1. P. 1140 in Furubotn, Eirik, and Pejovich, Svetozar (1972). "Property Rights and Economic Theory: A Survey of Recent Literature." *The Journal of Economic Literature 10* (December, No. 4): 1137–1162.
2. Ibid., p. 1140.

national arena. Finally, Chapter 10 deals with political structures in both autocratic and democratic societies.

The organization of Chapter 8 is as follows: We begin by introducing what we refer to as the *naive theory of property rights* and its application in several areas. The naive theory looks at the emergence or nonemergence of exclusive rights in terms of the costs and benefits of exclusion and the cost of internal governance when individuals share property rights. In a formal version of the naive model, Field (1986) uses this theory to analyze both the emergence of exclusive rights and the movement from communal exclusive rights toward individual exclusive rights. We discuss various applications of the naive model, for example: how it has been used to analyze the emergence of exclusive rights among North American Indians, the evolution of property rights on the American Frontier, and the rise of agriculture in prehistoric times. We also apply the model to situations where open access conditions have persisted in spite of the dissipation of rent, for example, in the fishery of modern economies.

We then go on to emphasize the limited usefulness of a model that attempts to explain the structure of property rights without reference to political factors and considerations of wealth redistribution. For this purpose we draw on studies by Gary Libecap and others, where the interplay between political and economic factors is used to explain the existence of elements of common property in various U.S. industries. The *interest-group theory of property rights* augments the naive theory of property rights by linking it with the theory of pressure groups that models institutions as exogenous. Finally, we take a brief look at the literature on rent seeking and try to place it in the context of Neoinstitutional Economics.

8.2 The naive model

McCloskey (1985) has pointed out that "the American institutionalists and the German historical school could argue truly in the early years of this century that modern economics had no theory of the origins of property and could therefore not claim to understand the long sweep of economic development."[3] But since the late 1960s or so, a group of scholars using the neoclassical apparatus has tried to remedy this deficiency by turning their techniques toward an examination of the origin of property itself. We refer to some of these early attempts as the *naive theory of property rights* because they seek to explain the development of exclusive property rights without explicitly modeling social and political institutions.

Demsetz's 1967 paper, "Toward a Theory of Property Rights," is the classic reference for the naive theory of property rights.[4] His thesis is the following:

> Property rights develop to internalize externalities when the gains of internalization become larger than the cost of internalization. Increased internalization, in the main, results from changes in economic values, changes which stem from the development of new technology and the opening of new markets, changes to which old property rights are poorly attuned. . . . [G]iven a community's tastes . . . [for private versus state ownership], the emergence of new private or state-owned property rights will be in response to changes in technology and relative prices.[5]

Demsetz (1967) uses his theory to explain the introduction of private ownership of land among Indian hunters in the eastern part of Canada who, in the early years of the eighteenth century, developed exclusive rights to take beaver furs from well-defined hunting grounds.[6] Initially, when the Indians hunted beavers only for

3. P. 339 in McCloskey, Donald N. (1985). *The Applied Theory of Price*, 2nd ed. New York: Macmillan.
4. Demsetz, Harold (1967). "Toward a Theory of Property Rights." *American Economic Review 57* (May, No. 2): 347–359.
5. Ibid., p. 350.
6. Demsetz's observations regarding the Indians of the American Northwest are based on the work of the anthropologist Eleanor Leacock.

their own consumption of meat and furs, exclusive rights were nonexistent, and, presumably, the opportunity cost of land was zero. With the development of commercial fur trade, an increase in demand led to a sharp increase in hunting, and wealth maximization required that investments be undertaken to protect the resource (i.e., the stock of game) and restore it to a level that maximized its present value. But optimal utilization of the resources over time was impractical unless individual hunters or bands of hunters had some control over the hunting of others: Without exclusive rights, the private value of animals running free was zero. As the introduction of exclusive rights was expected to increase the net wealth of the community, the Indians had an economic incentive to invest in exclusive rights.

Demsetz (1967) argues, further, that the Indians of the American Southwest failed to develop similar property rights because of the relatively high costs and low benefits from establishing private hunting lands. In the Southwest there were no animals of comparable commercial importance to beavers, and the animals of the plains were mostly grazing species who wandered over wide tracts of land.[7]

McManus (1972) has added an important postscript to Demsetz's (1967) work on the emergence of exclusive property rights among Indians involved in the North American fur trade.[8] McManus notes that "almost all the historians in the fur trade to whom I have referred remark that beaver populations were sharply reduced after the introduction of the fur trade into an area."[9] But Demsetz's theory suggests that, ceteris paribus, the beaver population should have stabilized, and possibly increased, when exclusive rights were introduced. McManus also cites evidence that the Hudson Bay Company, which at one point was an exclusive buyer of the furs,

7. Demsetz (1967) [op. cit., note 4], p. 353.
8. McManus, John C. (1972). "An Economic Analysis of Indian Behavior in the North American Fur Trade." *Journal of Economic History 32* (March, No. 1): 36–53.
9. Ibid., p. 39.

incurred costs to conserve the beaver population. This should not have been required, according to our theory, as the hunters had established exclusive rights to the hunting grounds.[10]

Furthermore, an examination of the evidence by McManus revealed no such changes in relative prices and technology, immediately following the opening of the fur trade, which (according to Demsetz's theory) might have created incentives for the hunters to return to common property.

Why this paradox? Why did property rights fail to protect the beaver population? McManus finds his answer by looking at details of the property rights structure. The Indian hunters in the eastern part of Canada were organized into small bands. "Individual members of the band had the right to exclude others from taking furs or meat from their territories for sale, but they did not have the right to exclude others from killing animals for consumption." In other words, "rights to use for direct consumption were common and . . . rights to use for exchange were exclusive" in the Indian communities.[11] As the hunters lived in an uncertain world and faced a real threat of starvation, the common right to kill for one's own consumption was an institutionalized form of insurance. McManus refers to it as the Good Samaritan (GS) constraint on the exercise of exclusive rights. This form of insurance was not without costs, and evidence of these costs is found in "reports of irresponsibility and laziness, and the depletion of beaver furs . . . "[12]

McManus also notes that the GS constraint reduced the cost of enforcing exclusive rights for use in exchange. If the insurance and enforcement benefits of the GS constraint were larger than the associated costs (and provided that less expensive forms of insurance were unavailable), then this particular structure of property rights was consistent with wealth maximization.

The naive theory of property rights was expanded to incorporate

10. Ibid., p. 46.
11. Ibid., pp. 48–49.
12. Ibid., p. 51.

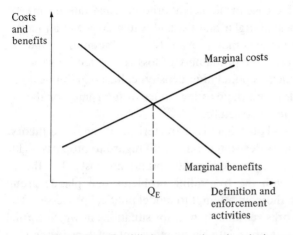

Figure 8.1. Equilibrium quantity of exclusion activity.

explicitly the costs of exclusion by Anderson and Hill (1975), who applied it to evolution of exclusive rights to the utilization of land, water, and cattle on the Great Plains of the American West during the second half of the nineteenth century.[13] The authors present a graphic model involving a marginal cost function and a marginal benefit function for investment in the definition and enforcement of property rights and identify critical shift parameters for each function. The model is reproduced in Figure 8.1.

The quantity axis of the diagram measures definition and enforcement (exclusion) *activities*, such as fencing. A fall in the price of exclusion inputs or a change in exclusion technologies (e.g., the introduction of barbed wire in 1874) shifts down the marginal costs function and, ceteris paribus, increases exclusion activity. The marginal benefit curve, representing the derived demand for exclusion, moves out when the value of an asset increases and also when the probability of encroachment by outsiders increases.

13. Anderson, Terry L., and Hill, P. J. (1975). "The Evolution of Property Rights: A Study of the American West." *Journal of Law and Economics 18* (No. 1): 163–179.

An increase in the neighborhood crime rate means
that locks, burglar alarms, and watch dogs will all have
higher benefits than previously. . . . In addition to the
crime rate, the probability of loss is affected by variables such as population density, cultural and ethical
attitudes, and the existing "rules of the game" or the
institutional structure.[14]

The Anderson–Hill model is characteristic of the naive theory:
The formulation of decision making with regard to property rights
is solely in terms of private benefits and private costs. The theory
does not deal with the free-riding problems that plague group
decision, nor is there an attempt to model political processes. The
naive model works reasonably well for situations in which formal
political processes are relatively unimportant, such as in the case
of the settlers of the American Great Plains, who, for various
reasons, partly bypassed the formal decision-making apparatus of
the United States, which was centered in the East. "As a result
various alternatives developed, including voluntary local agreements and extra-legal institutions."[15]

The naive theory of property rights is also useful for making
broad generalizations about changes in property rights institutions
in prehistoric times. For example, the theory has been used by
North and Thomas (1977) and North (1981) to "provide a new
explanation for the development of agriculture in human prehis-
tory," or the *first economic revolution*, which is the name given by
the authors to the gradual transition from hunting/gathering to
settled agriculture.[16]

The driving force of the North–Thomas model is population
pressures. While plants and animals were relatively abundant, the

---

14. Ibid., p. 167.
15. Ibid., p. 169.
16. P. 229 in North, Douglass C., and Thomas, Robert Paul (1977). "The First
    Economic Revolution." *Economic History Review 30*, second series (No. 2):
    229–241. Also see Chapter 7 in North, Douglass, C. (1981). *Structure and
    Change in Economic History*. New York: W. W. Norton.

costs of establishing exclusive rights to these resources exceeded the potential gains, and natural resources were used as common property. As the human population increased relative to the constant resource base, and competition among bands stiffened, open access led to diminishing returns in hunting. At the margin, settled agriculture gradually became more attractive than hunting, although agriculture required the costly establishment and enforcement of exclusive rights. North and Thomas have theorized that the first settled agricultural communities were based on *exclusive communal property* in land with individual bands sharing each commons. Within each commons, taboos and custom constrained, at least in part, the incentive to overexploit the resource.

The First Economic Revolution occurred about 10,000 years ago, and the span from the beginning of settled agriculture up to the peak of the Roman Empire is about 8000 years. Humans, in contrast to other animals, have inhabited the Earth for more than a million years, which implies that the period prior to the introduction of agriculture represents about 99.3 percent of man's chronological time. North and Thomas (1977) make the following point:

> The first economic revolution was not a revolution because it shifted man's major economic activity from hunting and gathering to settled agriculture. It was a revolution because the transition created an incentive change for mankind of fundamental proportions. The incentive change stems from the different property rights under the two systems. When common property rights over resources exist, there is little incentive for the acquisition of superior technology and learning. In contrast, exclusive property rights which reward the owners provide a direct incentive to improve efficiency and productivity, or, in more fundamental terms, to acquire more knowledge and new techniques. It is this change in incentive that explains the rapid progress made by mankind in the last 10,000 years in contrast to

his slow development during the long era as a primitive hunter/gatherer.[17]

Field (1986) presents a formal version of the naive theory of property rights. It emphasizes exclusion costs and expands the model to include, as a second cost variable, the costs of internal governance that arise when exclusive rights are shared.[18] Property rights have many dimensions, but the Field model emphasizes the *degree of exclusivity*, which can vary within a community from the sharing of a resource by the whole population to individual exclusive rights. Property rights emerge from attempts by *communities* to maximize their net wealth.

Field's story begins when a group of N individuals or families has acquired R units of a natural resource. The group seeks to maximize the rent from R by combining it in production with variable inputs, and it is assumed that political struggles over the distribution of income do not affect the member's behavior or the rules that evolve. Maximization requires adjustments at many margins, and one of the issues that the N families must settle is how to divide R among themselves. For example, if R is agricultural land, the families can treat the land as communal property and work it together. Or they can divide the land into N plots and give each family exclusive rights to one such. A third alternative is to design medium-size plots and have several families share the ownership of each plot. In other words, the potential structure of ownership is variable, and maximization requires finding the *optimal commons*. Field (1986) cites various cases from history of intermediate-size commons: town lands in early New England, grazing land in the American West, lobster regions of the inshore Maine fishery, traditional grazing areas in Botswana, and commons in the Hong Kong agricultural village.[19]

The purpose of Field's model is to isolate forces that drive the

---

17. North and Thomas (1977) [op. cit., note 16], pp. 240–241.
18. Field, Barry C. (1986). "Induced Changes in Property Rights Institutions." Research paper. Amherst: Department of Agricultural and Resource Economics, University of Massachusetts.
19. Ibid., pp. 22–32.

property rights system either away from or toward individual exclusive ownership. The model contains three types of cost functions: a neoclassical cost-of-production function, a cost-of-internal-governance function, and a cost-of-exclusion function.[20] In the model, governance costs are solely caused by the commons problem (which we discussed in Chapter 4, Section 4.2), namely the incentive to overutilize variable, individually owned inputs when several families share the ownership of a resource. The dissipation of the rent from the shared resource can be reduced by collective action, but such measures are costly and give rise to internal governance costs, costs that are justified if the limits on overutilization increase *net* output. It is assumed that governance costs vary directly both with the number of families on each commons and with the curbs on the use of variable inputs. Exclusion costs arise when property rights are defended against encroachment by outsiders. The benefits of exclusion are reflected in greater output for each level of input use. We would normally expect costs of exclusion to be related directly to the length of boundaries of the property – to peak when R is divided into N independent properties and to reach a minimum when R is undivided.

The assumptions of the model imply that R will be divided among identical commons. There are, therefore, three endogenous variables to be found simultaneously: the number of commons, the quantity of exclusion resources, and the level of variable input used on the representative commons. Assuming the latter to remain optimally adjusted, a reduced-form version of Field's model is shown in Figure 8.2.

The forces that determine the optimum number of commons, m, are channeled through two functions – $m = m^*(e)$ and $e = e^*(m)$ – and can either change the slope of the functions or shift them. The $m = m^*(e)$ function *defines the optimal number of commons for each level of exclusion expenditure*, $\hat{m}$, and the

---

20. It is assumed that the variable input, labor, is homogeneous, that the land can be divided into homogeneous plots of equal size, and that the production functions for all intermediate-size commons are identical.

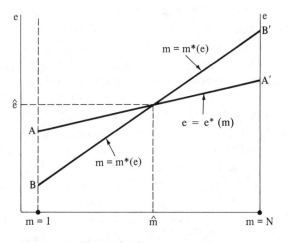

Figure 8.2. The optimal commons.

function $e = e^*(m)$ *maps the optimal level of exclusion expenditure for each number of commons,* $\hat{e}$.

Internal governance costs are likely to fall when a population becomes more homogeneous and adopts a common ideology. Adjustments in the group's formal decision procedures (such as the replacement of unanimity rule with majority rule in voting) can have the same effect. When internal governance costs fall, the new equilibrium outcome involves fewer but bigger intermediate commons. The reasoning is as follows: The logic of the model demands that the return on investment in internal governance and the return on investment in exclusion be the same at the margin. When exogenous change reduces internal governance costs, equilibrium is reestablished by associating larger commons (which have higher internal governance costs) with each level of expenditure on exclusion, e. In Figure 8.2, this process of adjustment is depicted as an upward shift in the $m = m^*(e)$ function.

Technological change of a type that makes exclusion easier can be treated as a fall in the price of exclusion resources, which implies a higher return on each dollar spent on exclusion. Optimization requires that more be spent on exclusion for each size commons, and the $e = e^*(m)$ function shifts upward. Now the equilibrium outcome is one of a larger number of (smaller) optimal commons than before.

An increase in trespassing has the opposite effect. Additional resources are now required to achieve the same effective level of exclusion as before, which is equivalent to an increase in the price of exclusion resources. At the margin, the return on a dollar spent on exclusion is now less than the return on a dollar spent on internal governance. Therefore, the $e = e^*(m)$ curve shifts downward, which implies fewer and larger commons. Extreme amounts of trespassing can lead to $m = 1$, where the resource is shared as communal property; and, on the other hand, very low exclusion costs can result in $m = N$ or individual exclusive property.[21]

Generally, it has been assumed in the property-rights literature that an increase in the value of a resource will foster exclusive rights. Perhaps the most interesting aspect of Field's model is that an increase in the value of the resource, R, either because of an exogenous increase in final demand for the commodity produced or because of population expansion, does not have an unambiguous effect on $\hat{m}$, the optimal number of commons. Let us consider the case of an increase in demand. First, an increase in the value of goods produced with R intensifies the internal governance problem and pushes the system toward more numerous and smaller (cheaper to govern) commons for each level of exclusion expenditures: The function $m^*(e)$ shifts downward.[22] Second, a higher value of land (R) increases the return to exclusion. Exclusion is aimed at preventing the theft of the fruits of the land, which are now more valuable. Optimization calls for more expenditure on

21. "In the case where both transaction costs [internal governance costs] and exclusion costs are zero, the optimal commons is governed strictly by the production function; with constant returns the size of the optimal commons is indeterminate within the model." Ibid., p. 18.
22. As exogenous change has increased internal governance costs, the marginal return on investment in exclusion exceeds the return on investment in internal governance. Output maximization requires that smaller commons (which have lower internal governance costs) be associated with each level of expenditure on exclusion, and, therefore, the $m^*(e)$ function shifts downward.

exclusion for all values of m, and the effect is to shift $e^*(m)$ upward. Both effects discussed so far work to move the property rights system toward individual exclusive commons. But there is a third effect. A greater value of R invites more trespassing, which, ceteris paribus, lowers the return on resources devoted to exclusion and suggests shortening of the total length of borders to be enforced by a move to larger and fewer commons. Other things being equal, more trespassing shifts the $e = e^*(m)$ function down and moves the system toward communal rights. As the relative strength of the three effects cannot be derived from the model, it is not possible to predict the impact on the degree of communalism from an increase in final demand, for example, due to the opening of new markets.

Finally, note that both internal governance and exclusion involve collective action, and that the costs of governance and exclusion are not independent of the political institutions of the community. For example, exclusion can be solely in the hands of the N/m owners of each commons, or all the N families may pool their resources and establish a specialized police force. Therefore, an autonomous institutional change can lead to a new size for the optimal commons, but this is not accounted for in the model that abstracts from political institutions.[23]

Field (1986) singles out for analysis only one of several dimensions of property-rights institutions, the *size* of the optimal commons. Another important margin of the rights structure is the degree of *precision* with which the rules are defined. For example, if rights are not clearly defined, it may be difficult for a proprietor to prove to a third party (e.g., the courts) that his rights have been violated. Posner and others have advanced the thesis that prop-

---

23. Field (1986) [op. cit., note 18] speculates about the potential influences of alternative political institutions. For example, were internal governance costs relatively low but exclusion costs relatively high under the political institutions of feudalism? Are various authoritarian political structures effective in reducing the commons problem in agriculture communities, and do democratic structures have the opposite effect? Can changes in property-rights institutions induce changes in political institutions?

erty rights will be made more precise as resources become more valuable.[24]

Libecap (1978) tested the precision hypothesis for Nevada's richest mining area, Comstock Lodge.[25] Before the discovery of the mining zone in 1859, the area was nearly uninhabited public land with no private ownership, but the mineral find brought in a hurried migration of prospectors. By the mid-1870s, the Comstock yielded about 50 percent of the total U.S. output of gold and silver.[26]

Libecap's (1978) study of the development of mineral laws, tracing their development from "unwritten rules in the 1850s to highly specified statutes and court verdicts by the end of the century," led him to conclude that private mineral laws did not evolve autonomously but were shaped by economic forces.[27] The owners of the largest mines, lobbying for clearer legislative and judicial definitions of property rights, were the major proponents of legal change. Libecap's statistical study reveals that in the early years, while the rights structure was still incomplete, the heated competition for land following new ore discoveries increased the miners' demand for more exclusivity, which in turn led to increased specificity of the mining law (measured on Libecap's statistical indices of legal change). But a long-run equilibrium was reached when the structure of legal rights had become highly defined and enforced, and the link between rising value of mineral land and more precise rules disappeared.

Libecap's findings are consistent with the naive theory of property rights. The state has a passive role and supplies rules in response to pressures from producers (who initially appropriated public land without payment). The structure of Western mineral

24. Posner, Richard A., and Ehrlich, Isaach (1974). "An Economic Analysis of Legal Rule Making." *Journal of Legal Studies 3* (January): 257–286; and Posner, Richard A. (1973). "An Economic Approach to Legal Procedure and Judicial Administration." *Journal of Legal Studies 2* (June): 399–458.
25. P. 341 in Libecap, Gary (1978). "Economic Variables and the Development of the Law: The Case of Western Mineral Rights." *Journal of Economic History 38* (No. 2, June): 399–458.
26. Ibid., p. 339.
27. Ibid., p. 261.

rights reflects concerns with the level of wealth rather than its distribution, or, to be more accurate, the issue of distribution was settled without recourse to rules that seriously interfered with the productivity in mining.[28]

Individuals can use the state in several ways for their personal gain: by lobbying for rules that increase the community's aggregate wealth, by seeking direct transfers that are not output enhancing and may have negative effects on incentives, and by obtaining property rights that create artificial scarcities and output losses. In a world of positive transaction costs, the basic logic of the naive model is consistent with all three types of wealth seeking, which implies that the cases we have listed so far in this chapter in support of the naive theory of property rights must represent special rather than general outcomes. This point is recognized by Libecap (1978):

> Given the high expected returns from exclusive
> control and the lack of an existing ownership structure
> when ore was discovered, one would expect economic
> events to outweigh other social and political factors
> in the formation of the legal structure.[29]

Now we go on to discuss attempts to modify the naive theory to account for the behavior of interest groups and nonproductive wealth seeking. But first let us consider yet another application of the naive model, cases where exclusive rights over valuable resources do *not* emerge.

8.3. When exclusive rights do not emerge

The naive model tells us that exclusive rights to an asset are established and enforced when potential owners expect positive

---

28. The mine owners did indeed use their political muscle to acquire property rights that represented transfers to them, but these rights did not lead to serious output restrictions. For example, in the initial years mining was exempt from taxation, and later, when taxation could no longer be avoided, the mine owners managed to obtain preferential tax rates. But the leading mine owners did *not* use the state to obtain monopoly control over Comstock. Libecap (1978) cites as one reason for the absence of cartelization that "competition among investors and variations in mine output prevented stable coalitions from forming." Ibid., p. 359.

29. Ibid., p. 341.

net gains from exclusivity. With rising marginal costs of enforcement and falling marginal benefits, exclusive rights are seldom complete. Furthermore, optimizing owners seek enforcement at margins where costs of measurement and enforcement are low.

The literature contains various examples of owners attempting to economize on enforcement expenditures. In the American West and in tribal Africa, exclusive rights to land have been enforced by controlling vital water supplies from rivers and wells rather than by fencing.[30] Demsetz (1964) explains the use of certain *combination sales* in terms of enforcement costs.[31] For example, suburban shopping plazas often provide "free" parking (which nonshoppers can take advantage of) but include the cost of this service in the prices of goods sold in the stores. This practice is consistent with wealth maximization, if the net gain from selling parking services separately is negative, which may be true of locations where the price of land is relatively low. In other cases of high enforcement and contracting costs, both separate and combination sales can be an unprofitable alternative, and then it is sometimes optimal to leave a scarce resource wholly or partly in the public domain. This is a theoretical possibility for joint products. Demsetz (1964) cites the example of an apple grower who provides a beekeeper with valuable and costly nectar free of charge because high transaction costs prevent the separate marketing of apples and blossoms, and lack of demand makes tie-in sales impractical.[32]

In most communities the uses of scarce and vital resources tend to be constrained by some form of exclusive rights. Yet there are exceptions, cases where valuable resources of major importance for an economy are wholly or partly in the public domain. The

30. I owe this example to Andrew Rutten.
31. Demsetz, Harold (1964). "The Exchange and Enforcement of Property Rights." *Journal of Law and Economics 3* (October): 11–26.
32. We can add that Cheung (1973) gives evidence of beekeepers and apple growers who overcame the costs of contracting and negotiated contracts that provided use of nectar for the bees in return for payment. Cheung, Steven N. S. (1973). "The Fable of the Bees: An Economic Investigation." *Journal of Law and Economics 16* (No. 1, April): 11–33.

utilization of fish stocks in the oceans is perhaps one of the best known examples of this phenomenon. In terms of our analysis three factors can push the ownership structure of an important resource, such as fish stocks, toward common property and open access: (1) high exclusion costs; (2) high internal governance costs, when exclusive rights are shared; and (3) an open-access constraint enforced by the state (for reasons of equity, for example).

Johnson and Libecap (1982) find evidence of common property characteristics in a study of the Texas shrimp industry and observe rent dissipation along several margins.[33] They explain the existence of the common pool problems in the industry primarily in terms of (2) and (3) above.

Private rights in fishing were common in the early period of U.S. history but were gradually taken away – early in the nineteenth century in the case of U.S. inshore waters.[34] Today, ocean fisheries are formally owned by the U.S. government for the common use of all citizens. U.S. federal and state governments have ruled out private rights to fish stocks, and the courts have prosecuted individuals and their organizations for attempting to control entry or effort, as such measures are judged to be in violation of the country's antitrust legislation.

Second, Johnson and Libecap (1982) emphasize the internal governance costs of commoners involved in fishing and argue that these costs block the emergence of effective exclusive communal rights. In the Texas shrimp industry, internal governance costs are high because the fishermen are heterogeneous with regard to fishing skills.[35] One implication of heterogeneous fishermen and open-

33. Johnson, Ronald N., and Libecap, Gary D. (1982). "Contracting Problems and Regulation: The Case of the Fishery." *American Economic Review 72* (No. 5): 1005–1022. "The Texas shrimp industry . . . is one of the nation's most valuable fisheries for a single species. . . . It is considered overcapitalized and catch per unit of effort is falling." (p. 1005)

34. Ibid., p. 1006.

35. "Repeated success by some fishermen (higher than average catches) is primarily attributed to knowledge of how to set nets and regulate their spread, correct trawling speed, and the location of shrimp." The capital equipment of the

access fishery is that fishermen with superior innate skills receive rent even though the marginally qualified receive no rent.[36] As individual efforts to exclude are illegal, government regulation is the only method available to increase the yield from the fishery, but Johnson and Libecap argue that heterogeneous fishermen can agree on only those regulations that recognize *existing ranking* of fishermen.[37] Heterogeneous fishermen will tend to oppose

> effort or catch quotas, corrective taxes, and transferable
> licenses . . . at least until the fishery is intensively
> depleted. Fishermen can be expected to rally for general
> regulations to raise total yields such as season closures
> or entry controls on outsiders. Those programs raise
> rents for existing fishermen above open access
> conditions, even though dissipation continues along
> other margins.[38]

In countries where private exclusive rights to species in the sea are legal and enforced by the state, exclusive rights are found in inshore waters for seaweed, shellfish, and other sedentary species. The case of the Japanese *inshore fisheries* is probably the best known of these.[39] In modern Japan, cooperative associations of fishermen have territorial rights to patches of the sea, which in

---

fishermen in the Texas bays is fairly homogeneous due to state regulations. Ibid., pp. 1010–1011.

36. Ibid., p. 1011.
37. The argument assumes that high transaction costs rule out side payments where reluctant fishermen are bribed to accept regulations that increase the net yield of the fishery.
38. Johnson and Libecap (1982) [op. cit., note 33], p. 1019. Finally, as the fishermen are opposed to precise communal rules, the politicians do not have an incentive to impose such regulations on the industry.
39. Comitini, Salvatore (1966). "Marine Resources Exploitation and Management in the Economic Development of Japan." *Economic Development and Cultural Change 14* (July): 414–427; and Hannesson, Rögnvaldur (1984). "Fishermen's Organizations and Their Role in Fisheries Management." Working paper. Bergen: Norwegian School of Economics and Business Administration. "The inshore waters of Japan are divided into 'fields,' and the right to harvest certain types of fish or use certain types of fishing gear belongs to somebody, usually a fishermen's cooperative, but individuals and companies can also hold fishing rights." Hannesson (1984), p. 14.

effect represent exclusive rights to bottom-dwelling species. The Japanese fishermen's associations seem to have overcome serious internal governance problems and appear to be able to undertake joint actions to increase the yield from their fish stocks. The introduction in modern times of territorial rights to the inshore waters of Japan was an attempt to limit disputes between fishermen over access, which often led to wasteful destruction of fishing gear. In fact, the system of territorial rights can be seen as an endogenous reduction in the optimal size of the commons caused by high internal governance costs for large units in the inshore fisheries. Later, when overfishing had become a more important issue, the fishermen's organizations began to manage the fish stocks.[40]

So far, we have not discussed the role of high exclusion costs in the fishery, which was the first factor listed above as promoting open access. High exclusion costs are of paramount importance in the case of migratory species in the ocean, such as the North Atlantic herring, which sometimes move during their life cycle throughout the territorial waters of one or even several coastal states. In the case of highly mobile fish stocks, exclusive individual rights to patches of the ocean – territorial use rights – may represent locational advantages but do not constitute exclusive rights to fishery resources.

Our analysis suggests that, other things being equal, high exclusion costs will push the ownership structure of a resource toward a large commons, which is consistent with the organization of ocean fisheries of today.[41] Most coastal states have organized the national

---

40. Hannesson (1984) [op. cit., note 39], pp. 14–19. Hannesson's review of the literature indicates that this system of fishing rights seems to prevent serious dissipation of resources. But he notes that some authors have expressed worries that "restraints [imposed by the fishermen's cooperatives] on fishing gear and methods delay or prohibit technological advance in the fisheries, without elaborating further." P. 16. In Chapter 7, Section 7.4, discussing the demise of the open-field system, we report that Dahlman and Fenoaltea have theorized that technical change and expanding markets strained the decision process of the European open-field village and made it inviable as an economic unit.
41. Political factors are also important. Clarkson (1974) surveyed the history of international law regarding resources of the ocean and found that "historically,

fishing zones as exclusive state property, with the government granting to individual fishermen fishing rights (user rights) that can be withdrawn or changed at short notice. It is striking to note that this system of exclusive ownership by the state typically has not given rise to rules that prevent large-scale dissipation at various margins.[42]

It is not clearly understood why a state tolerates that the rent from a valuable resource, such as a fishery, be dissipated when it has (at least formal) ownership rights over it. For one, the internal governance costs may be prohibitively large for all sizes of commons. Political considerations of equity may also perpetuate open-access conditions. And finally, little support comes from the fishermen for effective limits to dissipation if the Johnson–Libecap argument about the implications of heterogeneous fishermen is correct. Government regulation dominates, and Hannesson (1984), who examined worldwide the role of fishermen's organizations, found little or no evidence of involvement by the organizations in the management of *migratory* species.

Finally, institutional sophistication of fisheries regulation has been lacking, perhaps because of lack of knowledge. Until the 1970s, most fisheries economists ignored transaction costs and the logic of the property rights approach in their search for solutions to the institutional problems of the fishing industry. These economists "who had been brought up on Pigovian welfare economics favored taxes or subsidies to bridge the gap between private and

oceans policy has generally recognized only the highest valued use of the seas and has shifted from rules and regulations favoring the development and use of fisheries to those enhancing the use of oceans' services such as navigation." At various times in history, this has meant that open access to major fisheries has been enforced by national states. P. 118 in Clarkson, Kenneth W. (1974). "International Law, U.S. Seabeds Policy and Ocean Resource Development." *Journal of Law and Economics 17* (No. 1, April): 117–142.

42. Failure to maximize the value of fish stocks is understandable prior to the introduction of national fishing zones of 200 nautical miles in the 1970s. Then fishing fleets from several nations competed for the same resource, and the cost of enforcing agreements on limits to the exploitation was high, as in most cases effective third-party enforcement was unavailable.

social net marginal products."[43] Recently, economists have begun to pay attention to economic incentives and the enforcement costs of alternative forms of government regulation, and it is likely that institutional innovations may lower the transaction costs of establishing exclusive rights over fish stocks. Many economists now favor *individual transferable quotas* as a method of granting fishermen property rights in fish. New Zealand made a pioneering institutional change in 1984 by implementing transferable quotas in the country's deep sea fishery.[44] However, with individual transferable quotas, it is still the government that determines the allowable total catch, and not much is yet known about the enforcement costs of transferable quotas, particularly when individual quotas are frequently sold. Also, the impact of a transferable quota system on the location of a fishing industry and its concentration may be unacceptable to those who control the state.[45]

The case of the crude oil industry in the United States, which was introduced in Chapter 4, Section 4.2, is our final example of persistent common property conditions in a major economic sector of an advanced economy.[46] Open access conditions in the oil industry arise when the surface land above an oil reservoir is owned by several individuals who lease the land to a number of independent operators. As the oil is common property until it has been brought to the surface, several small firms on the same oil field give rise to competitive extraction. Firm Z, which shares a large

43. P. 726 in Scott, Anthony (1979). "Development of Economic Theory on Fisheries Regulation." *Journal of the Fisheries Resource Board of Canada 36*: 725–741.
44. Hannesson (1984), op. cit., note 39.
45. Scott (1986) speculates that transferable quotas may foster self-enforcement among the fishermen, when they develop a sense of proprietorship, and "a quota may become something like a share in a growing enterprise." P. 21 in Scott, Anthony (1986). "Emerging Markets in Fisheries' Rights." Working paper. Vancouver: University of British Columbia.
46. The discussion that follows is based on Wiggins, Steven N., and Libecap, Gary D. (1985). "Oil Field Unitization: Contractual Failure in the Presence of Imperfect Information." *American Economic Review 75* (No. 3): 368–385; also Libecap, Gary N. (1986a). "Property Rights in Economic History: Implications for Research." *Explorations in Economic History 23* (No. 3): 227–252.

reservoir with several other operators, finds itself in a prisoners' dilemma: If firm Z goes slow and decides not to join the race, the other firms are likely to drain the reservoir, and not only take the lion's share of the resource but also raise the marginal extraction costs for firm Z. This last effect comes about because the extraction of oil from the field weakens underground pressures that lift the oil to the surface. Tempered utilization of the field by firm Z, when the others hurry, implies that in the near future Z must use costly methods, such as pumps, for extracting oil. On the other hand, if all the other firms go slow, firm Z loses a golden opportunity to free-ride.

Competitive depletion of an oil reservoir by several independent firms leads to dissipation of rent from the resource along several margins. For example, too many wells are drilled, operations are not concentrated on wells with the lowest marginal cost of extraction, and only a relatively small share of the oil in the reservoir is economically recoverable.[47] The reason behind this last effect is as follows: A slow rate of utilization can maintain subsurface pressures longer than rapid exploitation does. With competitive extraction, pressure levels fall rapidly, and it becomes economical to abandon a field when only a relatively small proportion of the underground oil supplies has been brought to the surface.

Although the net gains from operating an oil field as a single commons, rather than as many intermediate commons, are often measured in tens or even hundreds of millions of dollars, the evidence tells us that the individual operators themselves very seldom take the initiative to organize the reservoir as one unit. Libecap and Wiggins (1985) report that in 1975, field-wide units in the Texas oil industry accounted for only 20 percent of the total state output, and for Oklahoma the comparable figure was 38 percent.[48] In a

---

47. "In 1937, the American Petroleum Institute estimated that excessive wells cost $200,000,000." Libecap (1986a) [op. cit., note 46], p. 243. Also see Chapter 4, Section 4.2, for estimates of the dissipation involved earlier in the century.
48. Libecap and Wiggins (1985) cite an oil industry study which predicted (in 1964) that the unitization of a particular Texas oil field would increase oil recovery by 130 million barrels. Furthermore, studies show that even partial unitization

theoretical context, the dilemma of the oil fields is rooted in high internal governance costs. Although very high exclusion costs for underground reservoirs (and important spillover effects) push an oil field with scattered ownership toward a single unified commons, high governance costs seem to prevent such a reorganization.

The reorganization of an oil field as a single operating unit can involve either *unitization*, where a single firm operates the field, acting as an agent for the old operators who share in net output; or *lease consolidation*. In either case, organizational change calls for estimates of lease values that are satisfactory to all sides.[49] Libecap and Wiggins (1985) report that high costs of ex ante estimating the value of leases are the major factor blocking spontaneous private contractual agreements on unitization or lease consolidation.

> Estimates are a function of surface acreage, number of wells, subsurface pressure, porosity and volume of the producing formation, oil migration, and estimated remaining oil reserves. Most of the parameters are not observable and involve subjective interpretation by company engineers, using limited and often controversial data. Moreover, there is no accepted procedure for mapping the parameters to lease values.[50]

can save tens of millions of dollars. Libecap Gary D., and Wiggins, Steven N. (1985). "The Influence of Private Contractual Failure on Regulation: The Cost of Oil Field Unitization." *Journal of Political Economy 93* (No. 4): 690–714.

49. Unitization requires estimates of the relative value of leases, and consolidation calls for estimates of the market value of leases. Note that some form of *output rationing* is a third approach to solve the common pool problems of oil fields.

50. Libecap (1986a) [op. cit., note 46], p. 244. Libecap and Wiggins (1985) [op. cit., note 48] report that the contracting costs of producing mutually acceptable estimates of lease values are highest when the extraction of oil has just begun, but the costs are lower both during the initial drilling stage and much later when the operating life of an oil field is near an end. The costs are low during the initial drilling stage because the limited information available is symmetrically distributed. The parties may then agree on lease values on the basis of surface areas. Information is cheap and plentiful on a mature field because information about lease values is a by-product of oil extraction. The costs are particularly high during the initial phase of extraction because information is asymmetrically distributed between inside owners and outside evaluators.

When high transaction costs block private contractual adjustments and lead to tremendous output losses, we would expect, on the basis of the naive theory of property rights, that the state would step in and adjust the structure of property rights, particularly if it involved only a simple organizational change, such as operating an oil field as one unit. Libecap and Wiggins (1985) and Libecap (1986b) have studied the role of the state in the U.S. oil industry.[51] We return to their findings in the next section.

8.4. Extending the naive model: the interest-group theory of property rights

The role of government in the naive theory of property rights is implicit. It is assumed that the state will create a general framework of property rights that permits individuals to maximize the community's net wealth by taking advantage of the division of labor and market exchange. In situations where transaction costs are high, the state maximizes wealth either by assigning property rights directly to individuals or by redefining the structure of rights in specific ways.[52] However, little ingenuity is needed to find cases from all parts of the world that contradict the naive theory. Let

---

51. Libecap and Wiggins (1985), op. cit., note 48; Libecap, Gary D. (1986b). "The Political Economy of Cartelization by the Texas Railroad Commission, 1933–1972." Working paper. Tucson: University of Arizona, Department of Economics.

52. This viewpoint characterizes much of the American economics of law (or law and economics) literature. For example, Posner (1987) states that the following premise guides some research in the economics of nonmarket law: "Common law (i.e., judge-made) rules are often best explained as efforts, whether or not conscious, to bring about either Pareto or Kaldor–Hicks efficient outcomes." (p. 5) The nonmarket areas of law include crime, torts, and contracts; the environment; the family; the legislative and administrative processes; constitutional law; jurisprudence and legal process; legal history; primitive law; and so on." (p. 4) Posner (1987) goes on to analyze, in terms of the wealth maximization hypothesis, recent rulings by the Supreme Court regarding regulation in the market for two "goods": ideas and religion. Posner, Richard A. (1987). "The Law and Economics Movement." *American Economic Review* 77 (No. 2, May): 1–13.

us briefly consider examples drawn from three countries: the United States, Norway, and Peru.

First, consider responses by the state to private contractual failures in the U.S. oil industry, which we discussed in the previous section. This question has been studied in detail by Libecap and Wiggins (1985) and Libecap (1986b), and we can only outline some of their most important findings.[53] Briefly, they find a complex set of responses at all levels of government to the common pool problem of the oil industry, but, in general, the state has *not* acted to minimize costs and maximize the community's net wealth. Libecap (1986b) describes the system used from 1933 to 1972 to restrict domestic crude output levels in the United States. During this period, output was prorationed on the basis of market demand among states, fields, and producers.[54] The Texas Railroad Commission was the prime mover of this cartel-type arrangement, and the rules governing the prorationing system were designed to *favor high-cost producers and small firms*. Libecap (1986b) reports that, in Texas, low-cost fields were held to less than half of their potential production, and, for example, figures for the year 1963 reveal that high-cost stripper wells were guaranteed 44 percent of the total Texas quota. Prorationing by the Texas Railroad Commission, a public body, was authorized under a Texas law, and the nation-wide system of rationing was backed by federal laws, regulations, and bureaus. Furthermore, Libecap and Wiggins (1985) report that the state governments of Texas and Oklahoma failed to design rules that encouraged the unitization of oil fields, whereas in Wyoming, where oil fields were mostly on federal land, the federal government designed a structure of property rights that *encouraged* unitization.

Next take the case of homogeneous, prosperous Norway. Norway is no different from other high-income countries of north-

53. Libecap and Wiggins (1985), op. cit., note 48; Libecap (1986b), op. cit., note 51.
54. See also Libecap, Gary D., and Wiggins, Steven N. (1984). "Contractual Responses to the Common Pool: Prorationing of Crude Oil Production." *American Economic Review 74* (No. 1): 87–98.

western Europe in that modest adjustments in its structure of property rights could lead to large increases in the country's net wealth. For example, Norwegian agriculture receives extensive subsidies and is protected from foreign competition through restrictions on imports, although production costs for many of the industry's products are well above world market prices. For instance, Norwegian consumers are constrained to buy costly Norwegian apples so long as they are available, and comparable restrictions on imported tomatoes and cucumbers have generated an unusual inverse relationship between their price and the height above the horizon of the midday sun, as one economist puts it.[55]

The Norwegian state has also taken measures to limit the size of firms, a policy that in many cases makes sense only if seen as preventing low-cost large-scale production (and protecting small, high-cost producers.) For example, boats longer than ninety feet are not permitted in one branch of the fisheries; a special license is required for operating a farm with more than 2000 chickens or 500 pigs; and, in the new and important industry of fish farming (aquaculture), the maximum size for each farm is 8000 cubic meters.[56] Finally, when foreign oil companies apply to the Norwegian government for a license to drill for and extract oil on the offshore oil fields of Norway, governmental rules require that priority be given to firms that have made valuable contributions to Norwegian society, without specifying clearly what constitutes a valuable contribution.

Third, consider the case of Peru, a developing country. Regulation in Peru (and in many other Third World countries) has reached mammoth proportions, and it is clear that the regulatory system does *not* stimulate economic growth and development. For example, the Peruvian state has erected high barriers that make legal entry into most lines of production very costly. An indepen-

---

55. The Norwegian examples are based on Hannesson, Rögnvaldur (1986). "Rent Seeking." Working paper [In Norwegian]. Bergen: Norwegian School of Economics and Business Administration.
56. Hannesson (1986); op. cit., note 39. The figures refer to the state of affairs in 1986.

dent Peruvian economic institute has estimated the cost of obtaining from the state the right to establish a small manufacturing firm in the domestic garment industry by actually making such an application. The individuals involved spent 289 days nearly full-time, negotiating the bureaucratic process. They were asked ten times for bribes by public officials but could avoid payment in all but two instances.[57] Similarly, it was found that a byzantine regulatory system governs applications for building homes on unoccupied government land in the Lima region, but some two thirds of the Peruvian population live in and around the capital city. The institute discovered that, in order to obtain all required permits to buy land that the government owns and has never been in private hands, the applicant must go through a bureaucratic process of *200 stages*, which takes a minimum of seven years.

The high costs of entry and extensive regulation of economic activity in Peru have given rise to an informal sector that operates outside or on the margin of the law. It is estimated that about half of the country's population works in the informal sector. For example, nearly half of the people of Lima live in informal housing, nine out of ten passengers ride on buses that belong to the informal sector, and informality dominates the activities of small commercial entrepreneurs, who typically operate as street vendors (obtaining informal but transferable property rights to slices of sidewalks) or in informal markets.

The costs of transacting are high in the informal sector of Peru, when compared to well-functioning markets. Ownership rights are uncertain and largely privately enforced; economic units tend to

---

57. The Peruvian examples are based on studies undertaken by the Institute for Liberty and Democracy in Lima, which is headed by Hernando De Soto. See Litan, Robert E., and Schuck, Peter H. (1986). "Regulatory Reform in the Third World: The Case of Peru." *Yale Journal on Regulation 4* (No. 1, Fall). De Soto has written about the work of the Institute and about Peru's informal sector. De Soto, Hernando (1986). *El Otro Sendero: La Revolucion Informal*. Lima: Editorial El Barranco. [Engl. Transl.: The Other Path: The Invisible Revolution in the Third World.]

be small as that makes it easier to hide illegal operations from the state; and an atmosphere of uncertainty discourages large-scale long-term investments. Operations that are illegal but receive de facto recognition by the state tend to be heavily regulated, and, similarly, the state imposes heavy costs of entry, operation, and exit on firms in the formal (legal) sector. We might add that structures of rights comparable to the Peruvian case are found today in many countries that generally tend to have stagnant economies. The system is sometimes referred to as "neomercantilism," which reminds us that it is well-known throughout history.[58]

It is clear that the examples listed above contradict the naive theory of property rights. A rudimentary knowledge of economic history or modern economic systems rules out the naive model as a general theory. In fact, it is doubtful whether any economist sees the model as a general theory in the positive sense, although attempts to provide an alternative to the naive model are relatively recent.[59] One of the first steps taken to modify the naive model of property rights involved linking it to the interest-group theory of legislation and government.[60] We refer to this extension of the naive model as the *interest-group theory of property rights*.

The interest-group theory of property rights takes the fundamental social and political institutions of the community as given, and seeks to explain the structure of property rights in various industries in terms of interaction between interest groups in the political market. Property rights, which serve the narrow self-

---

58. See Eklund Robert B., Jr., and Tollison, Robert D. (1982). *Mercantilism as a Rent-Seeking Society: Economic Regulation in Historical Perspective*. College Station: Texas A & M University Press.
59. Note that the naive theory can be taken as a general theory of how the government *should* define the property rights structure. In this book, we are not concerned with *normative* theories of property rights. As for positive theorizing, we do not deny that the naive model may be a powerful tool in certain restricted situations.
60. We introduced the interest-group theory of legislation and government in Chapter 3, in a discussion of the free-rider problem, information costs, and political processes; and in Chapter 5, where we looked at the economics of regulation.

interest of a special-interest group but cause substantial output losses to the community as a whole, typically are explained in terms of transaction costs, free-riding, and asymmetrical information.

The ability to influence elected representatives is often strong in the case of relatively small, compact special-interest groups, where each individual has much to gain by an adjustment in the structure of property rights, and when the group has an easy access to the relevant information and is able to control or manipulate it. The losers in the interest-group struggle tend to be individuals belonging to large groups: For consumers as a whole – for whom the adjustment in property rights (such as a new tariff) has a small impact on each person – the costs of organizing are high, free riding is a serious problem, and individual information costs are high relative to the stakes.

Individuals, acting alone or in groups, can maximize their wealth either by focusing solely on production within the existing framework of institutions or by seeking favorable changes in laws and regulations from rulers, legislatures, and government bureaus. The path chosen depends on the relative price of obtaining favorable changes in the structure of rights. When the price is low, wealth seeking by compact special-interest groups can generate economic institutions that allow a community to realize only a fraction of its technical capacity for production.

If we return to the Norwegian example, the evidence suggests that the structure of property rights in the country's agriculture is motivated by considerations of redistribution and equity, at least in part. One piece of evidence is a resolution passed in 1975 by the legislative assembly proclaiming that farmers have a right to the same pay as industrial workers.[61] Similarly, Libecap and Wiggins, in their studies of the U.S. crude oil industry cited above, explain the policies of the national oil cartel and the structure of rights on the oil fields of Texas and Oklahoma in terms of the political influence of numerous, small, high-cost producers. Li-

---

61. Hannesson (1986), op. cit., note 39.

becap (1986a) describes the interest-group approach to property rights in these words:

> Competitive forces tend to erode institutions that no longer support economic growth. Changing market conditions exert pressure for dynamic adjustments in the existing rights structure through refinement of rights and privileges or their transfer to others . . . to facilitate responses to new economic opportunities. Predictions regarding the way in which property rights arrangements respond over time to changing economic opportunities, however, must carefully consider political or equity factors. Distributional conflicts arise when property rights are coercively redistributed by the state with little or no compensation. . . . Disadvantaged parties will oppose the new arrangement, even though it allows for an aggregate expansion in production and wealth. Accordingly, analysis of the likely winners and losers of economic and institutional change and their interaction in the political arena in specific settings is necessary before the observed pattern of property rights can be understood.[62]

The interest-group theory of property rights is closely related to the *theory of rent seeking*. We end this chapter with a short note on the theory of rent seeking, which, in our opinion, tends to be unnecessarily narrow and carries with it, as an implicit assumption, the fundamental bias of the neoclassical approach and the naive theory of property rights.

8.5. A digression on rent seeking

The 1970s saw the emergence of the literature on rent seeking. The name was provided by Krueger (1974), who also supplied theoretical analysis and estimates of rent arising from

---

62. Libecap (1986a) [op. cit., note 46], pp. 227–228.

restrictive practices in India and Turkey.[63] A pioneering contribution was made by Tullock (1967). Tollison (1982) provides a readable survey, and several authors examine various aspects of the theory of rent seeking in Buchanan et al. (1980).[64]

The close relationship between the literature on rent seeking and the economics of property rights has often been pointed out. Buchanan (1980) sees rent seeking as an appropriate extension of the property rights approach.[65] Benson (1984) has demonstrated how the two approaches can yield identical conclusions, but he argues that the property-rights paradigm provides richer insights.[66]

Tollison (1982) makes clear that the rent-seeking literature contains two major lines of research. The first involves theoretical analysis and empirical estimates of the (neoclassical) social welfare losses resulting from the restriction of trade through tariffs, monopolies, and the like, which special-interest groups obtain from the government. The rent-seeking literature shows that the social costs of various government restrictions upon economic activity is greater than economists previously had assumed. In addition to the usual triangle representing the deadweight loss (lost consumer surplus) of restricting output and blocking mutually advantageous exchange, there are the resource costs of individuals seeking privileges from the government. The analysis is exactly equivalent to our discussion, in Chapter 4, of costs that can arise when individuals seek to obtain exclusive rights to a valuable resource. In either case, the individual is motivated by her expected personal gain from adjusting the structure of property rights. It is common to

63. Krueger, Anne O. (1974). "The Political Economy of the Rent-Seeking Society." *American Economic Review 64* (No. 3, June): 291–303.
64. Tullock, Gordon (1967). "The Welfare Costs of Tariffs, Monopolies, and Theft." *Western Economic Journal 5* (June): 224–232; Tollison, Robert D. (1982). "Rent Seeking: A Survey." *Kyklos 35* (No. 4): 575–602; and Buchanan, James M., et al., eds. (1980). *Toward a Theory of the Rent-Seeking Society.* College Station: Texas A & M University Press.
65. Buchanan, James M. (1980). "Rent Seeking and Profit Seeking." In Buchanan et al., eds. (1980), op. cit., note 64.
66. Benson, Bruce L. (1984). "Rent Seeking from a Property Rights Perspective." *Southern Economic Journal* (October): 388–400.

see several individuals compete for changes in property rights, and those who expect to lose from the proposed change fight back. It has been demonstrated theoretically that, when information is costly, the resource costs of such struggles can easily exceed the present value of the rent sought.[67]

The second major strand of the rent-seeking literature is concerned with deriving testable theories of the actual behavior of individuals and groups who are engaged in rent (or rather wealth) seeking. *Rent seeking* is defined as attempts by individuals to increase their personal wealth while at the same time making a negative contribution to the net wealth of their community. The approach is conceptually the same as the interest-group theory of property rights which we discussed in the previous section, as both are rooted in the interest-group theory of legislation and government.

The interest-group theory of government has supplied important insights, but it has weaknesses that are particularly apparent in many of its applications in the rent-seeking literature. The theory does not make clear what the state is, except presumably an aggregate of competing interest groups who somehow reach an equilibrium in the political market. Yet in much of the rent-seeking writings there seems to be a presumption that the state will somehow supply output-maximizing property rights, if only special-interest groups can be contained. This is evident in Olson's (1982) famous book, *The Rise and Decline of Nations*, which is perhaps the best known manifestation of the rent-seeking literature.[68] Olson draws on ideas developed in his classic *Logic of Collective Action* to demonstrate that special-interest groups require long periods of social tranquillity to overcome free riding and to organize as pressure groups.[69] Once pressure groups are organized, they are likely to seek various privileges that can strangle economic

67. See our discussion of these issues in Chapter 4, Section 4.3.
68. Olson, Mancur (1982). *The Rise and Decline of Nations*. New Haven: Yale University Press.
69. Olson, Mancur (1971). *The Logic of Collective Action*, rev. ed. Cambridge, Mass.: Harvard University Press.

growth. But, on the other hand, turbulent periods tend to uproot pressure groups and make rapid economic growth possible – for example, in Germany following World War II. In other words, when pressure groups are weak, the *state* provides a structure of property rights that is consistent with the naive theory of property rights.

We now turn to the final two chapters of this book to examine recent attempts to improve on the naive model and the interest-group theory of government by providing alternative theories of the state, which endogenize social and political institutions. Our concern is primarily with studies that emphasize the role of transaction costs.

9

Property rights in stateless societies

9.1. Introduction

In these two final chapters of the book, we are concerned with the economic logic of social institutions, particularly those formal and informal rules, norms, and customs of a community that affect economic behavior, the organization of production, and economic outcomes.[1] Chapter 9 looks at stateless societies and international property rights, and Chapter 10 deals both with autocratic states and with the political institutions of democracy. The approach is the same as in Chapters 6 and 7, where we examined the logic of various organizations in input and output markets, such as the firm, sharecropping, or warranties. As we see it, exchange in the *political arena* interacts with the environment (i.e., exogenous variables such as information technology, resource endowments, or geographical location) and gives rise to contractual arrangements – that is, social institutions. Again, in the political field, both the outcomes of contractual relationships and the structure of the contracts themselves are shaped by transaction costs. It is important to note that the NIE approach to social institutions does not require that the environmental (exogenous) variables be the same from one study or model to another. For example, de-

---

1. Note that we use the terms "social institutions" and "political institutions" interchangeably.

pending on circumstances we may want to treat population growth or technological change as either endogenous or exogenous variables. Laws, norms, and custom can be modeled either as endogenous variables or as a part of the environment (a constraint). The treatment of these critical variables depends in each case on the purpose of the study and on the availability of relevant theories.

At the outset it is necessary to define the task that we have set for ourselves in Chapters 9 and 10. First, our task is limited primarily to analyzing social institutions in terms of the transaction-costs approach, which is the common theme of this book. Second, we seek to model social institutions in terms of the economic approach, which involves optimization subject to constraints. As the discussion will make clear (particularly in Chapter 10), our approach does not imply that political institutions are always "efficient" in the neoclassical sense: that they always create conditions for maximizing the output of an economy subject to the constraints of resources, technologies, and tastes. Ultimately, NIE must strive to explain both the wealth of nations and the persistence of social institutions that impose high opportunity costs in lost output and stifled growth.

Let us assume that comparative statics analysis reveals that a particular society depends on relatively costly political institutions in terms of resource costs and net output foregone and, further, that alternative institutional arrangements are known and technically available. Neoinstitutional Economics suggests three responses to such findings. First, the investigator *reexamines* carefully the transaction costs dictated by the *physical environment* of the community and attempts to establish whether alternative institutional arrangements would *in fact* economize on resources and generate more wealth, even when the political costs of institutional change are ignored. Second, he or she seeks to model and investigate the *political environment* of the economy in order to identify political constraints on institutional change. The rudiments of an NIE model of the state have been developed on the basis of the new theory of the firm, and helpful contributions can be found in the public-choice literature; but much work lies ahead in this area.

Third, the investigator looks for strongly held values (perhaps relics from a prior environment) that get in the way of institutional change.

The organization of Chapter 9 is as follows. The next, or second, section constitutes the bulk of the chapter and deals, in terms of NIE, with cooperation and institutions in stateless societies. The cases discussed involve both primitive societies that anthropologists have investigated during the twentieth century, and early societies for which there are historical accounts. Prestate societies, like societies with formal government, must meet the minimum requirement of containing the open access problem by establishing individual exclusive rights or rules of internal governance for systems of communal rights. All societies depend on informal rules, conventions, and taboos for ensuring cooperation and enforcing the structure of property rights. Our understanding of the enforcement process and the fundamental nature of any property rights system can be advanced by looking at prestate societies, such as tribal societies, where privately enforced rules and custom are the critical social constraints on economic actors.

We begin Section 9.2 by examining whether production and exchange in stateless societies can be analyzed appropriately in terms of Neoinstitutional Economics (Section 9.2.1). Next the case of the Nuer of the Upper Nile region is used to introduce the issues of violence and deterrence in stateless communities. The discussion draws on research by anthropologists and, following Bates, uses the framework of a prisoners' dilemma game (9.2.2). We then look at private enforcement of law during the California gold rush of 1848 by examining Umbeck's well-known study of the economics of property rights in the mining districts (9.2.3). The case of the Nuer is used again to analyze how vengeance groups, compensation, arbitration, and ideology can help create order and solve the prisoners' dilemma of noncooperation (9.2.4). Up to this point various beliefs and norms that constrained behavior are treated as exogenous variables, but we present a short account of evolutionary models in economics seeking to endogenize these variables, primarily work by Hirshleifer (9.2.5). Then the discussion turns away from the basic question of order in stateless societies to a more general analysis of social institutions in terms of information and transaction costs. Our attention is directed at Posner's thesis regarding the insurance function of primitive law (9.2.6). Posner has also theorized about the basic constraints that create institutional equilibrium in stateless societies and block the evolution of formal governments. In the final part of Section 9.2, we examine the breakdown of a stateless society by looking at the demise in the thirteenth century of the Icelandic Commonwealth (9.2.7).

The chapter ends with a discussion about the establishment and enforcement of international property rights in the absence of world government (Section 9.3), a theme that is logically related to the question of order in stateless societies.

9.2. The origins of cooperation and the economics of institutions in stateless societies

9.2.1. The issues

No society is viable if it lacks institutional mechanisms for constraining open access to human and nonhuman capital and to natural resources. Open access reduces the wealth of a community and is inimical to survival in a world of scarce resources. The social mechanisms for constraining open access and establishing exclusive rights fall into four interrelated categories:

1. Exclusion by means of force or threats of force
2. Value systems or ideologies, which affect individual incentives and lower the costs of exclusion
3. Custom and customary law, such as the rules in prestate societies that define the clan, vengeance group, or eligible brides for a man and other forms of behavior
4. Rules imposed by the state and its agencies, including constitutions, statutes, common law, and executive decrees

All societies, the modern state included, depend vitally on self-enforcement, customary law, and value systems for preventing general conditions of open access and destructive wealth-seeking, but the role of these factors in shaping economic incentives is not well understood. Prestate societies – lacking formal institutions of government and specialists such as lawmakers, judges, police officers, investigators, and administrators – provide laboratory conditions for studying the way in which custom and private enforcement of law affect economic behavior.[2]

Attempts to explain the economic logic of primitive societies in terms of transaction costs and NIE have just begun. Until recently, primitive societies have been mostly the property of social scientists who reject the economic approach, frequently claiming that primitive man did not economize.[3] Karl Polanyi is perhaps the most distinguished of these critics.[4] He maintains that an economic analysis of exchange relationships is relevant for societies only when the allocation of resources is dominated by price-making markets, which he sees as a historical phenomenon of limited range, primarily characteristic of the nineteenth and, to a lesser degree, the twentieth century. Other allocation systems in history, "transactional modes" as Polanyi calls them, are not based on economizing behavior and can be understood only in terms of cultural, social, and psychological analysis for which he provides a conceptual framework. Although Polanyi exaggerates the lack of markets in history, he has a point: Until recently, economics has not made important contributions to the analysis of economic behavior and institutions, except in the context of price-making markets.[5]

2. The line between stateless societies and states is blurred, and various societies are, or have been, halfway houses in this respect, for example, the Icelandic Commonwealth from 930 to 1262, which had a law-making body and courts but relied on private enforcement of law, as it lacked an executive branch. This case is discussed below.
3. But the times are changing. For instance, see Behnke, Roy H., Jr. (1985). "Open Range-Management and Property Rights in Pastoral Africa: A Case of Spontaneous Range Enclosure in South Darfur, Sudan." London: Overseas Development Institute Paper.
4. For example, see the collection of Karl Polanyi's essays edited by George Dalton. (1971). *Primitive, Archaic and Modern Economies.* Boston: Beacon Press.
5. McCloskey has this to say about the alleged lack of markets for land in the Middle Ages: "Somewhere early in their educations most people acquire a view of the Middle Ages prevalent in the 19th century, of the medieval economy as

The challenge of Polanyi is taken up by North (1977), who argues that adding transaction-costs analysis to the economic approach makes it a useful tool for analyzing the whole range of allocation systems found in history.[6] Polanyi's various "transactional modes" – for example, administered trade, reciprocal obligatory gift giving between kin and friends, householding (production for use), ports of call – are not purely social and psychological institutions, according to North. Polanyi's transactional modes are substitutes for price-making markets and are used for the allocation of resources because they economize on costs, particularly transaction costs. Transactional modes vary because the measurement and enforcement costs of exchange vary, and in primitive or ancient societies high transaction costs typically limit or preclude impersonal exchange in price-making markets. North makes the point that Polanyi's approach offers no explanation why one transactional mode replaces another, whereas transaction-costs analysis (plus a theory of the state) may help us do so.[7]

We can add that a lack of specialization is a notable characteristic

a 'natural,' non-money economy in which such a thing as 'owning' land was foreign. Owning is supposed to have arrived with capitalism. . . . Since the early years of this century medievalists have been fighting a losing battle against the notion that the Middle Ages was innocent of markets. On sober consideration the subnotion that land was inalienable and common has never been very plausible: a society that marketed human beings and eternal salvation would be unlikely to have scruples about land. But speculation is unnecessary, since the evidence of an active market in land among peasants is ample." Pp. 43–44 in McCloskey, Donald N. (1986). "The Open Fields of England: Rent, Risk, and the Rate of Interest, 1300–1815." Working paper. University of Iowa. Forthcoming in Galinson, David, ed. *In Search of Historical Economics: Market Behavior in Past Times.* Cambridge: Cambridge University Press.

6. North, Douglass C. (1977). "Markets and Other Allocation Systems in History: The Challenge of Karl Polanyi." *Journal of European Economic History* 6 (No. 3, Winter): 703–716.

7. North acknowledges that the transaction-costs approach has far to go: "To the degree that we can develop an ordinal ranking of transactions costs, then changes at the margin should produce predictable pressure for institutional rearrangement. The caveat to such an optimistic statement is that while we can and should be able to predict the direction of institutional change, the precise form it will take is still beyond the scope of the state of the art." North (1977) [op. cit., note 6], 716. North's caveat is still valid.

of primitive societies, involving not only production and exchange but also institutions. The same institution may serve simultaneously to lower the cost of information in exchange, to substitute for formal governmental enforcement mechanisms, and to meet individual emotional and spiritual needs. Therefore, the conflicting conclusions of political scientists, anthropologists, and economists regarding the institutions of primitive society sometimes remind the impartial reader of the story of the five blind men and the elephant.

9.2.2. *The question of order: violence and deterrence*
Let us begin our exploration by considering the central question of *order* in stateless societies.

> All over the world there are societies which have no
> governmental institutions. That is, they lack officers
> with established powers to judge on quarrels and to
> enforce their decisions, to legislate and take admin-
> istrative action to meet emergencies, and to lead wars
> of offence and defence.... We know that some of them
> have existed over long periods with some kind of
> internal law and order, and have successfully defended
> themselves against attacks by others.... Therefore when
> anthropologists came to study these societies, they were
> immediately confronted with the problem of where
> social order and cohesion lay.[8]

Some of the most valuable insights into the preservation of property rights in stateless societies are found in the work of anthropologists, particularly in the work of a number of investigators who studied primitive societies in Africa in the first half of the century. Pioneering contributions were made by Evans-Pritchard, and the work of Gluckman is particularly insightful for our purposes.[9]

8. Pp. 2–3 in Gluckman, Max (1956). *Custom and Conflict in Africa.* Oxford: Basil Blackwell.
9. Evans-Pritchard, E. E. (1937). *Witchcraft, Oracles and Magic Among the Azande of the Anglo-Egyptian Sudan.* Oxford: Clarendon Press; idem (1940). *The Nuer: A Description of the Modes of Livelihood and Political Institutions*

The gains from secure property rights, compared with open access, can be explained with the help of the prisoners' dilemma in the theory of games.[10] Bates (1983) has formulated in terms of game theory Evans-Pritchard's explanation of the maintenance of order among the African Nuer, a pastoral people of the Upper Nile region.[11] The Nuer economy is based on the raising of cattle, which is exclusively owned by a joint family – the basic ownership unit being a father, his sons, and their wives. The Nuer cannot rely on any institutional authority to protect his cattle; he can depend only on private enforcement of his rights.

Let us consider an imaginary case of two joint families, X and Y, each with equal violence potential and propensity for violent behavior, and each holding net wealth equal to 10 cattle (a Nuer monetary unit). Each family is faced with a choice between aggression, A, and nonaggression, N, against the other family. The payoff from each strategy, A or N, depends on whether the other family will resort to aggression, so there are four possible outcomes. A hypothetical payoff matrix is presented in Matrix 9.1.[12]

		Family Y	
		A	N
	A	(4, 4)	(18, 2)
Family X			
	N	(2, 18)	(10, 10)

Matrix 9.1

of a Nilotic People. Oxford: Clarendon Press; idem (1951). *Kinship and Marriage Among the Nuer*. Oxford: Clarendon Press; idem (1956). *The Nuer Religion*. Oxford: Clarendon Press. See also Gluckman's (1956) excellent six essays dealing with the question of order in primitive societies, beginning with his classic "The Peace in the Feud." Gluckman draws on his own work and that of other anthropologists dealing with Africa, and provides a good bibliography of this early work. Gluckman, Max (1956), op. cit., note 8.

10. The prisoners' dilemma is a noncooperative, variable-sum game.
11. Bates, Robert H. (1983). "The Preservation of Order in Stateless Societies: A Reinterpretation of Evans-Pritchard's *The Nuer*." Chapter 1 in *Essays on the Political Economy of Rural Africa*. Cambridge: Cambridge University Press.
12. This example is based on Bates (1983) [op. cit., note 11], p. 9.

Peaceful coexistence results in a joint wealth of 20 cattle equally divided between the two families. Aggression by both sides uses up resources and reduces the joint wealth of X and Y to 8 cattle, again equally divided. Finally, if aggression is limited to one of the two parties, the joint wealth of X and Y is not reduced, but wealth is redistributed from (10,10) to (18,2) or (2,18). The dilemma arises when each player must make an irreversible choice between violence and nonviolence without knowing what the other side will choose. Then, no matter whether the other family chooses A or N, each player maximizes his expected wealth by choosing aggression – as 4 > 2, and 18 > 10. The equilibrium outcome is (A,A), a world where property rights are insecure, perhaps to the point of rendering cattle rearing and herding inviable economically.

The solution to this basic social dilemma calls for facing the "players" with *external constraints* or introducing *internalized values* that change the relative weight of the payoffs in the matrix, making outcomes (A,N) unattractive or unavailable to a potential aggressor. For example, the off-diagonal cells of the matrix, (18,2) and (2,18), could be removed outright: If the rules of the game were modified – and each party let it be known, perhaps through an unrelated third party (an arbitrator), that he would always retaliate – then outcomes (A,N) and (N,A) would no longer be possible, and we would have:[13]

		Family Y	
		A	N
Family X	A	(4, 4)	(0, 0)
	N	(0, 0)	(10, 10)

Matrix 9.2

---

13. Ibid., p. 13. Among the Nuer the leopard-skin chief provided such arbitration. His role was to lower the cost of information between feuding parties, and his influence on the disputants does not seem to have depended on threats of violence. Ibid., pp. 11–12.

The rational, wealth-maximizing household now chooses non-violence, N, if the threat of violent retaliation is certain. There is only one possible outcome associated with each strategy, and (10,10) is clearly preferable to (4,4).

9.2.3. A digression on the California gold rush

Deterrence and threats of private violence were also used by Umbeck in his well-known analysis of the formation and initial distribution of property rights during the California gold rush of 1848.[14]

Gold was discovered in California in 1848, the same year that the peace treaty with Mexico transferred nonprivate land in the region to the U.S. government, that the U.S. military governor abolished Mexican law without offering an alternative system of law, and that most U.S. government employees deserted to the gold fields.[15] In three years the population of the once desolate mining areas had reached a quarter million, but federal laws pertaining to property rights in mining land were not introduced until 1866. Nevertheless, the miners succeeded in avoiding open access, chaos, and excessive violence, and established a stable system of exclusive rights at relatively low costs of enforcement.

Umbeck (1981a, 1981b) develops a model whereby he seeks to endogenize the size of each miner's claim and also explain the mechanism or forces that made the gold diggers respect each other's property. Umbeck's basic thesis is that potential violence constrains all forms of rationing: *"The agreed upon contract must initially endow each individual with the same amount of wealth as [he] could have had through violence."*[16]

---

14. Umbeck, John R. (1978). "A Theory of Contractual Choice and the California Gold Rush." *Journal of Law and Economics 21*: 421–437; idem (1981a). "Might Makes Rights: A Theory of the Formation and Initial Distribution of Property Rights." *Economic Inquiry 20* (No. 2): 38–59; idem (1981b). *A Theory of Property Rights with Applications to the California Gold Rush*. Ames: Iowa State University Press.
15. Umbeck (1981a) [op. cit., note 14], p. 49.
16. Ibid., p. 40.

The model abstracts from the restraining influences of social norms, and simplifies by assuming that individuals have full information about each other's productivity in mining and in violence, the only two uses of labor recognized in the model. Violence takes the form of using labor to exclude others from a piece of land. If two individuals with identical potential for violence compete for a marginal piece of land, then the person who is ready to allocate more labor hours to the conquest will acquire the plot.

The decision to allocate labor time to violence rather than to mining depends on marginal costs and benefits. The opportunity cost of labor in violence is determined by the value of the marginal product of labor (VMP_l) in gold mining.[17] VMP_l is relatively high for a worker who already has a large claim; land complements labor and raises its productivity. The VMP_l of a miner who has almost no land is relatively low, and his opportunity cost of taking time off for conquest is low. The marginal benefits of allocating labor to violence depend on the value of the marginal product of the incremental land that is at stake. The VMP_c of an addition to a claim falls as the plot grows larger. In Umbeck's model, no violence occurs because potential outcomes are known with certainty. Competing individuals calculate marginal costs and benefits and carve the land into plots of equilibrium sizes, thus removing all incentives to use violence.

Consider two individuals, X and Y, who have the same production functions in mining and violence and compete for mining land of equal quality. Let us assume that initially X has a small claim and Y has a large claim. This means that the marginal gain of additional land is relatively high for X, and the marginal value of time allocated to violence is relatively low. Therefore, X will take over some of Y's land and continue his transgressions until he has half of the available mining land. Note that $(VMP_c/VMP_l)_X$ measures how much labor time individual X is willing to assign to

---

17. Umbeck assumes that there is no work–leisure substitution and the amount of labor supplied to mining is constant. Note that no labor time is ever allocated to violence. Ibid.

enforcing exclusive rights to a marginal unit of his claim. For example, a ratio of 1/2 implies that X is willing to assign 1/2 labor unit to defend a marginal land unit. In equilibrium, the quantity of labor that each party is willing to assign to a conflict over a marginal land unit must be the same; that is, $(VMP_c/VMP_l)_X = (VMP_c/VMP_l)_Y$. Equilibrium is established by varying the distribution of land.

The Umbeck model generates various hypotheses:

1. With N identical individuals and land of identical quality, each individual will hold $1/N$ of the total land.
2. When the quality of land varies, the size of claims will vary inversely with the per unit quality of land.
3. Other things being equal, individuals with relative advantage in violence will hold larger claims than other miners.
4. Other things being equal, individuals with a relative advantage in mining will hold smaller claims than other miners.

The miners of the California gold rush used simple technology to mine placer deposits – superficial accumulations of gold dust and small nuggets.[18] Mining districts were established, through explicit contract in each case, at the site of several hundred gold deposits. Each miner was assigned a parcel of land, a claim, and the claim size varied inversely with the expected value per unit of the land.[19] No political coalitions for taking over mining districts were formed, and the mining was undertaken mostly by individual operators (unitary firms). Umbeck's data, however, do not allow direct testing of hypotheses 3 and 4 above. He concludes that there was insignificant variation in the miners' violence potential: They were all mature males of considerable physical strength, and nearly all carried a pistol: "The six shooter was not called the 'equalizer'

18. Ibid., p. 51.
19. The expected yield of a parcel of land depended on the distance separating a claim from a source of water because most of the placer deposits had been formed by the actions of moving water, and water was used to separate gold dust and nuggets from the paydirt. Ibid., p. 54.

for nothing."[20] In fact, Umbeck's study does not permit a direct test of his thesis that *might makes rights*.[21]

9.2.4. The question of order: customary law and ideology

Umbeck's solution to the prisoners' dilemma is based on his assumption that each miner has certain knowledge: Forceful usurpation of mining land will bring retaliation when the threatened property is more valuable to its possessor than his required labor time for defending it. In fact, Umbeck's solution can be compared to the previous case of the Nuer if every cattle thief faces certain retaliation. In general, however, models of man as a purely egoistic rational being cannot explain all social cooperation in terms of individual cost–benefit calculations. This is recognized by Hirshleifer (1980), who makes the following point:

> Economic study of market interactions may yield satisfactory results while postulating purely egoistic men, acting within an unexplained social environment of regulatory law. But as the power of economic analysis comes to be employed outside the traditional market context, for example in the area of public choice, the egoistic model of man (as in "social contract" theories) will not suffice.[22]

Therefore, in modeling nonmarket interaction and the economics of institutions, it is often helpful to incorporate in the model

20. Ibid., p. 51. The evidence also suggests that the miners were approximately homogeneous with respect to mining skills.
21. Umbeck's data are also consistent with other models than with his own theory of violence. He himself suggests an alternative explanation (p. 46). Furthermore, the Umbeck model does not explain why, after a point, new entrants to the mining regions were turned away. The model suggests that the contracts would be renegotiated as additional miners showed up, with each person's claim getting smaller and smaller. In fact, the mining districts did set up organizations for regulating entry and for trying and punishing miners who violated their rules.
22. P. 663 in Hirshleifer, Jack (1980). "Privacy: Its Origin, Function and Future." *Journal of Legal Studies* 9 (No. 4, December): 649–664. Some game theorists may disagree with Hirshleifer's conclusion. See Section 9.2.5, below.

some of the myriad innate and social factors that constrain the behavior of egoistic man. Evans-Pritchard, in his study of the Nuer and other African societies, discovered a whole set of customary law and ideological beliefs, which can be seen either as reinforcing the mutual nonaggression solution [outcome (10,10) of Matrix 9.2] or as introducing new games. Bates (1983) has modeled the implications of Nuer societal institutions in terms of game theory. Let us briefly consider some of these mechanisms.

The presence of *vengeance groups* in many stateless societies increases the likelihood of retaliation by the injured parties against transgressors. Vengeance groups, which among the Nuer are kinship groups of members related by blood through males, reduce the expected gains from ambushing and killing one's neighbor because it is highly likely that his kinsmen will take revenge. But the prisoners' dilemma plagues all forms of collective action: Unless they are somehow constrained, the members of a vengeance group have an incentive to free-ride rather than risk their lives on behalf of others in violent confrontations, and the institution of a vengeance group does not, per se, solve the problem of conflict among its members. Anthropologists have documented various constraints, such as religious beliefs, that work to support order. In many tribal societies, it is a common belief that transgressions by an individual against his social group will bring collective misfortunes, such as droughts and plagues. Gluckman (1956) provides a fascinating account of how the set of beliefs surrounding the institution of witchcraft works to overcome the prisoners' dilemma in small social groups. Furthermore, a vengeance group is *collectively responsible* for each of its members, and revenge can take the form of strikes against any member of a vengeance group. Therefore, even a self-centered individual may find it advantageous to control violent members of his vengeance group, as Posner (1980) has emphasized.[23]

Another arrangement, which also works to create order and

---

23. Posner, Richard A. (1980). "A Theory of Primitive Society, with Special Reference to Law." *Journal of Law and Economics 23* (No. 1, April): 1–53.

lower the cost of enforcing property rights in stateless societies, is the institution of *compensation*. Under a system of compensation, those who violate property rights are required to reimburse their victims, which changes the structure of the game and alters the participants' payoff matrix. A Nuer cattle thief now can expect either of two scenarios: (1) a violent and destructive retaliation by his victim's vengeance group, or (2) payment of costly compensation as a means of escaping retaliation. If the vengeance group is capable of costly retaliation and makes credible threats, an offender is likely to agree to pay compensation, and disruptive violence is prevented. Both vengeance and compensation act as a deterrent to potential transgressors and lower the cost of enforcing property rights.

However, the process of compensation may require direct communication between vengeance groups. The high transaction costs of negotiating compensation between hostile groups can be lowered by introducing a neutral *arbitrator*. Among the Nuer arbitration was in the hands of the leopard-skin chief, who lowered the costs of transacting in disputes but did not rely on coercive power.

Finally, *cross-cutting allegiances* introduce secondary costs for those who violate property rights in a stateless society or refuse to participate in the compensation process. This is the theme of Gluckman's lecture on "The Peace in the Feud," and indeed of all six lectures in his *Custom and Conflict in Africa*: "Customary forms for developing relations of kinship, for establishing friendships, for compelling the observance through ritual of right relations with the universe, and so forth – these customary forms first divide and then unite men."[24]

For example, the customary law of *exogamy* can give rise to conflicting allegiances. If custom requires a man to take a wife from outside his vengeance group, the members of feuding venge-

---

24. Gluckman (1956) [op. cit., note 8], p. 1. Gluckman's analysis of social cohesion and multiple interest among individuals in small-scale societies owes much to Elizabeth Colson's studies of the Plateau Tonga. For references, see Gluckman (1956), p. 166.

ance groups may find that they are fighting their wives' fathers and brothers. Evans-Pritchard reports that among the Nuer the curse of a maternal uncle is among the worst a Nuer can receive.[25] Conflicting relationships lower the net returns from aggressive acts against the property of other persons and create incentives for settling disputes through arbitration. The secondary costs of conflicting allegiances are *specific to individuals* and, with other customs and beliefs, stabilize the internal order in stateless societies. Bates (1983) shows how the presence of these secondary costs can alter the payoff matrix and make it less costly to change the players' dominant strategy from noncooperation and aggression to cooperation. The secondary costs tend to be stronger, the closer the relationship between the individuals involved. If the ties are strong, the secondary effects may even shift the dominant strategy of the players from the prisoners' dilemma to one of cooperation. Bates illustrates the effect with the following hypothetical case.[26] In Matrix 9.3 the payoff matrix of Matrix 9.1 has been modified to allow for the secondary costs to an individual in a small-scale stateless society of committing an act of aggression against his neighbor. It is assumed that the secondary effects of aggression (including psychic costs) reduce the direct gains of an aggressive act by 9 cattle, which gives us the following payoff matrix:

		Family Y	
		A	N
Family X	A	(−5, −5)	(9, 2)
	N	(2, 9)	(10, 10)

Matrix 9.3

In Matrix 9.3, social ties cutting across vengeance groups (or villages) have eliminated the prisoners' dilemma by imposing secondary social costs on prospective violators of property rights. For

25. Ibid., p. 13. See also Evans-Pritchard (1940) and (1951), op. cit., note 9.
26. Bates (1983) [op. cit., note 11], p. 16.

each agent the dominant strategy is now N, and the equilibrium outcome, (NN), maximizes the agents' joint wealth. The strength of the secondary effects will depend on the closeness of the social ties involved. In Matrix 9.3, strong secondary effects are postulated. If the secondary effects are small – for example, equivalent to 1 instead of 9 units of wealth – the prisoners' dilemma may still be in place. But any positive secondary effect raises the cost of violence and lowers the level of punishment (compensation) needed to create incentives for peaceful solutions.

9.2.5. Evolutionary models and game theory

The theme of our discussion so far has been the need for property rights and some enforcement mechanisms and constraints even in the most elementary agricultural and pastoral societies. By reference to the literature on cultural anthropology, we have tried to sketch the bare outlines of a system of order in stateless societies, but the various beliefs and norms that constrain behavior were treated as exogenous variables. The process of endogenization can be taken even further by attempting to explain the emergence of particular personal traits (tastes) and social customs.

In an earlier chapter, we mentioned attempts by several authors to model the evolution of (Anglo-Saxon) common law – typically, in order to show theoretically how law that maximizes output arises.[27] Hirshleifer has used theories of natural selection and mathematical sociobiology to model the evolution of institutions that promote cooperation in human affairs.[28] According to Hirshleifer, the pattern of institutional change involves natural selection as

---

27. Hirshleifer (1982) provides references and a thoughtful discussion of models that purport to show how the law evolves. He does not support the wealth maximization hypothesis. See pp. 46–49 in Hirshleifer, Jack (1982). "Evolutionary Models in Economics and Law." In Zerbe, R. O., Jr., and Rubin, P. H., eds. *Research in Law and Economics*, Vol. 4, pp. 1–60. Greenwich, Conn.: JAI Press.

28. See Hirshleifer (1982), which is the theme paper of a 220-page conference volume dealing with evolutionary models in economics and law. The volume contains viewpoints of leading experts and an extensive bibliography. See also Hirshleifer (1980), op. cit., note 22.

well as revolutionary and designed changes. In this context, he has also examined the question whether an innate drive, which helps man overcome the prisoners' dilemma, has emerged and become established by the process of natural selection. A careful examination of evolutionary models in economics is outside the scope of this book, but below we summarize some of Hirshleifer's conclusions regarding the *privacy ethic* and implanted social controls.

1. For the most part, man's genetic controls are not hard-wired but soft-wired; in other words, human beings are constrained by genetic factors, but they have a wider range of choice than other animals. Humans are characterized by their relatively greater ability to learn.[29]

2. Both cultural and genetic factors are simultaneously under the sway of natural selection.[30]

3. Genetic adaptation is slower than cultural adaptation: Early prehistoric generations of man may have left us with genetic traits ill-suited to modern living conditions.[31]

4. "Three main social principles – dominance, sharing, and private rights – have evolved in Nature, each as an adaptation to a particular type of social niche. Each principle tends to be associated with an ingrained supporting ethic, since a mere 'social contract' entered into by purely egoistical individuals is unlikely to survive the free-rider problem. Typically, strands of all three may be woven together in the behavior pattern of each species. And of course the merely egoistic element probably never totally disappears."[32]

5. "Evolution might have 'hard-wired' defensive belligerence into proprietors together with the

29. Hirshleifer (1980) [op. cit., note 22], pp. 652–653.
30. Ibid., p. 652.
31. Ibid., p. 659.
32. Ibid., p. 658.

complementary traits of reluctance to intrude
and willingness to retreat on the part of
potential challengers – the two together
comprising what I have called the privacy ethic."[33]

The point of this short digression on evolutionary models is that
rational-choice explanations of cooperation – whether in the context of sharing, dominance, or private rights – ultimately require
the assumption of individual taste for some form of cooperation.
But so far economics and social science have failed to evolve an
accepted theory of tastes and ideology. Possibly, evolutionary
models are a step toward such a theory.[34]

Our discussion of various solutions to the problem of collective
action would be incomplete without mention of recent work by
game theorists, who have examined whether voluntary cooperation
among egoists is at all possible in situations where the players are
not faced with external or internal constraints, including evolutionary constraints. The problem of collective action is often characterized by the payoff matrix of a prisoners' dilemma (PD) game
– like the payoff matrix of the Nuer families in Section 9.2.2 above.
As we pointed out there, the dominating strategy for each player
in a two-person PD game is to defect, and the outcome of the
game is Pareto inferior. Both parties would prefer an alternative
outcome, the one associated with mutual cooperation, although
transaction costs prevent them from reaching this preferred outcome. In fact, it is the nature of the collective action problem that
decisions by rational individuals lead to outcomes that no one
desires.

But how would it affect the outcome, if the players did not play
each other at random in one-shot games but each set of players
repeated their game ad infinitum? Game theorists refer to such
games as iterated games or as supergames. If a PD game is played

---

33. Ibid., p. 657.
34. See North's (1981) discussion of ideology. North, Douglass C. (1981). *Structure
and Change in Economic History*. New York: W. W. Norton.

repeatedly with no end in sight, each player can develop a conditional strategy based on the previous moves by the other player. Let us say that the other player appears to follow a strategy, called Tit for Tat, of being nice initially – that is, she cooperates, but then simply repeats the opponent's most recent move. The rational player now compares the once-for-all benefits of defecting, with the present value of an infinite time series of benefits that are associated with cooperation. The discount rate, which is used to discount future benefits, reflects both the usual factors of intertemporal evaluation in economics and the probability that the two players will not meet again.

		Player B	
		Cooperate	Defect
	Cooperate	(3, 3)	(0, 5)
Player A			
	Defect	(5, 0)	(1, 1)

Matrix 9.4

In terms of Matrix 9.4, a player, facing an opponent who appears to follow a Tit for Tat strategy, will consider the benefits of a gain of 5 in the current period against the discounted present value of an infinite stream of benefits, each amounting to 3. Therefore, if the future is not heavily discounted, the shadow of the future may bring cooperation to the players: A rational player may choose to cooperate.

These issues were discussed by Taylor in *Anarchy and Cooperation* (1976) and are developed further in his more recent book, *The Possibility of Cooperation* (1987).[35] Schofield (1985) has written an authoritative survey of recent applications of game theory to the problem of collection action.[36] The work of Axelrod, which

35. Taylor, Michael (1976). *Anarchy and Cooperation*. London: John Wiley; idem (1987). *The Possibility of Cooperation*. Cambridge: Cambridge University Press.
36. Schofield, Norman (1985). "Anarchy, Altruism and Cooperation." *Social Choice and Welfare 2*: 34–44.

is summarized in *The Evolution of Cooperation* (1984), has drawn much attention.[37] Axelrod organized a computer tournament where the outcomes of alternative strategies were tested in iterated PD games. The computerized strategies were designed by experts from various countries, and all strategies were matched in a series of bilateral games. Axelrod found that the winning strategy was also the simplest, namely Tit for Tat (T), which we described above.

Axelrod also studied whether a community of T players can withstand an invasion of players who follow different strategies, that is, whether such an invader would do better in an iterated game against a T player than two T players would do when playing each other. Axelrod found that Tit for Tat was stable under such attacks (evolutionary stable, in his words), given certain assumptions about the structure of the payoff matrix and the discount factor. Similarly, a group of T players can invade a noncooperative society, if certain conditions are met. However, *single* nice players cannot get cooperation started in a noncooperative society.

The relevance of Axelrod's model is critically evaluated by Schofield (1985) and also by Taylor (1987). The latter extends the iterated PD game from a two-person game to an *N*-person PD game, which is more relevant for studying the problem of supplying public goods. Taylor (1987) also makes the case that "important classes of public goods provision problems are better represented by Assurance and especially Chicken games, and in the continuous case by hybrids of these two. In all these games, arguably, if the game is played only once, *some* cooperation is more likely to be forthcoming than in cases for which the prisoners' dilemma is the appropriate model."[38]

---

37. Axelrod, Robert (1984). *The Evolution of Cooperation*. New York: Basic Books; idem (1981). "The Emergence of Cooperation Among Egoists." *American Political Science Review 75:* 306–318.
38. Taylor (1987) [op. cit., note 35], p. 31.

Finally, Schofield (1985) emphasizes that information and transaction costs are at the heart of the problem of cooperation:

> The theoretical problem underlying cooperation can be stated thus: what is the minimal amount that one agent must know in a given mileu about the beliefs and wants of other agents, to be able to form coherent notions about their behavior, and for this knowledge to be communicable to others?[39]

Before concluding the discussion of the structure of property rights in prestate societies, we want to draw attention to two issues: first, how primitive societies often seem to evolve systems of property rights that over time smooth the consumption pattern of individual households, thus providing insurance against hunger; and, second, how institutional equilibrium in stateless societies requires the blocking of social and economic developments, which would lead to the evolution of a state.[40]

9.2.6. The insurance function of primitive law

The property rights structure of primitive societies is highly variable, but in many cases a close look reveals certain regularities, as Posner (1980) has emphasized in an important study that applies the economics of transaction costs to the institutions of primitive and archaic societies.[41]

Posner's main point is that relatively high costs of information in these societies shape their institutions and give them common characteristics. Primitive technologies of measurement and communications, a lack of a system of writing, no written records, and a limited knowledge of the laws of nature shrink the set of relevant institutions.[42] Without our inferring anything about cause and ef-

---

39. Schofield (1985) [op. cit., note 36], p. 219.
40. The discussion below of these issues draws on Posner (1980), op. cit., note 23.
41. Ibid.
42. In order to simplify, Posner downplays many significant differences among primitive societies and organizes his analysis in terms of an informal model or an ideal type of primitive society. The basic assumptions of his model are the

fect, it should also be noted that the simple production technology of primitive societies along with home production and lack of specialization make relatively few demands on measurement and contractual enforcement. Posner points out, for example, that the potential domain of the law of contracts in primitive societies is limited primarily to "the formation of marriage, exchanges within the household or kin group, and gift-giving . . . , the most important forms of exchange."[43]

There is one form of complex transactions, however, that the primitive household has a strong demand for, namely *insurance against hunger*. This is particularly true of an autarkic society, where the annual output of food is near the subsistence level, the vagaries of Nature cause substantial annual variations in the food production of each household, and the primitive technology does not allow the storage of surplus harvest for more than one production period. Furthermore, in prestate societies it is not possible to use regular taxes and bounties to affect the distribution of food among households, and formal insurance markets are also impracticable.

Posner argues that a whole range of social institutions in primitive societies helps to provide this vital insurance service. The sharing of surplus harvest, gift giving, reciprocal exchange, interest-free loans, marriage rules and kinship obligations, norms specifying the size of the kinship group, the assignment of respect-

following: (1) The society does not have a written language. (2) There is almost no specialization in economic and political activities; the society is without formal government. (3) The economy produces a narrow range of products, mostly food products. Almost no physical capital is used in production, except simple hand tools, but farm animals are common. (4) The state of technology permits that food be stored for only a brief period of time. (5) There is no external trade that could increase the variety of consumer commodities. (6) Knowledge of science and technology corresponds to the earliest stages of human experience. Labor productivity is low, and random factors result in a life-threatening variance in the output of individual households. Posner (1980) [op. cit., note 23], pp. 8–10.

43. Ibid., p. 35.

ability and prestige to giving rather than to accumulation, and many other institutions of primitive society can be analyzed in terms of the insurance principle.

In prestate societies, the economic rationale for exchange is usually not specialization in production; the main function of exchange is rather to meet the community's demand for insurance against hunger. The primitive household is too small for spreading the risk of harvest failure or animal disease, so the larger kinship group has become the primary insurance collectivity. The classical insurance problem of adverse selection is minimized by social norms that make it costly to leave one's kinship group, and by the fact that the kinship group is also the insured's vengeance group. Primitive societies tend to allocate a considerable amount of their scarce resources toward defining their kinship groups. A large group reduces the covariance in household outputs and provides more insurance, but, on the other hand, incentive problems and moral hazard become more serious issues as the group becomes larger. Finally, note that inability to store surpluses, a narrow range of available commodities, and limited investment opportunities in primitive societies make the opportunity cost of giving relatively low.[44]

9.2.7. Institutional disequilibrium and the breakdown of stateless societies

In all societies, variations in individual abilities and tastes, along with random "luck" factors, tend over time to generate unequal distribution of wealth. Wealth is correlated with political power, and, for example, a stateless society might soon be on a path toward concentrated power, and possibly some form of feudalism, unless the process of wealth concentration is constrained by the institutional structure.

Posner (1980) discusses some of the constraints that limit the concentration of wealth over time and create institutional equilibrium in stateless societies. The custom of reciprocal gift-giving and

---

44. Ibid., pp. 10–19.

various norms for sharing, the association of social stigma with accumulation and prestige with giving – these and other institutions and values of the insurance principle work to equalize wealth. Certain primitive societies have evolved institutions of outright wealth dissipation – for example, extravagant feasts or the custom, when people die, of destroying some of their wealth or burying it with them. Posner also argues that customary laws of inheritance in stateless societies typically limit accumulation over time, and he makes a convincing case that the institution of polygamy tends to equalize wealth in the long run. Finally, in primitive society, property rights in land are often restricted to user rights: A household has exclusive rights to use certain plots of agricultural land, and the land can be inherited, but the right to sell the property does not exist. Therefore, an individual cannot use surplus harvests to reduce a neighbor to a state of dependence by purchasing his land. Also note that in many primitive societies high transaction costs make large units of production unattractive – just as high transaction costs eat up the gains from trade across price-making markets.

But the institutional equilibrium of stateless societies has, in most cases, eventually given way, and the state in its various forms has emerged.[45] In the case of the Icelandic Commonwealth, A.D. 930–1262, the breakdown of a stateless society was documented by contemporaries to the event.[46] The Commonwealth had many

---

45. "The analysis of the origins of order in decentralized societies is perhaps the most famous contribution of African studies to the study of politics. Yet recent scholarship has argued that too much emphasis has been placed upon decentralized systems. On the one hand, their occurrence appears to be relatively infrequent; on the other, even in so far as decentralized societies do exist, they can arguably be regarded as transitory – as societies which once were centralized or which are in the early stages of a movement toward more centralized political forms." Bates (1983) [op. cit., note 11], p. 21.

46. The laws of the Commonwealth, called *Grágás*, were put in writing early in the twelfth century (but cover an earlier period) and survive in three manuscripts. They are considered "the most extensive and detailed of the surviving Germanic law codes." P. 96 in Miller, William Ian (1984). "Avoiding Legal Judgment: The Submission of Disputes to Arbitration in Medieval Iceland. *American Journal of Legal History 28:* 95–134. The so-called *Sturlunga Sagas*

characteristics of the Posnerian primitive society, but there were important differences, including literacy (and eventually written law), legislative and judicial bodies, and voluntary political associations. In fact, early Icelandic society had taken a step toward statehood, except that it lacked an executive branch of government – a principal who would monopolize the legitimate use of violence.

In early Iceland, Posner's insurance problem was in part handled directly by geographical associations of farmers, called *hreppar*. Membership in one's local hreppur was compulsory, which solved the problem of adverse selection. The farmers were required to help each other in case of damages to houses or livestock, and they had to feed and take care of the indigent in their district.[47]

The preservation of order and the enforcement of exclusive rights depended on a political system that involved a system of courts of justice (local, regional, and national) and a legislative

deal directly with the disputes and feuds that preceded the collapse of the Commonwealth as seen by contemporaries, and the *Bishop Sagas* tell the story of Icelandic bishops from the eleventh to the fourteenth century. The Icelanders also wrote sagas of the kings who ruled in Norway during the age of the Commonwealth and earlier.

The thirty or more Icelandic Family Sagas deal primarily with events of the tenth and early eleventh centuries, but they were written mostly in the thirteenth century and probably contain a strong fictional element. Many scholars argue, however, that the family sagas give a fair account of the country's political system at the time of their writing. For example, Turner (1971) theorizes that the famous *Njál's Saga*, which describes events on each side of the year 1000, was written after the collapse of the Commonwealth to demonstrate how the old order had no means of keeping the peace (p. 370).

Other sources include Icelandic Chronicles, which go back to the thirteenth century. As for secondary sources and modern historical research, see Jóhannesson, Jón (1974). *A History of the Icelandic Commonwealth*. Transl. by Haraldur Bessason. Winnipeg: University of Manitoba Press. Finally, in view of our discussion of the Nuer, it is interesting to note that Turner (1971) links the Icelandic data with the theories of Evans-Pritchard. Turner, Victor W. (1971). "An Anthropological Approach to the Icelandic Sagas." In T. O. Beidelman, ed. *The Translation of Culture. Essays to E. E. Evans-Pritchard*. London: Tavistock Publications.

47. The origins of *hreppar* are unknown, but they may date back to the tenth century. *Grágás* contains clauses referring to hreppar. The duties of each farmer were related to his means, and from 1097 the hreppar shared in the tithe. This type of organization apparently did not exist in the other Nordic countries.

assembly – all controlled by thirty-six (later thirty-nine) chieftains.[48] Each independent farmer was required to become a liegeman of one of the chieftains, but he was free to change his allegiance at any time. The chieftaincies were exclusive private property: They could be inherited, bought, and sold. An individual had the right to own several chieftaincies and appoint his agents as chieftains but could be chieftain himself only over one.[49]

The relationship between liegemen and chieftains was one of mutual rights and duties, particularly in processing disputes. In this system, individuals whose rights had been violated could seek three types of redress: They could (1) take the law into their own hands and seek revenge; (2) place the case in arbitration; or (3) litigate the case.[50] Miller (1984) provides an interesting analysis of the early Icelanders' choice among arbitration, blood, and law, and why arbitration was in many cases a favored alternative.[51]

The history of early Iceland adds evidence against the viewpoint, favored by some social scientists, that economically motivated exchange is basically a modern phenomenon. The early Icelanders not only established exclusive rights to economic resources and

48. See Jóhannesson (1974), op. cit., note 46. The Icelandic word for such a chieftain is *goði* (plural *goðar*). *Goði* is related to the English word "god," as the chieftains also had a religious function prior to the introduction of Christianity in A.D. 1000. The Icelandic word for chieftaincy is *goðorð*.

49. Women could own a chiefdom, but they were not allowed to be chieftains.

50. David Friedman (1979) has made the case that the structure of property rights in the Icelandic Commonwealth was relatively effective, even when compared with public enforcement in societies that have developed formal institutions of law enforcement. Friedman, David (1979). "Private Creation and Enforcement of Law: A Historical Case." *Journal of Legal Studies 8* (No. 2): 399–415.

51. Miller, William Ian (1984), op. cit., note 16. Wormald (1981) looks at bloodfeuds in Scotland and the early history of modern law, particularly the relationship between private and royal justice. She shows that, over a long period in Scottish history (from about 1400 to 1600), the justice of the feud was accepted by the government, and customary and private methods for dealing with crime or civil disputes coexisted harmoniously with public justice. The substitution in history of private and public law in the context of a theory of the state is yet another important topic awaiting the application of neoinstitutional economics. Wormald, Jenny (1981). "Bloodfeud, Kindred and Government in Early Modern Scotland. *Past and Present 87* (May): 54–97.

commodities and exchanged these rights nationally and internationally (e.g., exported woolens and imported grain), but they also created unusual transferable rights in the political arena.[52] As we just said, the chieftaincies, which represented control over the legislature and the courts of justice, were transferable private property. But also the right to prosecute a case could be traded, and even court verdicts were a marketable private property: Plaintiffs could transfer to a third party the right to enforce judgments in their favor (e.g., confiscate the defendant's property or kill him).

The political arena of the early Commonwealth can be seen as a competitive market of thirty-nine firms of similar sizes. Each firm involved contracts between the chieftain and his liegemen for the joint production and protection of property rights. The power of a chieftain was constrained in various ways. He could not tax his followers like a feudal lord, and there was some flexibility: A farmer was free to cancel his contract with a chieftain and take up association with another.[53]

The various forces that helped to solve the prisoners' dilemma and establish order among the Nuer and other traditional societies of Africa were also at work in early Iceland: repeated play, deterrence, arbitration, cross-cutting ties, and ideology. But various factors that Posner sees as creating stability were *not* present. His insurance problem was to a large extent handled directly, land could be bought and sold, and there were no important institutions of wealth dissipation. Also, food could be stored, a surplus could be spent on internationally traded commodities, and there were ample investment opportunities for the first generations of settlers.

The Commonwealth lasted from 930 to 1262 and enjoyed reasonable stability for the first 200 years of its existence. The eventual breakdown of the system was preceded by (1) a strengthening of

---

52. For information on the economy of the Icelandic Commonwealth, see Gelsinger, Bruce E. (1981). *Icelandic Enterprise: Commerce and Economy in the Middle Ages*. Columbia, S.C.: University of South Carolina Press.
53. The evidence suggests that the chieftains did not tax their followers, except for a small tax to cover the costs of attending official functions (assemblies) with a delegation of freeholders.

the relative position of the chieftains vis-à-vis their liegemen, and (2) the merger of the thirty-nine competitive firms (chieftaincies) into a few oligarchic firms.

The position of the chieftains was strengthened by a population expansion which put pressure on land, increased its price relative to labor, and created a new class of tenants and paupers. Also, the introduction of the tithe in 1097, the beginning of large-scale taxation in Iceland, transformed the country's power structure. Half of the tithe, which was a net wealth tax of 1 percent, was assigned to churches and to priests, but typically this sum went to chieftains who built churches on their land and provided priestly services (by hiring priests at subsistence wages). The chieftaincies were exempt from the tax because they were "not wealth but dominions," as the law code stated! It was, of course, the chieftains themselves who had passed the tax law in Althing.[54]

One fourth of the tithe went to the country's two bishops, who thus became wealthier than any chieftain. The church had become a new force in the community, but the constitution of the Commonwealth was not amended to allow for this change in the power structure. It has been noted that the merger of chieftaincies began in the rich agricultural districts around the two Episcopal seats, presumably as attempts by chieftains to redress the balance of power. By the year 1220, all the chieftaincies of the Commonwealth were owned by six families, who then fought one another for more power.[55] The bloody civil strife ended in 1262, when the Icelanders contracted with Hákon the Old, King of Norway, to restore order:

54. The introduction of the tithe in Iceland was a relatively peaceful event, whereas in neighboring countries it caused much political turbulence. In the other countries of Northern Europe, the tithe was a 10 percent tax on net income rather than a 1 percent tax on net wealth as in Iceland.

55. Jóhannesson (1974) [op. cit., note 46], p. 228. The causes of the Commonwealth's collapse are still debated by historians. The case is complicated by the simultaneous occurrence of several factors that might have contributed to the breakdown: the econometric problem of multicolinearity. In addition to the factors that we have mentioned, the climate became colder, the country's foreign markets collapsed, and the international terms-of-trade moved against Iceland, the chieftains became imbued with notions of royalty, and the Nor-

The covenant [the Old Pact of 1262] was a mutual one:
The Icelanders became the king's liegemen and promised him fixed annual taxes, but they were released
from their obligations if the sovereign, in the opinion of
the "best men," broke faith with them and failed to
carry out his side of the bargain. The main requirement
stipulated on the Icelandic side was the preservation of
peace and the retention of their own laws.[56]

Thus Iceland acquired a head of state through contractual arrangements that correspond closely to North's (1981) theory of the
state, introduced in Chapter 3 and taken up again in Chapter 10.

The students of the Icelandic Commonwealth frequently note
how essentially the same constitution and the same laws generated
widely different behavior at different times. During the early Commonwealth, the law appears to have functioned well, but toward
the end of the period the chieftains either ignored the law or
manipulated it for their personal ends. The evidence suggests, as
we have outlined, that various changes in relative prices altered
the payoff matrix and contributed to the breakdown of the cooperative solution to the political game in early Iceland. Some
historians argue that a change in taste for law-abiding behavior
was a crucial causal variable in this institutional change. So far,
NIE does not have a workable theory of ideology, which limits
our ability to study *operational* behavioral constraints rather than
formal constitutional and contractual constraints. In the modern
world, we see how similar formal rules can create different behavior and outcomes – for example, in Third World countries that
have copied in considerable detail the constitutions of the United

wegian kings grew increasingly more interested in Iceland and stirred up political troubles in the country.
56. P. 40 in Jóhannesson, Thorkell (1975). "An Outline History." In Nordal, J.,
and Kristinsson, V., eds. *Iceland 874–1974*. Reykjavík: Central Bank of Iceland. "Such a relationship between Iceland and Norway, and later Iceland and
Denmark, lasted nearly 700 years in one form or another. All along the Icelanders maintained that they had direct contractual relations with the Nordic
heads of state (the kings) but the contract did not involve the Danish or
Norwegian peoples."

States or Britain or, on a lesser scale, the traffic regulations of cities such as Geneva.

9.3. A digression on international property rights

Before leaving the topic of stateless societies, let us briefly digress on international property rights and exchange across national borders. Few countries are utterly isolated. Members of households, firms, and governments in one country contract and exchange property rights with people in other countries. Therefore, the structure of international property rights affects the behavior of agents in foreign transactions and the wealth of interrelated nations. Owing to the absence of an effective world government, international relations are in some ways comparable to the property rights system of stateless societies; for in neither case is there ultimate recourse to a third party for the enforcement of contracts. Perhaps the early Icelandic model, rather than the case of the Nuer, is a better mirror of the system of international property rights: Chieftaincies; courts of law and justice; an active choice among submissiveness, blood, private arbitration, or law for settling disputes; and self-policing are institutional arrangements that resemble the world order.

The structure of international property rights takes many forms and reflects the relative strength of states, the objective functions and constraints of rulers and leaders, and various information and transaction costs, which tend to be high in international relations.

First, powerful states often exploit small or weak nations and appropriate their wealth. At one end of the continuum of exploitation, the dominant state taxes the weaker states but provides nothing in return. But even the most powerful state is constrained by measurement costs and agency problems, which give rise to contractual relationships and organizational forms amenable to analysis in terms of NIE. In intermediate cases, forced exchange takes place, bringing some net gain to the weaker nations but less than they could obtain through free international trade. Finally, at the other end of the spectrum, we have exchange between countries on an equal basis – for example, in a competitive world market.

Second, states often engage in various types of collective actions, which benefit them all, but to a varying degree. Such cooperation can involve military alliances or, for instance, cartels designed to limit the production of certain commodities in order to raise their prices in the world market. The gains from a collective action by a group of nations are often at the expense of other states. Successful collective action augments the net wealth of the countries involved, raising the question of how costs and benefits are shared.

Third, international exchange is facilitated by international public goods. Serving as an example of such goods are the various standards of measurement, including the metric system, the gold standard, the earth's time zones, and standardized wool, coffee, steel, or pitch of the screw thread. Standardized railway gauges and rules of navigation in the air and on the oceans are also international public goods.[57] It is characteristic of standards that they become more valuable as more people use them, that exclusive rights to standards often cannot be enforced, and that their introduction may involve substantial costs. The start-up costs of national and international standards are typically relatively small when a technology is new. Then standards may emerge as positive externalities of individual firms – for example, in the aircraft or computer industry. A world-wide standardization of revolutions per minute (r.p.m.) for records and record players emerged from the interaction between firms.[58]

Kindleberger (1982) makes the case that in nineteenth-century

---

57. See Kindleberger, Charles P. (1982). "Standards as Public, Collective and Private Goods." Seminar Paper No. 231. Stockholm: Institute for International Economic Studies; idem (1986). "International Public Goods Without International Government." *American Economic Review 76* (No. 1): 1–13.

58. Kindleberger (1982) [op. cit., note 57], p. 11. Note that there are three levels of rules affecting exchange between individuals of different states: (1) supranational laws and regulations; (2) national law, for example, regarding imports, and also national laws of great powers often have extraterritorial applications; (3) private rules (private contracts), which regulate direct contacts between individual firms in different countries.

England industrial standards failed to emerge in many areas because the country's industries typically were not dominated by a single large firm.[59] The same logic applies when international leadership is lacking: "When countries are more evenly matched in size and importance, agreement on international standards for output regulation, taxation and the like is likely to be weakened by compromise."[60]

When individual firms or states already have invested in their own standards, a change to international standards can be very costly, except for the party whose measures are being adopted by others. Economies of scale suggest that the best course for a small country (firm) is often voluntarily to adopt the standards of a leading country (firm). Ancient Rome provided the Justinian and Gregorian calendars; Great Britain in its heyday gave rise to the gold standard and Greenwich mean time; postrevolutionary France supplied the metric system and the Napoleonic law code; and the United States gave us the dollar exchange standard.[61] Safe conduct is our final example of an international public good. The elimination of piracy on the high seas can bring gains to all traders, but a single powerful state may find it advantageous to carry the full cost of pacification when other states free-ride and collective action is unlikely or costly – and thus provide Pax Romana, Britannia, or Americana.

In sum, international property rights can lower transaction costs in international exchange and encourage specialization in production and exchange among nations. And, conversely, when the system of international property rights fails, the joint wealth of nations is adversely affected. Kindleberger (1986) argues that the Great Depression may have run unchecked because Britain was unable

---

59. Kindleberger (1982) informs us that in Britain at one point "there were 200 types of axle boxes, 40 different handbrakes in railway wagons, perhaps 200 sizes and specifications for manhole covers. . . . In World War I Britain was found to have 70 electricity generating companies with 50 different systems of supply, 24 voltages and 10 different frequencies." Ibid.
60. Ibid., p. 23.
61. Ibid., pp. 22–23.

to provide the international leadership required to halt it. Similarly, in recent years the world economic order has become fragile, in his view, because the United States has reduced its supply of international public goods:

> The point of all this is that after about 1971, the United States, like Britain from about 1890, had shrunk in economic might relative to the world as a whole, and more importantly, has lost its appetite for providing international public goods – open markets in time of glut, supplies in times of acute shortage, steady flows of capital to developing countries, international money, coordination of macroeconomic policies and last-resort lending.[62]

The complex structures of international rules and norms constitute a ripe field for Neoinstitutional Economics. Again, we envision three levels of analysis, involving (1) the behavior of economic actors as a function of international property rights, contractual arrangements, and transaction costs; (2) the logic of economic organizations and contractual arrangements in international exchange emphasizing transaction costs and structures of international property rights; and (3) the economic logic of the political institutions of the international order.

So far, economists, working with the tools of NIE, have paid scant attention to international property rights, but, given the importance of information and transaction costs in this area, the field offers promising research opportunities. Frey and Schneider (1982) survey applications of public-choice theory to international political economy and consider the formation of tariffs and trade restrictions, foreign trade flows, foreign direct investments, international aid, economic nationalism and warfare, and international organizations and bargaining.[63] Of these areas, the most interesting

---

62. Kindleberger (1986) [op. cit., note 57], p. 9.
63. Frey, Bruno S., and Schneider, Friedrich (1982). "International Political Economy: An Emerging Field." Seminar Paper No. 227. Institute for International Economic Studies, University of Stockholm. See also Frey, Bruno S. (1984). *International Political Economy.* Oxford: Blackwell.

work deals with the formation of tariffs and trade restrictions. Frey and Schneider make clear that until recently, international economic issues have been dominated, on the one hand, by economists applying the standard neoclassical model and, on the other hand, by political scientists who reject the rational-choice model.

Recently, political scientists using the rational-choice model have made important contributions to the study of international order. Many of these studies approach the question of order with the help of game theory in a way reminiscent of our previous discussion of the Nuer. Typically, the relationship between states is modeled as a repeated prisoners' dilemma game where the payoff matrixes of the players are symmetrical, and each player has full knowledge of his opponent's set of potential strategies and associated payoffs. In order to show how states have succeeded in various cooperative efforts, attempts have been made to find successful strategies that can, in the long run, overcome the prisoners' dilemma.[64] For Axelrod, for example, a successful strategy includes the rules of never being first to defect, keeping the rules of the game simple to avoid misunderstanding, and being willing to retaliate against any transgression.[65]

Alt et al. (1986) argue that the prisoners' dilemma approach is poorly suited for dealing with international politics, particularly with *hegemony*, which has been an important part of the international order throughout history.[66] A hegemon is a powerful state that has the resources to coerce weaker states to adhere to an

64. Those working in international political theory refer to structures of property rights, which govern exchange between nations, as regimes. For a recent survey of applications of game theory to world politics, see Snidal, Duncan (1985). "The Game Theory of International Politics." *World Politics* 38 (No. 1): 25–57.

65. See Section 9.2.5, above; also Axelrod, Robert (1984), op. cit., note 37.

66. Alt, James E., Calvert, Randall L., and Humes, Brian D. (1986). "Game Theory and Hegemonic Stability: The Role of Reputation and Uncertainty." Political Economy Working Paper 106. St. Louis: Center in Political Economy, Washington University. Keohane's work on hegemony and the international order has drawn much attention. For example, see Keohane, Robert (1984). *After Hegemony: Cooperation and Discord in the World Political Economy.* Princeton: Princeton University Press.

international structure of property rights – for example, by applying selective incentives to force compliance with collective action. The hegemony game is characterized by asymmetries: One of the parties, the hegemon, has more coercive capacity than the others, and it also has more information about its own ability to coerce than the others. The asymmetries in power and in information give rise to investment in *reputation building, bluffing*, and other related behavior.

In some cases the hegemon is too weak to punish all transgressions, but then it can pay to invest in punishment in early periods of the game, even when it brings more costs than benefits in the short run. The argument is that the hegemon, by establishing reputation for toughness, can lower policing costs and earn a positive return in the long run. The smaller states, in turn, find it to their advantage to challenge the hegemon in order both to update their estimates of its strength and to make sure that they will not be taken for granted. Alt et al. (1986) emphasize that in the hegemony game it can be rational to be the first to defect, to play a game with obscure rules, and punish only some of the time. The behavior of the actors depends on the strength of the hegemon and on the smaller states' estimate of the hegemon's costs of punishing, represented in the model by a random variable. One of the interesting outcomes suggested by the model is that it sometimes pays to follow a mixed strategy – namely, to defect or punish randomly but in the context of a given probability distribution.

Finally, we note that the relationship between a legislative leader and the rank-and-file can also be characterized as a hegemony game. Calvert (1986) has used game theory to examine reputation building, leadership strength, and the nature of legislative outcomes.[67] In fact, the model should also be applicable to the relationship between rulers of countries and their subjects.

---

67. Calvert, Randall L. (1987). "Reputation and Legislative Leadership." *Public Choice* 55 (Nos. 1–2): 81–119.

10

The state in Neoinstitutional Economics

10.1. Introduction

In Chapter 9, we examined the system of property rights in stateless societies, particularly how informal rules, values, and taboos constrain behavior and limit the waste associated with open access to resources. However, the embryonic institutional structure of prestate societies is not capable of supporting the complex exchange relationships among unrelated individuals that are associated with highly developed specialization in production and large markets, advanced technology, and time-intensive production patterns.[1]

Without the state, its institutions, and supportive framework of property rights, high transaction costs will paralyze complex production systems, and specific investments involving long-term exchange relationships will not be forthcoming. But the state is a two-edged sword: "The existence of a state is essential for economic growth; the state, however, is the source of man-made decline."[2]

1. This point has been made by North, for example: North, Douglass C. (1987). "Institutions, Transaction Costs and Economic Growth." *Economic Inquiry 25* (No. 3): 419–428.
2. P. 20 in North, Douglass C. (1981). *Structure and Change in Economic History.* New York: W. W. Norton. To a large extent this chapter is based on North's

Section 10.2 elaborates North's (1979) theory of the state, which was introduced in Chapter 3.[3] His approach is based on the modern theory of the firm (see Chapters 5 and 6) and emphasizes how transaction costs and agency problems affect political behavior and the structure of property rights. We present a formal version of a North-type model of the state (due to Findlay and Wilson), and consider various ramifications of the approach.

Section 10.3 is given to empirical applications of the theory. Our purpose is primarily to outline critical variables and suggest a research agenda rather than to settle debates in economic history and development. Following an introduction (Section 10.3.1), the link between political coalitions and property rights is examined in Section 10.3.2. The discussion is organized about Bates's study of markets and states in Tropical Africa. In Section 10.3.3, we consider the agency problems of the principals who control the state, illustrating, with studies by Winiecki, the issues of reforms and counterreforms in Soviet-type economies. Finally, Section 10.3.4 cites studies by several authors, and the case of early modern Europe, to discuss the links among methods of public finance, property rights, and economic outcomes. Predatory public finance, with its devastating long-term consequences, is seen as constrained optimization by rulers who have few choices.

The chapter's final section (10.4) looks at applications of Neoinstitutional Economics to the study of democratic institutions. Rather than surveying the emerging field of "neoinstitutionalism" within Public Choice and Political Science, the discussion is limited to two issues and two important studies that display the potential of the NIE approach in this area. First, we examine a formal model, by Denzau and Munger, of the importance of information costs for the behavior of legislators. Second, we consider a model by Weingast and Marshall that uses the new theory of economic organizations to explain the internal structure of the U.S. Congress.

theories of the relationships among the productive forces of an economy, the structure of property rights, and the political system.
3. North, Douglass C. (1979). "A Framework for Analyzing the State in Economic History." *Explorations in Economic History* (July): 249–259.

10.2. Theory of the state: the model

We turn now to a discussion of the state in the context of Neoinstitutional Economics. Our concern is with the interaction between the state and the system of property rights; the approach, which is due to North (1979, 1981), involves combining the economics of transaction costs and agency theory in a rational-choice analysis of political institutions and processes.

North's vision of the interrelationship between the state, property rights, and productivity can be described as follows. The stock of knowledge in society and the endowment of resources determine the technical upper limits for productivity and output, the economy's *technical production frontier*. However, for each structure of property rights there is a *structural production frontier*, which is reached by selecting, from the set of feasible organizations, those structures that minimize costs and maximize output. The set of feasible forms of economic organization is defined by the system of property rights (given the state of technology and other exogenous factors), and the system of property rights depends on the community's political structure. And, finally, some political systems create incentives that place the structural production frontier close to the technical production frontier; other political systems do not. Usually, a political change is required to move the structural production frontier closer to the technical frontier, and, therefore, a benefit–cost evaluation of economic reforms must include both the costs of political change and the costs of maintaining (enforcing) each system.[4]

Modern technology creates the potential for very high levels of productivity. These high levels of output cannot be reached without

4. The argument could also be stated in terms of growth rates – that is, how fast the production frontier moves out under alternative systems of property rights. Note that we treat technology and population as exogenous variables in this chapter, although these factors are fundamental sources of economic and political change. The NIE approach suggests that the rate of investment in technological change is inversely related to the investors' cost of capturing the potential returns on their investments. However, except for general statements, economists working in the NIE tradition have not contributed important new theories of population and technological change.

elaborate specialization in production and complex webs of exchange among unrelated individuals, extending across both time and space. In general, we can say that the more advanced the technology, the more complex the transactions, and the higher the transaction costs of utilizing the technology.[5] Appropriate structures of property rights are needed to reduce transaction costs of advanced technologies to manageable levels, and the state has a relative advantage in supplying the required structure: "The economies of scale associated with devising a system of law, justice, and defense are the basic underlying source of civilization."[6]

In sum, the willingness of individual owners to supply specific appropriable assets, essential for economic growth and full utilization of advanced technologies, depends directly on the social rules structure, including the availability of relatively consistent and impartial dispute processing by a third party, which in most cases can be supplied only by the state.

North (1981) argues that there is overwhelming historical evidence to support the proposition that states typically do not supply structures of property rights that are appropriate for placing the economy close to the technical production frontier. For example, he maintains that various historical cases of relative and absolute economic decline can be explained only as *failures of organization*. We now turn to North's theory of the state, which is intended to provide an explanation for such failures, and begin by examining the theory in terms of a formal model due to Findley and Wilson (1984).[7]

Let us assume that an economy produces a composite commodity Y, which is supplied by private firms. The only inputs are labor services, L, and the services of a fixed capital stock, K. The input–

5. But note that technical change also works to lower transaction costs – for example, by advancing the technologies of measurement and communications.
6. North (1981) [op. cit., note 2], p. 27.
7. Findlay, Ronald, and Wilson, John D. (1984). "The Political Economy of the Leviathan." Seminar Paper No. 285. Stockholm: Institute for International Economic Studies. Their model can be used to discuss alternative positive theories of the state in terms familiar to economists.

output relationship is represented by a conventional production function, $f(L,K)$. However, the output of the economy can be enhanced by a third input, which we can call public order, P (the services rendered by the system of property rights). Public order can be supplied effectively only by the state, and government workers, G, are the sole input used. The production function for public order is $p(G)$, and the aggregate production function for a community where the state supplies public order can then be written as:[8]

$$Y = f(L,K)\, p(G) \qquad (10.1)$$

Findlay and Wilson (1984) assume that the supply of homogeneous labor to the economy, H, is constant, and people work in either the public or the private sector. So we have:

$$H = L + G \qquad (10.2)$$

Because the total supply of labor services is a constant, H, and $G = H - L$ we can write:

$$Y = y(G) \qquad (10.3)$$

In Figure 10.1, we graph the relationship between Y and G.[9] The graph shows how expansion of the public sector first increases the national output, Y, and then, after a point, reduces it. Maximum output, Y^*, is reached at a level of public employment, G^*, where the marginal products of workers in the public sector and in the private sector are equal.[10]

Contractual theories of the state, associated with Locke, Rousseau, and some of the traditional public finance literature (the Pigou–Meade tradition), view the state as a contractual arrangement among equals for providing productive public services. In terms of the Findlay–Wilson model, the level of G would then be

8. It is assumed that $p(0) = 1$. Therefore, in a stateless society the community's production function would be $Y = f(L,K)$.
9. It is assumed that $p_g > 0$, $p_{gg} < 0$, and that $f(L,K)$ is homogeneous of the first degree in L and K.
10. The optimization problem is comparable to that of a firm that operates two plants and must divide its fixed labor force between the two plants so as to maximize output.

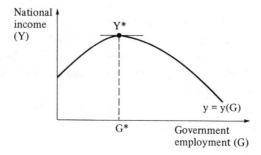

Figure 10.1. National income as a function of the level of public employment.

decided in terms of a common goal. Let us assume that the goal is the one of maximizing the community's joint income, which calls for $G = G^*$. However, the state must tax in order to pay wages for G^* hours of work in the public sector (as the sector's output is a public good and cannot be marketed). Findlay and Wilson assume that the state levies a proportional tax, t, on all incomes. The government's tax revenue is equal to tY. Now the optimization problem involves finding both G^*, and the corresponding tax rate t^*, which exactly covers the government's wage bill (and balances the budget). It is assumed that the labor market is competitive, which constrains the wage to be the same in the public and private sectors: $W_G = W_L$. Figure 10.2 presents the revenue function and the expenditure function of a contractual state when $t = t^*$.[11]

North's model of the state is of another variety, a relation of Hobbes's predatory theory of the state, recognizing *both* the productive and the potentially predatory nature of government.[12]

---

11. The government's expenditure function reflects the equality of wages in the two sectors, $W_G = W_L$, and also the assumption that wages in the private sector are equal to the value of the marginal product of private sector workers, $W_G = W_L = VMP_L$. Note that the public sector workers are also taxed. The expenditure function is then $(1 - t^*)VMP_L G$. The revenue function can be written as $t^*Y(G)$.
12. North (1981) [op. cit., note 2] concedes that the contract theory can serve as an explanation of the origin and the productive function of the state. However, the nature of the social contract is likely to change over time as events influence

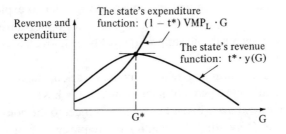

Figure 10.2. Equilibrium public employment in the contract state.

North defines the state as "an organization with comparative advantage in violence, extending over a geographic area whose boundaries are determined by its power to tax constituents."[13] The state is controlled by a ruler who monopolizes both the use of violence and the supply of public services and acts as a discriminating monopolist. The ruler has a long-term contractual relationship with his or her subjects, which stipulates the terms for the exchange of public services in return for taxes. The price that the ruler can set for such services is limited by the extent of his or her monopoly power. In particular, the ruler's ability to raise monopoly profits is constrained by three factors, the first being threats of entry from potential domestic and foreign rivals or, in other words, the availability to the subjects of substitutes for the ruler. As the availability of substitutes varies from one group to another, their ability to resist taxation also varies, and it is therefore rational for the ruler to follow a policy of price discrimination (e.g., exempt ranking members of the military from taxation and place heavy taxes on scattered, unorganized rural populations).

the potential power of the contractors. A look at the state in history does not suggest that "contracts among equals" is an appropriate characterization of the relationships involved. Also note that the introduction of transaction costs and agency problems (for instance, bureaucrats out of control) can alter the outcome of the contract model and make it less ideal than suggested by Figure 10.2. In fact, transaction costs blur the distinction between the contractual and predatory models.

13. Ibid., p. 21.

The second factor limiting the ability of the ruler to exploit his or her monopoly is rooted in the propensity for opportunistic behavior of the agents of the state who must be employed to provide public services and collect taxes.

The third constraining factor involves various measurement costs, particularly the cost of measuring the tax base.

The ruler maximizes his or her wealth, subject to the constraints listed above. Only after allowing for the requirements of survival does he or she take measures to increase the tax base. North's central point is that the ruler's maximization – constrained by survival consideration, agency problems, and measurement costs – easily can lead to methods of collecting taxes and systems of property rights that place the economy well inside its technical production frontier.[14] In extreme cases, the ruler's optimum strategy can give rise to structures of property rights that bring stagnation and economic collapse.

Now let us return to the Findlay–Wilson model. Their formal model does not capture the full flavor of North's theory, but some of the basic elements of that theory are represented in Figure 10.3. Let us assume that the ruler holds the power to tax but does not control the tax rate, t, which is exogenously set at t_0. We can imagine, for instance, that t is controlled by some representative body or is protected by custom stronger than the ruler. In terms of the formal model, the fixing of t at t_0 means that employment in the public sector is the ruler's only control variable. In Figure 10.3, the ruler seeks to maximize his or her wealth by selecting an employment level in the public sector, G_R, that maximizes the state's surplus of revenue over expenditure. By "expenditure," we refer to the net wage bill of the public sector. In the diagram, maximizing the surplus involves finding a level for G that corresponds to the greatest vertical distance between the tax revenue function and the expenditure function.

This elementary model gives us the following results:

14. North provides a recent statement of his theory in North, Douglass C. (1984). "Government and the Cost of Exchange in History." *Journal of Economic History 44* (No. 2, June): 255–264.

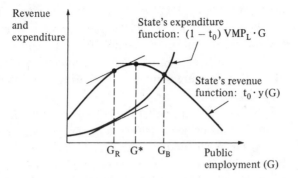

Figure 10.3. Failure to maximize national income when the tax rate is exogenous (t_0) or when bureaucrats are out of control.

1. G_R will always be to the left of G^*. As G^* corresponds to Y^*, the economy's maximum output, this implies that Y_R will always be smaller than Y^*.

2. A higher value for t_0 raises the revenue function and lowers the expenditure function (by lowering the net income of government workers), and, similarly, a lower value for t_0 lowers the revenue function and raises the expenditure function. But the *ruler's* optimum size of the public sector, G_R, will never correspond to G^*, the level that maximizes the output of the economy; hence $Y_R < Y^*$.[15]

3. The ruler undersupplies public services to the economy. A move from G_R to G^* (and hence from Y_R to Y^*) appears to be Pareto efficient. The output of the economy could be maximized by changing the rules of taxation. For example, rather than being provided with residual tax revenue, the ruler could be given the revenues either from a lump-sum

15. An optimizing ruler will increase G while marginal revenue (incremental tax revenue) is greater than marginal cost (the addition to the wage bill). The ruler will never take the economy to the point where Y peaks (to Y^*), because at that point marginal revenue ($t \times$ the change in income) is zero, but the marginal wage cost of expanding the public sector will always be positive, given Findlay and Wilson's assumptions.

tax or from a separate proportional tax on incomes. The change could provide simultaneously a greater net tax revenue for the ruler and a higher after-tax income for the subjects. North argues that such adjustments are often blocked by measurement costs, the costs of contracting, and power politics.

4. Finally, let us assume that the ruler is not fully in control of his or her agents, the public sector workers. For instance, the chiefs of bureaus in the state bureaucracy may seek to enhance their power and prestige by increasing their staff. One scenario might involve public-sector employment expanding out of control until government wages have eaten up all tax revenues. In Figure 10.3, this point is reached at G_B. The state now oversupplies the economy with public services, and again we have $Y < Y^*$.

10.3. Theory of the state: applications

10.3.1. Introduction

If an economy is to operate close to its technical production frontier, economic agents must be given the appropriate incentives. Incentives depend on the structure of property rights, and the state has a central role in determining the structure of property rights. The actual incentives and structures, which are required to place an economy close to its technical production frontier, will depend on the available technology and other circumstances, but certain generalizations can be made. The structural frontier of an economy will depend on the following factors:

1. The degree to which decision makers bear the full social costs and benefits of their actions. In general, productivity is enhanced when the system of property rights encourages decision makers to internalize the full costs and benefits of their actions.[16]

16. This statement may not be true if our definition of output is the same as found

2. The degree to which present and future ownership rights are clearly defined and secure and the extent to which disputes over ownership and contractual performance can be settled in an orderly manner and at a low cost. Secure property rights encourage investors to increase the economy's stocks of productive capital.

3. The degree to which the structure of property rights contributes to the lowering of both the cost of measuring valuable margins of assets and commodities and the cost of transferring from one owner to another the ownership rights over resources. Structures that lower the costs of transacting can move the economy closer to its technical production frontier.

4. The degree to which the state directly assigns ownership rights to assets to the uses of highest value in situations where high transaction costs prevent voluntary exchange. A state that uses a neoclassical criterion of wealth maximization in settling disputes over conflicting uses of resources can contribute to higher productivity.

The theory of the state presented above gives various reasons for the propensity of states to create property rights that are inconsistent with economic prosperity, but all the explanations are derived from the joint effects of information and transaction costs, on the one hand, and struggles over the distribution of wealth, on the other. As North (1981) notes, "Under the condition of zero transaction costs, the ruler could always devise first an efficient set of rules and then bargain for his rents, but this postulate from welfare economics simply ignores positive transaction costs, which is what the game is all about."[17]

in standard national income accounts that fail to account fully for various spillovers such as pollution. "Economic organization that induces economic growth may very well do so by internalizing the benefits and externalizing the costs and hence raising the private rate of return to 'productive' economic activity at the expense of costs lumped on other groups in society." North (1981) [op. cit., note 2], p. 62.

17. Ibid., p. 28.

Below we apply the theory of the state to examine how *political coalitions*, the state's internal *agency problems*, and systems of *public finance* affect the structural production frontiers of economies. Although empirical studies are used to illustrate these issues, our purpose is not to settle debates in economic history but rather to highlight critical linkages among political systems, property rights, and economic performance, and outline an important research agenda for Neoinstitutional Economics.

10.3.2. Political coalitions and property rights in Tropical Africa

All rulers depend on the support of influential social groups to maintain their power. We do not attempt here to present a comprehensive theory of political coalitions, but the discussion elsewhere in the book suggests the following points: Other things being equal, the political weight of social groups is directly related to the strength of their economic base. Second, the costs of collective action tend to be relatively high for large groups, especially when the members are scattered over large geographical areas, and high costs of collective action reduce the political influence of a group. Third, rulers will often divide and rule by strategically supplying goods and property rights to select individuals and groups.[18] Fourth, as North has emphasized, a common ideological fervor, for instance, arising from a pervasive sense of unjust treatment, lowers the cost of collective action and increases the political weight of groups.

Our interest in political coalitions derives from the link between the structure of coalitions and the property rights systems that result. Usually, the ruler (or the ruling group) of a state must deal with individuals and factions that possess substantial bargaining power. An increase in the bargaining power of a group often leads to demands for renegotiating the group's contract with the ruler, and changes in the structure of the social contract can affect economic performance.

---

18. Of course, no one can be excluded in the case of pure public goods, but many goods supplied by the state are not public goods.

Throughout history, changes in population and military technology have been a driving force behind shifts in the bargaining power of social groups. In his *Structure and Change in Economic History*, North (1981) uses historical examples going back to the city states of Mesopotamia and the kingdoms of ancient Egypt to illustrate a chain of causation, which begins with changes in population and military technology and ends with new economic organizations and outcomes.

For example, North argues that in the past, shifts in bargaining power caused by changes in military technology were a major (but not the only) causal factor in the rise of pluralistic government:

> The transformation of the Greek city-state from monarchy to oligarchy to democracy (in the case of Athens) occurred as a consequence of a change in military technology (the development of the phalanx) which could only be accomplished with a citizen army; the price the ruler paid was a dilution of his rule-making powers. Similarly in early modern Europe, alterations in military technology (the pike, the longbow, and gunpowder) led in some instances to the delegation of rule-making powers to parliament or Estates General in return for the increased revenue needed for survival.[19]

In turn, pluralism has various implications for property rights, which are explored by North (1981). In the modern era, North sees pluralism and changes in the control of the state rise primarily from the "Second Economic Revolution," namely the systematic development of science and its application to technology in the nineteenth century. However, he makes clear that no simple one-way line of causation dominates. In fact, economic growth (or lack of it) often has feedback effects on relative prices and the bargaining power of social groups, and no simple model explains the complex interactions involved in political and economic change.[20]

19. North (1981) [op. cit., note 2], p. 30.
20. Furthermore, in explaining collective action, North (1981) puts a major emphasis on changes in ideology – that is, people's stylized view of the world, particularly their conception of fairness. When political changes are brought about by voluntary actions of large groups, North argues that strong ideological

In the remainder of this subsection, we turn to an examination of the static (rather than dynamic) relationship between political coalitions and economic variables, using as an illustration Bates's (1981) study of *Markets and States in Tropical Africa*, which addresses the political origin of economic stagnation and decline in various African states.[21]

Economic structures and economic outcomes in Tropical Africa are far from being uniform, but certain generalizations can be made. The industrial structure of these countries is characterized by dependence on the production and export of cash crops, yielding products such as cocoa, coffee, palm oil, sisal, and cotton. Recently these vital industries have entered a path of stagnation, and Bates reports "that during the 1970s the volume of agricultural exports from all of Africa has declined."[22] Furthermore, the states of Tropical Africa, just like so many states in the Third World, have embarked upon a course of industrialization that has given rise to a small, state-sponsored manufacturing sector, which is sheltered from foreign competition and often from domestic competition as well. The production methods tend to be excessively capital intensive as a result of various government subsidies for capital inputs, and high costs and low quality make the products uncompetitive on world markets.

Bates's (1981) study of political structures in Tropical Africa reveals that three groups form the ruling coalition: individuals associated with the state bureaucracy (including members of the armed forces), firms of the state-sponsored capitalist sector, and local industries (firms that process agricultural products). Fur-

beliefs are instrumental in overcoming the free-riding problem. He has criticized Marx for both neglecting the free-riding problem in his analysis of group (class) action, and for overplaying the role of production technology in political change prior to industrial revolution. See North, Douglass C. (1986). "Is It Worth Making Sense of Marx?" *Inquiry* 29 (No. 1): 57–63.

21. Bates (1981) emphasizes that, in addition to domestic political causes, there are other complementary explanations of agricultural shortfalls in Africa. (p. 2) Most of the data used in his study are drawn from the English-speaking territories of West Africa. Bates, Robert H. (1981). *Markets and States in Tropical Africa*. Berkeley: University of California Press.

22. Ibid., p. 2.

thermore, and this is of crucial importance, all these groups seek privileged access to the resources of farmers. In fact, the position of urban workers (a small minority) is stronger than the position of farmers (the majority of voters) because of the state's concern with urban riots.

Bates (1981) also reports on the structure of property rights generated by political alliances in Tropical Africa, particularly the structures found in the markets for agricultural outputs, agricultural inputs, and domestic manufacturing products. He cites a variety of evidence suggesting that:

1. In these countries the system of property rights is very unfavorable for farmers.
2. The system tends to favor urban dwellers, bureaucrats, owners of manufacturing firms, and local industries.
3. The state has strong preferences for direct controls rather than measures that affect incentives indirectly through changes in relative prices; the state also has strong interest in mammoth projects, apparently for reasons of prestige.
4. The state uses *selective incentives* for evoking support for the government in the countryside – for example, through strategic allocation of agricultural inputs, such as fertilizers, and rural services (schools, hospitals etc.).
5. The state is ready to use violence against political entrepreneurs who try to capitalize on rural discontent.

Let us consider more closely the status of farmers who produce the vital cash crops and the disincentives that they face. In the output market, the producers of cash crops are usually required to deal exclusively with state-sponsored *monopsonies* (state marketing boards or agencies), which offer low prices for the products. The marketing boards, which were established during the colonial period and initially were used to stabilize prices, are now major instruments of taxation. At present, the farmers receive only a fraction of world-market prices for their products, and the bulk of the marketing boards' net incomes is transferred to the ruling coalitions rather than plowed back into the rural sector.

Although rural dwellers form a majority of the voting population, they have relatively little political influence, for example, compared with individuals belonging to the small manufacturing sector. There are several explanations for this. In the rural sector, the cost of collective action is high, selective incentives (political rationing of inputs and social services) weaken the resolve of potential leaders to take action against the governing coalition, and the state uses force to quell political entrepreneurs who seek to make political capital out of rural discontent. However, even though the farmers do not organize in opposition to the ruling coalition, they can minimize the losses of an adverse system of property rights by economic adjustments.

In Chapter 4, we discussed how owners of resources respond to restrictions on their property rights (e.g., to rent control) by minimizing, subject to the relevant constraints, the potential dissipation of nonexclusive income. Similarly, African producers of cash crops, when faced with severe restrictions on the right to income from their assets, adjust the use of these assets so as to maximize their value under the new constraints. Bates finds that the adjustments include withdrawal of inputs from the production of cash crops, the substitution of unregulated food crops for regulated products, the allocation of labor time to work outside agriculture including migration to urban areas.[23] The adjustment has been massive and the economic costs have been large: Even though the farmers have sought to maximize the private value of their assets by shifting them into new uses, according to the criterion of social productivity these are inferior uses. In Tropical Africa, the system of property rights works against the region's vital industries, and, in many cases, the economic impact has been devastating.

23. Bates reports that African states have strong interest in low food prices for their urban populations. However, attempts to push food prices below equilibrium market prices have met with little success. Plans to channel food crops through monopsonistic marketing boards have not been successful because of high enforcement costs. (In the case of cash crops for export, enforcement is usually manageable, as the transaction costs of controlling exports are usually relatively low.) Furthermore, most of these countries lack foreign monies to purchase food on international markets.

10.3.3. Agency problems and Soviet-type economies

If a state is to prosper and stay close to the economy's technical production frontier, it must have the political strength to adjust the structure of property rights to changes in the economic environment. However, adjustments are often blocked by *agents of the state* who believe that reforms threaten their self-interest. When structural changes are expected to raise society's aggregate wealth, both ruler and subjects may find it in their self-interest to offer state agents compensation for expected losses and to attempt to buy their compliance. Yet high transaction costs are likely to prevent such side payments. For the proponents of structural change, the transaction costs in question include not only the costs of collective action, such as the problem of free riding, but also the cost of making credible commitments to the agents. For their part, the agents fear that yielding privileges and strategic positions, even in return for reasonable compensation, will weaken their bargaining position and eventually lead to an uncompensated loss of all privileges through political action.[24]

Below we use the history of economic reforms in Soviet-type economies to illustrate how agents serving the state's ruling group can obstruct structural change. The discussion draws on a series of articles by Winiecki (1986a, 1986b, 1986c) dealing with the Soviet Union and the other Soviet-type economies (STEs) of Eastern Europe.[25]

In our times, centrally managed STEs are of great significance in terms of the world economy, and the study of STEs is a field to which Neoinstitutional Economics could make important contributions. In the STEs, the principals ruling the state attempt to

24. The same reasoning also applies to the behavior of members of political coalitions who obstruct changes in property rights, even when they are expected to increase the community's total wealth.

25. Winiecki, Jan (1986a). "Are Soviet-Type Economies Entering an Era of Long-Term Decline?" *Soviet Studies 38* (No. 3, July): 325–348; idem (1986b). "Soviet-Type Economies: Considerations for the Future." *Soviet Studies 38* (No. 4, October): 543–561; idem (1986c). "Why Economic Reforms Fail in the Soviet System: A Property Rights-Based Approach." Seminar Paper No. 374. Stockholm: The Institute for International Economic Studies.

manage the industrial sector and, partly, the agricultural sector of their economies as a single gigantic firm.[26] The evolution of the centrally managed economy can be compared to the evolution of the corporation in the Western economies; each form of organization has shaped the economic history of the twentieth century. In the West, the introduction of marketable shares and complex capital markets lowered the potential for debilitating agency costs in the corporation, which has flourished as an organizational form despite the separation of ownership and control.[27] In STEs, the institution of the Communist Party, one of the most significant institutional developments of this century, made it possible to manage complex economies from the center.[28]

The structure of the STE has a unique feature: Branching from the center of the Soviet state are two organizational trees, populated by party apparatchiks and agents of the multilevel management bureaucracy.[29] The parallel hierarchies are designed to lower the transaction costs of managing an industrial economy as one administrative unit, and the double structure remains the singular characteristic of the STEs. In this scheme, party agents monitor agents of the management bureaucracy and report back to the center. The party apparatchiks also have the important role of selecting managers at all levels, using loyalty to the principals and the Party as the overriding criterion for selection. In addition to these two sets of agents, the rulers of the STEs rely on the agents of the police and the military – in all, four agency networks.

This organizational form, chosen in the late 1920s and early 1930s by the leaders of the Soviet Union, was well suited for rapid mobilization of resources, forced industrialization, and for taking advantage of economies of scale in various basic industries. In spite of high agency costs, the system was suited for extensive growth,

---

26. See our discussion, in Chapter 2, of the Soviet economy as a single firm.
27. These issues are discussed in Chapters 5 and 6.
28. See p. 240 in Lindblom, C. E. (1977). *Politics and Markets: The World's Political Economic System.* New York: Basic Books.
29. For details of the organization of the Soviet system, see for example, Nove, Alec (1986). *The Soviet Economic System,* 3rd ed. London: Allen & Unwin.

and it served the leaders well: There are few who question the military and economic might of the Soviet Union. However, Winiecki (1986a) and other observers argue that for some time the basic organizational structure of the STEs has been dysfunctional from the viewpoint of the ruling groups of the STEs for two reasons: the cumulative effects of the system's *agency problems* and *increases in transaction costs* caused by changes in the technological environment.

First, there is the *cumulative* effect of an incentive structure that does not encourage cost minimization in the production sector but emphasizes meeting (volume or value) output quotas.[30] The long-run effects of these incentives on the economic structures of the STEs stand out, for example, when we examine their resource intensity per unit of output. Winiecki (1986a) compares energy intensity and steel intensity per U.S. dollar of GDP in East European STEs and West European market economies, and finds that the resource intensity is 2–2.5 times higher in the STEs. Furthermore, time series studies show that the resource intensity of market economies *decreases* as they mature whereas the STEs do not display a comparable trend.[31] In addition to rising resource

30. The emphasis on output quotas at the expense of cost minimization represents a constrained choice by the leadership of an STE for whom it is too costly to measure all margins. The resulting problems are good examples of what we referred to as *moral hazard*, in Chapter 2 when the theory of agency was introduced. The lack of regard for costs by enterprises in STEs has given rise to the term, *soft budget constraints*. See Kornai, Janos (1979). "Resource-Constrained Versus Demand-Constrained Systems." *Economica* 47 (No. 4) 801–819. Furthermore, the incentive structure of STEs does not encourage innovation, which becomes increasingly troublesome as these economies catch up with advanced industrial economies and economic growth depends increasingly on complex technological industries.

31. The high resource intensity of the STEs is partly related to their lack of specialization. All the small STEs of Eastern Europe have followed Stalin's model of national self-sufficiency and each built a self-contained industrial base without regard for economies of scale and comparative advantage. Also, high transaction costs make it attractive for each enterprise to be self-sufficient rather than rely on the central-management mechanism for inputs. Therefore, Winiecki refers to the *twofold lack of specialization* in STEs. Winiecki (1986a) [op. cit., note 25], p. 337.

intensity, Winiecki (1986a) analyzes various other malfunctions that are endogenous to the central management system and over time cause mounting difficulties. For example, the STEs display high and increasing transport intensity in freight ton-kilometers per unit of GNP compared with market economies, even after allowance is made for differences in income per capita, and the STEs' ability to compete in international markets for industrial products seems to have fallen over time, whereas the evolving industrial structure of these countries has created increasing demand for imports of industrial inputs.[32]

Second, changes in the technological environment have raised transaction costs and rendered the organizational structure of the STEs dysfunctional. The hierarchical central management structure of the STE works best when (1) final outputs have relatively few quality dimensions; (2) when the vertical phases of processing a commodity are few; (3) when there are substantial economies of scale at the enterprise level; and (4) when the technology does not require horizontal linkages between enterprises with each unit acting as both supplier and purchaser of inputs.[33] However, recent technological developments have worked against the central management structure:

> The trend in the world economy during the 1970s and the 1980s has been for industries in which vertical relations predominate (steel, cement, bulk chemicals) to be replaced as an engine of growth by industries in which enterprises are typically linked horizontally and act as both suppliers of inputs and purchasers of outputs from each other. These less material-using, more value-adding industries (electrical and non-electrical engineering, instrument making, fine chemicals) where complex, non-linear intra- and inter-industry linkages

---

32. Ibid., pp. 337–340. Also note that "by the late 1970s the source of labor provided by the shift of agriculture into industry had largely dried up. On the other hand, intra-industry movement of labor from slow- to fast-growing branches in a basically autarkic economy is almost non-existent " (p. 329).
33. Ibid., pp. 326–327.

predominate depend much more for their performance
upon features that are the antithesis of central
planning.[34]
In sum, the long-run effect of central management appears to be
economic stagnation.[35]

For some time, the leadership of the STEs has been aware that
their economies may be on a path of long-term decline and there
is no turning around unless the command-rationing system is replaced with decentralized management in the state sector and/or
an expanded private sector. In order to restore their economies,
the leaders have introduced a series of reforms but with little or
no success. Winiecki (1986c) advances the thesis that the reforms
have been sabotaged primarily by middle-level agents of the party
and the management bureaucracy. The reason is simple: The common theme of the proposed reforms is the replacement of commands with autonomous parameters, such as prices. Bureaucrats,
who are asked to implement reforms where parametric adjustments replace command-rationing by agents of the state, are,
in fact, asked to show inventiveness in making themselves obso-
lete and forego the *rents* which their current property rights give
rise to.

There are two reasons why middle-level agents of the Party and
the management bureaucracy have a strong interest in keeping the
basic institutional structure of the STE intact. First, the Communist
Party apparatus holds property rights over managerial positions in
all administrative and enterprise units through the *nomenklatura*
system. A competitive market for managers would represent a
huge transfer of wealth away from Party functionaries.[36] Second,

34. Ibid., p. 328.
35. "The predictable outcome has been stagnation of real – as distinct from officially
    reported – economic growth, higher inflation – open, hidden, and repressed –
    and falling living standards, with the latter affected more strongly than overall
    growth by decision makers' preferences, the working of the central planning
    mechanism, and the necessity to pay foreign debt." Winiecki (1986c) [op. cit.,
    note 25], p. 543.
36. By a "competitive market for management" we imply a system in which se-
    lection is based on managerial skills rather than loyalty to the Party. Winiecki

the agents benefit from an elaborate system of kickbacks involving managers primarily of industrial enterprises. The STEs have been characterized as *shortage economies*, and the kickbacks tend to be goods and services in short supply provided at list prices or at even lower prices, bypassing the rationing-by-waiting system. A detailed description of the system of privileges enjoyed by the agents of the two networks is found in any text on the Soviet system, but the basic point is that these privileges are *system-specific to the STEs*: The management agents and their monitors, the Party apparatchiks, are substitutes for the decentralized systems of parametric adjustments, and the rewards they enjoy arise from their monopoly over top positions and opportunistic behavior which the center is unable to control.[37]

However, as Winiecki (1986c) emphasizes, the privileges accruing to members of the other two networks of agents, the military and the police, are system-specific not to central management but rather to *autocratic* forms of government. As the STEs enter a path of long-term decline, the call for a fundamental change in the structure of property rights comes from both the rulers and the public, whereas the military and the police either are largely neutral or support change, and opposition comes primarily from two segments of the ruling stratum: party apparatchiks and management bureaucrats.[38]

The first signs of slowdown in Eastern Europe were seen early in the 1960s, but the traditional sources of extensive economic

(1986c) argues that in the STEs the pool of talent included in *nomenklatura* is below average competence relative to the pool of talent that non-STEs can draw on to fill positions of management. He maintains that entry into nomenklatura is characterized by adverse selection. Ibid., p. 7.

37. Reforms face the strongest opposition in industry, as the most lucrative management positions are found there. The STEs have been relatively more successful in reforming agriculture. Ibid., p. 12.

38. Extensive economic reforms in the STEs would require the introduction of equilibrium prices. It is not clear how the general public would react, at least in the short run, if a large increase in prices replaced rationing by waiting. Opponents of reforms have also warned that they will increase inequality. Winiecki reports that in Poland the price of a car on the free market is 110–130 percent higher than list prices. Winiecki (1986b) [op. cit., note 25], p. 11.

growth were still available and partial economic reforms still worked. Difficulties in the 1970s were met with Western technology and credit, but by the 1980s the choice seemed to involve radical political change or economic decline: By themselves, investment expansion, technological change, changes in industrial composition, and more international trade could not revive the failing European STEs.[39] If political reforms are to create conditions for sustained growth they must involve a system "of checks and balances constraining the freedom of party apparatchicks to interfere in and sponge the economy . . . "[40]

A survey of attempts at reforms in European STEs reveals the following:[41] First, attempts to decentralize these systems, beginning shortly after the death of Stalin in 1953 and accelerating in recent years, have not removed control by party apparatchiks over economic enterprises, particularly control over appointments to managerial positions.

Second, the strategy employed by agents of the state who seek to preserve the nomenklatura and the kickback system varies, depending on political constraints such as the extent of public discontent. At times, the agents have been able to ensure from the start that the reforms are no more than pseudo-reorganization. For example, a program of reforms may involve shedding a few middle-level organizations but adding other comparable institutions or limiting the number of obligatory plan indicators for enterprises but adding new classes of "orienting" and "auxiliary" indicators.

Third, in other instances, reforms have raised the cost to the agents of controlling enterprises, rather than eliminating their control. For example, although direct commands have been eliminated, the agents' right to ration inputs has been retained; alternatively, commands and rationing have been abolished but not the right to appoint and dismiss managers of enterprises. In

---

39. Winiecki (1986b) gives the details of this argument.
40. Ibid., p. 558.
41. See Winiecki (1986c), op. cit., note 25.

many cases, the agents have managed partly to reverse this process, thus confounding the situation by creating uncertainty about the effective structure of property rights.

Finally, only in Hungary have both formal commands and rationing been abolished, but still the party apparatchiks remain in control:

> Thus, since the market did not substitute for central planning, the void was filled by "suggested" auxiliary or orienting indicators covering the whole range of enterprise activities, and bargaining between managers and economic bureaucracy for change in the value of these indicators, by informal rationing and bargaining for inputs, by participation of economic bureaucracy and party apparatchiks in the preparation of enterprises' "autonomous" plans, as well as by an amalgam of disguised or undisguised, formal or informal, persistent or ad hoc interference in enterprise activity.[42]

The analysis above suggests that a necessary condition for increasing the dynamic efficiency of the STEs is to destroy, in its present form, the now dysfunctional monitoring agency, the Communist Party, which previously was the key to the system's success. One suggested scenario has the Party somehow fade into the background; another scenario has the ruling strata form a coalition with the military and the police against the Party, turning the systems into market-oriented dictatorships.[43]

---

42. Ibid., p. 24. Winiecki (1986b) argues that the high living standards of Hungary, relative to the other STEs, are explained by a decision by the top leadership, responding to the massive uprising in 1956, to give higher priority to consumer goods. The emphasis on consumer goods predates the first Hungarian reforms. Hungary shows the same structural weaknesses as the other STEs, according to Winiecki.

43. In this context, Winiecki (1986c) speculates whether the Chinese Cultural Revolution managed to weaken the power of the middle-level Party apparatus and lay the groundwork for the successful replacement of commands with parameters, and elimination of the Party's control over management positions in enterprises, or whether counterreformation is unavoidable.

10.3.4. Public finance and property rights: the case of early modern Europe

Long-term investments tend to be vulnerable to appropriation and forthcoming only when potential investors see present and expected future ownership rights as reasonably secure. The question of stable exclusive private ownership rights is not an issue in the STEs, where the state, through its agents, directly controls major physical investments.[44] However, in countries where ownership of the means of production is decentralized, the stability of private ownership rights is of critical importance for the performance of the economy.

The way in which the state conducts its finances affects the definition and stability of exclusive rights. Predatory public finance creates de facto incomplete exclusive rights, and wealth-maximizing individuals respond to uncertain property rights by making various adjustments to minimize the risk of appropriation. These adjustments tend to lower the level of investment activity and change its nature.[45] In other words, predatory public finance can move the economy's structural production frontier away from its technical production frontier.

In Europe, during a period of 200 years ending in the mid-seventeenth century, the nation-state rose from the ruins of the former feudal/manorial structures. The gradual emergence of the nation-state was in response to various forces, including military technology, which had increased the optimal size of the political unit and multiplied the state's military and bureaucratic expenditures.[46] However, as the crown was typically constrained by an

---

44. However, the delegation of investment decisions by the state raises a host of agency problems, as we touched upon in the previous subsection.
45. See our discussion, in Chapter 4, of common and incomplete property rights. The adjustments to reduce the risk of appropriation are likely to involve several margins, such as type of technology employed, time profiles of investments, type of inputs used, and nature of commodities produced. One possible reaction is to avoid long-term investments altogether.
46. "Whether the development of an exchange economy was a sufficient condition for expanding the optimum scale of warfare or [whether] technological inno-

archaic revenue system, and as the costs of measuring the tax base were high, the early nation-state suffered chronic financial deficits and relied heavily on credit.

To repeat, in addition to political constraints, measurement and other transaction costs limited taxation. Land was taxed, but high transaction costs restricted taxes on the growing wealth of the merchant class except when large volumes of trade passed through a few specified points, such as ports in the case of English foreign trade. As for income taxes, the concept of annual income was still poorly defined and the costs of measuring incomes were high. Later developments of organizational forms in business and associated commercial law required the definition and measurement of annual incomes and reduced the costs of effective income taxation. Similarly, general property taxes were impeded by the high cost of maintaining measures of current property values: The measurement cost fell later when property, to a considerable extent, came to be in the form of transferable securities. And, finally, an unsophisticated monetary and banking system, along with economic and political considerations, limited inflationary financing through manipulation of the money supply.[47]

In order to survive, the typical ruler resorted to predatory public finance, which created uncertainty about property rights, reduced the tax base and lowered the crown's credit ratings, and further weakened the state's ability to finance its activities. For instance,

---

vations augmented the scale may still be argued. What cannot be argued is that it expanded. As a consequence, the conditions for political survival were drastically altered. Survival now required not only a large army, but a trained disciplined fighting force supported by costly equipment in the form of cannons and muskets. The age of the amored knight with lance passed; the age of chivalry was ended. Warfare on land and at sea (where the size and armaments of naval ships increased dramatically) had dramatically altered the size of the financial resources necessary for survival." North (1981) [op. cit., note 2], p. 138. See also Tilly, Charles, ed. (1975). *The Formation of National States in Western Europe.* Princeton: Princeton University Press.

47. See "The Finances of the Sovereign," Chapter 6 in Hicks, John (1969). *A Theory of Economic History.* Oxford: Oxford University Press.

in early seventeenth-century England under the Stuarts prior to the Civil War, public finance involved the sale of crown lands to raise revenue, the sale of monopoly rights to industries, the sale of peerage and knighthood, the seizure of goods for public purposes without paying the owners the full market value of the goods, the sale to specific individuals of the right to dispense with certain public rules, and outright confiscation of private property. The Stuarts also secured loans under force of threat and, later, unilaterally rewrote loan contracts to make the terms more favorable for the state.[48]

There is ample historical evidence to show that predatory public finance often has shrunk the state's tax base, reduced its credit and tax revenues, and contributed to economic decline.[49] Therefore, let us recall why a rational ruler might ever resort to such self-defeating measures. First note that, according to the theoretical model of the state presented in the second subsection of this chapter, a ruler who is not constrained by competition, agency problems, and measurement costs will seek to maximize the state's tax base.[50] However, in the real world, rulers do face the constraints just listed: Their control (ownership) of the potential tax

48. See pp. 5–9, and 21–22 in North, Douglass C., and Weingast, Barry R. (1987). "Constitutions and Commitment: The Evolution of Institutions Governing Public Choice in 17th Century England." Working paper. St. Louis: Washington University. The European sovereigns, as a rule, were not creditworthy. They frequently repudiated their promises, creditors (particularly minorities) were persecuted and expelled from their country, and outright bankruptcies were not unusual. "The Spanish declared bankruptcy in 1575, 1596, 1607, 1627, and 1647." See p. 1 in Root, Hilton L., and Ingberman, Daniel E. (1987). "Tying the King's Hands: Credible Commitments and Royal Fiscal Policy During the Old Regime." Working Paper. Philadelphia: University of Pennsylvania.

49. For example, the selling of monopoly rights over major industries will bring stagnation in the long run, and extensive selling of tax-free status will limit future tax revenues. "Parting with State property, and parting with taxing power, obviously weaken government." Hicks (1969) [op. cit., note 47], p. 87.

50. The wealth of his or her subjects is the potential tax base of a ruler. The dissipating ruler can be compared to fishermen in an open-access fishery or landlords subject to rent controls. See our discussion in Chapter 4.

base is incomplete and uncertain, and, under certain circumstances, dissipation becomes rational behavior for a wealth-maximizing ruler.

Although the constraints of competition and transaction costs often create incentives for rulers to dissipate the state's potential wealth, the addition of *further constraints* can both create stable property rights and increase public and private revenues. A ruler who appropriates the quasi-rents from investments, initially made by private investors who believed that ownership rights were secure, can be compared to an opportunistic party to a private long-term contract. In our discussion of the nature of the firm (Chapter 5), it was pointed out that reneging on contracts, holding up investors, and confiscating their quasi-rents not only curtails vulnerable investments and reduces wealth, but also makes it worthwhile to make arrangements that prevent appropriation.[51]

There are two fundamental ways of protecting quasi-rents. One is vertical integration, which, in the political arena, is the road of Soviet-type states and many developing countries: The state acquires the vulnerable assets. The other approach is to constrain potential appropriators. Potential appropriators can either make credible commitments and bond themselves by means such as long-term contracts and collaterals ("hostages"), or they can be deprived of power and have constraints forced on them. The early history of the nation-state provides examples of both kinds of constraints.

The case has been made that relative economic success or failure of the countries of Europe in the past 200 or so years is related to the resolution of the financial crisis in the early nation-states.[52] In some instances, the crisis was resolved through the emergence of

51. For an authoritative discussion of these issues see Williamson, Oliver (1985). *The Economic Institutions of Capitalism*. New York: Free Press.
52. See North, Douglass C., and Thomas, Robert (1973). *The Rise of the Western World: A New Economic History*. Cambridge: Cambridge University Press; North, Douglass C. (1981), op. cit., note 2; idem (1986a). "Institutions, Economic Growth and Freedom: An Historical Introduction." Political Economy working paper. St. Louis: Washington University.

representative government, the distribution of powers, an independent judiciary, and other institutions supportive of secure property rights. In other cases a centralist bureaucratic tradition evolved, and dissipating property rights structures became institutionalized. Furthermore, during the colonial era, the European powers exported their alternative systems which thus came to affect world development.[53]

Finally, let us briefly consider the different responses of England and France to the financial crisis of the early nation-state.

> A king could rely on loans to tide the government through a war; but facing the awesome task of repayment, he required fiscal revenues. The necessity to establish a regular source of revenue to repay war loans influenced and then determined the relationship between the state and the private sector. . . . In most cases the crown was initially forced to grant to "representative" bodies (Parliament, Estates General) control over tax rates in return for the revenue they voted. In some instances these representative bodies retained this privilege; in others, they lost it. This last point requires special emphasis and further elaboration since it is the key to future differential patterns of development which we observe within Europe.[54]

North and Weingast (1987) examine how constraints were forced on the English crown during the seventeenth century, leading to the separation of powers and an independent judiciary. Toward the end of the century, various changes were made in the way in which the government sought credit, and the new institutions, including the Bank of England, ushered in modern capital markets. The new political institutions and the fiscal revolution made cred-

---

53. North examines divergent institutional change in England and Spain in early modern Europe and discusses how these structures influenced property rights in British North America and Spanish imperial policies in the Indies and Latin American colonial development. North (1986a), op. cit., note 52.

54. North (1981) [op. cit., note 2], pp. 140–141.

ible the government's commitment to honor its credit contracts, and the new structures demonstrated how: "Rules that can readily be revised by the sovereign differ significantly in their implications for performance from exactly the same rules when not subject to revision."[55]

The new limits on the crown's ability to control property rights, and the balance of powers, increased enormously the government's capacity to borrow at very low rates of interest. Furthermore, the new institutions not only took away the crown's incentives to renege on its contracts, but also lowered the cost to private individuals of making credible commitments to long-term contracts among themselves. Looking beyond the seventeenth century, "It is clear that these institutional changes underpinned the drive towards British hegemony and dominance of the world. England could not have beaten France without its financial revolution. These changes also provided the institutional underpinnings of the industrial revolution."[56]

In fifteenth-century France, Charles VII unified France after the devastations of the Hundred Years' War. To finance the pacification of the country and the recovering of more than half his claimed kingdom, the representative body, the Estates General, granted Charles VII special power to tax. However, the sovereign's control over public finance outlived the emergency, and the crown retained rights to grant and alter property rights until the Revolution.[57]

For lenders an unsecured loan to a sovereign, who is above the law and cannot be sued, is a risky venture. Hicks (1969) shows how European sovereigns sought to make credible commitment to repayment by pawning physical assets such as crown jewels and royal estates and, more importantly, by pawning less tangible assets such as the right to collect certain taxes, the right of appointment to high offices, the right to monopolize trade, and the right to claim tax exemptions.[58]

55. North and Weingast (1987) [op. cit., note 48], p. 1.
56. Ibid., p. 28.
57. North (1981) [op. cit., note 2], pp. 148–150.
58. "There is indeed not much difference between pawning an asset, with little

Root and Ingberman (1987) discuss how the crown, during the Old Regime in France, sought to make credible commitments to lenders. The commitment technology evolved from using a few financial families as intermediaries, to relying on bureaucratic corporations. The financiers, who made a network among themselves through intermarriage, were not above the law, and could be held responsible if the king failed to honor his debts. However, the crown's abuses of the financiers created incentives for their organizing themselves into corporations in order to increase the cost to the crown of repudiating its debts and to constrain kingly discretion. "Among the intermediaries the king called upon were the traditional corps: the village communities, the guilds and the provincial estates. In return for official recognition and privileges, these corporate groups acted as bankers for the sovereign."[59] Typically, the privileges involved the assignment of monopoly rights protected by the state and the right to tax the movement of goods at the local level.

However, the king's claim to absolute power undermined the government's fiscal credibility. In the eighteenth century, France could not make credible commitments to a national bank (an experiment that failed), the old practice of selling tax exemptions had come to a dead end, and the country could not satisfactorily finance its wars. The French were aware that institutional change in England, including the separations of powers, and a fiscal revolution, had put English finances on a sound footing, and major social and political reforms were needed in France to raise tax revenues and improve the government's credit standing:[60] "Informed members of the public insisted on the need to subject economic policy to public discussion and to design institutions

---

prospect of redemption, and outright sale. Thus borrowing against a tax-farm slides into selling tax-farms; and that slides into selling exemptions from future taxation." Hicks (1969) [op. cit., note 47], p. 87.

59. Root and Ingberman (1987), p. 14.
60. For a discussion of why a parliament has less incentive than a king to default on government loans, see Root and Ingberman (1987) [op. cit., note 48], pp. 19–20.

that would limit the crown's discretion over finance. The discussion of how to design such institutions led to the Revolution [of 1789]."[61]

We conclude with a few generalizations. First, society's stock of institutional capital changes through obsolescence and new investments, but changes tend to be marginal. Existing institutions shape the course of future institutional developments. Second, credible commitment by the state to stable property rights both promotes private investments and lowers the transaction costs to the state of raising revenue. In modern nation-states, such commitments seem to require an effective separation of powers. Finally, generalizations about the separation of powers are hard to make. In history, the separation of powers has depended partly on factors, such as the existence (or non-existence) of a standing army controlled by the crown, structural features of the economy that affect the transaction costs of regular taxation, and various domestic and foreign political factors, which affect the bargaining strength of social groups.

10.4. The institutions of representative government and transaction costs

10.4.1. Introduction

In the industrial democracies of our times, public rules prescribing exchange in factor and output markets have multiplied in the past 100 years. In general, there is vast involvement by the state in economic life, spanning both the definition and the enforcement of property rights and direct allocation of resources. Ultimately, a behavioral theory of representative government and its institutions is needed to explain the allocation of resources in modern industrial states.

The positive study of representative government has been the domain of two related disciplines, Political Science and Public Choice. The Public Choice school extends the rational-choice

61. Ibid., p. 26.

model to the study of politics, and since the 1960s the economic approach is increasingly used by political scientists in general.[62] The early work applying the rational-choice model to politics tended to mirror neoclassical economics in that transaction costs were assumed to be zero and the role of institutions was neglected. Furthermore, the scholars of the 1960s and 1970s rediscovered, and became preoccupied with, the classical voting paradox.[63] According to the voting paradox, outcomes are unstable under majority rule because a new majority preferring some other alternative can always be found.[64] In fact, Schwartz (1987) surveys this literature and concludes that almost all collective choice environments are unstable.

As we discussed in Chapter 3, when this topic was introduced, actual political outcomes are not as unstable as the early rational-choice models suggest. Recently, political theorists have reintroduced institutions into their models and, using the tools of Neoinstitutionalism, sought to explain how rules constrain legislators and induce stability:

> The importance of procedural rules became more obvious in all sorts of rational-choice models of politics. Students of Congress argued that creating subject-area committees in Congress, with a seniority rule for determining committee chairmanship, resulted in quite different outcomes than an alternative set of internal

62. For an early classic in the Public Choice field, see Buchanan, James, and Tullock, Gordon (1962). *The Calculus of Consent*. Ann Arbor: University of Michigan Press. A pioneering application of the rational-choice model to government is found in Downs, Anthony (1957). *An Economic Theory of Democracy*. New York: Harper and Row. The early public choice literature is surveyed by Mueller, Dennis C. (1979). *Public Choice*. Cambridge: Cambridge University Press.
63. The Marquis De Condorect discovered in the eighteenth century the paradox associated with majority-rule decisions.
64. The theoretical literature dealing with the instability of outcomes in voting is reviewed by Schwartz, Thomas (1987). "Votes, Strategies, and Institutions: An Introduction to the Theory of Collective Choice." In McCubbins, Mathew D., and Sullivan, Terry, eds. (1987). *Congress: Structure and Policy*. Cambridge: Cambridge University Press.

procedural rules based on, for instance, party discipline.
. . . Rational-choice theorists became fascinated with
examples which demonstrated the coercive nature of
such institutional rules on group choice. . . . [W]ith the
renewed interest in institutions came a renewed interest
in history, since institutions (as opposed to individual
attitudes and behavior) seemed grounded in history.[65]

The next logical step for political theorists was to apply the tools
of Neoinstitutionalism to the question of how the institutions themselves were chosen. This work has just begun.

It is beyond this book to give a comprehensive view of attempts
to use the tools of NIE to endogenize the political outcomes and
institutions of representative government.[66] Our task in this section
is to suggest the potential of our approach to political theory
through the example of two studies. The first study attempts to
model formally the role of transaction costs in explaining how the
influence of interest groups and the behavior of legislators depend
on the nature of the assumptions about the cost of information.
The second study uses NIE and the new theory of business organization to explain the internal structure of the U.S. Congress.

10.4.2. Information costs and interest groups

The interest-group theory of legislation was introduced in
Chapter 3. The puzzle of an excessive influence over legislators by
a relatively small special-interest group was explained informally
in terms of an asymmetrical distribution of information and by the
majority group's high costs of collective action relative to expected
benefits. Denzau and Munger (1986) have formalized these issues
in a model that shows how policies chosen by legislators, and the

---

65. See p. 8 in Knott, Jack H., and Miller Gary J. (1987). *Reforming Bureaucracy: The Politics of Institutional Choice.* Englewood Cliffs, N.J.: Prentice Hall.
66. We refer the reader to leading journals, such as *Public Choice, American Journal of Political Science,* and *American Political Science Review.* Also, some twenty papers representative of the neoinstitutional approach are found in McCubbins and Sullivan (1987), op. cit., note 64.

influence of organized interest groups, depend on the assumptions that are made about the availability of information to voters.[67]

In the Denzau–Munger model, legislators maximize votes (V). The legislators' activities are constrained by a scarce resource, effort (E), an exogenous variable. Each legislator allocates her $\bar{E}$ to various activities so as to maximize the chances of reelection. A legislator can affect the votes of her geographical constituency in three ways: (1) by policies and actions directed explicitly to benefit the district's unorganized constituency; (2) by promoting policies of interest groups that don't vote – policies that may be liked or disliked by the voters; and (3) by advertising and otherwise controlling the flow of information to voters.

In order to control the flow of information to her voters (through advertising and other forms of campaigning), the legislator requires resources R. R is available only from nonvoting interest groups in return for support in promoting their policies, P. A legislator produces policy results by allocating some effort E_i to policy P_i. The legislator's effectiveness in getting results is represented by a production function, $P_i(E_i)$. The productivity of legislators varies both from one person to another and, for an individual, across policies. For example, the productivity of a legislator is relatively high for policy P_i, if she is a member of a legislative committee with jurisdiction over P_i.

Any policy, P_i, can increase or decrease the welfare of the legislator's geographical constituency. The legislator will support a policy that affects potential voters negatively, only if by doing so she can raise advertising revenue, R, from organized groups. Therefore, the model also contains both a revenue function, $R_i(P_i)$, representing the prices paid by organized groups for services rendered; and a production function, relating votes to advertising expenditure, $V(R)$.

The legislator's optimization problem involves allocating effort,

67. Denzau, Arthur T., and Munger, Michael (1986). "Legislators and Interest Groups: How Unorganized Interests Get Represented." *American Political Science Review 80* (No. 1, March): 89–106.

$\bar{E}$, to policies and services for the geographical constituency, P_u, and to policies, P_i, favored by organized groups in order to raise advertising revenue, R. We assume that there are only two organized interest groups, each promoting a single policy program. Then a legislator maximizes the following equation:[68]

$$V = V[P_u(E_u), P_1(E_1), P_2(E_2), R] + \lambda(\bar{E} - E_u - E_1 - E_2)$$
(10.4)

Now consider two extreme assumptions about information available to voters: (1) *rational ignorance*, and (2) *full information*. The concept of rational ignorance implies that voters find it costly themselves to collect information about the activities of their representative and depend for information on her advertising. In the limit, when all information comes from the legislator (a case of pure rational ignorance), the response function for voters is $V(R)$, and Eq. 10.4 becomes:

$$V = V\{R_1[P_1(E_1)], R_2[P_2(E_2)]\} + \lambda(\bar{E} - E_1 - E_2)$$
(10.5)

In situations depicted by Eq. 10.5, interest groups control the legislator's activities, and her production function for producing alternative policies, $P_i(E_i)$, becomes the central issue. Pressure groups will seek out legislators with high productivity in their policy area (committee chairpersons, individuals with expert knowledge in the field, etc.) in an attempt to minimize the resource cost of obtaining and preserving favorable laws and regulations.[69] Note, however, that the model exaggerates the power of interest groups over legislators in a world of complete rational ignorance. A legislator does not have a monopoly over the flow of information to the geographical constituency. If she can advertise, so can her

---

68. Note that in the following equation $R = R_1(P_1) + R_2(P_2)$. Also note that E_u represents the effort that the legislator allocates to the promotion of policies and services for her geographical constituency, P_u.

69. Denzau and Munger derive from their model that "the more adept the legislator is at producing policy services for a group, the lower the minimum price he will require for doing so." Denzau and Munger (1986) [op. cit., note 67], p. 97.

political competitors, and the news media also polices the actions of incumbents.[70]

Next consider the implications of introducing a world of full information where, at no cost to themselves, all the members of a constituency have full knowledge of the activities of their representative. As there is no room for manipulating information, political advertising by the legislator is pointless. Therefore the vote productivity of advertising resources, R, falls to zero, and interest groups have nothing to offer the legislator.[71] R drops out of the voters' reaction function, which becomes:

$$V = V(P_u, P_1, P_2) \qquad (10.6)$$

Furthermore, a legislator will not allocate effort to policies P_1 and P_2 unless they directly promote the welfare of her constituency, which means that a legislator will represent only the interests of her voters.

In real life, the situation lies somewhere between the assumptions of rational ignorance and full information. Denzau and Munger (1986) point out that various phenomena, ranging from political advertising, preferences by members of the U.S. Congress for positions on committees, and the behavior of organized interest groups, are inconsistent with both extreme assumptions. Well-funded interest groups are, indeed, influential, as a result of positive transaction costs, but their influence is constrained by the geographical constituency because some information does filter through to the voters, and voters do react.

10.4.3. Transaction costs and the structure of democratic institutions

In Chapters 6 and 7, the tools of Neoinstitutional Economics were used to explain the structure of firms and contracts in various markets in terms of cost minimization. We emphasized how measurement and enforcement problems may prevent owners of valuable resources from realizing potential gains from trade,

70. Ibid., p. 100.
71. It is assumed that the legislator cannot use R for personal consumption.

and also how trade can be thwarted by the difficulty of foreseeing future environments and writing contingent contracts when exchange has a substantial time dimension. Incomplete contracts give rise to opportunistic behavior. When the gains from exchange cannot be realized because of high transaction costs, traders have an incentive to lower these costs by introducing new institutions, which constrain and prescribe individual action. These new institutions include, for example, vertical integration, franchising, or the traditional entrepreneurial firm.

It is reasonable to believe that the NIE approach may be useful also in modeling the structure of political institutions under representative government, but work in this area has just begun. As we just said, the introduction of the rational-choice model into political science in the 1960s was, in part, a reaction to the old institutionalism. The early work tended to emphasize exchange across implicit or explicit markets, ignored transaction costs, and did not focus on the structure of institutions or their constraining influence. Recently, this has changed, and scholars using the label Neoinstitutionalism have begun to apply the tools of NIE to the study of government. For example, the twenty papers by various authors in *Congress: Structure and Policy* (1987) provide a good summary of the current understanding of the institutional structure of the U.S. Congress.[72] The authors represent different schools of thought, but, in one way or another, the papers are concerned with the effect of institutions on individual behavior, particularly institutional innovations in Congress that organize the business of legislating, the effects of institutions on policy choices, and how the U.S. Congress designs institutions to control the execution of delegated authority.

A model of the organization of the U.S. Congress by Weingast and Marshall (1988) illustrates the potential of the NIE approach to democratic institutions.[73] A great variety of interests are rep-

---

72. McCubbins and Sullivan (1987), op. cit., note 64.
73. The remainder of this section is based on their study. See Weingast, Barry R., and Marshall, William J. (1988). "The Industrial Organization of Congress;

resented in a legislature, but few have the automatic support of a majority of the members. If we assume that reelection is the primary goal of legislators, and that the promotion of appropriate policies enhances their reelection, then legislators can gain by trading votes: A legislator seeks votes for bills that make the largest positive impact on her reelection in return for giving her vote to bills with minimal negative impact on her election fortunes.

The pioneering studies of vote trading (logrolling) all assume implicit or explicit markets in votes.[74] Although these studies have provided valuable insights, Weingast and Marshall (1988) argue that they fail to account for the high transaction costs of exchanging votes. In fact, the organizational structure of legislative bodies can (at least in part) be explained in terms of designs for lowering the transaction costs of exchanging votes and building coalitions. Let us pause and consider why transaction costs of trading votes should be high.[75]

First, legislators, unlike traders in markets for goods and services, cannot rely on third-party enforcement of their agreements. Legislator A who reneges on her promise to vote for the bill of legislator B (in return for some favor) cannot be taken to court for breach of contract.

Second, legislators A and B may agree to support each other's policies, but the voting on their bills need not take place simultaneously. Legislator A may vote for B's bill, but B may refuse to return the favor weeks or months later, when A's bill comes up for voting.

Third, many things can happen before A's bill comes up for voting, such as changes in the preferences of voters who benefit

or, Why Legislatures, like Firms, Are Not Organized as Markets." *Journal of Political Economy 96* (No. 1): 132–163.

74. For example, see Tullock, Gordon (1967). *Towards a Mathematics of Politics.* Ann Arbor: University of Michigan Press; Wilson, Robert (1967). "An Axiomatic Model of Logrolling." *American Economic Review 59* (June): 331–341; and Koford, Kenneth J. (1982). "Centralized Vote-trading." *Public Choice 39* (No. 2): 245–268.

75. Weingast and Marshall (1988) [op. cit., note 73], pp. 137–142.

by the bill or other political circumstances. Legislator A may need to amend her bill to protect her reelection chances, or the new circumstances may create incentives for B to ask for changes in the bill. In either case, asymmetrical information makes it hard for each legislator to judge whether the other's behavior is opportunistic or a genuine response to changing circumstances.[76] High transaction costs preclude the writing of complete contracts that cover all contingencies, and the role of repeat play and reputation in facilitating enforcement is undermined.

Fourth, the flow of electoral benefits from their programs to legislators A and B need not coincide in time. A's program may involve dams and bridges, and B's program may constitute a new regulatory agency. Once the dams and bridges are built, A can join a new coalition and vote for a bill abolishing B's regulatory agency and deprive him of future benefits.

These factors can impose high costs on exchange and limit trade, but Weingast and Marshall (1988) use the new theory of the firm to analyze how institutional structures within the U.S. Congress help make agreements between members enforceable and facilitate the forming of durable coalitions. The committee system is the centerpiece of their model, and the basic features of the analysis are summarized below.[77]

In Congress, the political agenda is divided into clearly defined jurisdictions. Committees are assigned property rights over jurisdictions, and they control what alternatives, if any, to the status quo, come up for vote by the whole assembly. The system also involves rules for proper amendments.

Legislators compete for positions on committees that best suit their reelection chances. The competitive process reveals the leg-

---

76. The resulting problems of measurement reduce the effectiveness of investment in reputation as an instrument of lowering the transaction cost of trading in legislative IOUs. Weingast and Marshall (1988) emphasize, however, that reputation complements formal legislative institutions rather than substitutes for them. Ibid., pp. 141–142.
77. See ibid., pp. 143–148.

islators' preferences, and the assignment of committee positions reflects these preferences. Seats on committees cannot be traded, and members keep their positions as long as they wish, subject to their reelection.

A committee is an agent of the whole legislature, and various rules are designed to constrain the power of committees in order to limit agency problems. The most important of these constraints is the requirement that committee proposals must command a majority of votes in the legislature to become public policy.

Now reconsider the previous example of an exchange of votes for dams and roads in return for votes in support of a new regulatory agency, and the possibility that legislators may renege and abolish the agency once their dams and roads have been built. With the committee system in place, the original coalition that supported the regulatory agency had to include a majority of members on the committee with jurisdiction over the relevant regulations. Even when a new majority emerges in Congress for revoking the regulations, the committee can use its veto power over changes in the status quo and refuse to bring bills to the floor for vote. A new majority on the *committee* is required to bring about a change in this area.

Furthermore, the committee system limits opportunistic behavior in vote trading, when voting is not simultaneous and some legislators have an incentive to renege by rewriting the original bill. The committee, which has jurisdiction in the area, can control which of several alternatives, supported against the status quo by a majority, comes up for voting. The committee system does not solve all problems, and agreements across committees are still costly (and this should affect the structure of jurisdictions), but the assignment of property rights over jurisdictions, through a process of competition and self-selection, lowers the cost of forming coalitions and enforcing agreements.[78] The

78. Note that the membership of a committee does not change except after elections to Congress. The decision to move between committees is comparable to an

institutionalization of the system gives permanence to policies.[79]

Finally, Weingast and Marshall (1988) suggest that the transaction costs of trading in legislative IOUs can also be reduced with the help of a party system in the legislature. In fact, a strong committee system may be a substitute for strong political parties and party discipline. Enforcement through reputation and repeated dealings is more effective in the case of political parties than individual legislators, provided the parties control the access of their members to political resources.

> investment, and is taken only in response to substantial changes in the legislator's environment. Weingast and Marshall (1988) report empirical evidence which "supports four implications that follow from our model of legislative institutions but do not follow from a simple market exchange mechanism. First, committees are composed of 'high demanders,' that is, individuals with greater than average interest in the committee's policy jurisdiction. Second, the committee assignment mechanism operates as a bidding mechanism that assigns individuals to those committees that they value most highly. Third, committee members gain a disproportionate share of the benefits from their policy area. This appears to hold across widely differing policy jurisdictions. Fourth, there exists important evidence supporting a comparative statistics prediction of the model, namely, that as the interests represented on the committee change, so too will policy, with the interest of the non-committee members held constant."

79. One question remains. Why do the legislative institutions themselves survive? If outcomes depend on institutions, why don't majorities first vote to change the institutions and then vote for the policies they favor? The reader is referred to Chapter 3, where these issues were introduced. Note that political institutions can be seen as a set of complementary capital goods, some involving time-consuming investments in understanding the nature of outcomes generated by the institutional complex. An institutional change at one margin can destroy capital values at other margins. Institutions do change, but usually in response to fundamental changes in the environment.

REFERENCES

Chapter 1

Alchian, A., and Demsetz, Harold (1972). "Production, Information Costs, and Economic Organization." *American Economic Review 62* (December): 777–795.

Arrow, Kenneth J. (1962). "Economic Welfare and the Allocation of Resources for Invention." In Universities-National Bureau Committee for Economic Research. *The Rate and Direction of Inventive Activity.* Princeton: Princeton University Press.

Buchanan, James M. (1959). "Positive Economics, Welfare Economics, and Political Economy. *Journal of Law and Economics 2* (October): 124–138.

——— (1964). "What Should Economists Do?" *Southern Economic Journal 30* (No. 3, January): 213–222.

Buchanan, J. M., and Stubblebine, W. Craig (1962). "Externality." *Economica 29* (November): 371–384.

Cheung, Steven N. S. (1974). "A Theory of Price Control." *Journal of Law and Economics* (April): 53–71.

Coase, Ronald H. (1937). "The Nature of the Firm." *Economica 4* (November): 386–405.

——— (1960). "The Problem of Social Cost." *Journal of Law and Economics 3* (No. 1): 1–44.

——— (1984). "The New Institutional Economics." *Journal of Theoretical and Institutional Economics 140* (No. 1): 229–231.

Dahlman, Carl J. (1979). "The Problem of Externality." *Journal of Legal Studies 22* (No. 1): 141–162.

De Alessi, Louis (1980). "The Economics of Property Rights: A Review of the Evidence." *Research in Law and Economics 2*: 1–47.

——— (1983a). "Property Rights, Transaction Costs, and X-Efficiency: An Essay in Economic Theory." *American Economic Review 73*, (No. 1, March): 64–81.

——— (1983b). "Reply." *American Economic Review 73* (September, No. 4): 843–845.

(1983c). "The Role of Property Rights and Transaction Costs: A New Perspective in Economic Theory." *Social Science Journal 20* (No. 3, July): 59–70.

Demsetz, Harold (1969). "Information and Efficiency: Another Viewpoint." *Journal of Law and Economics 12* (No. 1): 1–22.

(1972). "Wealth Distribution and the Ownership of Rights." *Journal of Legal Studies 1* (No. 2, June): 13–28.

(1980). *Economic, Political, and Legal Dimensions of Competition*. Amsterdam: North-Holland.

Goodhart, C. A. E. (1975). *Money, Information and Uncertainty*. London: Macmillan.

Hayek, Friedrich A. (1937). "Economics and Knowledge." *Economica* (February): 33–54.

(1945). "The Use of Knowledge in Society." *American Economic Review* (September): 519–530.

Hirshleifer, Jack (1988). *Price Theory and Applications*, 4th ed. Englewood Cliffs: Prentice-Hall.

Johansen, Leif (1981). "Interaction in Economic Theory." *Economie Appliquée 34* (Nos. 2–4): 229–267.

Knudsen, Christian (1986). "Normal Science as a Process of Creative Destruction: From a Microeconomic to a Neo-institutional Research Program." Paper presented at the *International Symposium on Property Rights, Organizational Forms and Economic Behavior*. Lund: The Swedish Collegium for Advanced Study in the Social Sciences.

Lakatos, Imre (1970). "Falsification and the Methodology of Scientific Research Programs." In Lakatos and Musgrave, eds. *Criticism and the Growth of Knowledge*. Cambridge: Cambridge University Press.

Leibenstein, Harvey (1983). "Property Rights and X-Efficiency: Comment." *American Economic Review 73* (No. 4, September): 831–842.

Malinvaud, Edmond (1972). *Lectures on Microeconomic Theory*. Amsterdam: North-Holland Publishing.

Matthews, R. C. O. (1986). "The Economics of Institutions and the Sources of Growth." *Economic Journal 96* (December): 903–910.

North, Douglass C. (1968). "Sources of Productivity Change in Ocean Shipping, 1600–1850." *Journal of Political Economy 76* (September/October): 953–970.

(1981). *Structure and Change in Economic History*. New York: W. W. Norton.

(1984). "Government and the Cost of Exchange in History." *Journal of Economic History 44* (No. 2, June): 255–264.

(1986). "The New Institutional Economics." *Journal of Institutional and Theoretical Economics 142* (No. 1): 230–237.

North, Douglass C., and Thomas, Robert Paul (1973). *The Rise of the Western World: A New Economic History*. Cambridge: Cambridge University Press.

North, Douglass C., and Wallis, John J. (1986). "Measuring the Transaction Sector in the American Economy, 1870–1970." In *Long-Term Factors in American Economic Growth*, vol. 51 of *The Income and Wealth Series*, Stanley L. Engerman and Robert E. Gallman, eds. Chicago: University of Chicago Press.

Pigou, A. C. (1932). *The Economics of Welfare*, 4th ed. London: Macmillan.

Simon, Herbert (1957). *Models of Man*. New York: Wiley.

Smith, Adam (1776). *An Inquiry into the Nature and Causes of the Wealth of Nations*. [Reprint ed. R. H. Campbell and A. S. Skinner. Oxford: Oxford University Press, 1976.]

Staten, Mike, and Umbeck, John (1986). "Economic Inefficiency of Law: A Logical and Empirical Impossibility." Working Paper: Department of Economics, University of Delaware, and Department of Economics, Purdue University.

Stigler, George J. (1961). "The Economics of Information." *Journal of Political Economy 69* (June): 213–225.

Stoebe, Wolfgang, and Frey, Bruno S. (1980). "In Defense of Economic Man: Towards an Integration of Economics and Psychology." *Schweizerische Zeitschrift für Volksvirtschaft und Statistik 116* (No. 2, June): 119–148.

Veblen, Thorstein (1919). "Why Is Economics Not an Evolutionary Science?" In his *The Place of Science in Modern Civilization*. New York: B. W. Huebsch, pp. 56–81.

Veljanovski, Cento G. (1982). "The Coase Theorems and the Economic Theory of Markets and Law." *Kyklos 35* (No. 1): 53–74.

Williamson, Oliver E. (1974). *Markets and Hierarchies*. New York: The Free Press.

(1985a). *The Economic Institutions of Capitalism: Firms, Markets, Relational Contracting*. New York: The Free Press.

(1985b). "Reflection on the New Institutional Economics." *Journal for Theoretical and Institutional Economics 141* (No. 1): 187–195.

Chapter 2

Alchian, Armen A. (1950). "Uncertainty, Evolution and Economic Theory." *Journal of Political Economy 58* (No. 3, June): 211–221.

(1965). "Some Economics of Property Rights." *Il Politico 30* (No. 4): 816–829. (Originally published in 1961 by the Rand Corporation.) Reprinted in Alchian, Armen A. (1977). *Economic Forces at Work*. Indianapolis: Liberty Press.

(1977). *Economic Forces at Work*. Indianapolis: Liberty Press.

Alchian, Armen A., and Demsetz, Harold (1972). "Production, Information Costs, and Economic Organization." *American Economic Review 62* (December): 777–795.

Berle, Adolf A., and Means, Gardner C. (1932). *The Modern Corporation and Private Property*. New York: Macmillan.

Calabresi, Guido (1961). "Some Thoughts on Risk Distribution and the Law of Torts." *Yale Law Journal 70* (No. 4, March): 499–553.

Cheung, Steven N. S. (1968). "Private Property Rights and Sharecropping." *Journal of Political Economy 76* (No. 6, December): 1107–1122.

(1969a). *The Theory of Share Tenancy*. Chicago: University of Chicago Press.

(1969b). "Transaction Costs, Risk Aversion, and the Choice of Contractual Arrangements." *Journal of Law and Economics 12* (No. 1, April): 23–42.

(1970). "The Structure of a Contract and the Theory of a Non-exclusive Resource." *Journal of Law and Economics 13* (No. 1, April): 49–70.

(1983). "The Contractual Nature of the Firm." *Journal of Law and Economics* 26 (April): 1–21.

Coase, Ronald C. (1937). "The Nature of the Firm." *Economica 4* (November): 386–405.

(1960). "The Problem of Social Cost." *Journal of Law and Economics 3* (No. 1): 1–44.

De Alessi, Louis (1980). "The Economics of Property Rights: A Review of the Evidence." *Research in Law and Economics*: 1–47.

Demsetz, Harold (1964). "The Exchange and Enforcement of Property Rights." *Journal of Law and Economics 3* (October): 1–44.

Eggertsson, Thráinn (1984). "A Neoinstitutional Model of the Soviet Political and Economic System." Photocopy. St. Louis: Department of Economics, Washington University.

Furubotn, Eirik G., and Pejovich, Svetozar (1970). "Property Rights and the Behavior of the Firm in a Socialist State: The Example of Yugoslavia." *Zeitschrift für Nationalökonomie 30* (Nos. 3–4): 431–454.

(1972). "Property Rights and Economic Theory: A Survey of Recent Literature." *Journal of Economic Literature 10* (December): 1137–1162.

Jensen, Michael C. (1983). "Organization Theory and Methodology." *Accounting Review 58* (No. 2, April): 319–339.

Jensen, Michael C., and Meckling, William H. (1976). "Theory of the Firm: Managerial Behavior, Agency Costs and Ownership Structure." *Journal of Financial Economics 3* (No. 4, October): 305–360.

Moe, Terry M. (1984). "The New Economics of Organization." *American Journal of Political Science 28* (No. 4): 739–777.

North, Douglass C. (1981). *Structure and Change in Economic History*. New York: Norton.

Nove, Alec (1977). *The Soviet Economy*. London: George Allen & Unwin.

Pejovich, Steve (1982). "Karl Marx, Property Rights School and the Process of Social Change." *Kyklos 35* (No. 3): 383–397.

Ross, Stephen A. (1973). "The Economic Theory of Agency: The Principal's Problem." *American Economic Review 62* (May): 134–139.

Spence, Michael, and Zeckhauser, R. (1971). "Insurance, Information and Individual Action." *American Economic Review 61* (No. 2, May): 380–387.

Wiles, Peter J. D. (1977). *Economic Institutions Compared*. Oxford: Basil Blackwell.

Chapter 3

Alchian, Armen A. (1950). "Uncertainty, Evolution, and Economic Theory." *Journal of Political Economy 58* (No. 3): 211–221.

Arrow, Kenneth J. (1951). *Social Choice and Individual Values*. New York: Wiley.

Cohen, Linda, and Matthews, Steven (1980). "Constrained Plot Equilibria, Directional Equilibria and Global Cycling Sets." *Review of Economic Studies 47* (No. 5, October): 975–986.

De Alessi, Louis (1983a). "Property Rights, Transaction Costs, and X-Efficiency:

An Essay in Economic Theory." *American Economic Review 73* (March, No. 1): 64–81.

(1983b). "Reply." *American Economic Review 73* (September, No. 4): 843–845.

Field, Alexander J. (1979). "On the Explanation of Rules Using Rational Choice Models." *Journal of Economic Issues 13* (No. 1): 49–72.

(1981). "The Problem with Neoclassical Institutional Economics: A Critique with Special Reference to the North/Thomas Model of Pre–1500 Europe." *Explorations in Economic History 18* (No. 2): 174–198.

Friedman, David (1979). "Private Creation and Enforcement of Law: A Historical Case." *Journal of Legal Studies 8* (No. 2): 399–415.

Leibenstein, Harvey (1983). "Property Rights and X-Efficiency: Comment." *American Economic Review 73* (September, No. 4): 831–842.

McCubbins, Mathew D., and Schwartz, Thomas (1984). "Congressional Oversight Overlooked: Police Patrols Versus Fire Alarms." *American Journal of Political Science 2* (No. 1, February): 165–179.

McKelvey, R. D. (1976). "Intransitivities in Multidimensional Voting Models and Some Implications for Agenda Control." *Journal of Economic Theory 12* (No. 3): 472–482.

Moore, John H. (1981). "Agency Costs, Technological Change, and Soviet Central Planning." *Journal of Law and Economics 24* (October): 189–214.

Musgrave, Richard A., and Musgrave, Peggy M. (1976). *Public Finance in Theory and Practice*. New York: McGraw-Hill.

North, Douglass C. (1981). *Structure and Change in Economic History*. New York: W. W. Norton.

Olson, Mancur (1965). *The Logic of Collective Action*. Cambridge, Mass.: Harvard University Press.

Romer, Thomas, and Rosenthal, Howard (1979). "Bureaucrats Versus Voters: On the Political Economy of Resource Allocation by Direct Democracy." *Quarterly Journal of Economics 93* (No. 4, November): 563–587.

Shepsle, Kenneth A. (1983). "Institutional Equilibrium and Equilibrium Institutions." Working Paper No. 82. St. Louis: Center for the Study of American Business, Washington University.

Shepsle, Kenneth A., and Weingast, Barry R. (1981). "Structure-Induced Equilibrium and Legislative Choice." *Public Choice 37* (No. 3): 503–519.

(1983). "Rational Choice Explanations of Social Facts." Working paper. St. Louis: Washington University.

(1987). "The Institutional Foundations of Committee Power." *American Political Science Review 81* (No. 1, March): 85–104.

Simon, Herbert A. (1957). *Models of Man*. New York: John Wiley.

(1978). "Rationality as Process and as Product of Thought." *American Economic Review 68* (May): 1–16.

Stigler, George J. (1961). "The Economics of Information." *Journal of Political Economy 69* (June, No. 3): 213–225.

(1971). "The Economic Theory of Regulation." *Bell Journal of Economics and Management Science 2* (No. 3): 3–21.

Stigler, George J., and Friedland, Claire (1962). "What Can Regulators Regulate? The Case of Electricity." *Journal of Law and Economics 5* (No. 1): 1–16.

Tullock, Gordon (1971). "The Paradox of Revolution." *Public Choice 9* (Fall): 89–99.

Weingast, Barry R. (1983). "Bureaucratic Discretion or Congressional Control? Regulating Policymaking by the Federal Trade Commission." *Journal of Political Economy 91* (October, No. 5): 766–800.

———— (1984). "The Congressional-Bureaucratic System: A Principal–Agent Perspective." *Public Choice 44* (No. 1): 147–192.

Chapter 4

Andersen, Peder, and Sutinen, Jon G. (1984). "The Economics of Fisheries Law Enforcement." In Skog, Göran, ed. *Papers Presented at the First Meeting of the European Association for Law and Economics*. Department of Economics, University of Lund.

Anderson, Terry L., and Hill, Peter J. (1975). "The Evolution of Property Rights: A Study of the American West." *Journal of Law and Economics 18* (No. 1, April): 163–179.

———— (1983). "Privatizing the Commons: An Improvement?" *Southern Economic Journal 50* (No. 2, October): 438–450.

Barzel, Yoram (1974). "A Theory of Rationing by Waiting." *Journal of Law and Economics 17* (No. 1, April): 73–95.

Cheung, Steven N. S. (1970). "The Structure of a Contract and the Theory of a Non-exclusive Resource." *Journal of Law and Economics 13* (April): 49–70.

———— (1974). "A Theory of Price Control." *Journal of Law and Economics 17* (No. 1, April): 53–71.

———— (1975). "Roofs or Stars: The Stated Intents and Actual Effects of Rent Ordinance." *Economic Inquiry 13* (March): 1–21.

———— (1976). "Rent Control and Housing Reconstruction: The Postwar Experience of Prewar Premises in Hong Kong." *Journal of Law and Economics 19* (No. 1): 27–53.

Clarkson, Kenneth W. (1974). "International Law, U.S. Seabeds Policy and Ocean Resource Development." *Journal of Law and Economics 17* (No. 1): 117–142.

Coase, Ronald N. (1959). "The Federal Communications Commission." *Journal of Law and Economics 2* (No. 1, October): 1–40.

———— (1960). "The Problem of Social Cost." *Journal of Law and Economics 3* (No. 1, October): 1–44. Reprinted in Breit, William, and Hochman, Harold, eds. (1968). *Readings in Microeconomics*. New York: Holt, Rinehart, and Winston, pp. 423–456.

Cooter, Robert (1982). "The Cost of Coase." *Journal of Legal Studies 11* (No. 1, January): 1–34.

Crutchfield, J. A. (1961). "An Economic Evaluation of Alternative Methods of Fishery Regulation." *Journal of Law and Economics 4* (No. 1): 131–141.

Demsetz, Harold (1972). "When Does the Rule of Liability Matter?" *Journal of Legal Studies 1* (No. 1, February): 13–28.

Furubotn, Eirik G. (1985). "The Gains from Privatization. A General Equilibrium

Perspective." Working paper. University of Texas at Arlington, Department of Economics.

(1987). "Privatizing the Commons. Comment and Note." *Southern Economic Journal 54* (No. 1): 219–224.

Gordon, H. S. (1954). "The Economic Theory of a Common Property Resource: The Fishery." *Journal of Political Economy 62* (April): 124–142.

Haddock, David, and Spiegel, Menahem (1984). "Property Rules, Liability Rules, and Inalienability: One View of the Edgeworth Box." In Skog, Göran, ed. *Papers Presented at the First Meeting of the European Association for Law and Economics*. University of Lund, Department of Economics.

Libecap, Gary D. (1984). "The Political Allocation of Mineral Rights: A Reevaluation of Teapot Dome." *Journal of Economic History 44* (June): 381–391.

Libecap, Gary D., and Johnson, Ronald N. (1979). "Property Rights, Nineteenth-Century Federal Timber Policy, and the Conservation Movement." *Journal of Economic History 39* (No. 1, March): 129–142.

(1980). "Legislating Commons: The Navajo Tribal Council and the Navajo Range." *Economic Inquiry 18* (January): 69–86.

McCloskey, David N. (1985). *The Applied Theory of Price*, 2nd ed. New York: Macmillan.

Posner, Richard A. (1977). *Economic Analysis of Law*, 2nd ed. Boston: Little, Brown.

Samuels, Warren J. (1971). "Interrelations Between Legal and Economic Processes." *Journal of Law and Economics 14* (October, No. 2): 435–450.

Scott, Anthony (1979). "Development of Economic Theory on Fisheries Regulation." *Journal of the Fisheries Research Board of Canada 36*: 725–741.

(1983). "Property Rights and Property Wrongs." *Canadian Journal of Economics 16* (No. 4): 555–573.

Veljanovski, Cento G. (1982). "The Coase Theorems, and the Economic Theory of Markets and Law." *Kyklos 35* (No. 1): 66–81.

(1984). "The Impact of the Employers' Liability Act 1880." In Skog, Göran, ed. (1984). *Papers Presented at the First Meeting of the European Association for Law and Economics*. University of Lund, Department of Economics.

Warming, Jens (1911). "Om 'Grundrente' af Fiskegrunde." *Nationalökonomisk Tidsskrift*: 495–506. See also Andersen, P. (1983). " 'On Rent of Fishing Grounds': A Translation of Jens Warming's 1911 Article, with an Introduction." *History of Political Economy 15* (Fall, No. 3): 391–396.

(1931). "Aalgaardsretten." *Nationalökonomisk Tidsskrift*: 151–162.

Chapter 5

Alchian, Armen A., and Kessel, Reuben A. (1962). "Competition, Monopoly and the Pursuit of Money." In National Bureau of Economic Research, *Aspects of Labor Economics*. Princeton: Princeton University Press.

Averch, H., and Johnson, L. L. (1962). "Behavior of the Firm Under Regulatory Constraints." *American Economic Review 52* (December): 1053–1069.

Berle, Adolf A., and Means, Gardner C. (1932). *The Modern Corporation and Private Property*. New York: Macmillan.

Cook, Richard E. (1987). "What the Economics Literature Has To Say About Takeovers." Working Paper No. 106. St. Louis: Center for the Study of American Business, Washington University.

De Alessi, Louis (1980). "The Economics of Property Rights: A Review of the Evidence." *Research in Law and Economics 2*: 1–47.

(1982). "On the Nature and Consequences of Private and Public Enterprise." *Minnesota Law Review 67* (No. 1, October): 191–209.

Demsetz, Harold (1980). *Economic, Political, and Legal Dimensions of Competition*. Amsterdam: North-Holland.

(1983). "The Structure of Ownership and the Theory of the Firm." *Journal of Law and Economics 26* (June): 375–393.

Fama, Eugene F., and Jensen, Michael C. (1983). "Agency Problems and Residual Claims." *Journal of Law and Economics 26* (June): 327–349.

(1985). "Organizational Forms and Investment Decisions." *Journal of Financial Economics 14* (No. 1): 101–119.

Frech, Harry E. III (1976). "The Property Rights Theory of the Firm: Empirical Results from a Natural Experiment." *Journal of Political Economy 84* (February): 143–152.

Goldberg, Victor P. (1976a). "Toward an Expanded Economic Theory of Contract." *Journal of Economic Issues 10* (No. 1, March): 45–61.

(1976b). "Regulation and Administered Contracts." *Bell Journal of Economics 7* (No. 2): 426–441.

Jensen, Michael C., and Meckling, William H. (1976). "Theory of the Firm: Managerial Behavior, Agency Costs and Ownership Structure." *Journal of Financial Economics 3* (No. 4): 305–360.

(1979). "Rights and Production Functions: An Application to Labor-Managed Firms and Codetermination." *Journal of Business 52* (No. 4): 469–506.

Jensen, Michael C., and Ruback, Richard S. (1983). "The Market for Corporate Control: The Scientific Evidence." *Journal of Financial Economics 11* (Nos. 1–4): 5–50.

Kahn, Alfred E. (1983). "Deregulation and Vested Interests: The Case of Airlines." In Noll and Owen, eds. (1983), pp. 132–151.

Kalt, Joseph P. (1981). *The Economics and Politics of Oil Price Regulation*. Cambridge, Mass.: MIT Press.

(1983). "The Creation, Growth, and Entrenchment of Special Interests in Oil Price Policy." In Noll and Owen, eds. (1983), pp. 97–114.

Manne, H. G. (1962). "The 'Higher Criticism' of the Modern Corporation." *Columbia Law Review 62* (March): 399–432.

(1965). "Mergers and the Market for Corporate Control." *Journal of Political Economy 73* (April): 110–120.

Nicols, Alfred (1967). "Stocks Versus Mutual Savings and Loan Associations: Some Evidence of Differences in Behavior." *American Economic Review 57* (May): 337–347.

(1972). *Management and Control in the Mutual Savings and Loan Association.* Lexington, Mass.: Lexington Books.

Noll, Roger G., and Owen, Bruce M., eds. (1983a). *The Political Economy of Deregulation: Interest Groups in the Regulatory Process.* Washington, D.C.: American Enterprise Institute.

(1983b). "Conclusions: Economics, Politics, and Deregulation." In Noll and Owen, eds. (1983), pp. 155–162.

Shelton, John (1967). "Allocative Efficiency v. 'X-Efficiency': Comment." *American Economic Review 57* (No. 5): 1252–1258.

Chapter 6

Alchian, Armen A. (1965). "The Basis of Some Recent Advances in the Theory of Management of the Firm." *Journal of Industrial Economics 14*: 30–41.

(1984). "Specificity, Specialization, and Coalitions." *Journal of Institutional and Theoretical Economics 140* (No. 1): 34–49.

Alchian, Armen A., and Demsetz, Harold (1972). "Production, Information Costs, and Economic Organization." *American Economic Review 62* (December, No. 5): 777–795.

(1977). "Production, Information Costs, and Economic Organization." *American Economic Review 62* (No. 5, December): 211–221.

Alchian, Armen A, and Woodward, Susan (1987). "Reflections on the Theory of the Firm." *Journal of Institutional and Theoretical Economics 143* (No. 1): 110–136.

Arrow, Kenneth J. (1974). *The Limits of Organization.* New York: W. W. Norton.

Barzel, Yoram (1987a). "The Entrepreneur's Reward for Self-Policing." *Economic Inquiry 25* (No. 1): 103–116.

(1987b). "Knight's Moral Hazard Theory of Organization." *Economic Inquiry 25* (No. 1): 117–120.

Becker, Gary S. (1964). *Human Capital: A Theoretical and Empirical Analysis with Special Reference to Education.* New York: National Bureau of Economic Research.

(1965). "A Theory of the Allocation of Time." *Economic Journal 75* (September): 494–517.

Chamberlin, Edward H. (1953). "The Product as an Economic Variable." *Quarterly Journal of Economics 67* (February, No. 1): 1–29.

Chandler, Alfred D., Jr. (1962). *Strategy and Structure: Chapters in the History of the Industrial Enterprise.* Cambridge, Mass.: MIT Press.

Cheung, Steven N. S. (1983). "The Contractual Nature of the Firm." *Journal of Law and Economics 26* (April): 1–21.

Coase, Ronald H. (1937). "The Nature of the Firm." *Economica 16*, new series (November): 386–405. Reprinted in Stigler, George J., and Boulding, Kenneth E., eds. (1952). *Readings in Price Theory.* Chicago: Richard D. Irwin, pp. 331–351.

Demsetz, Harold (1983). "The Structure of Ownership and the Theory of the Firm." *Journal of Law and Economics 26* (June): 375–393.

Fama, Eugene F., and Jensen, Michael C. (1983a). "Agency Problems and Residual Claims." *Journal of Law and Economics 26* (June): 327–349.

(1983b). "Separation of Ownership and Control." *Journal of Law and Economics 26* (June): 301–325.

(1985). "Organizational Forms and Investment Decisions." *Journal of Financial Economics 14* (No. 1): 101–119.

Furubotn, Eirik G. (1985). "Codetermination, Productivity Gains, and the Economics of the Firm." *Oxford Economic Papers 37* (No. 1): 22–39.

Jensen, Michael C., and Meckling, William H. (1976). "Theory of the Firm: Managerial Behavior, Agency Costs, and Capital Structure." *Journal of Financial Economics 3* (No. 4, October): 305–360.

Klein, Benjamin (1983). "Contracting Costs and Residual Claims: The Separation of Ownership and Control." *Journal of Law and Economics 26* (No. 2, June): 367–374.

Klein, Benjamin, Crawford, Robert G., and Alchian, Armen A. (1978). "Vertical Integration, Appropriable Rents, and the Competitive Contracting Process." *Journal of Law and Economics 21* (No. 2): 297–326.

Knight, Frank H. (1921). *Risk, Uncertainty and Profit.* Boston: Houghton Mifflin.

Lancaster, Kelvin J. (1966). "A New Approach to Consumer Theory." *Journal of Political Economy 74* (No. 2, April): 132–157.

LeRoy, Stephen F., and Singell, Larry D., Jr. (1987). "Knight on Risk and Uncertainty." *Journal of Political Economy 95* (No. 2, April): 394–406.

McNulty, Paul J. (1984). "On the Nature and Theory of Economic Organization: The Role of the Firm Reconsidered." *History of Political Economy 16* (No. 2): 233–253.

Williamson, Oliver E. (1980). "The Organization of Work: A Comparative Institutional Assessment." *Journal of Economic Behavior and Organization 1* (March): 5–38.

(1975). *Markets and Hierarchies: Analysis and Antitrust Implications.* New York: Free Press.

(1981). "The Modern Corporation: Origins, Evolution, Attributes." *Journal of Economic Literature 19* (December): 1537–1568.

(1983a). "Organizational Form, Residual Claimants, and Corporate Control." *Journal of Law and Economics 22* (No. 2): 233–261.

(1983b). "Credible Commitments: Using Hostages To Support Exchange." *American Economic Review 73* (September): 519–549.

(1985). *The Economic Institutions of Capitalism: Firms, Markets, Relational Contracting.* New York: Free Press.

Chapter 7

Akerlof, George A. (1970). "The Market for 'Lemons': Quality, Uncertainty and the Market Mechanism." *Quarterly Journal of Economics 84* (August): 488–500.

Allen, Robert C. (1982). "The Efficiency and Distributional Consequences of Eighteenth Century Enclosures." *Economic Journal 92* (December): 937–953.

Alston, Lee J. (1979). "Costs of Contracting and the Decline of Tenancy in the South, 1930–1960." *Journal of Economic History 39* (No. 1, March): 324–326.

(1981). "Tenure Choice in Southern Agriculture." *Explorations in Economic History 18* (July): 211–232.

Alston, Lee J., and Higgs, Robert (1982). "Contractual Mix in Southern Agriculture Since the Civil War: Facts, Hypotheses, and Tests." *Journal of Economic History 42* (No. 2, June): 327–353.

Amid, M. J. (1986). "The Theory of Sharecropping: A Survey." Paper presented at *The International Symposium on Property Rights, Organizational Forms and Economic Behavior*. Uppsala: Swedish Collegium for Advanced Study in the Social Sciences.

Barzel, Yoram (1977). "An Economic Analysis of Slavery." *Journal of Law and Economics 20* (April): 87–110.

(1982). "Measurement Costs and the Organization of Markets." *Journal of Law and Economics 25* (April): 27–48.

(1985). "Transaction Costs: Are They Just Costs?" *Journal of Institutional and Theoretical Economics 141* (No. 1): 4–16.

Bergstrom, T. (1971). "On the Existence and Optimality of Competitive Equilibrium for a Slave Economy." *Review of Economic Studies 38*: 23–36.

Brunner, Karl, and Meltzer, Allan H. (1971). "The Uses of Money: Money in the Theory of an Exchange Economy." *American Economic Review 61* (December): 784–805.

Cheung, Steven N. S. (1968). "Private Property Rights and Sharecropping." *Journal of Political Economy 76* (No. 6, December): 1107–1122.

(1969a). *Theory of Share Tenancy*. Chicago: University of Chicago Press.

(1969b). "Transaction Costs, Risk Aversion, and the Choice of Contractual Arrangements." *Journal of Law and Economics 13* (April): 49–70.

Clower, R. W., ed. (1969). *Monetary Theory*. London: Penguin.

(1967). "A Reconsideration of the Microfoundations of Monetary Theory." *Western Economic Journal 6*: 1–9. Reprinted in Clower, ed. (1969).

Dahlman, Carl J. (1980). *The Open Field System and Beyond: A Property Rights Analysis of an Economic Institution*. Cambridge: Cambridge University Press.

Domar, Evsey D. (1970). "The Causes of Slavery or Serfdom: A Hypothesis." *Journal of Economic History 30* (March): 18–32.

Engerman, Stanley L. (1973). "Some Considerations Relating to Property Rights in Man." *Journal of Economic History 33* (No. 1, March): 43–65.

(1986). "Slavery and Emancipation in Comparative Perspective: A Look at Some Recent Debates." *Journal of Economic History 46* (No. 2, June): 317–339.

Fenoaltea, Stefano (1976). "Risk, Transaction Costs, and the Organization of Medieval Agriculture." *Explorations in Economic History 13* (No. 2, April): 129–151.

(1977). "Fenoaltea on Open Fields: A Reply." *Explorations in Economic History 14* (No. 4, October): 405–410.

(1982). *"The Open Field System and Beyond*: A Review." *Speculum 57*: 125–128.

(1984). "Slavery and Supervision in Comparative Perspective: A Model." *Journal of Economic History 44* (No. 3, September): 635–668.

(1986). "The Economics of the Common Fields: The State of the Debate." A paper prepared for the *International Symposium on Property Rights, Organizational Forms and Economic Behavior*. Uppsala: The Swedish Collegium for Advanced Studies in the Social Sciences.

(1987). "Transaction Costs, Whig History, and the Common Fields." Working paper. Princeton: Institute for Advanced Study.

Fischer, Stanley (1986). "Friedman Versus Hayek on Private Money." *Journal of Monetary Economics 17* (No. 3): 433–439.

Friedman, Milton (1959). *A Program for Monetary Stability*. New York: Fordham University Press.

Goodhart, C. A. E. (1975). *Money, Information and Uncertainty*. London: Macmillan.

Gray, L. C., et al. (1924). "Farm Ownership and Tenancy." In *Yearbook 1923*. Washington D.C.: U.S. Department of Agriculture.

Hayek, Friedrich A. (1976). *Denationalization of Money*. Hobart Paper. London: The Institute of Economic Affairs.

Higgs, Robert (1973). "Race, Tenure, and Resource Allocation in Southern Agriculture, 1910." *Journal of Economic History 33* (March): 149–169.

Ho, S. P. S. (1976). "Uncertainty and the Choice of Tenure Arrangements: Some Hypotheses." *American Journal of Agricultural Economics 58* (No. 1): 88–92.

Holler, Manfred J. (1984). "Quality Enforcement by the Invisible Hand of Prices and Costs." In Skog, Göran, ed. *Papers Presented at the First Meeting of the European Association for Law and Economics*. Lund: Lund University, Department of Economics, pp. 76–88.

Jevons, W. S. (1910). *Money and the Mechanism of Exchange*, 23rd ed. London: Kegan Paul.

Johnson D. G. (1950). "Resource Allocation Under Share Contracts." *Journal of Political Economy 58* (No. 1, February): 111–123.

King, Robert G. (1983). "On the Economics of Private Money." *Journal of Monetary Economics 12* (No. 1): 127–158.

Klein, Benjamin (1974). "The Competitive Supply of Money." *Journal of Money, Credit and Banking 6* (No. 4, November): 423–454.

Klein, Benjamin, and Leffler, Keith B. (1981). "The Role of Market Forces in Assuring Contractual Performance." *Journal of Political Economy 89* (No. 4, August): 615–641.

Leffler, Keith B. (1982). "Ambiguous Change in Product Quality." *American Economic Review 72* (No. 5, December): 956–967.

(1985): "Quality Assurance: Manufacturer and Retailer Incentive Compatibility." Working paper. Seattle: University of Washington.

Lucas, R. E. B. (1979). "Sharing, Monitoring, and Incentives: Marshallian Misallocation Reassessed." *Journal of Political Economy 87* (No. 3): 501–521.

Marshall, Alfred (1920). *Principles of Economics*, 8th ed. London: Macmillan.

McCloskey, Donald N. (1972). "The Enclosure of Open Fields: Preface to a Study of Its Impact on the Efficiency of English Agriculture in the Eighteenth Century." *Journal of Economic History 32* (March): 15–35.

(1975). "The Persistence of English Common Fields," and "The Economics of Enclosure: A Market Analysis." In Parker, W. N., and Jones, E. L., eds. *European Peasants and Their Markets: Essays in Agrarian Economic History.* Princeton: Princeton University Press, pp. 73–119.

(1976). "English Open Fields as Behavior Toward Risk." In Uselding, P., ed. *Research in Economic History*, Vol. 1. Greenwich, Conn.: JAI Press, pp. 124–171.

(1977). "Fenoaltea on Open Fields: A Comment." *Explorations in Economic History 14* (No. 4, October): 402–404.

(1985). *The Applied Theory of Price*, 2nd ed. New York: Macmillan.

(1986). "The Open Fields of England: Rent, Risk, and the Rate of Interest, 1300–1815." University of Iowa: Departments of Economics and of History. Forthcoming in Galenson, David, ed. *In Search of Historical Economics: Market Behavior in Past Times.* Cambridge: Cambridge University Press.

Nelson, Phillip (1970). "Information and Consumer Behavior." *Journal of Political Economy 78* (No. 2, March/April): 311–329.

(1974). "Advertising as Information." *Journal of Political Economy 82* (No. 4, July/August): 729–754.

Niehans, Jürg (1969). "Money in a Static Theory of Optimal Payment Arrangements." *Journal of Money, Credit and Banking 1* (No. 4, November): 706–726.

(1971). "Money and Barter in General Equilibrium with Transaction Costs." *American Economic Review 61* (No. 5, December): 773–783.

North, Douglass C., and Thomas, Robert P. (1971). "The Rise and Fall of the Manorial System: A Theoretical Model." *Journal of Economic History 31* (No. 4, December): 777–803.

Ostroy, J. M. (1973). "The Informational Efficiency of Monetary Exchange." *American Economic Review 63* (No. 4): 597–610.

Salin, Pascal, ed. (1984). *Currency Competition and Monetary Union.* Norwell, Mass.: Martinus Nijhoff Publishers.

Stiglitz, Joseph E. (1974). "Incentives and Risk Sharing in Sharecropping." *Review of Economic Studies 41* (No. 2): 219–255.

Thompson, E. P. (1963). *The Making of the English Working Class.* New York: Random House.

Williamson, Oliver E. (1983). "Credible Commitments: Using Hostages to Support Exchange." *American Economic Review 73* (No. 4, September): 519–540.

Chapter 8

Anderson, Terry L., and Hill, P. J. (1975). "The Evolution of Property Rights: A Study of the American West." *Journal of Law and Economics 18* (No. 1): 163–179.

Benson, Bruce L. (1984). "Rent Seeking from a Property Rights Perspective." *Southern Economic Journal* (October): 388–400.

372   References

Buchanan, James M. (1980). "Rent Seeking and Profit Seeking." In Buchanan et al., eds. (1980). *Toward a Theory of the Rent Seeking Society.*

Buchanan, James M., et al., eds. (1980). *Toward a Theory of the Rent-Seeking Society.* College Station: Texas A & M University Press.

Cheung, Steven N. S. (1973). "The Fable of the Bees: An Economic Investigation." *Journal of Law and Economics 16* (No. 1, April): 11–33.

Clarkson, Kenneth W. (1974). "International Law, U.S. Seabeds Policy and Ocean Resource Development." *Journal of Law and Economics 17* (No. 1, April): 117–142.

Comitini, Salvatore (1966). "Marine Resources Exploitation and Management in the Economic Development of Japan." *Economic Development and Cultural Change 14* (July): 414–427.

De Soto, Hernando (1986). *El Otro Sendero: La Revolucion Informal.* Lima: Editorial El Barranco.

Demsetz, Harold (1964). "The Exchange and Enforcement of Property Rights." *Journal of Law and Economics 3* (October): 11–26.

(1967). "Toward a Theory of Property Rights." *American Economic Review 57* (May, No. 2): 347–359.

Eklund Robert, B., Jr., and Tollison, Robert D. (1982). *Mercantilism as a Rent-Seeking Society: Economic Regulation in Historical Perspective.* College Station: Texas A & M University Press.

Field, Barry C. (1986). "Induced Changes in Property Rights Institutions." Research paper. Amherst: University of Massachusetts, Department of Agricultural and Resource Economics.

Furubotn, Eirik, and Pejovich, Svetozar (1972). "Property Rights and Economic Theory: A Survey of Recent Literature." *Journal of Economic Literature 10* (December, No. 4): 1137–1162.

Hannesson, Rögnvaldur (1984). "Fishermen's Organizations and Their Role in Fisheries Management." Working paper. Bergen: Norwegian School of Economics and Business Administration.

(1986). "Rent Seeking." Working paper. [In Norwegian.] Bergen: Norwegian School of Economics and Business Administration.

Johnson, Ronald N., and Libecap, Gary D. (1982). "Contracting Problems and Regulation: The Case of the Fishery." *American Economic Review 72* (No. 5): 1005–1022.

Krueger, Anne O. (1974). "The Political Economy of the Rent-Seeking Society." *American Economic Review 64* (No. 3, June): 291–303.

Libecap, Gary (1978). "Economic Variables and the Development of the Law: The Case of Western Mineral Rights." *Journal of Economic History 38* (No. 2, June): 399–458.

(1986a). "Property Rights in Economic History: Implications for Research." *Explorations in Economic History 23* (No. 3): 227–252.

(1986b). "The Political Economy of Cartelization by the Texas Railroad Commission, 1933–1972." Working paper. Tucson: University of Arizona, Department of Economics.

Libecap, Gary D., and Wiggins, Steven N. (1984). "Contractual Responses to the

Common Pool: Prorationing of Crude Oil Production." *American Economic Review 74* (No. 1): 87–98.

(1985). "The Influence of Private Contractual Failure on Regulation: The Case of Oil Field Unitization." *Journal of Political Economy 93* (No. 4): 690–714.

Litan, Robert E., and Schuck, Peter H. (1986). "Regulatory Reform in the Third World: The Case of Peru." *Yale Journal on Regulation 4* (No. 1, Fall).

McCloskey, Donald N. (1985). *The Applied Theory of Price*, 2nd ed. New York: Macmillan.

McManus, John C. (1972). "An Economic Analysis of Indian Behavior in the North American Fur Trade." *Journal of Economic History 32* (March, No. 1): 36–53.

North, Douglass, C. (1981). *Structure and Change in Economic History*. New York: W. W. Norton.

North, Douglass C., and Thomas, Robert Paul (1977). "The First Economic Revolution." *Economic History Review 30*, second series (No. 2): 229–241.

Olson, Mancur (1971). *The Logic of Collective Action*, rev. ed. Cambridge, Mass.: Harvard University Press.

(1982). *The Rise and Decline of Nations*. New Haven: Yale University Press.

Posner, Richard A. (1973). "An Economic Approach to Legal Procedure and Judicial Administration." *Journal of Legal Studies 2* (June): 399–458.

(1987). "The Law and Economics Movement." *American Economic Review 77* (No. 2, May): 1–13.

Posner, Richard A., and Ehrlich, Isaach (1974). "An Economic Analysis of Legal Rule Making." *Journal of Legal Studies 3* (January): 257–286.

Scott, Anthony (1979). "Development of Economic Theory on Fisheries Regulation." *Journal of the Fisheries Resource Board of Canada 36*: 725–741.

(1986): "Emerging Markets in Fisheries' Rights." Working paper. Vancouver: University of British Columbia.

Tollison, Robert D. (1982). "Rent Seeking: A Survey." *Kyklos 35* (No. 4): 575–602.

Tullock, Gordon (1967). "The Welfare Costs of Tariffs, Monopolies, and Theft." *Western Economic Journal 5* (June): 224–232.

Wiggins, Steven N., and Libecap, Gary D. (1985). "Oil Field Unitization: Contractual Failure in the Presence of Imperfect Information." *American Economic Review 75* (No. 3): 368–385.

Chapter 9

Alt, James E., Calvert, Randall L., and Humes, Brian D. (1986). "Game Theory and Hegemonic Stability: The Role of Reputation and Uncertainty." Political Economy Working Paper No. 106. St. Louis: Center in Political Economy, Washington University.

Axelrod, Robert (1981). "The Emergence of Cooperation Among Egoists." *American Political Science Review 75*: 306–318.

(1984). *The Evolution of Cooperation*. New York: Basic Books.

Bates, Robert H. (1983). *Essays on the Political Economy of Rural Africa*. Cambridge: Cambridge University Press.

Behnke, Roy H., Jr. (1985). "Open Range-Management and Property Rights in Pastoral Africa: A Case of Spontaneous Range Enclosure in South Darfur, Sudan." London: Overseas Development Institute Paper.

Calvert, Randall L. (1987). "Reputation and Legislative Leadership." *Public Choice 55* (Nos. 1–2): 81–119.

Evans-Pritchard, E. E. (1937). *Witchcraft, Oracles and Magic Among the Azande of the Anglo-Egyptian Sudan*. Oxford: Clarendon Press.

(1940). *The Nuer: A Description of the Modes of Livelihood and Political Institutions of a Nilotic People*. Oxford: Clarendon Press.

(1951). *Kinship and Marriage Among the Nuer*. Oxford: Clarendon Press.

(1956). *The Nuer Religion*. Oxford: Clarendon Press.

Frey, Bruno S. (1984). *International Political Economy*. Oxford: Basil Blackwell.

Frey, Bruno S., and Schneider, Friedrich (1982). "International Political Economy: An Emerging Field." Seminar Paper No. 227. Institute for International Economic Studies, University of Stockholm.

Friedman, David (1979). "Private Creation and Enforcement of Law: A Historical Case." *Journal of Legal Studies 8* (No. 2): 399–415.

Gelsinger, Bruce E. (1981). *Icelandic Enterprise: Commerce and Economy in the Middle Ages*. Columbia, S.C.: University of South Carolina Press.

Gluckman, Max (1956). *Custom and Conflict in Africa*. Oxford: Basil Blackwell.

Hirshleifer, Jack (1980). "Privacy: Its Origin, Function and Future." *Journal of Legal Studies 9* (No. 4, December): 649–664.

(1982). "Evolutionary Models in Economics and Law." In Zerbe, R. O., Jr., and Rubin, P. H., eds. *Research in Law and Economics*, Vol. 4, pp. 1–60. Greenwich, Conn.: JAI Press.

Jóhannesson, Jón (1974). *A History of the Icelandic Commonwealth*. Transl. by Haraldur Bessason. Winnipeg: University of Manitoba Press.

Jóhannesson, Thorkell (1975). "An Outline History." In Nordal, J., and Kristinsson, V., eds. *Iceland 874–1974*. Reykjavík: Central Bank of Iceland.

Keohane, Robert (1984). *After Hegemony: Cooperation and Discord in the World Political Economy*. Princeton: Princeton University Press.

Kindleberger, Charles P. (1982). "Standards as Public, Collective and Private Goods." Seminar Paper No. 231. Stockholm: Institute for International Economic Studies.

(1986). "International Public Goods Without International Government." *American Economic Review 76* (No. 1): 1–13.

McCloskey, Donald N. (1986). "The Open Fields of England: Rent, Risk, and the Rate of Interest, 1300–1815." Working Paper. University of Iowa. Forthcoming in Galinson, David ed. *In Search of Historical Economics: Market Behavior in Past Times*. Cambridge: Cambridge University Press.

Miller, William Ian (1984). "Avoiding Legal Judgement: The Submission of Disputes to Arbitration in Medieval Iceland." *American Journal of Legal History 28*: 95–134.

North, Douglass C. (1977). "Markets and Other Allocation Systems in History: The Challenge of Karl Polanyi." *Journal of European Economic History 6* (No. 3, Winter): 703–716.

——— (1981). *Structure and Change in Economic History.* New York: W. W. Norton.

Polanyi, Karl (1971). *Primitive, Archaic and Modern Economies.* Boston: Beacon Press.

Posner, Richard A. (1980). "A Theory of Primitive Society, with Special Reference to Law." *Journal of Law and Economics 23* (No. 1, April): 1–53.

Schofield, Norman (1985). "Anarchy, Altruism and Cooperation." *Social Choice and Welfare 2*: 207–219.

Snidal, Duncan (1985). "The Game Theory of International Politics." *World Politics 38* (No. 1): 25–57.

Taylor, Michael (1976). *Anarchy and Cooperation.* London: John Wiley.

——— (1987). *The Possibility of Cooperation.* Cambridge: Cambridge University Press.

Turner, Victor W. (1971). "An Anthropological Approach to the Icelandic Sagas." In T. O. Beidelman, ed. *The Translation of Culture: Essays to E. E. Evans-Pritchard.* London: Tavistock Publications.

Umbeck, John R. (1978). "A Theory of Contractual Choice and the California Gold Rush." *Journal of Law and Economics 21*: 421–437.

——— (1981a). "Might Makes Rights: A Theory of the Formation and Initial Distribution of Property Rights." *Economic Inquiry 20* (No. 2): 38–59.

——— (1981b). *A Theory of Property Rights with Applications to the California Gold Rush.* Ames: Iowa State University Press.

Wormald, Jenny (1981). "Bloodfeud, Kindred and Government in Early Modern Scotland. *Past and Present 87* (May): 54–97.

Chapter 10

Bates, Robert H. (1981). *Markets and States in Tropical Africa.* Berkeley: University of California Press.

Buchanan, James, and Tullock, Gordon (1962). *The Calculus of Consent.* Ann Arbor: University of Michigan Press.

Denzau, Arthur T., and Munger, Michael (1986). "Legislators and Interest Groups: How Unorganized Interests Get Represented." *American Political Science Review 80* (No. 1, March): 89–106.

Downs, Anthony (1957). *An Economic Theory of Democracy.* New York: Harper and Row.

Findlay, Ronald, and Wilson, John D. (1984). "The Political Economy of the Leviathan." Seminar Paper No. 285. Stockholm: Institute for International Studies.

Hicks, John (1969). *A Theory of Economic History.* Oxford: Oxford University Press.

Knott, Jack H., and Miller Gary J. (1987). *Reforming Bureaucracy: The Politics of Institutional Choice.* Englewood Cliffs, N.J.: Prentice Hall.

Koford, Kenneth J. (1982). "Centralized Vote-trading." *Public Choice 39* (No. 2): 245–268.

Kornai, Janos (1979). "Resource-Constrained Versus Demand-Constrained Systems." *Economica 47* (No. 4): 801–819.

Lindblom, C. E. (1977). *Politics and Markets: The World's Political Economic Systems.* New York: Basic Books.

McCubbins Mathew D., and Sullivan, Terry, eds. (1987). *Congress: Structure and Policy.* Cambridge: Cambridge University Press.

Mueller, Dennis C. (1979). *Public Choice.* Cambridge: Cambridge University Press.

North, Douglass C. (1979). "A Framework for Analyzing the State in Economic History." *Explorations in Economic History* (July): 249–259.

(1981). *Structure and Change in Economic History.* New York: W. W. Norton.

(1984). "Government and the Cost of Exchange in History." *Journal of Economic History 44* (No. 2, June): 255–264.

(1986a). "Institutions, Economic Growth and Freedom: An Historical Introduction." Political Economy working paper. St. Louis: Washington University.

(1986b). "Is It Worth Making Sense of Marx?" *Inquiry 29* (No. 1): 57–63.

(1987). "Institutions, Transaction Costs and Economic Growth." *Economic Inquiry 25* (No. 3): 419–428.

North, Douglass C., and Thomas, Robert (1973). *The Rise of the Western World: A New Economic History.* Cambridge: Cambridge University Press.

North, Douglass C., and Weingast, Barry R. (1987). "Constitutions and Commitment: The Evolution of Institutions Governing Public Choice in 17th Century England." Working paper. St. Louis: Washington University.

Nove, Alec (1986). *The Soviet Economic System*, 3rd ed. London: Allen & Unwin.

Root, Hilton L., and Ingberman, Daniel E. (1987). "Tying the King's Hands: Credible Commitments and Royal Fiscal Policy During the Old Regime." Working paper. Philadelphia: University of Pennsylvania.

Schwartz, Thomas (1987). "Votes, Strategies, and Institutions: An Introduction to the Theory of Collective Choice." In McCubbins Mathew D., and Sullivan, Terry, eds. (1987). *Congress: Structure and Policy.* Cambridge: Cambridge University Press.

Tilly, Charles, ed. (1975). *The Formation of National States in Western Europe.* Princeton: Princeton University Press.

Tullock, Gordon (1967). *Towards a Mathematics of Politics.* Ann Arbor: University of Michigan Press.

Weingast, Barry R., and Marshall, William J. (1988). "The Industrial Organization of Congress; or, Why Legislatures, like Firms, Are Not Organized as Markets." *Journal of Political Economy 96* (No. 1): 132–163.

Williamson, Oliver (1985). *The Economic Institutions of Capitalism.* New York: Free Press.

Wilson, Robert (1967). "An Axiomatic Model of Logrolling." *American Economic Review 59* (June): 331–341.

Winiecki, Jan (1986a). "Are Soviet-Type Economies Entering an Era of Long-Term Decline?" *Soviet Studies 38* (No. 3, July): 325–348.

(1986b). "Soviet-Type Economies: Considerations for the Future." *Soviet Studies* *38* (No. 4, October): 543–561.

(1986c). "Why Economic Reforms Fail in the Soviet System: A Property Rights-Based Approach." Seminar Paper No. 374. Stockholm: The Institute for International Economic Studies.

AUTHOR INDEX

SUBJECT INDEX